I0161392

Jackson Hole
Hiking Guide

A Hiking Guide to Grand Teton, Jackson,
Teton Valley, Gros Ventre, Togwotee Pass,
and more.

by
Aaron Linsdau

Sastrugi Press
Jackson, WY

©2021 Aaron Linsdau
Jackson Hole Hiking Guide: A Hiking Guide to Grand Teton, Jackson, Teton Valley, Gros Ventre, Togwotee Pass, and more.

Interior image copyrights © Aaron Linsdau unless otherwise noted
All rights reserved. No part of this book may be reproduced or transmitted in any form or by any means, electronic or mechanical, including photocopying, recording, or by any information storage and retrieval system without the written permission of the author, except where permitted by law.

Sastrugi Press / Published by arrangement with the author
Sastrugi Press: PO Box 1297, Jackson, WY 83001, United States
www.sastrugipress.com
The activities described in this book are inherently dangerous. The publisher does not have any control over and does not assume any responsibility for author or third-party websites or their content. No content in this book is to be construed as legal advice. Seek out a qualified and licensed legal advisor.

Modern medical treatment is a constantly evolving field—recommended treatment and drug therapy are always changing. All medical treatment discussed in this book must be evaluated using the most current product information provided by the manufacturer to verify the recommended dose, the proper administration, and contraindications. It is always the responsibility of the licensed practitioner, relying on training and knowledge of the patient, to determine the best treatment and proper dosages for each individual. Neither the publisher nor the author assume any liability for any injury, illness, or death related to the medical discussions in this publication.

Any person participating in the activities described in this work is personally responsible for learning the proper techniques and using good judgment. You are responsible for your own actions and decisions. The information contained in this work is subjective and based solely on opinions. No book can advise you of all potential hazards or anticipate the limitations of any reader. Participation in the described activities can result in severe injury or death. Neither the publisher nor the author assume any liability for anyone participating in the activities described in this work.

Library of Congress Cataloging-in-Publication Data
Linsdau, Aaron
Jackson Hole Hiking Guide / Aaron Linsdau. First Edition.
Jackson, WY : Sastrugi Press, [2021]
LCCN 2021021921 (print) | LCCN 2021021922 (ebook) | ISBN 9781649221742 (Hardback)
ISBN 9781649222732 (Paperback) | ISBN 9781649221759 (eBook)
Subjects: LCSH: 1. Hiking--Wyoming--Jackson Hole--Guidebooks. 2. Day hiking--Wyoming--Jackson Hole--Guidebooks. 3. Mountaineering--Wyoming--Jackson Hole--Guidebooks. 4. Walking--Wyoming--Jackson Hole--Guidebooks. 5. Backpacking--Wyoming--Jackson Hole--Guidebooks.
6. Camping--Wyoming--Jackson Hole--Guidebooks. 7. Trails--Wyoming--Jackson Hole--Guidebooks.
8. Jackson Hole (Wyo.)--Description and travel. 9. Jackson Hole (Wyo.)--Guidebooks.
LCC GV199.42.W82 L56 2021 (print)
LCC GV199.42.W82 (ebook)
DDC 796.52209787/55--dc23
LC record available at https://lccn.loc.gov/2021021921
LC ebook record available at https://lccn.loc.gov/2021021922

ISBN-13: 978-1-64922-027-1 (paperback)
ISBN-13: 978-1-64922-174-2 (hardback)

Summary: This book contains everything hikers need to know for hiking and backpacking in the greater Jackson Hole, Wyoming area. The book provides maps, GPS coordinates, and detailed directions for every trail.
Thank you to Nancy Takeda for making this book possible.
15 14 13 12 11 10 9 8 7

Table of Contents

"Enjoy the adventure of hiking in Jackson Hole!"
— Aaron Linsdau, Polar Explorer

Map Legend

Major Road/Highway	══════
Local/Dirt Road	──────
Buildings	■
Boat Ramp	
Parking Area	P
Pass/Bridge	)(
Main Trail	– – – – –
Alternate/Secondary Trail	··········
Trailhead	
Camping Zone	
Campground	▲
Creek/River	
Cave	
Marsh	
Mountain	
Summit	▲
Viewpoint	
Park Boundary	– · – · –
Restroom	
Map Orientation	↑ N
Map Scale	Miles 0 0.5 1 / Kilometers 0 0.75 1.5

JACKSON HOLE OVERVIEW MAP

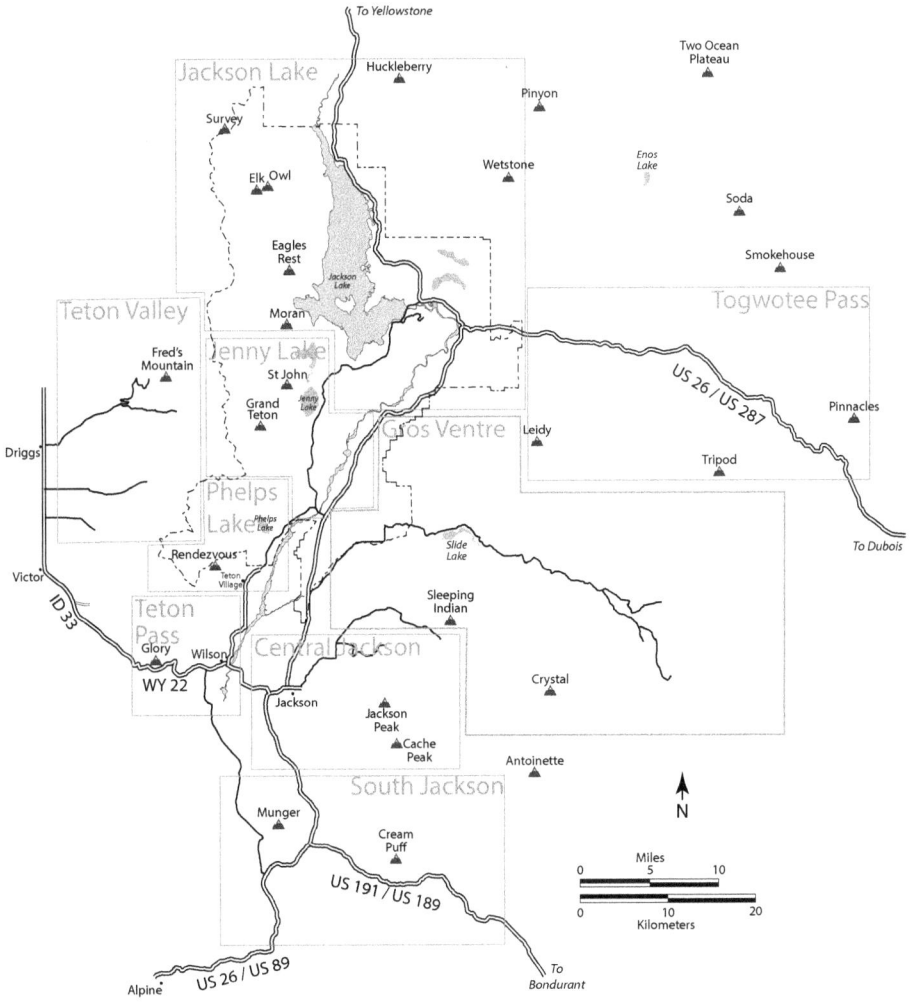

To Yellowstone

Jackson Lake

Huckleberry

Two Ocean Plateau

Pinyon

Survey

Wetstone

Enos Lake

Elk Owl

Soda

Eagles Rest

Smokehouse

Jackson Lake

Moran

Togwotee Pass

Teton Valley

Fred's Mountain

Jenny Lake

St John

US 26 / US 287

Pinnacles

Grand Teton

Jenny Lake

Gros Ventre

Leidy

Driggs

Tripod

To Dubois

Phelps Lake

Phelps Lake

Rendezvous

Slide Lake

Victor

Teton Village

ID 33

Sleeping Indian

Teton Pass

Glory

Wilson

Central Jackson

Crystal

WY 22

Jackson

Jackson Peak

Cache Peak

Antoinette

South Jackson

N

Munger

Cream Puff

Miles

0   5   10

US 191 / US 189

0   10   20

Kilometers

Alpine

US 26 / US 89

To Bondurant

Enjoying a sunset from Toppings Lake Ridge (9,036 feet / 2,754 m) after a long day of hiking.

Introduction

Jackson Hole, the town of Jackson, Grand Teton, and the areas surrounding this outdoor playground are visited by over four million people every year. There is a good reason. Yellowstone is a short drive to the north, wildlife is plentiful, the landscapes are awe-inspiring, and the locals are friendly.

Jackson Hole is named after David "Davey" E. Jackson. He was a fur trapper who worked the area in the 1820s, so much so that it became known as "Jackson's Hole." The name soon shortened to Jackson Hole that is so familiar today.

If you visit the Craig Thomas Discovery & Visitor Center in Grand Teton, look for the three-dimensional map of the area. The reason it is named a "hole" will be obvious. The ring of mountains circling the region creates a relatively flat hole in the landscape.

Glaciers shaped the region by raking across the landscape, creating mountain canyons and broad flats. A fault line runs across the eastern base of the Tetons, creating the uplift that sculpted the famous mountains visitors enjoy today. The mountains are still rising and Jackson Hole is still dropping according to local geologists.

Visitors come to experience the wildlife, too. Wolves, moose, bear, elk, bighorn sheep, and other animals are common sights throughout Jackson Hole. Hikers must be prepared to handle wildlife encounters safely and responsibly. Big animals are thrilling to encounter on the trail.

Winter defines the region. Because of the high altitude and proximity to the high Yellowstone caldera, snow can stay well into summer. It has snowed every day of the year in Jackson. One summer day may be warm and comfortable while the next is downright chilly. Often, there are weeks in winter when the high temperature never rises above 0° F (−18° C). In 1979, the temperature dropped to −63° F (−53° C). The thermometers in the park froze at −50° F (−46° C).

Jackson is a popular ski destination for alpine downhill, backcountry, and cross-country skiing. It's a top stop for amateurs and pros alike. Winter arrives early and melts of late, making hiking up high a challenge through June. The payoff is high alpine flowers that last well into August.

The valley is a destination for artists and art lovers. The September Arts Festival, coupled with smaller crowds, fall colors, and chilly mornings, is perfect for hiking enjoyment. People travel from all over the world to visit Jackson and experience the wonders that it has to offer.

Enjoy the hikes in this book!

Using this guide

Tabs on the page's edge and text on the top header demarcate major areas of the book in Jackson Hole. Sub-areas in each area are marked at the bottom of the page. This provides the reader with a better understanding of what area they are in while searching the book.

The goal of this book was to provide readers with information as quickly as possible. All hikes are self-contained. Simply photocopy or take images of only the pages you need for the hike and head outdoors. The table of contents is designed to help you make a quick decision about what trail to tackle.

Each area page provides a map with each sub-area marked. There are more detailed views of nearby trails and other navigational features. For many areas, travel is simple and understandable. Other trails are challenging to follow and poorly signed, if at all. Trails in Grand Teton are generally easy to navigate. Gros Ventre Range trails may have no signs at all and require a GPS plus map and compass skills.

Locally used names do not always match up with official government names or names on maps. This makes finding certain features of interest challenging for the first-time visitor. One example of inconsistent naming is Sheep Mountain. Locals call Sheep Mountain by the name Sleeping Indian. Once you identify the mountain, you may visualize where the name comes from. Wherever possible, the trail notes these name variances in the text to further aid the reader.

Trail numbers are clustered by major areas. Inside each area, the trails are listed alphabetically for convenience. There is no particular priority given to some trails over others. Each trail described in this book has its highlights and features. Notes are listed in the table above the trail description.

Units and Distances

Distances are provided in both standard/imperial and metric. Elevations are provided in feet and meters. Adding both metric and standard/imperial units eliminates the mental gymnastics required to convert between whichever system you are familiar with.

Table of Contents

The name, distance to complete the trail, and difficulty are noted in the table of contents. This makes it easy for readers to find hikes they have time or energy for without having to thumb through the entire book. With a glance, you can find the area you want to go to, the distance, and the difficulty of trails in that area. Do you only have time for a short hike or are you ready to walk all day? In moments, the table of contents provides you with information to make that decision.

Ratings: Easy, Mod (moderate), Stren (Strenuous), Ex Stren (Extremely Strenuous).

Trail Descriptions

This book is designed so every trail description is self-contained rather than relying on multiple sections to piece together longer hikes. The design makes it easy for readers to learn about a hike in a single description.

The trail's title has the round trip or loop distance required to complete the hike for easy reference. It also notes the difficulty. This distance is included in the table of contents as a rapid reference for hikers looking for quick answers. This information reduces time-consuming searching for a hike in a particular area based on the amount of time available.

The trail descriptions contain distances, trail markers, and obvious major geographic locations. Overviews give you the one-sentence snap of what this trail is about.

Overview

The overview contains a one-sentence quick overview of the major trail highlights. Some trails feature a particular destination. Other trails are about the sights along the journey.

Trip Style

There are different types of hiking trips in this book which are described below:

Out and back: This is the most common type of trip. You hike to a particular destination, turn around, and return along the same trail.

Loop: Loop trails start and end at the same trailhead. There is little if any ground that the trail covers on both the outbound and the return journey.

Lollipop: Trails of this nature have a starting section of trail that will be walked twice when returning to the trailhead. However, much of the trail is a loop. The basic trail shape resembles a lollipop.

Shuttle: These trails start at one trailhead and end at another. It is possible to return via the same trail. However, the distance is substantial enough to warrant using a vehicle or bicycle to return to the originating trailhead. If you can schedule or have communication, you can have someone pick you up at the ending trailhead, saving the double driving back and forth. The trail description discusses ways to make this trail style work well.

Trail Distances

Where possible, a quality GPS was used to measure the trail distance. Minor variations in a trail can add up to a significant distance over what a map shows. Often signage in Grand Teton matches well with GPS-measured distances. In other locations, sign distances may not match up to what is on the map and both will not match up to the actual ground distance. The difference is rarely more than 10% but is normally far less. Every trail has minor variations that can add up to more distance than the maps may show.

If the measured trail distances do not match your device's distances, don't become too worried. Some GPS units are less accurate than others. Sampling frequency, measurement error, and elevation integration failures all add to the distance beyond the stated trail distance. Note that whatever the distance may be, the difficulty of the trail is not only its distance but the elevation gain and terrain it covers. Give yourself plenty of time and avoid overestimating your ability.

Elevation gain/loss and max. elevation

The elevation difference between the lowest and highest point on the trail is the number provided. Every trail has up and down travel that adds up. This variation is often far more than what maps indicate. Refer to the elevation profile to better understand the amount of gain and loss experienced on a trail.

For loop and complex trails, total elevation gain and loss are reported. The style of measurement is noted in the trail overview. The maximum elevation of a trail is the highest point attained on that trail. Some trails have a high point that is not the endpoint. The Teton Crest Trail, Teton Traverse, and other trails have high points along the path rather than at the end.

Trail difficulty

There are four ratings used in this book. These categories are based on what moderately fit middle-aged adults with some hiking experience report. People who have never hiked the Rockies will feel a moderate trail as the toughest thing they've ever done. Others with substantial experience will feel the opposite. The greatest difficulty in the Jackson Hole area is finding easy and moderate hikes. Many hikes lead straight up into the Tetons, automatically making them strenuous trails.

Trail ratings are primarily affected by elevation gain, ruggedness, and the amount of route finding required. Distance is a secondary factor, as a nearly level trail of several miles (kilometers) is far easier for a human to walk than a steep climb with slip and fall exposure. Inexperienced hikers will attempt to rush a steep trail and burn themselves out rather than pacing themselves to reach a high point.

Below are the trail ratings and their criteria:

Easy: These trails have little to a slight elevation gain. They may cover a short distance to several miles (kilometers). Over that distance, there will be no route-finding or difficulty in returning to the trailhead.

Moderate: Longer, graded hills with moderate elevation gain covering longer distances. There may not be much elevation gain but the distance will be more significant. Little to no route finding is required.

Strenuous: Hikes that will test your stamina and fitness. They are steep, long, and rugged. They may be multi-day trips and will have substantial elevation gains. There may be some route finding required.

Extremely strenuous: Trails that travel straight up mountains. They may have substantial exposure and can require significant route-finding effort.

Often trails feel much longer in the Jackson Hole region due to three factors: elevation, terrain ruggedness, and elevation gain. Each of these factors will affect how long a trail "feels" to a hiker. First-time visitors often remark that official trail distances are not correct. "The trail felt much farther than that," is the common refrain.

The below three points help explain the ratings.

Elevation: All trails in the Jackson Hole area are above 6,000 feet (1,828 m) above mean sea level (MSL). The air has ~20% less oxygen in Jackson Hole than at sea level. If you are not acclimated to this altitude, the thin air can make hiking one mile (1.6 km) feel like two miles (3.2 km). Avoid underestimating the effort and time required to cover distances.

Elevation gain: The second factor is the elevation gain of many of the trails in the area. Every trail has gain and loss along its length. Some trails feature a substantial amount of gain and loss, increasing the time and effort required to complete them. Some trails are incredibly steep which will slow hikers down far more than they are used to. This gain coupled with the absolute elevation will tax even the fittest athletes.

Ruggedness: Often visitors to Jackson Hole remark that trails are far more rugged than their home mountains. A dramatic tectonic uplift created the Teton Range. This geologic feature causes many trails to be rocky. The landscape has not had time to erode and smooth out. The toughness of this northwest Wyoming landscape cannot be understated.

Visitors want to enjoy these strenuous hikes but find the trails are beyond their fitness or skill level. There is no shame in turning around and declaring that the trail is too tough. It is far better to accept the trail is too difficult, turn around, and return home safely. Avoid pushing through a misery fest and becoming injured or lost, requiring a dangerous and expensive evacuation.

Trailhead location

The overview uses the official trailhead name where available. Trailheads without official or local names use the trail's name. Some starting points do not have a name and the trail's name simply becomes the name of the trailhead.

GPS Coordinates

GPS coordinates are provided in WGS 84 DD.DDDD, WGS 84 DD°

MM' SS", and UTM coordinate systems. Depending on the accuracy of your GPS, the coordinates and distances may not exactly match the information noted in the trail description. With a strong signal, the error should be less than 30 feet (9 m).

Be mindful of local conditions. Do not blindly follow your GPS device or phone. Avoid being completely dependent on a device for navigation. Devices may fail for many reasons, including software failure, device failure, breakage, user error, battery failure, weather, or terrain.

Trail Traffic

Trail traffic ratings are based on the author's experience, local knowledge, and what official sources have reported over the years. Some traffic ratings have changed from light to heavy over the years from online media exposure. Below are the subjective trail traffic ratings:

None: The chance of meeting another hiker along this trail is unlikely. You will be rewarded with wilderness solitude by taking the trail less traveled.

Light: There may be a hiker or two along this trail. More often than not, hikers will rarely see others along this route.

Moderate: Hikers will encounter a few others along the route. The trail will not feel busy but the chance of solitude is unlikely.

Heavy: You will frequently encounter hikers along this trail. Some trails are so popular that they feel like social events. These highly popular trails are busy due to ease of access or where they go.

Maps and Notes

This book uses United States Geologic Survey (USGS) 7.5' 24k topo maps for hikers to refer to. These maps are the most common and are easy to find at local stores or online. They are the basis for all trail descriptions.

Arrows on trail maps coordinate with the distances marked between those arrows. The arrows are normally situated where there are trail junctions, summits, or other major waypoints. Maps are to scale except where noted. Refer to official US National Park, Forest Service, and USGS maps for the latest updated official information.

Trail notes include any additional information or things hikers need to watch for. Some of these may be dangers to be prepared for. Other notes are helpful tidbits to give you a better idea if the trail is appropriate for your group's skill level.

Trailhead Directions

All driving distances begin at the Town Square in Jackson. The farthest away trails in this book are no more than a two-hour drive from town. Be mindful of local conditions, detours, construction, and seasonal changes. If you are using a map on your cellular device, plan to lose the signal. Often there is no cellular coverage at trailhead locations. Be prepared.

Trailhead Facilities

Many trailheads have an information kiosk with a map. A few locations have general stores where supplies can be purchased. Other trailheads are simply a dirt track that leads off into the wilderness without even a sign.

Trail Descriptions

Cardinal directions are referred to by their first initial where appropriate in the trail descriptions: North (N), South (S), East (E), West (W).

The more complex or confusing a trail is, the more detailed the description will be. Some trails travel for miles (kilometers) with little chance of becoming lost. Other trails are particularly difficult to follow, requiring cross-country travel. Where off-trail travel is required, this is noted in the trail overview and description. Unless you are confident in your outdoor skills, be mindful that off-trail travel in the Jackson Hole area is challenging.

Waypoints

Distance waypoints are added for longer trails to aid in understanding the total distance to particular destinations. The first number is miles and the second is kilometers.

Distances are measured from the trailhead unless noted otherwise.

Right of Way Rules and Etiquette

Hikers traveling uphill have the right of way. Those struggling up a steep trail will appreciate downhill travelers stepping to the side. Hikers have the right of way over bike riders.

All travelers must give way to horse, mule, and stock traffic. Safely step off the trail on the downhill side and talk with the riders. This is especially important if you are carrying a backpack. Some pack animals perceive people carrying backpacks as a threat. Riders appreciate you speaking and showing you're a human. Ask permission before touching or petting any animal.

Let bike riders know how many are in your group if they're not immediately behind you.

Consider avoiding portable speakers to avoid disturbing other people's outdoor enjoyment. Some hikers use them as a tool to announce their presence to bears. They are ineffective and create a false sense of security. Popular Bluetooth speakers cannot project enough sound far enough ahead of you to be effective.

Fees

There are entrance fees for Grand Teton National Park. If you think you might ever visit another national park, monument, or recreational area in the next year, the national parks pass, also officially known as the America the Beautiful Pass, is well worth the money. It allows you quicker entrance and can be used in several federal jurisdictions.

If you are old enough, consider purchasing an America the Beautiful Senior Pass. Once purchased, this pass is good for the life of the pass holder. Park passes cannot be replaced if lost. They must be repurchased.

A permit is required for camping in the national parks. Plan well in advance for these, as popular sites fill up well ahead of time. Check the latest park regulations to learn more about walk-up and advance purchase camping permits.

Location Names

Highly popular locations like Jackson Hole have naming conflicts between official and local names. Due to historical usage, overlapping agencies, and local vernacular, the names of some trails and locations may not match the official record.

For the sake of communicating with locals, the local name has been selected as the trail or place name where it adds more understanding. The official name is noted in the text or on the map as well for the reader's convenience.

Road numbers, names, and local pronunciations

The roads through Jackson Hole have multiple US and Wyoming highway numbers and names. There are also names that locals use, confusing first-time visitors. It is common for locals not to know a highway number. Below are some common names to help when reading or obtaining directions.

The road heading north from Jackson, US 26 / US 89 / US 191, is called "The Highway" or "The Park Road." Teton Park Road, between Moose and Jackson Lake, is sometimes called the "Inner Park Road." The road between Hoback Junction and Alpine, US 89 / US 26, is called "The Canyon." The road between Gros Ventre Junction and the town of Kelly is called "The Kelly Road." The dirt road leading into the Elk Refuge from the east end of Broadway is called "The Refuge Road." Highway 22 between Wilson and Victor is called "The Pass."

Highway 390 from Highway 22 to Teton Village (Jackson Hole Mountain Resort) is called "The Village Road." The dirt road north of the Grand Teton south entrance leading to Moose and the Teton Park Road is called "The Moose-Wilson Road." The dirt road that passes by the Moulton Barn is called "Mormon Row." US 26 / US 287 from Moran Junction to Dubois is called "Togwotee Pass." This particular name covers a long stretch of road. The actual pass is short but locals generally call it "going to/over Togwotee."

The French word "Teton" is pronounced "tea-tawn" with the "tea" dragged out a bit longer than expected and "tawn" sounding like the word "yawn." Teton is not pronounced "tea-tun," with "tea" cut short and "tun" sounding like a "ton of bricks." The town of Dubois is pronounced "dew boys," as in the soda drink "Mountain Dew" and "boys", as in boys and girls. It is not pronounced "du-boys", as in "no duh" plus "boys." The French phrase Gros Ventre is pronounced "grow-vont" as in "grow a garden" and "computer font." Togwotee is pronounced "toe-guh-tea."

Local newspaper with updated information

The free daily newspaper is the Jackson Hole News and Guide, called "The Daily." It is an excellent resource for daily Jackson Hole information. It has weather reports, local events, incident reports, and discount coupons that hikers and travelers will want to be aware of. It is available at most hotels, gas stations, coffee shops, and many stores.

The weekly edition of this paper is distributed Wednesday and is called "The Weekly" by locals. It has in-depth articles and more substantial information that a visitor will be interested in. This weekly paper is sold for a nominal cost at hotels and grocery stores. Both papers are well worth seeking out.

Best Season

The "best" season for general hiking is summer in Jackson Hole. All other seasons can and will have substantial snow depending on the year. Snow stays late into the spring and often well into summer at altitude. Winter conditions often arrive before the start of fall. Snow has fallen in July and August and caught many cold, unprepared hikers by surprise.

The weather in Jackson Hole is highly unpredictable. Temperatures can drop below freezing at night, even in the summer. One day can be warm and the next day requires a down jacket and gloves. Many people have spent unplanned substantial sums of money on winter clothing in July.

Late May through mid-June is a great time to enjoy alpine flowers in the lower elevations. Flowers may be present well into late August in the high elevations. Animals will often migrate to upper elevations during mid-summer to escape the valley heat. Early spring and late summer are best for viewing the large animals of Jackson Hole.

Wilderness Area Regulations

Special regulations and rules apply to all wilderness areas in this book. Wilderness areas are special use designated areas with greater restrictions than the national parks. This includes no mechanized travel at all (bikes included), no drones, paragliders, or anything else mechanical. Check with the Forest Service for other use restrictions.

Minimize Impact

The Jackson Hole area is heavily used due to its beauty. To keep the area as pristine as possible, consider the following leave no trace principles:

Plan and prepare: Honestly evaluate your skill and impact. Hacking down a section of the forest for a survival shelter leaves long-lasting impacts.

Camp lightly: Avoid crushing plants with your campsite. High alpine vegetation can take years to recover from being squashed under a tent.

Carry out waste: Carry everything out that was brought in. Bury toilet paper at least 200 feet (60 m) from any water or consider carrying it out.

Leave what is there: Though tempting to take a souvenir, leave all items in the forest as you found them. Collecting anything in the national park is prohibited, even pine cones and rocks.

Minimize campfires: Avoid leaving burned logs and blackened rocks. They make the area look like a garbage dump. Use established fire pits to minimize the impact. Check local regulations.

Respect wildlife: Life is tough for animals in Jackson Hole. Winters are long and brutal. They only have a few months to prepare their young for winter.

Be considerate: Millions of people visit the area every year. Follow the golden rule and treat others and the area as if you were visiting a respected friend's home.

Pets and service animals

Pets are not allowed on national park trails. See the park's website for updated ADA-permitted service animal information. Native animals perceive pets as predators and a dangerous threat. Owners often do not understand that pets are in danger in the wilderness. There have been many recorded instances of pets being killed by wolves, bears, moose, and other wildlife.

The scent of a pet that passed by hours ago will disturb the local animals. Wild animals, especially protective mothers, may react negatively to the scent of a pet's urine spot days later.

Be considerate when bringing pets on trails where allowed. Respect local trail regulations and customs. Not all people appreciate a pet invading their space. What some may think is fun, others may find intrusive and threatening. An unexpected encounter with an unleashed pet on a narrow trail can result in serious injury or worse.

Note that some wild animals carry rabies or bubonic plague. Bats, squirrels, chipmunks, etc., have infected humans and pets before. Should a pet encounter and contact a small mammal, there may be serious consequences. Consider a pet's health and safety by leaving them at home or in a safe location. All pets must be under control at all times. Many off-leash pets have been tragically killed when confronting wild animals.

Carry out all pet waste in a bag and dispose of it at home. Bring your own bags. Trash bags are often left along trails by inconsiderate owners. These make this beautiful area look like a disgusting garbage dump. Do not leave bags "to be picked up later." They are often forgotten, polluting the forest and leaving a mess for others to deal with. Wild animals often take waste bags and spread them into the forest.

In 2015, the Forest Service counted 168 piles of dog feces and trash bags left at the Cache Creek trailhead in one month. 6 per day. This prompted a closure of the area due to pollution and garbage in the creek. There are constant trash bags and feces piles discarded in the Cache Creek area every day by irresponsible owners. Please don't pollute the forest with pet waste and trash from it.

Forest Service Trail Numbers

The forest service trail numbers are added to the maps when possible. They are referred to in the trail description and the heading table to help clarify directions. Forest service trail numbers are sometimes physically marked with a sign. Often these signs are in trees, so look around when encountering a trail junction in forest service areas.

The Forest Service website has useful information. Check this book's web page for the latest updated links to forest service web pages.

SAFETY

General Safety

Hiking during a warm summer day in Jackson Hole is an exquisite experience. Travelers from all over the world visit to enjoy the landscape, animals, and plant life. However, there are some dangers visitors must be aware of. For virtually all hikers, a walk will go exactly as planned. It's the seemingly minor stumble, overestimation of ability, or unexpected weather that changes a pleasant walk into an ordeal.

Water

Bring water or be prepared to treat water collected in the backcountry. All water sources should be considered contaminated, no matter how crystal clear a source may look. Be prepared to boil, filter, or chemically treat water to prevent Giardia and Cryptosporidium. Both parasites can land inattentive hikers in the hospital.

Satellite beacons and emergency transponders

Avoid being reliant on a satellite beacon to keep your friends and family updated on your whereabouts. Devices fail. Batteries run out of power. The mountainous nature of Jackson Hole routinely blocks satellite signals. Emergency personnel regularly receive calls from panicked family or friends back home who haven't received satellite updates in hours or days. Often hikers forget to send an update because they become engrossed in their wilderness experience. Avoid creating panic by tempering expectations.

The park and emergency services routinely receive messages from hikers who believe they are in mortal danger. What often happens is hikers find themselves out ill-prepared after dark or are heavily fatigued. An emergency beacon is meant for just that—a real, life-threatening emergency. Being tired and hiking in the dark is a non-event for some. Others may feel that they are on death's doorstep. Strongly consider your experience, equipment, and time required.

Emergency rescue

Rescues are costly and dangerous for all involved. Helicopter rescues are only used when emergency medical service (EMS) personnel determines there is no other safe way to rescue a stranded or injured hiker. Air rescues are risky. If EMS determines the risk to be too great, be prepared to stay put through the night. This said, if you are seriously injured or require rescue, do not hesitate to signal for help in a safe manner. If you break a bone and cannot walk, do not allow the sit-uation to worsen by delaying a call for help. Many sad circumstances could have been avoided by a timely call for help.

Ten Essentials

Derived from the Scouting program, carrying the items on the ten essentials list improves the likelihood a person will survive an unexpected event. They provide a person with an improved chance of survival.

Without the understanding of how to use the ten essentials, they can seem a burden to the untrained hiker. Spend a little time familiarizing yourself with how to use each of these items. This invested time can make the difference between an exciting family story and a tragic local newspaper story.

Below is a list of essentials to bring on any hike:

Map and compass: A physical map and compass are key tools to helping you navigate out of the woods, as they are not dependent on electronics. These take practice to learn to use properly. GPS units and phones have batteries that will fail at the worst possible time and are easily damaged.

Pocket knife: A basic pocket knife, Swiss army-style knife, or multi-tool with a blade is an essential tool. You do not need a large sheath knife.

Extra clothing: A light jacket, spare socks, and a hat can help you through an unexpected cold front.

Rain gear: A light rain jacket and rain pants can make all the difference in preventing hypothermia in unexpected weather changes.

Water bottle (with purification): Bring extra water beyond what you expect to use. Water purification will greatly extend your hiking range.

Extra food: Bring extra food that requires no cooking. Basic trail snacks, bars, or dried meat will provide energy.

Flashlight/headlamp: Bring at least one flashlight of any type and ideally two. Headlamps are doubly handy. Lithium batteries work to −40° F/C and last far longer than alkaline or NiMH batteries, especially in the cold.

First aid kit: A small quality first aid kit will take care of most minor injuries in the field. The ability to take care of blisters and minor sprains is most important.

Matches or fire starters: The ability to create a fire in an emergency is helpful. Matches in a waterproof case are ideal. Change them out yearly, as they can deteriorate over time. A small votive candle can be a lifesaver.

Sun protection: The sun and its ultraviolet radiation (UV) are intense in Jackson Hole due to the high elevation. Unprotected skin can sunburn in an hour. Serious skin sunburns and UV eye damage are possible without protection. Sunscreen, hats, and glasses are a wise investment for your health and safety.

Other handy items to have:
Whistle and signal mirror
Toilet paper plus trash bag
Trekking poles

The goal of this list is to have what you need to take you through a chilly night in the summer while waiting for rescue. If you plan on being in Jackson Hole in the winter, the additional safety gear list substantially expands. Temperatures in the −30° F (−35° C) range during the day are common during the winter.

Weather and Lightning

Weather cannot be seen approaching over the Tetons until it is on top of you. A surprise thundershower has caught many hikers off guard, soaking and chilling them to the point of mild hypothermia. Temperatures can drop below freezing at night in the middle of a hot summer. It can be 95° F (35° C) in the day and 25° F (−4° C) in the middle of the night. This is especially true at higher elevations in exposed, breezy conditions.

Hikers have experienced a sunburn in the late morning only to find it snowing in the afternoon. Most of the time, summer weather is pleasant and enjoyable. Other times, you can find yourself soaked, freezing, and miserable in a snow flurry at a high mountain lake.

Before venturing out, check the latest weather forecast in the daily paper, the park service, and the National Weather Service at https://www.weather.gov/. Forecasts can be unreliable due to the nature of the mountain terrain. The best bet is to know that if a 20% or more chance of precipitation is predicted, there is a decent chance of being rained on.

Afternoon monsoon weather patterns develop in July and August with regularity. Mornings will be clear and then afternoon rain and lightning appear out of nowhere. Storm clouds cannot be seen west of the Tetons until they are right above you. It is a scary experience to be above the tree line in the Tetons when clear skies turn dark in mere moments and lightning booms overhead.

The mountains surrounding Jackson Hole create an unpredictable rain and lightning shadow. If thundershowers or lightning are predicted, be extremely cautious. Lightning has killed many hikers and climbers over the years here. Immediately abandon your plans and move to a protected area if you hear thunder and are in an exposed location. Your life may truly depend upon your actions.

Hypothermia

It is easy to develop hypothermia in Jackson Hole. A passing rain shower in the afternoon far from the trailhead can leave hikers soaked and chilled. Add a breeze, fatigue, and sweat and you have a potentially fatal combination. Slipping into a creek during a crossing late at night a few miles (kilometers) from help is all it takes to put yourself in danger.

The common signs of hypothermia are uncontrollable shivering, slurred speech, incoherence, fumbling with basic tasks like tying shoelaces, stumbling while walking (similar to intoxication), inability to stand up after resting, and strong drowsiness. Should you or your hiking partners want to fall asleep, make every effort to warm up and stay awake. Falling asleep while hypothermic is a sure recipe for death.

Should someone suffer from mild hypothermia, dry them off, and warm them up. Should the symptoms become severe, have the victim climb into a sleeping bag with another person. If none is available, huddle together out of the wind in a sheltered location. Call for help if possible while trying to rewarm the victim following modern first aid guidelines.

Often adults will hide symptoms out of embarrassment until the situation is serious or dire. They may become combative, claiming everything is fine. Be honest and open with your hiking partners. There is no shame in asking for help when in need.

Wild animals

Wild animals are a big part of the attraction of Jackson Hole. Over the decades, some animal populations have expanded, making it easier than ever to find and enjoy seeing them.

Do not feed any wild animal. It is illegal to feed wild animals, even chipmunks. The fines and penalties are steep. Plus, a fed animal quickly associates humans with food. They can become aggressive, forcing authorities to kill these habituated animals. Humans are almost always the cause of wild animals becoming dependent on human food sources.

Bears

Bears now inhabit all parts of Jackson Hole and, by extension, northwest Wyoming. There are popular grizzly bears that people travel from all around the world to observe. Cubs are wonderfully gregarious and playful when observed from afar. Bears are powerful apex predators that require the utmost respect and lots of space. The wilderness is the bear's domain and you are a guest passing through.

There are two species of bears in Jackson Hole: black and brown bears. The common species name of the bear does not correlate to the color of their fur. Their dispositions are also different. Never think that a seemingly docile bear is tame. All animals in Jackson Hole are wild and tough.

Black bears (*Ursus americanus*) can be any number of colors, including blond, tan, cinnamon, brown, or black. They have long muzzles, relatively short claws (1"-2" / 2.5cm-5cm), and have little to no pronounced shoulder hump. Their ears are relatively tall and pointed. They have a comparatively mild disposition, though black bears have killed people and their pets.

Grizzly bears (*Ursus arctos horribilis*), known as the brown bear, also come in a variety of colors. They have a pronounced shoulder hump, a flatter face with ears that are short and round. Their claws are long (2"-4" / 5cm-10cm). These bears are highly territorial and will attack for no apparent reason.

You may never see a bear on your hike. When you do see one nearby, it is an experience you will never forget. There is much written on bear safety and traveling in bear country. Refer to the up-to-date national park and forest service guidelines for keeping safe. Note that bears act aggressively because they perceive humans as a dangerous intruder, especially mothers with cubs. Given enough warning, bears will tend to avoid encounters and disappear silently into the forest. They are large animals but travel with amazing stealth.

There are a few guidelines that will help you reduce the chance of a negative bear encounter:

Encounters: If you should come across a bear, DO NOT RUN. DO NOT CROUCH DOWN. You cannot climb a tree faster than a bear.

Stay calm, avoid eye contact, talk to the bear in a calming, monotone voice, and slowly back away while facing the bear. Bears often bluff charge. You won't know until they pass or hit you if it's a bluff or a defensive attack.

Angry bears may huff, stomp, snap their jaws and teeth, growl, or otherwise let you know they are uncomfortable. They may do none of these things, simply walk away, or charge you. There are no absolute rules. Bears are wild and thus unpredictable.

Should a bear stalk you and act overly interested, you are in serious jeopardy. The bear may be curious but it may have also decided you are prey. Please refer to the national park and forest service information for the latest in bear conflict avoidance techniques.

Bear cubs: Should you find yourself between a female grizzly (sow) and her cubs, you are in mortal danger. Never put yourself in this situation. Bear cubs are cute to see and are thoroughly entertaining. However, sows will perceive you as a threat. They will do everything in their power to render you as a non-threat. To her, you are a danger to her cubs. If you see bear cubs while hiking, immediately and calmly vacate the area and notify a ranger.

Bear cubs are likely not abandoned though they appear to be. A natural human reaction is to help a seemingly endangered baby animal. If you see a baby bear, imme-diately vacate the area. The mother is likely nearby and will viciously defend her young. Notify rangers that you have seen bear cubs along a trail.

Noise: Make as much noise as possible while hiking. Sing, clap, call out, and do whatever you can to make sure you are heard. Surprise encounters are a primary reason for bear charges and attacks.

Sightlines: If you are in dense brush and cannot see far ahead and to the side, slow down. Make even more noise. Yell, announcing your presence.

Cooking: Cook at least 100 feet (30 m) from your campsite. If possible, eat dinner on the trail a full hour before setting camp to distance yourself from your food smell. Though not practical, it's the best you can do. Thoroughly clean your dishes. Note that cleaning dishes in creeks, rivers, and lakes is not allowed in the national park. The easiest method for avoiding dirty dishes is to bring food that only requires boiled water.

Food storage: The national park requires bear-resistant food canisters for food storage. Hanging food in trees is no longer allowed in Grand Teton as a food storage method. Finding a proper hang location takes skill, time, and effort. An appropriate tree may be impossible to find. An approved bear container, when properly used, is simple to use. They dramatically reduce the stress of backpacking in bear country. Make sure to place your locked bear food container far away from your tent, ideally 100 yards/meters.

Use this rule when thinking about food storage and bears: never underestimate an animal that can learn to ride a motorcycle. Only heavy steel and concrete can stop bears. Coolers and vehicles are no match for these motivated and powerful animals.

Smell items: Bears can smell everything. They can smell your triple-bagged beef jerky as though it were not in a bag at all. Store all items with a scent in your bear container, including toothpaste, gum, candy, deodorant, etc. The only exception is DEET-based bug repellent. This chemical can damage some bear containers and render your food inedible.

Trash: What you bring with you must come out of the forest. Do not bury trash. Animals can easily dig up what you have left, habituating them to human food. This often leads to aggressive animals that tragically have to be euthanized due to human carelessness.

Groups: Hike in groups of four or more whenever possible. The larger the group, the more likely a bear is to vacate the area rather than acting defensively.

Fixation: Look as far down and around the trail as possible. It is easy to become fixated on the trail 10 feet (3 m) in front of you, increasing the chance of walking into a surprised bear or moose.

Dead animal carcass: If you encounter a dead animal carcass that is anything other than dry bones on a trail, immediately vacate the area. Both grizzlies and black bears will violently defend the food they have claimed. Idle curiosity can cost you your life. Notify a ranger of the carcass. It can save someone else's life.

Bear spray: Be ready to deploy bear spray in 1–2 seconds. Carry it in your hand while in thick brush or where you cannot see a significant distance. Keep it accessible in a cargo pocket so you can draw it in one second if it's not in hand already. Bears can cover 100 yards/meters in 7 seconds. They can run 50 feet (15 m) in 2 seconds. If bear spray is dangling on your pack or is packed away, you might as well be carrying a rock.

The National Park and Forest Service visitor centers have training materials regarding bear charges. Contact them and ask what the current best methods are for dealing with a bear charge and how best to avoid them.

While sleeping, place bear spray so it's immediately accessible. In windy conditions, bear spray effectiveness will be limited and may incapacitate you. Should you be walking into a breeze, consider what you will do before you need to do something.

Bear spray seems expensive. However, it is far less expensive than having your face sewn back on after an attack. Bear spray can be rented in Jackson. Airlines will not allow you to fly with bear spray, so you will be forced to abandon it at the airport.

Firearms: Current regulations may or may not allow loaded firearms to be carried in national parks. Check for the latest regulations. Areas outside the national parks have different rules and may allow firearms. The overriding philosophy in Jackson Hole is to carry bear spray at all times. Unlike a firearm, bear spray will not permanently injure a bear, yourself, or those around you. Bear spray is simply concentrated pepper spray.

The tragic bear fatality event near Togwotee Pass in 2018 changed some people's approach in the Jackson Hole area to bear defense. Speak with forest service personnel about the latest recommendations and regulations. Should you use a firearm against a bear, there will be a thorough investigation. Grizzlies are a federally protected species. If you are found negligent, there can be serious penalties. *This book is not meant to be legal advice and should not be construed as such.*

Note that the above bear defense approaches are generally considered effective in the Jackson Hole area. Always refer to the latest laws and regulations in the area you are visiting. The philosophy and approach to bear encounters in Alaska and Canada is different than in Jackson Hole. Always observe local regulations and customs for the best, non-lethal outcome.

Author's note: *This will help you understand the power of bears. I once saw a small black bear lift a solid log with one paw multiple times looking for grubs. This log was larger than a big coffee table, 6 feet long and 3 feet in diameter (1.8 m / 1 m). After doing this several times, it became annoyed and, with a huff, tossed the log away with little effort. It was the same effort as me tossing aside a book. I hiked by the same spot the next day and tried to move the log myself. I could barely rock it.*

Moose

Moose (*Alces alces*) are the largest species of the deer family. Weighing upwards of 1,000 pounds (454 kg), these magnificent animals roam much of Jackson Hole. They lose their antlers (rack) every year during the winter. They are usually found by the water, as moose eat aquatic plants in the summer. In the winter, they can be seen in Jackson living off of the buds of twigs on trees.

Though they appear awkward and slow, they are neither. Should you encounter a moose on the trail, speak calmly and back away. If a moose feels threatened, they will defend themselves. People have been seriously injured or killed over the years by not giving moose enough space. Female moose (cows) may defend their young. Nearly every year, there is a tragic story of a pet being killed by moose. Pets fail to understand that moose feel threatened by their presence. A moose may stomp an uncontrolled, off-leash pet that is harassing the moose. The owner may be found liable for the actions of their pet harassing wildlife.

Bison

Bison (*Bison bison*) are a symbol of the American west and are on the Wyoming flag. Though often referred to as buffalo, their true name is bison. These herd animals are large, powerful, and fast. They can weigh over 2,000 pounds (907 kg) and can run upwards of 40 MPH (64 KPH). A running herd is a sight to behold.

These cantankerous federally protected animals can be seen throughout the lower elevations of Jackson Hole. Maintain a minimum distance of 25 yards/meters and abide by the latest national park wildlife regulations. These herd animals are powerful and can run faster than expected.

Mountain Lions

Mountain lions (*Puma concolor*), also known as pumas, catamounts, cougars, or panthers, are present in the Jackson Hole area. The chances of a visitor seeing them are exceedingly rare and are a special treat to see. A sighting will generate ex-citement and press. Should you encounter this powerful cat up close, do everything you can to appear larger and threatening. Let the cat know you are not an easy target. Do not crouch down, as this may initiate an attack. Fight back with anything you have. Let wildlife officials know of any sighting along a trail.

Wild Animal Diseases

Some wild animals carry rabies. Others can carry the Bubonic plague, the same disease that killed millions in medieval Europe. Avoid contact with all wild animals, especially seemingly tame raccoons, rodents like squirrels and chipmunks, and other mammals.

Bats also carry rabies. If you find a bat, never touch it. Bat teeth are tiny and you may not even feel a minute scratch from their teeth. The tiniest scratch is all that it takes to infect humans with rabies. The saliva of bats and other wild mammals contacting broken skin (even a hangnail) can infect you with rabies. You may not even realize it has happened. The same thing can happen to a pet. Often people infected with rabies will be unable to drink though desperately thirsty. They may become hydrophobic (fearful of water).

There is no known cure for rabies. Once a person shows symptoms of rabies, death is almost certain. Rabies is 100% fatal in humans if it is not diagnosed and treated in time.

Sun Exposure

The sun is intense in Jackson Hole. It is easy to sunburn due to the elevation and thin atmosphere. Bring clothing that protects skin and use sun protection products when necessary. Avoid temporary and even permanent eye damage by using proper eye protection.

Altitude Sickness

Due to the steepness and elevation of trails in Jackson Hole, it is possible to develop altitude sickness. Also called Acute Mountain Sickness (AMS), this condition can make people feel ill or even put them in the hospital.

The primary cause of altitude sickness is gaining elevation too quickly. If you fly into Jackson, give yourself a few days to acclimate before going on a long hike. Seek professional advice on this matter.

The most effective treatment for altitude sickness is descending to a lower elevation. Should you feel more than slightly ill, seek professional treatment. AMS will make you miserable and may land you in the hospital.

Dehydration

The air in Jackson Hole sucks the moisture out of humans. People often underestimate how much water is needed for a hike. A small half-liter bottle is completely inadequate for long hikes with elevation gain. In the summer, you will soon be out of water and feeling terrible. Avoid heat exhaustion or worse by bringing more water than you need.

Author's note: *I have provided water to countless unprepared hikers over the years. People I've helped were exhausted, sitting in the dirt, and even stumbling. This often happens on Snow King and near Hidden Falls at Jenny Lake. Please avoid injury by carrying more water than you need. Avoidable rescues are costly and risk all involved.*

Hiking Boots

Bring broken-in footwear that protects feet and ankles. Jackson Hole is far more rugged than people realize. Many trails are rocky for long stretches. The number of people with debilitating blisters from new boots starting on a long backpacking trip on the Teton Crest Trail is uncountable.

Twisted ankles from improper footwear are a daily occurrence in Jackson Hole. Often hikers purchase boots the day before a multinight trip. Soon, their feet are covered in painful, open sores. Avoid this agony by planning ahead.

Emergency Satellite Beacons

Modern technology has allowed humans to travel farther than ever before. It has also enabled inexperienced hikers to get themselves into substantial danger.

Also, the park receives calls from distressed relatives about hikers who have not checked in with their tracking beacon. Avoid creating an unnecessary and expensive emergency call by setting realistic expectations for communications. Technology often fails in the backcountry.

Do not promise you'll send daily messages via satellite beacons to someone. This promise may be impossible to keep, creating unnecessary panic. Hikers relying on these devices are unaware of the impacts.

Cell Phone Reception

Do not rely on a cell phone for emergency communications in the areas covered in this book. The cell phone coverage in this region is spotty at best. Cellular service can be affected by weather, geography, or outages.

Always let someone responsible know where you are going and when to expect you back.

Courtesy of Randy Isaacson

Taggart Lake Trail.

JACKSON LAKE

Jackson Lake is the dominant body of water in Grand Teton National Park. Covering nearly 40 square miles (104 sq km), the lake temperature averages 60 °F (16 °C). It is covered with ice and snow for months at a time during the winter.

The southeast and eastern portions of the lake are readily accessible by vehicles and hikers. However, the western side of the lake is inaccessible. It requires a boat or substantial bushwhacking in the summer if you wish to climb Mt. Moran.

Jackson Lake Lodge, located 4.9 miles (7.8 km) northwest of Moran Junction, is an excellent spot to start your exploration of the lake. This lodge is historically famous and provides sheltered views of Willow Flats, Jackson Lake, and the Cathedral Group. There are gift shops and restaurants located in-side the lodge to fuel up before or after a long hike.

The 438 feet (134 m) deep lake has several hiking areas around it. South Jackson Lake, Colter Bay, and North Jackson Lake are each distinctive in what they offer hikers for an outdoor experience.

Much of the western side of the lake is also a prime grizzly bear habitat. World-famous bears regularly wander alongside the road with their cubs, offering visitors a closer look from their vehicles at these powerful animals.

Due to the nature of the grizzlies, it's imperative to make sure to bring bear spray and have it at the ready. Some forest areas around Jackson Lake are dense, restricting your line of sight. Being prepared with bear spray will help reduce the chance of an unpleasant encounter with North America's largest predator.

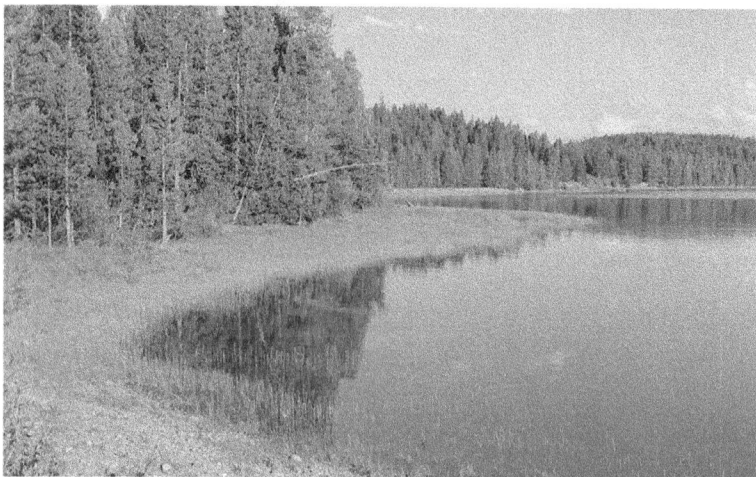

Lakeshore Loop at Colter Bay.

JACKSON LAKE AREA HIKES

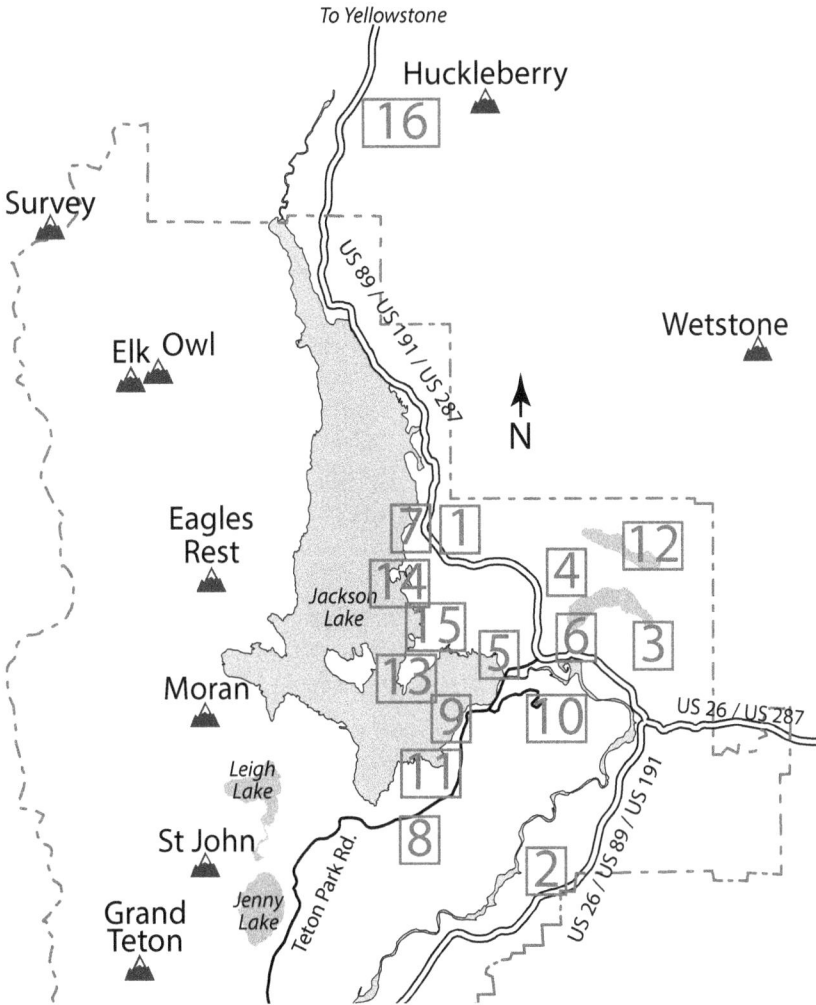

To Yellowstone

Huckleberry
16

Survey

US 89 / US 191 / US 287

Elk Owl

Wetstone

N

Eagles
Rest

7 1

Jackson
Lake

14 4 12

15 6 3

5

13 9 10

US 26 / US 287

Moran

Leigh
Lake

11

St John

8

Teton Park Rd.

2

US 26 / US 89 / US 191

Grand
Teton

Jenny
Lake

South Jackson Lake
1. Christian Pond
2. Cunningham Cabin
3. Emma Matilda Lake
4. Grandview Point
5. Jackson Lake Dam
6. Lookout Rock
7. Lunch Tree Hill
8. Potholes
9. Signal Mountain Marina Cliff

10. Signal Mountain Summit
11. South Landing
12. Two Ocean Lake

Colter Bay
13. Hermitage Point
14. Lakeshore Loop
15. Swan Lake and Heron Pond

North Jackson Lake
16. Huckleberry Fire Tower

South Jackson Lake

South Jackson Lake is where most of the hiking activity around the huge lake occurs. Between Colter Bay, Two Ocean, and Emma Matilda lakes, plus the area around Jackson Lake Lodge, there are a large variety of trails to enjoy.

A visit to the historic Jackson Lake Lodge is well worth the time, whatever your hiking plans may entail. The gift shops, dining options, animal displays, and stunning views are well worth the extra few minutes for a visit.

Although Oxbow Bend doesn't have any official hiking trails around it, stopping here is well worth it any time of year. This is especially true in the fall. The colorful aspens at the far end of the bend make for memorable photographs.

Signal Mountain Lodge is another location at the south end of the lake that is worth a visit. It has a general store, gas station, restaurant, gift shop, and boat ramp. Several hiking trails start from the Signal Mountain Lodge area.

Grizzlies are highly prevalent in the south Jackson Lake Area. Make sure to be prepared with bear spray and have it in hand at all times. Check with the park service for recent bear activity updates.

Grandview Point looking toward the Cathedral Group, 16.3 miles (26.3 km) away.

JACKSON LAKE

1 CHRISTIAN POND (1 mi / 1.6 km / Easy)

Overview: A lightly-used trail to an overlook of a waterfowl pond.
Trip style: Out and back
Distance: 0.46 mile (0.74 km) one way, 0.92 mile (1.48 km) total
Elevation gain: 69 feet (21 m)
Max. Elevation: 6,878 feet (2,096 m)
Difficulty: Easy
Trailhead: Jackson Lake Lodge horse corrals
43.8781°N, -110.5726°W / 43°52'41"N, -110°34'21"W
12T 0534334E 4858423N
Traffic: Light
Maps: Two Ocean Lake, Moran 7.5' USGS topos

Trailhead Directions

Drive north from Jackson on US 191 for 30.3 miles (48.8 km). Turn left (west) at Moran Junction. Continue for 4.9 miles (7.8 km) and turn left (west) into Jackson Lake Lodge. Turn left at the gas station and park in the southeast parking lot. Alternatively, park 900 feet (266 m) south of Jackson Lake Lodge in the dirt turnouts along the road north of the Christian Creek Bridge to access the trail.

Trailhead Facilities

General store, gas station, water, restrooms, bike rack.

Hike Description

Start hiking from the southeast corner of the Jackson Lake Lodge horse corral parking lot. The trail passes under the Christian Creek bridge. In 600 feet (183 m), take the right trail fork at the junction heading away from the highway.

The trail passes through tall shrubbery and marshy wetlands. At 0.3 mile (0.4 km), the trail travels uphill toward a ridge. Christian Pond will be visible at the first saddle. Continue south to the top of the ridge to enjoy a commanding view of Christian Pond.

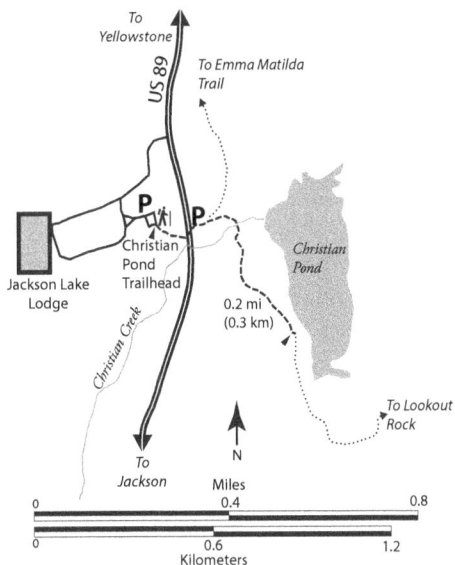

2 CUNNINGHAM CABIN (0.4 mi / 0.7 km / Easy)

Overview: Historical cabin with commanding views of the Tetons.
Trip style: Loop
Distance: 0.43 mile (0.69 km) round trip
Elevation gain: 23 feet (7 m) (total trail gain/loss)
Max. Elevation: 6,768 feet (2,062 m)
Difficulty: Easy
Trailhead: Cunningham Cabin
43.7777°N, -110.5575°W / 43°46'40"N, -110°33'27"W
12T 0535609E 4847278N
Traffic: Light
Maps: Moran 7.5' USGS topo
Notes: The information kiosk has more info about this historic area.

Trailhead Directions

Drive north from Jackson on US 191 for 27.1 miles (43.6 km). Turn left at the Cunningham Cabin sign and continue 0.36 mile (0.58 km) to the parking area.

Trailhead Facilities

Information kiosk.

Hike Description

Starting at the trailhead under the wood arch, walk 400 feet (122 m) toward the creek, through the tall shrubs, and on to the cabin.

On the north side of the cabin, the loop trail travels northwest in a counterclockwise direction. Using the history brochure, you can learn more about the cabin, its history, and the surrounding ruins.

The area is open and is easy to navigate. The signs and kiosks help hikers better understand the im-portance and value of the location. This is a short, family-friendly walk.

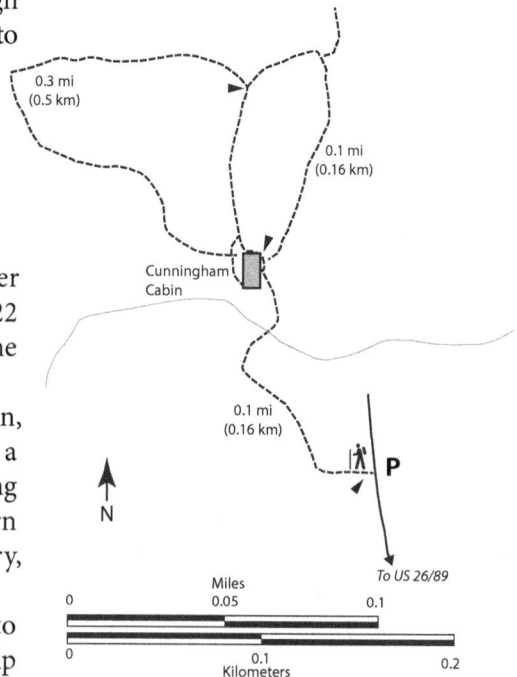

3 EMMA MATILDA LAKE (11.4 mi / 18.3 km / Mod)

Overview: A lightly-used trail around a spectacular backcountry lake.

Trip style: Out and back

Distance: 11.37 miles (18.3 km)

Elevation gain: 1,351 feet (412 m) (total trail gain/loss)

Max. Elevation: 7,313 feet (2,229 m)

Difficulty: Moderate

Trailhead: Pacific Creek Road
43.8701°N, -110.5017°W / 43°52'12"N, -110°30'06"W
12T 0540040E 4857562N

Traffic: Light

Maps: Two Ocean Lake, Moran 7.5' USGS topos

Notes: The trailhead is not marked. Other lake access trailheads to Emma Matilda exist but have longer approaches.

Trailhead Directions

Drive north from Jackson on US 191 for 30.3 miles (48.8 km). Turn left (west) at Moran Junction. Drive 1.2 miles (1.9 km) and turn right (northeast) on Pacific Creek Road. Drive 1.5 miles (2.4 km) and park in the unmarked turnout on the left (north) side of the road.

Trailhead Facilities

None.

Hike Description

Start hiking north from the trail leading from the dirt pullout. This trailhead is not official, so it is not signed. However, it is the fastest way to access the trail around the lake. The trail goes over a slight hill toward the lake through a grove of mixed trees and open grassland.

Bear markings on trees will be apparent along the entire hike. Have bear spray ready to use in a holster or pocket, not in or on your backpack.

At 0.6 mile (1 km), you will encounter a signed junction in an open grassland area with a few small aspen trees. Follow the sign toward North Emma Matilda Lake Trail to follow the trail around the lake counterclockwise. The sign does not provide distances.

The trail continues for another 1.6 miles (2.6 km) over two rolling hills through mostly open aspen groves with mixed conifers at the next trail junction. The trail is roughly 0.3 mile (0.5 km) from the edge of the lake along the north section. This section gains and loses 270 feet (82 m). The right fork leads to Two Ocean Lake 1 mile (1.6 km) north. Continue straight, following the sign toward Lookout Rock.

This next section of trail continues around the lake with direct views of Mt. Moran and the Cathedral Group. At the edge of a thick stand of conifers, the trail begins gently gaining elevation. The trail breaks out of the trees in 0.4 mile (0.8 km) and continues gaining elevation through a sagebrush and grassy area.

The trail enters another conifer stand in 0.4 mile (0.8 km) and continues through this tree area for 1.1 miles (1.8 km). From the top of the hill, the trail loses 400 feet (122 m) over 0.4 mile (0.6 km) to the junction.

Follow the sign toward Lookout Rock at the junction. The trail goes for 0.9 mile (1.5 km), gaining and losing 140 feet (43 m) through mostly open sagebrush and some trees to the next trail junction.

The trail passes a few "TRAIL NOT MAINTAINED" signs. Bypass these trails and stay on the main trail.

Follow the next sign toward Lookout Rock. The view from Lookout Rock at 6,887 feet (2,099 m) above sea level is a major highlight of the trail.

Continue on the trail down the rock for 67 feet (20 m) which then veers east. Hike 450 feet (135 m) to the Jackson Lake Lodge Junction and continue on the Emma Matilda Lake Trail heading east. In another 430 feet (131 m), cross a small bridge that spans a seasonal creek and swampy area.

The trail passes through a thickly wooded old-growth area until it drops to the lake with a tiny rocky beach. From there, the trail continues through thick forest for another 1.8 miles (2.9 km) and reconnects near the lake with many fallen trees.

Walk near the lakeshore for another 1.1 miles (1.7 km) to a bridge over a seasonal creek, then on to the first trail junction in another 0.3 mile (0.5 km). Turn right (south) and hike the remaining 0.6 mile (1 km) to the parking area.

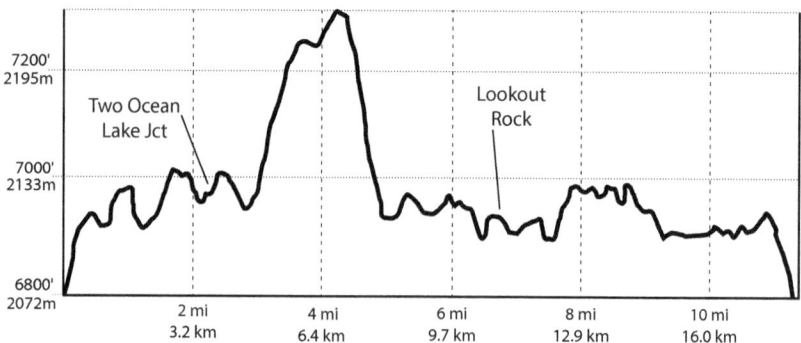

SOUTH JACKSON LAKE

EMMA MATILDA LAKE

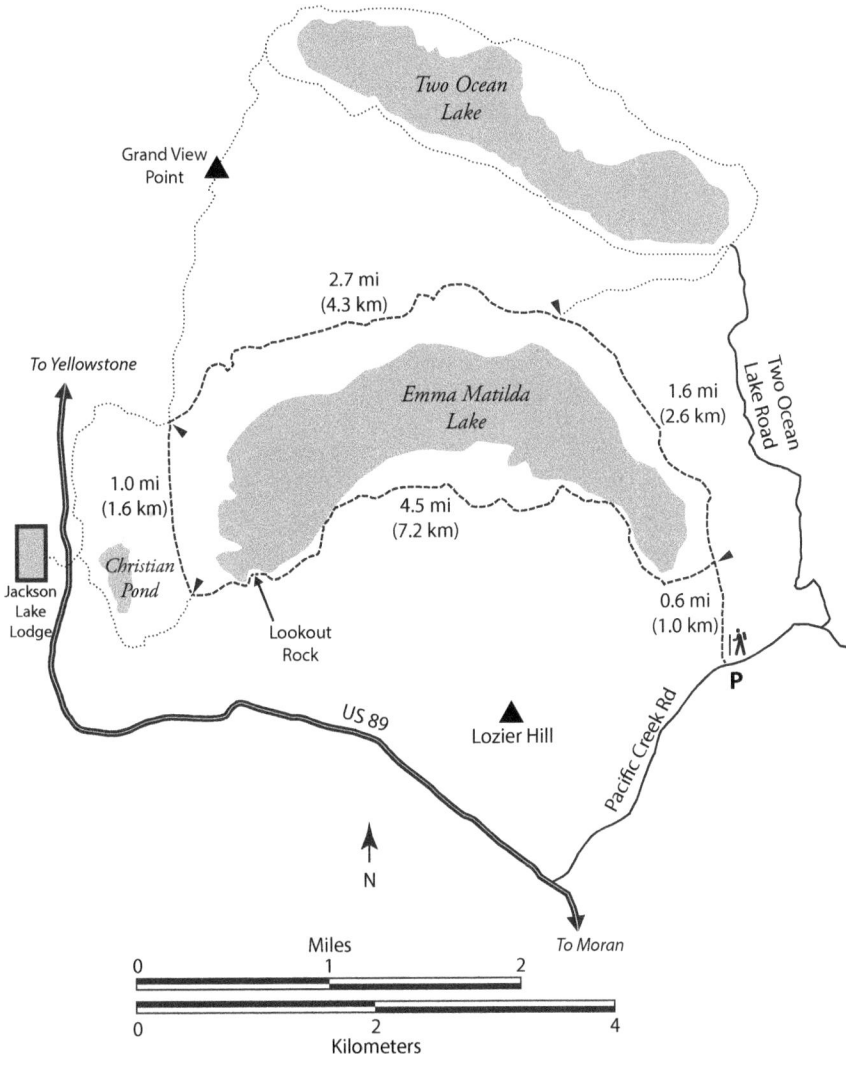

Two Ocean Lake

Grand View Point

2.7 mi (4.3 km)

To Yellowstone

Emma Matilda Lake

1.6 mi (2.6 km)

Two Ocean Lake Road

1.0 mi (1.6 km)

4.5 mi (7.2 km)

Jackson Lake Lodge

Christian Pond

Lookout Rock

0.6 mi (1.0 km)

P

US 89

Lozier Hill

Pacific Creek Rd

N

To Moran

Miles
0   1   2

Kilometers
0   2   4

SOUTH JACKSON LAKE

JACKSON LAKE

4 GRANDVIEW POINT (3.6 mi / 5.8 km / Mod)

Overview: A short sunset hike to a spectacular viewpoint with commanding views of Two Ocean Lake and Jackson Lake.

Trip style: Out and back

Distance: 1.8 miles (2.9 km) to summit, 3.6 miles (5.8 km) total

Elevation gain: 719 feet (219 m)

Max. Elevation: 7,823 feet (2,384 m)

Difficulty: Moderate

Trailhead: Grand View Road
43.8943°N, -110.5688°W / 43°53'39"N, -110°34'08"W
12T 0534631E 4860220N

Traffic: Light

Maps: Moran USGS topo 7.5' USGS topo

Notes: The turnoff to the road to the trailhead was unsigned at the time of publication.

Trailhead Directions

Drive north from Jackson on US 191 for 30.3 miles (48.8 km). Turn left (west) at Moran Junction. Drive 5.8 miles (9.3 km) and turn right on an unsigned road. This turnoff is 0.9 mile (1.5 km) north of the Jackson Lake Lodge turnoff. Continue 0.15 mile (0.24 km) and park in the dirt lot.

Trailhead Facilities

None.

Hike Description

Start hiking at the steel gate with the large two-track trail headed northeast. The two-track reduces to a single-track and crosses a road at 0.67 mile (1.1 km) that leads to a visible remote measurement station. There is a trail sign indicating which direction to walk.

In another 0.25 mile (0.4 km), the trail connects with the Emma Matilda Lake Trail. Turn left (north) and walk 0.7 mile (1.1 km) to Grand View Point.

There are two summits. The first encountered overlooks Jackson Lake. Continue on for a short distance to the northern, higher summit marked by the easily missed Grand View Point sign. It is on the west edge of the summit clearing.

The hike takes 45 minutes if you are fit and motivated. Give yourself adequate time to catch the sunset. The sun drops below the mountains well before the official local sunset time, up to an hour before, depending on the time of year.

GRAND VIEW POINT

Two Ocean Lake

Grand View Point

0.7 mi
(1.1 km)

To Yellowstone   0.9 mi
(1.4 km)

P

Emma Matilda Lake

Two Ocean Lake Road

Jackson Lake Lodge

Christian Pond

US 89

Lozier Hill

Pacific Creek Rd

N

To Moran

Miles
0   1   2

0   2   4
Kilometers

7400'
2255m

7200'
2194m

7000'
2133m

Emma Matilda Lake Trail

0.5 mi
0.8 km

1 mi
1.6 km

1.5 mi
2.4 km

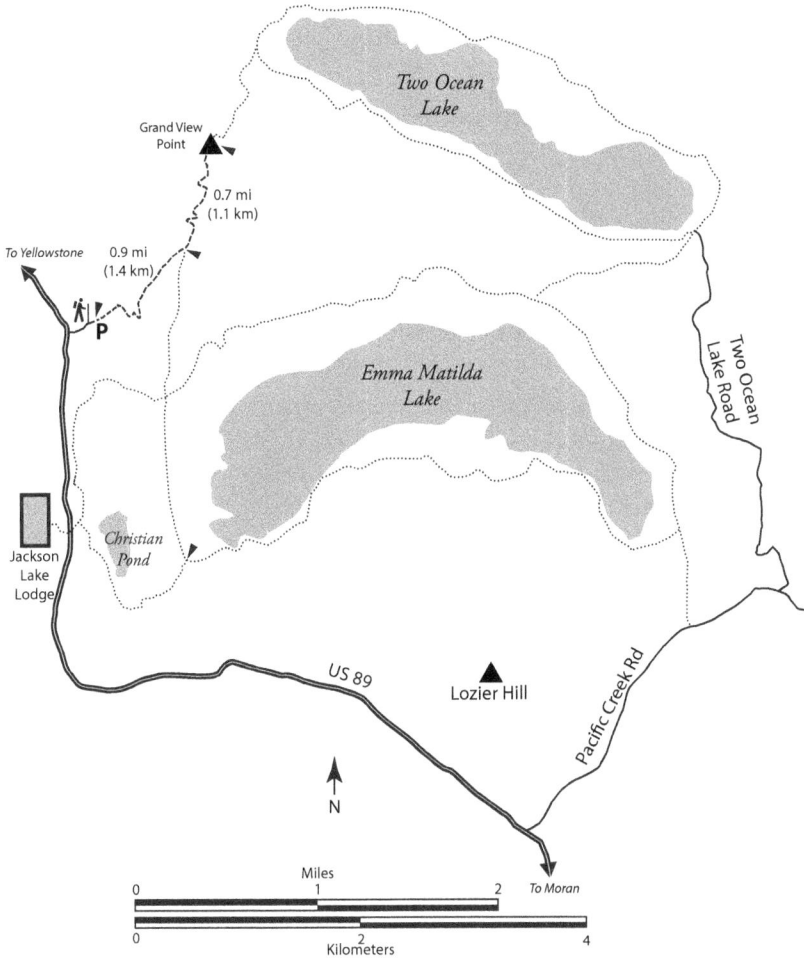

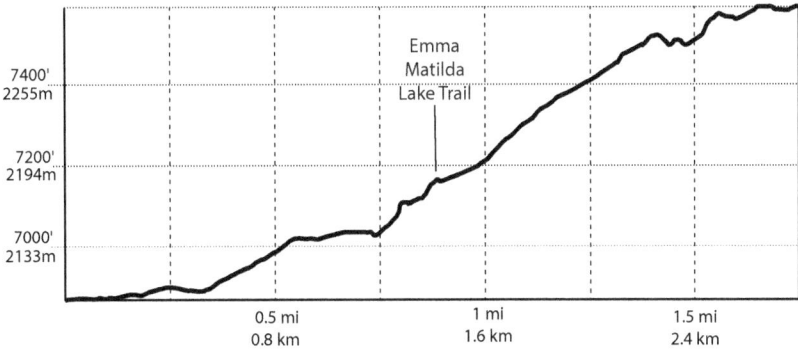

SOUTH JACKSON LAKE

5 JACKSON LAKE DAM (1.8 mi / 2.9 km / Easy)

Overview: A flat, easy, short hike along the top of Jackson Lake Dam.

Trip style: Out and back

Distance: 0.9 mile (1.4 km) to end of dam, 1.8 miles (2.9 km) total

Elevation gain: Negligible

Max. Elevation: 6,783 feet (2,067 m)

Difficulty: Easy

Trailhead: Jackson Lake Dam parking lot
43.8569°N, -110.5893°W / 43°51'25"N, -110°35'22"W
12T 0533010E 4856064N

Traffic: Light

Maps: Moran USGS topo 7.5' USGS topo

Notes: It is easy to walk along the wide top of the dam.

Trailhead Directions

Drive north from Jackson on US 191 for 30.3 miles (48.8 km). Turn left (west) at Moran Junction. Drive 4 miles (6.4 km) and turn left at Jackson Lake Junction. Continue for 1.4 miles (2.2 km) and park in the lot south of the dam.

Trailhead Facilities

Information kiosks.

Hike Description

Cross the roadway to the lakeside of the road. Walk north on the lakeside of the dam along the sidewalk. Once over the dam, continue to the stepped surface of the dam.

Continue hiking along the concrete dike northwest until it turns north, then walk to the end for a total of 0.9 mile (1.4 km).

There is no shade or weather protection along this short walk. The views of Willow Flats are expansive and worth the walk.

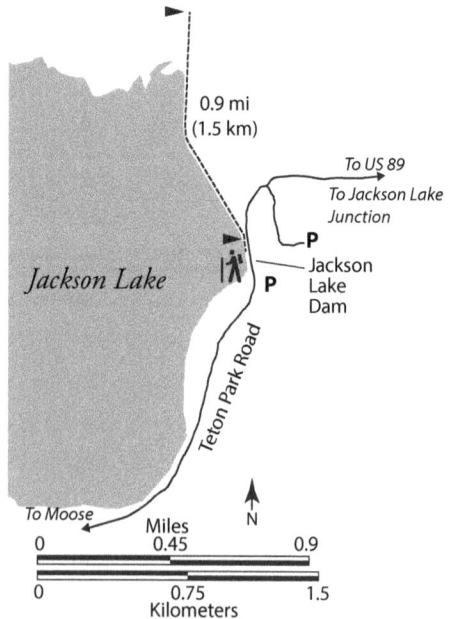

0.9 mi
(1.5 km)

To US 89
To Jackson Lake Junction

P

Jackson Lake Dam

P

Jackson Lake

Teton Park Road

To Moose

Miles
0   0.45   0.9

Kilometers
0   0.75   1.5

N

6 LOOKOUT ROCK (3.2 mi / 5.2 km / Mod)

Overview: A hike through a lightly-used section of Grand Teton National Park to a rock that overlooks Emma Matilda Lake.

Trip style: Out and back

Distance: 1.6 miles (2.6 km) one way, 3.2 miles (5.2 km) round trip

Elevation gain: 343 feet (104 m)

Max. Elevation: 6,967 feet (2,124 m)

Difficulty: Easy to moderate

Trailhead: Signal Mountain Marina Road.
43.8409°N, -110.6121°W / 43°50'27"N, -110°36'44"W
12T 0531183E 4854280N

Traffic: Light

Maps: Two Ocean Lake, Moran 7.5' USGS topos

Notes: The official start of the trail is at the Jackson Lake Lodge horse corrals. If parking is unavailable, park alongside the dirt pullout on the main road and access the trail.

Trailhead Directions

Drive north from Jackson on US 191 for 30.3 miles (48.8 km). Turn left (west) at Moran Junction. Continue for 4.9 miles (7.8 km) and turn left (west) into Jackson Lake Lodge. Turn left at the gas station and park in the southeast parking lot. Alternatively, park 900 feet (266 m) south of Jackson Lake Lodge in the dirt turnouts along the road north of Christian Creek Bridge to access the trail.

Trailhead Facilities

General store, gas station, water, restrooms, bike rack.

Hike Description

Start hiking from the southeast corner of the Jackson Lake Lodge horse corral parking lot. The trail passes under the Christian Creek bridge. In 600 feet (183 m), take the right trail fork at the junction heading away from the highway.

The trail passes through tall shrubbery and marshy wetlands. Continue past the Christian Pond Overlook to the first trail junction at 1.2 miles (1.9 km).

Continue to follow the signs to Lookout Rock. The rock is a minor climb and has a nearly cliff-like drop-off overlooking the southern portion of Emma Matilda Lake.

Note

Be aware that bears often frequent this area. Obvious tree markings abound. Keep bear spray ready in hand to deploy at a moment's notice.

LOOKOUT ROCK

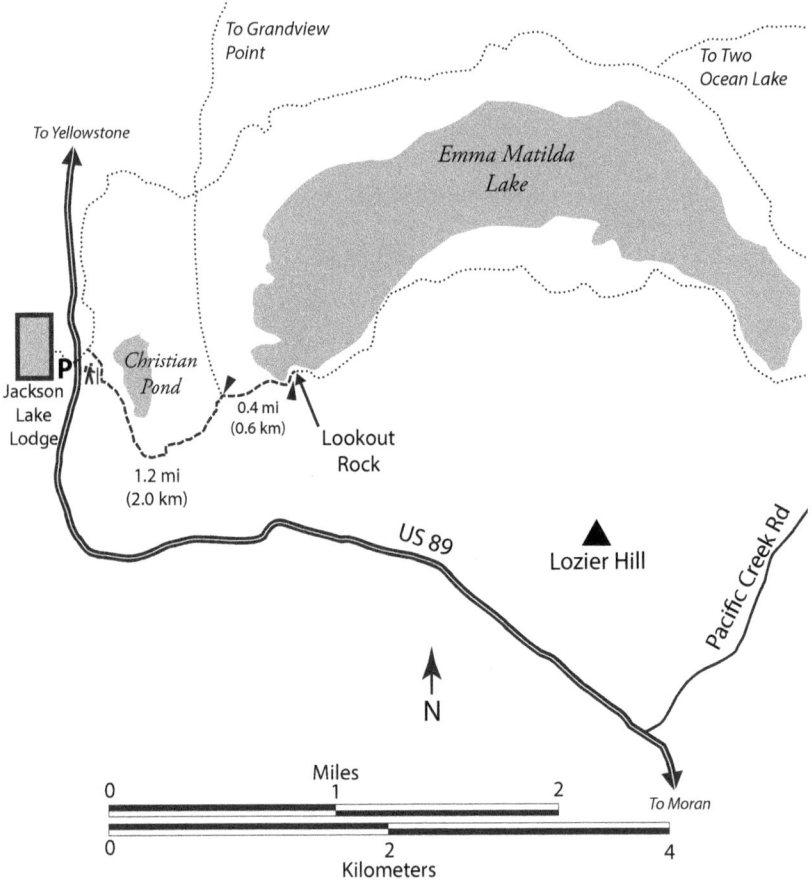

To Grandview
Point

To Two
Ocean Lake

To Yellowstone

Emma Matilda
Lake

P

Christian
Pond

Jackson
Lake
Lodge

0.4 mi
(0.6 km)

Lookout
Rock

1.2 mi
(2.0 km)

US 89

Lozier Hill

Pacific Creek Rd

N

Miles
0   1   2

0   2   4
Kilometers

To Moran

SOUTH JACKSON LAKE

7 LUNCH TREE HILL (0.4 mi / 0.8 km / Easy)

Overview: A path to the famous overlook commemorating John D. Rockefeller Jr.'s vision of Grand Teton as a park.

Trip style: Out and back

Distance: 0.2 mile (0.4 km) one way, 0.4 mile (0.8 km) total

Elevation gain: 93 feet (28 m)

Max. Elevation: 6,955 feet (2,120 m)

Difficulty: Easy

Trailhead: Jackson Lake Lodge viewing deck
43.8777°N, -110.5780°W / 43°52'40"N, -110°34'41"W
12T 0533899E 4858371N

Traffic: Medium

Maps: Two Ocean Lake 7.5' USGS topo

Notes: The pathway is partially paved and family friendly.

Trailhead Directions

Drive north from Jackson on US 191 for 30.3 miles (48.8 km). Turn left (west) at Moran Junction. Continue for 4.9 miles (7.8 km) and turn left (west) into Jackson Lake Lodge. Park near the main lobby.

Trailhead Facilities

General store, gas station, water, restrooms, bike rack, lodge.

Hike Description

Walk into the entrance of Jackson Lake Lodge and proceed up the stairs. Walk to the main window and take the door outside to the left of the main window. Walk to the wooden fence, then turn right and walk north along the sidewalk to the trail sign under the conifers.

From here, follow the marked trail signs toward Lunch Tree Hill.

There are multiple interpretive signs along the pathway up to the top of the hill. There is a large rock with the plaque dedicated to John D. Rockefeller Jr.'s vision for the park.

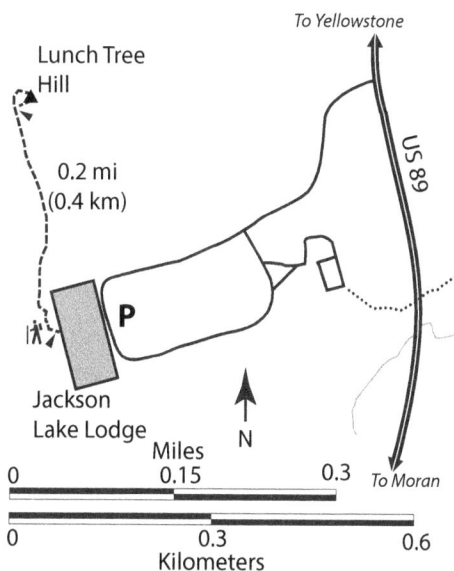

To Yellowstone

Lunch Tree Hill

0.2 mi (0.4 km)

US 89

P

Jackson Lake Lodge

Miles N
0   0.15   0.3   To Moran

0   0.3   0.6
Kilometers

8 POTHOLES (0.6 mi / 1 km / Easy)

Overview: A short, easy hike to a unique glacial geologic formation.

Trip style: Out and back

Distance: 0.3 mile (0.5 km) one way, 0.6 mile (1 km) total

Elevation gain: 26 feet (8 m)

Max. Elevation: 6,900 feet (2,103 m)

Difficulty: Easy

Trailhead: Potholes turnout
43.8068°N, -110.6283°W / 43°48'24"N, -110°37'42"W
12T 0529897E 4850477N

Traffic: Light

Maps: Jenny Lake 7.5' USGS topo

Notes: The trail leads from the parking lot into the sagebrush field.

Trailhead Directions

Drive north from Jackson on US 191 for 12.3 miles (19.8 km) to Moose Junction and turn left on Teton Park Road. Continue past the entrance station for a total of 15.2 miles (24.4 km) to the Potholes turnout. Drive to the end of the lot.

Trailhead Facilities

None.

Hike Description

Start at the trail leading south from the parking lot into the open sagebrush field. Soon the trail passes the first pothole that has two clusters of trees inside the pothole. It is possible to circumnavigate the first pothole. There is a faint trail to follow but will require some off-trail travel.

From there, continue walking southwest along the trail as it be-gins to disappear into the sagebrush. Once the trail curves to the southwest, it becomes increasingly difficult to follow, ultimately leading toward another large pothole. The last 160 feet (49 m) into the pothole is off-trail, traveling through the sagebrush.

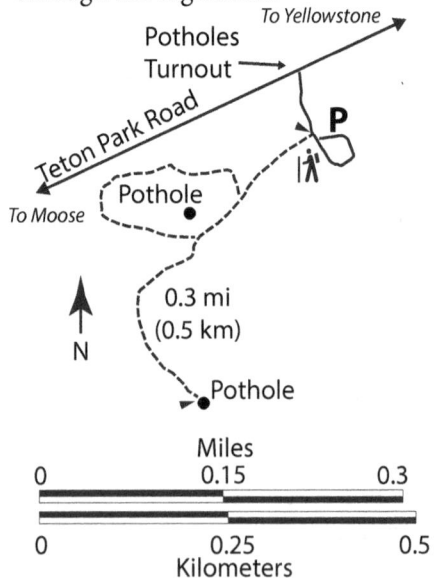

9 SIGNAL MOUNTAIN MARINA CLIFF
(2.8 mi / 4.6 km / Mod)

Overview: A lightly hiked trail along a high cliff over Jackson Lake.

Trip style: Out and back

Distance: 1.4 miles (2.3 km) one way, 2.8 miles (4.6 km) total

Elevation gain: 317 feet (97 m) (total trail gain/loss)

Max. Elevation: 6,869 feet (2,094 m)

Difficulty: Moderate

Trailhead: Signal Mountain Marina Boat Launch
43.8385°N, -110.6164°W / 43°50'19"N, -110°36'59"W
12T 0530842E 4854010N

Traffic: Light

Maps: Jenny Lake, Moran 7.5' USGS topo

Notes: Avoid standing on the cliff edge as it can crumble.

Trailhead Directions

Drive north from Jackson on US 191 for 12.3 miles (19.8 km) to Moose Junction and turn left on Teton Park Road. Continue past the entrance station for a total of 17.8 miles (28.7 km) to the Signal Mountain Lodge entrance.

Trailhead Facilities

General store, gas station, water, restrooms, bike rack, restaurant, gift shop.

Hike Description

Start at the trail leading south from the boat dock. The trail has a bear warning sign and a no pets sign but no trail name or distance signs.

The trail stays slightly above the beach shoreline for 0.14 mile, then rapidly rises 84 feet (26 m) to the peak elevation in 0.1 mile (0.16

km). The trail rolls along for 1.4 miles (2.3 km) along the cliff. There are views of the lake for nearly the entire hike until it turns southeast.

The trail drops down to the beach level and ends at a group camp and single campsite with bear boxes.

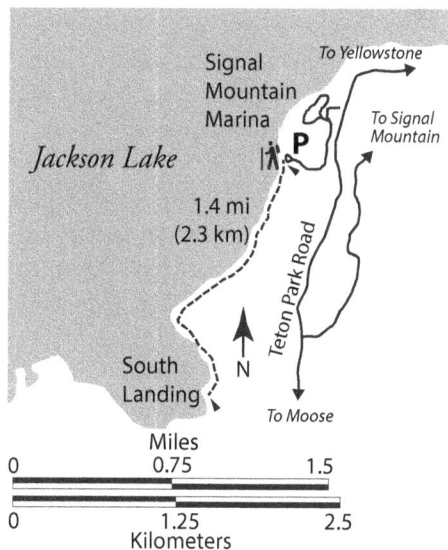

SOUTH JACKSON LAKE

10 SIGNAL MOUNTAIN SUMMIT (9.4 mi / 15 km / Mod)

Overview: A longer family-friendly hike that takes hikers to a central viewpoint of Grand Teton National Park.

Trip style: Out and back

Distance: 4.7 miles (7.5 km) to summit, 9.4 miles (15 km) round trip

Elevation gain: 909 feet (277 m)

Max. Elevation: 7,726 feet (2,355 m)

Difficulty: Moderate

Trailhead: Signal Mountain Marina Road
43.8409°N, -110.6121°W / 43°50'27"N, -110°36'44"W
12T 0531183E 4854280N

Traffic: Light

Maps: Moran 7.5' USGS topo

Notes: The official start of the trail is on Signal Mountain Marina Road. Starting on Signal Mountain Road from the dirt pullout eliminates crossing the park road.

Trailhead Directions

Drive north from Jackson on US 191 for 12.3 miles (19.8 km) to Moose Junction and turn left on Teton Park Road. Continue past the entrance station for a total of 17.8 miles (28.7 km) to the Signal Mountain Lodge entrance. Park in the main lot at the Signal Mountain Lodge.

Alternative Trailhead Directions

Turn in at the Signal Mountain Summit Road and drive 1.2 miles (1.9 km) and park at the large road-side turnout. Walk south 250 feet (77 m) and start the trail. Use this approach to avoid the traffic of the lodge and the difficulty of finding the official trailhead.

Trailhead Facilities

General store, gas station, water, restrooms, bike rack, restaurant, gift shop.

Hike Description

Start from the parking lot, walk past the gas station, through the intersection, past the Signal Mountain RV dump station, turn left (south), and walk for 385 feet (117 m) to reach the official summit trailhead.

Hike 245 feet (75 m) and cross to the east side of the park road to the signed trail. Continue for 0.25 mile (0.4 km) to the Signal Mountain Summit Road. Cross the road and continue on the trail past a marshy pond north of the trail for 0.27 mile (0.43 km) to the first trail junction.

Take the ridge trail (left, N) and continue for 1.3 miles (2.1 km) along a slowly rising trail through a partially forested area to the next trail junction.

Take the left fork at the junction toward the summit. Hike another 1.5 miles (2.4 km) along a ridge with a wide view of Jackson Lake. The trail switches back south, then north again to reach the overlook.

To continue on to the summit, walk along the shoulder of the road for 1 mile (1.6 km). Be cautious of distracted drivers on this narrow road. The summit view overlooks the wide expanse of northern Jackson Hole and looks like a scene out of a movie.

Return down the trail and take the left (S) fork at the junction via the lakes. Enjoy the small lake nestled among the trees on the south side of the trail. This side diversion adds 0.1 mile (0.16 km) to the hike and is worth it.

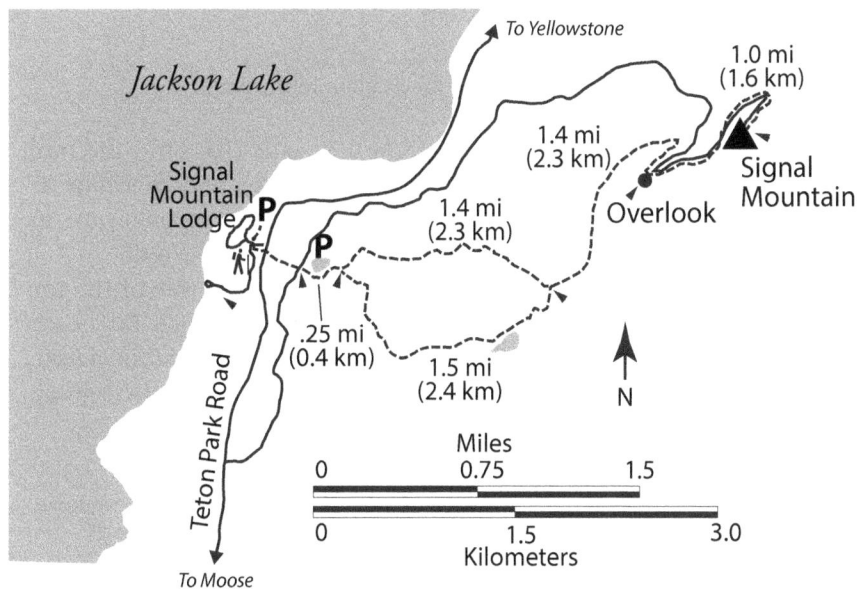

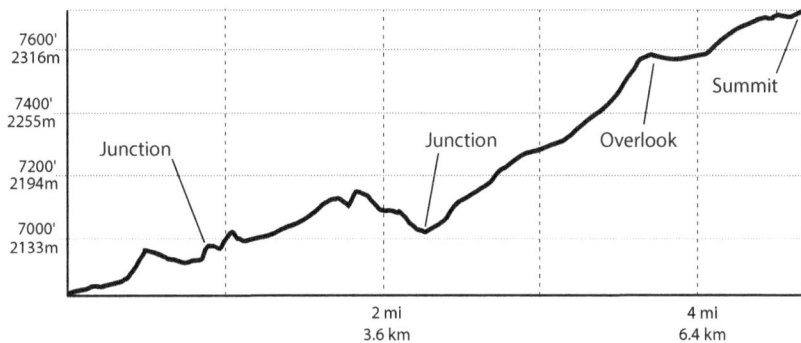

SOUTH JACKSON LAKE

JACKSON LAKE

11 SOUTH LANDING (1.2 mi / 1.8 km / Easy)

Overview: A lightly hiked trail to a secluded beach on Jackson Lake.
Trip style: Out and back
Distance: 0.6 miles (0.9 km) one way, 1.2 miles (1.8 km) total
Elevation gain: –128 feet (-39 m)
Max. Elevation: 6,896 feet (2,102 m)
Difficulty: Easy
Trailhead: South Landing Pond
43.8230°N, -110.6156°W / 43°49'23"N, -110°36'56"W
12T 0530913E 4852284N
Traffic: Light
Maps: Moran 7.5' USGS topo
Notes: Avoid blocking the access gates to the pond.

Trailhead Directions

Drive north from Jackson on US 191 for 12.3 miles (19.8 km) to Moose Junction and turn left on Teton Park Road. Continue past the entrance station for a total of 16.5 miles (26.6 km) to an unmarked junction. Turn left and park in the dirt lot with a wood fence and trail sign.

Trailhead Facilities

None.

Hike Description

Start on the trail leading south from the dirt lot. The trail turns gently west over 300 feet (91 m) and continues losing elevation toward Jackson Lake.

The trail turns southwest and enters a stand of trees at 0.25 mile (0.4 km). This forest area is thin, so it is possible to see some distance into the woods and along the trail.

At 0.37 mile (0.6 km), the trail turns northwest and continues as Jackson Lake becomes visible in the last section of the trail.

The trail breaks free of the forest and opens up to a rocky beach and secluded cove on Jackson Lake. There is a campsite and also a group campsite at this cove.

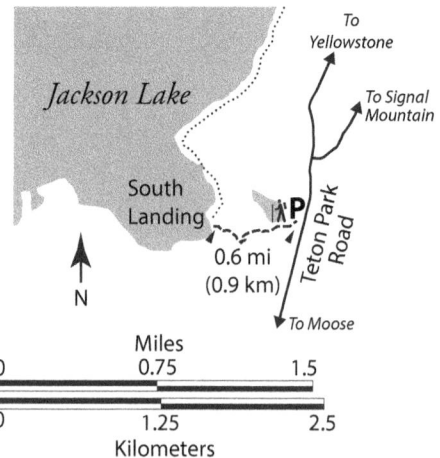

SOUTH JACKSON LAKE

12 TWO OCEAN LAKE (6.2 mi / 10 km / Mod)

Overview: An uncrowded hike around a large back-country lake with the chance to view wildlife and enjoy solitude.

Trip style: Loop

Distance: 6.2 miles (10 km)

Elevation gain: 550 feet (168 m) (total trail gain/loss)

Max. Elevation: 7,041 feet (2,146 m)

Difficulty: Moderate

Trailhead: Two Ocean Lake parking area
43.9011°N, -110.5017°W / 43°54'04"N, -110°30'06"W
12T 0540021E 4861012N

Traffic: Light

Maps: Two Ocean Lake, Whetstone Mountain 7.5' USGS Topos

Notes: High bear activity in the area.

Trailhead Directions

Drive north from Jackson on US 191 for 30.3 miles (48.8 km). Turn left (west) at Moran Junction. Drive 1.2 miles (1.9 km) and turn right (northeast) on Pacific Creek Road. Drive 2.1 miles (3.3 km) and turn left toward Two Ocean Lake. Continue 2.4 miles (3.9 km) on the dirt road to the parking lot.

Trailhead Facilities

Restrooms, information kiosk.

Hike Description

Start the hike by walking down the trail at the north end of the parking lot. It leads over a small bridge at the outlet of Two Ocean Lake and continues northeast.

In 0.3 mile (0.5 km), the trail turns northwest and continues following a generally straight path.

At 0.9 mile (1.4 km), the trail continues straight while the lakeshore falls away to the south, at times being 0.3 mile (0.5 km) from the trail.

Once the path sweeps south and connects with Grand View Point Trail at 3.3 miles (5.3 km), the trail enters and stays in a heavily forested area. Continue the 2.9 miles (4.6 km) to the trailhead.

Side Trips

At the western junction, divert from the loop trail to hike 1 mile (1.6 km) to reach Grand View Point that overlooks Two Ocean, Emma Matilda, and Jackson lakes.

Notes

Bears are highly active in this area. Bring bear spray and have it ready. Insects can be intense. Bring an appropriate insect repellent.

TWO OCEAN LAKE

3.3 mi
4.8 km

Two Ocean
Lake

1 mi
1.6 km

Grand
View Point ▲

2.9 mi
4.6 km

P | 🚶

To
Yellowstone

1 mi
1.6 km

Two Ocean Lake Road

Emma Matilda
Lake

Christian
Pond

Jackson
Lake
Lodge

US 89

▲
Lozier Hill

Pacific Creek Rd

↑
N

Miles

| 0 | | 1 | | 2 |

| 0 | | 2 | | 4 |
Kilometers

To Moran

7000'
2133m

Grand View
Point Jct

6920'
2109m

2 mi
3.2 km

4 mi
6.4 km

6 mi
9.7 km

SOUTH JACKSON LAKE

Colter Bay

Colter Bay is the busy hub of activity in the South Jackson Lake area. It has a general store, fishing license sales, multiple parking lots, visitor centers, boat launches, restaurants, restrooms, a gas station, and just about anything a visitor to the area may need.

The large network of trails that lead south from the parking lot offers many options for hikers and wildlife enthusiasts. There are multiple, easy trail options for families and the adventurous alike.

The Jackson Lake Lookout along the Heron Pond Trail is a pleasant and short diversion up a small hill to a broad lookout. Note that this viewpoint is relatively far from the lake. The geography of the area makes it easy to try out cross-country, off-trail hiking as well. The forest is generally open, making it easy to try forest travel off-trail.

There are multiple loops for campsites at Colter Bay as well. They are highly popular and making reservations well in advance is recommended.

Bald eagles can be seen nesting high in the trees above Hermitage Point. Ospreys are in the area as well, making for an interesting birdwatching experience. Their flight patterns are mesmerizing.

Keep your eyes up and out, as grizzly bears regularly wander through this area, too.

Bald eagle, Colter Bay.

Grizzly bear claw marks, Colter Bay.

JACKSON LAKE

13 HERMITAGE POINT (9.6 mi / 15.4 km / Mod)

Overview: A long family-friendly hike with minimal elevation gain to an isolated point to view Jackson Lake.

Trip style: Loop

Distance: 9.6 miles (15.4 km)

Elevation gain: 111 feet (34 m) net gain, 922 feet (281 m) gain/loss

Max. Elevation: 6,886 ft (2,099 m)

Difficulty: Moderate

Trailhead: Colter Bay Marina
43.9006°N, -110.6420°W / 43°54'02"N, -110°38'31"W
12T 0528751E 4860899N

Traffic: Light to moderate

Maps: Two Ocean Lake, Colter Bay, Jenny Lake 7.5' USGS Topos

Notes: Trail signs can be confusing and are not consistent.

Trailhead Directions

Drive north from Jackson on US 191 for 30.3 miles (48.8 km). Turn left (west) at Moran Junction. Drive 9.3 miles (14.9 km) and turn left at the Colter Bay Junction. Drive to the end of the road, turn left (S) and park near the Hermitage Point Trailhead kiosk.

Trailhead Facilities

General store, gas station, water, restrooms, bike rack, restaurant, ranger station, fishing supplies, gift shop.

Hike Description

Note that the trail signs in this section of Grand Teton are not as well marked as other areas. Take the widest trail fork at each junction which will lead you to Hermitage Point. Refer to the map.

There are two options for starting the trail: follow the lakeshore to the first trail junction or walk 100 feet (30 m) north to the trailhead and travel over the hill. Either route takes 0.4 mile (0.6 km) to the first trail junction.

This first junction is a triangle (see map) and can lead to Heron or Swan Ponds. Take the right fork and continue for 0.1 mile (0.2 km) and take the left trail fork at the junction. (It was unmarked at the time of this writing.) Either route reconnects at the NW end of Heron Pond, then continues 0.4 mile (0.6 km) along Heron Pond to the next junction.

Heron Pond is large and easily accessible from the trail. Travel through the sparse forest cover to the shore for the chance to see the extensive lily pads, water birds, and amphibians.

Turn right (S) and continue 0.8 mile (1.3 km) up a hill that gains 95 feet (29 m) to the next trail junction. This junction connects the east and west sides of the trails around the peninsula that Hermitage Point sits on.

Take the right trail and continue 2.2 miles (3.5 km) to Hermitage Point. The trail travels up and down minor hills along the way. Hermitage Point is a rocky beach 50 feet (13 m) south of the trail along a well-traveled dirt path.

From the point, continue counterclockwise around the peninsula along the eastern shore for 2.2 miles (3.5 km) to the eastern peninsula crossing junction. (It is possible to bypass the northeast overlook and cut 0.1 mile (160 m) off the hike.)

Continue northeast along the trail for 1.3 miles (2.1 km). The trail passes an unmarked (at the time of this writing) junction that forks north toward Jackson Lake Lodge. The southeast portion of Swan Lake comes into view along this portion of the hike.

Continue following the loop counterclockwise (left) to the junction near Heron Pond. Take the right fork (NW) toward Swan Lake and continue for 1.2 miles (1.9 km) mostly along the shore of Swan Lake that is substantially covered in lily pads.

At the final junction, turn right and travel over a minor hill for 0.4 mile (0.6 km) to reach the parking lot. To bypass the hill, turn left at the junction and retrace the beginning of the trail.

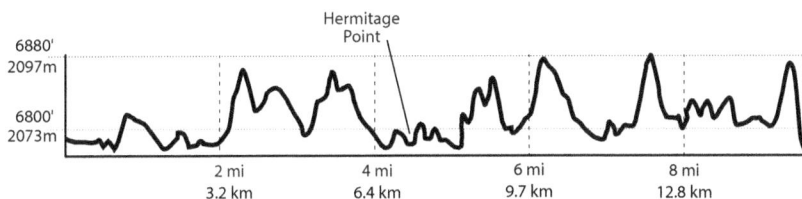

Hermitage Point looking toward Mt. Moran, 6.4 miles (10.3 km) away.

HERMITAGE POINT

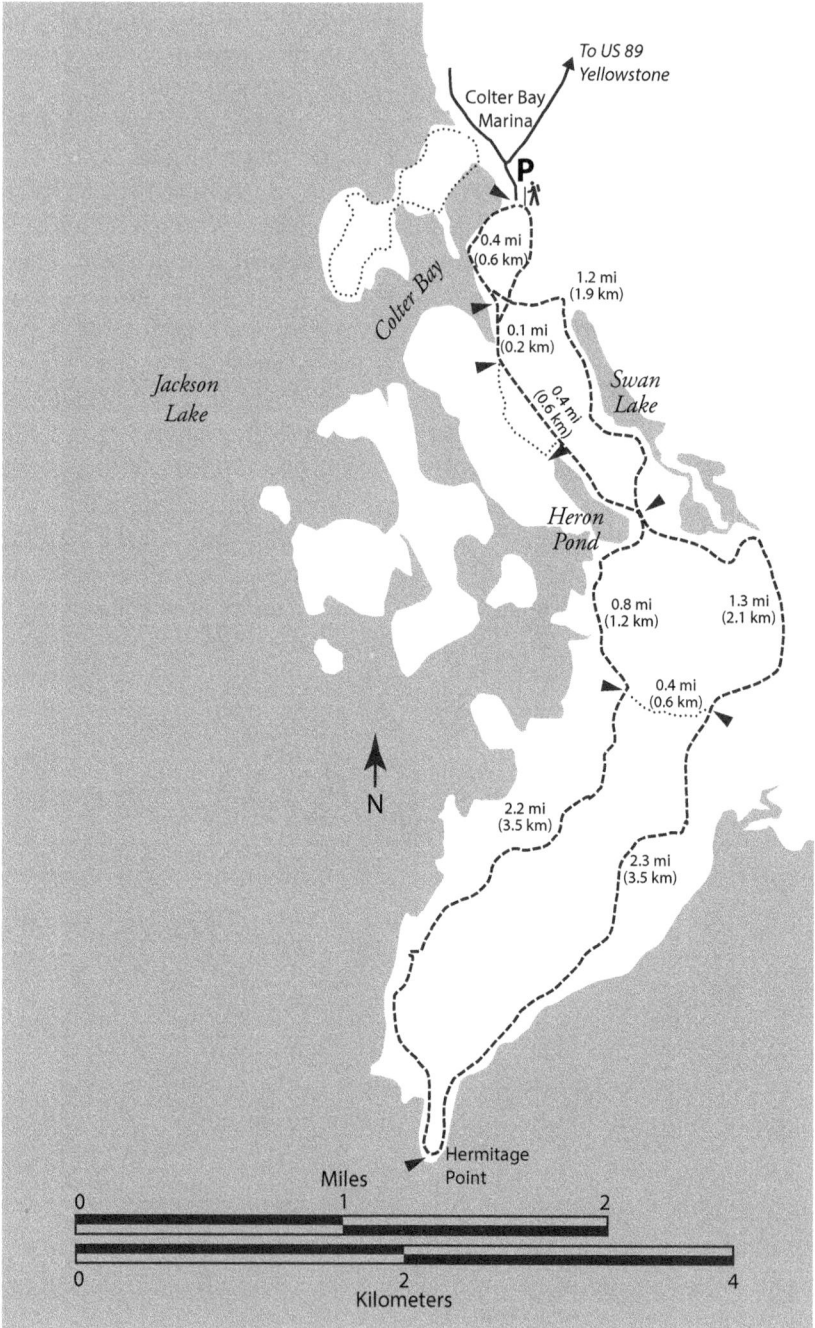

To US 89
Yellowstone

Colter Bay
Marina

P

Colter Bay

Jackson
Lake

0.4 mi
(0.6 km)

1.2 mi
(1.9 km)

0.1 mi
(0.2 km)

0.4 mi
(0.6 km)

Swan
Lake

Heron
Pond

0.8 mi
(1.2 km)

1.3 mi
(2.1 km)

0.4 mi
(0.6 km)

N

2.2 mi
(3.5 km)

2.3 mi
(3.5 km)

Hermitage
Point

Miles

| 0 | 1 | 2 |

Kilometers

| 0 | 2 | 4 |

COLTER BAY

14 LAKESHORE LOOP (2.2 mi / 3.5 km / Easy)

Overview: A short, family-friendly hike on a small peninsula.

Trip style: Loop

Distance: 2.2 miles (3.5 km)

Elevation gain: 207 feet (63 m) gain/loss

Max. Elevation: 6,834 feet (2,083 m)

Difficulty: Easy

Trailhead: Colter Bay Marina
43.9043°N, -110.6448°W / 43°54'16"N, -110°38'41"W
12T 0528520E 4861307N

Traffic: Light

Maps: Colter Bay 7.5' USGS topo

Notes: The trail is highly trafficked and easy to follow.

Trailhead Directions

Drive north from Jackson on US 191 for 30.3 miles (48.8 km). Turn left (west) at Moran Junction. Drive 9.3 miles (14.9 km) and turn left at the Colter Bay Junction. Drive to the end of the road, turn left (S) and park near the visitor center.

Trailhead Facilities

General store, gas station, water, restrooms, bike rack, restaurant, ranger station, fishing supplies, gift shop.

Hike Description

Start at the Colter Bay visitor center, walk 425 feet (129 m) to the signed concrete stairs with steel handrails, then follow the trail northwest toward the lake. Continue along the lakeshore for a total of 0.5 mile (0.8 km) to the junction on the dike. It is possible to bypass the peninsula and return to the parking lot or continue farther on.

Cross the dike and take the path 1.1 miles (1.8 km) path around the peninsula with a minor elevation gain and loss around the loop. Hiking in either direction does not change the difficulty. The views of the mountains are slightly better in the counterclockwise direction.

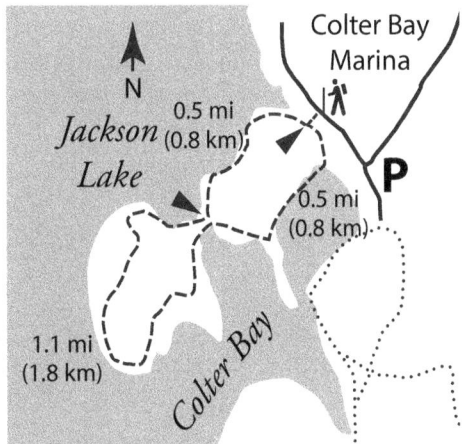

COLTER BAY

15 SWAN LAKE AND HERON POND
(3 mi / 4.8 km / Easy)

Overview: A hike to several lakes and ponds with wildlife.

Trip style: Loop

Distance: 3 miles (4.8 km)

Elevation gain: 330 feet (101 m) gain/loss

Max. Elevation: 6,883 ft (2,098 m)

Difficulty: Easy

Trailhead: Colter Bay Marina
43.9006°N, -110.6420°W / 43°54'02"N, -110°38'31"W
12T 0528751E 4860899N

Traffic: Light to moderate

Maps: Colter Bay 7.5' USGS Topo

Notes: The trail signs can be confusing on this trail.

Trailhead Directions

Drive north from Jackson on US 191 for 30.3 miles (48.8 km). Turn left (west) at Moran Junction. Drive 9.3 miles (14.9 km) and turn left at the Colter Bay Junction. Drive to the end of the road, turn left (S) and park near the Hermitage Point Trailhead kiosk.

Trailhead Facilities

General store, gas station, water, restrooms, bike rack, restaurant, ranger station, fishing supplies, gift shop.

Hike Description

Note that the trail signs in this section of Grand Teton are not as well marked as other areas. Take most all right turn forks at each junction. This will bring you to the lakes. Refer to the map.

There are two options for starting the trail: follow the lakeshore to the first trail junction or walk 100 feet (30 m) north to the trailhead and travel over the hill. Either route takes 0.4 mile (0.6 km) to the first trail junction.

This first junction is a triangle (see map) and can lead to Heron or Swan Ponds. Take the right fork and continue for 0.1 mile (0.2 km) and take the left trail at the junction. (It was unmarked at the time of this writing.) Either route reconnects at the NW end of Heron Pond, then continues 0.4 mile (0.6 km) along Heron Pond to the next junction.

Heron Pond is large and easily accessible from the trail. Walk through the sparse forest cover to the shore for the chance to see the extensive lily pads, water birds, and amphibians.

Turn left at the next junction (NW) toward Swan Lake and continue for 1.2 miles (1.9 km) mostly along the shore of Swan Lake that is substantially covered in lily pads, making the water dark.

At the final junction, turn right and travel over a minor hill for 0.4 mile (0.6 km) to reach the parking lot. To bypass the hill, turn left at the junction and retrace the beginning of the trail. Though the signs are confusing, it is difficult to become lost in the area.

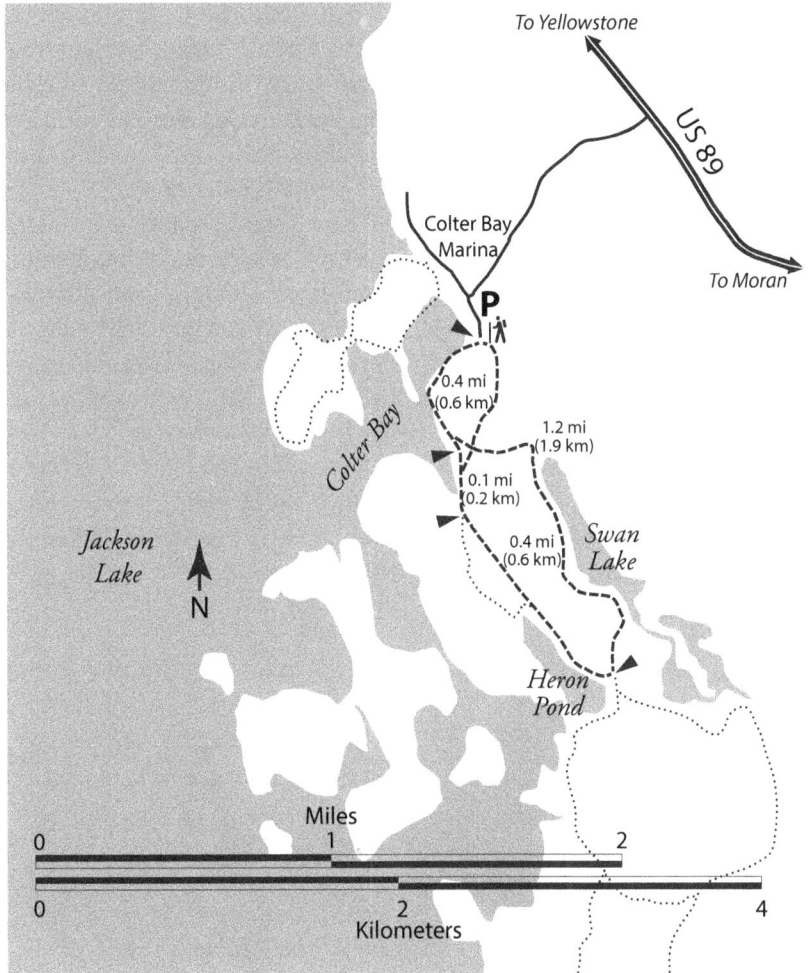

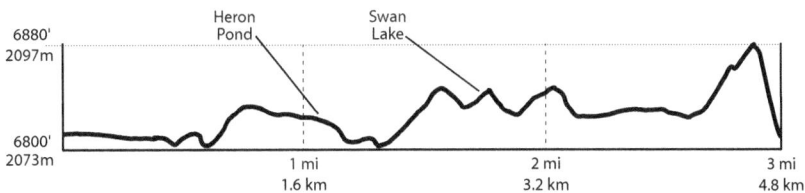

COLTER BAY

North Jackson Lake

The north Jackson Lake area is the most northerly trail area in this book. There are trails inside and outside Grand Teton National Park, providing hikers with a variety of terrain and options for exploration.

The geography at the north point of Jackson Lake is interesting, as the higher mountains disappear in the area northwest of the lake, giving way to a series of creeks, rivers, and lakes in the lumpy hills.

Yellowstone marks the northernmost edge of hikes in this guidebook. The geography of the land changes as you drive up into the Yellowstone caldera, marking the edge of Jackson Hole.

Due to being farther north than the other popular hiking areas, this area receives far less visitation than the more popular areas to the south.

This does not mean that the hikes in the area are any less enjoyable. They are often more interesting because of the solitude they offer.

Instead of the large crowds in south Grand Teton, explore the trails in the northern area of Jackson Lake. They offer a quiet only found here and on Togwotee Pass. It is worth the drive.

The rugged area to the northwest of Jackson Lake has few official trails. This region outside of Grand Teton National Park is part of the Bridger-Teton National Forest. Much of this area is part of the Teton Wilderness, a special use zone that has the rules and regulations of other designated wilderness areas. If you want to try your skill at tough, off-trail travel, this area is for you.

Panorama looking south from the Huckleberry Fire Tower.

16 HUCKLEBERRY FIRE TOWER
(12.6 mi / 20.2 km / Stren)

Overview: A historical hike around one of the only remaining fire lookout towers in the Jackson Hole area.

Trip style: Out and back

Distance: 6.3 miles (10.1 km) one way, 12.6 miles (20.2 km)

Elevation gain: 3,133 feet (955 m)

Max. Elevation: 9,625 feet (2,934 m)

Difficulty: Strenuous

Trailhead: Sheffield Campground
44.0912°N, -110.6633°W / 44°05'28"N, -110°39'48"W
12T 0526956E 4882053N

Traffic: Light

Maps: Flagg Ranch, Huckleberry Mountain 7.5' USGS Topos

Notes: Some route-finding is required to find the cliff trail.

Trailhead Directions

Drive north from Jackson on US 191 for 30.3 miles (48.8 km). Turn left (west) at Moran Junction. Drive 24.3 miles (39.1 km) and turn into Sheffield Campground. Continue 0.6 mile (1 km) to the trailhead.

Trailhead Facilities

Horse corral, restrooms, information kiosk.

Hike Description

The trail begins near the horse corrals and is marked by a sign. The trail begins traveling east and southeast through a medium cover forest for 0.3 mile (0.5 km). At this point, the trail begins a series of switchbacks that makes its way up the mountain, bypassing the old direct trail. The trail breaks free of the heavy forest cover for 0.3 mile

(0.5 km) before entering another heavily forested area. At 0.7 mile (1.1 km), the trail makes several long switchbacks to work its way up the steepening hill.

At 1.3 miles (2.1 km), the trail crosses over an open area of unique-looking layered sedimentary rock as it continues up a wide ridgeline, in and out of tree cover.

A minor creek crossing is at 2.3 miles (3.7 km) where the trail then changes directions. It travels southeast through a short series of switchbacks in a more open forest. At 2.7 miles (4.3 km), the forest gives way to an open area and enters a large burned area at 3 miles (4.8 km).

The trail drops down a small hill at 3.4 miles (5.5 km), crosses a minor creek, then continues the climb. The trail turns southeast, crossing a

JACKSON LAKE

small ravine at 4.5 miles (7.2 km).

The relatively flat area continues for 0.7 mile (1.1 km) before encountering an unmarked junction at 5.4 miles (8.7 km) in a grassy area. Stay to the right and walk up a short hill. As the hill levels out slightly, look for a faint trail to the right in the grass, sometimes marked by a cairn or a wooden arrow (the sign was missing at the time of this writing) near these coordinates:

44.0875°N, -110.5932°W
44°05'15"N, -110°35'36"W
12T 0532563E 4881674N

Hike on an average bearing of 260° W and look for plastic markers on trees, as the trail disappears in the grassy areas. Ascend the steep, crumbly cliff on the switchback trail. Avoid a direct climb, as the loose rock is dangerous. On the ridge, turn left and ascend 0.25 mile (0.4 km) to the fire tower through thin tree cover.

Take care while ascending the stairs, as they are not maintained. This unique protected structure has a spectacular view of northern Jackson Hole.

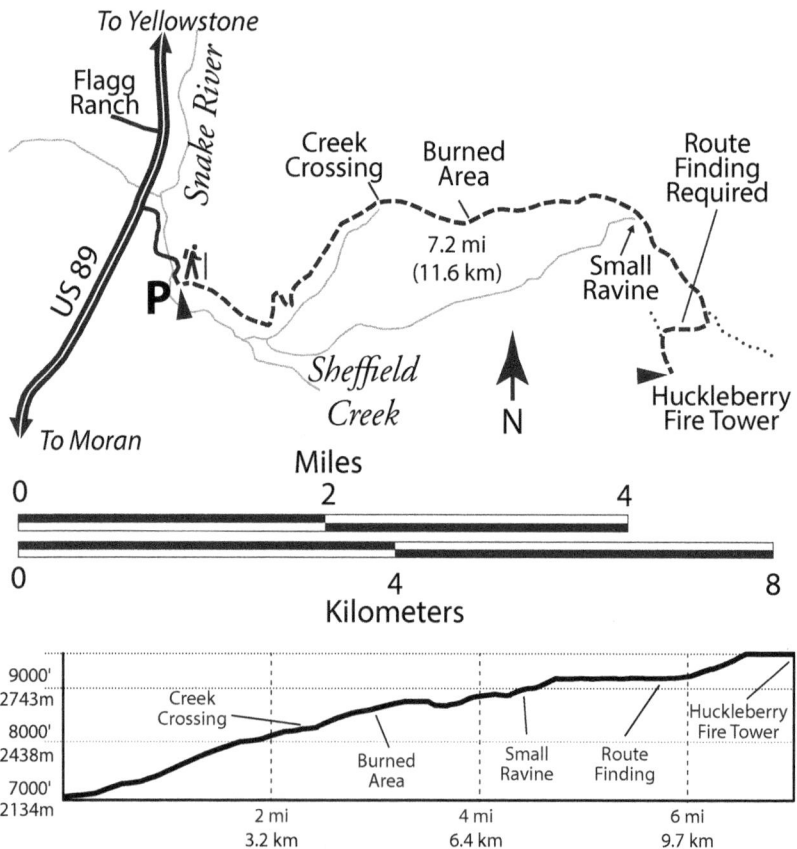

NORTH JACKSON LAKE

JENNY LAKE

The Jenny Lake area is one of the busiest and most popular hiking areas in all of Jackson Hole. Popular year-round with hikers, boaters, and adventurers in the summer, the area also provides winter visitors with recreation opportunities.

With dozens of hiking and recreating possibilities, where should one start? If you are new to the area, consider taking the popular shuttle boat across the lake. Hidden Falls and Inspiration Point are short, moderately steep hikes that bring you to a stunning view of the Jackson Hole area.

Should you be ready for an adventure, hike into Cascade Canyon, travel past Lake Solitude, and climb up to Paintbrush Divide. The views of the western side of the Cathedral Group are stunning.

For history lovers, explore the Bar BC Ranch, the Lucas-Fabian homesteads, and Menors Ferry. Each of these hikes is easy and provides visitors with a better understanding of how Grand Teton came to be.

Stop in at the Craig Thomas Discovery & Visitor Center south of the four-way stop when entering the park near the Moose entrance. You can pick up backcountry permits, handle moose and elk antlers, and gain a better appreciation of the grandeur of Grand Teton. The three-dimensional relief map of the park will help you plan your day's activities. The rangers are highly knowledgeable and can answer any question you may have about your visit to the area.

Stock up supplies at Dornans near the Moose entrance or at the Jenny Lake general store. You can pick up everything you need for an easy picnic or a substantial outing in the park. Dornans also has a supply store where you can purchase last-minute clothing. The stores at Dornans also rent some climbing, boating, and adventure equipment should you need something.

Jenny Lake south shore visitor complex.

JENNY LAKE AREA HIKES

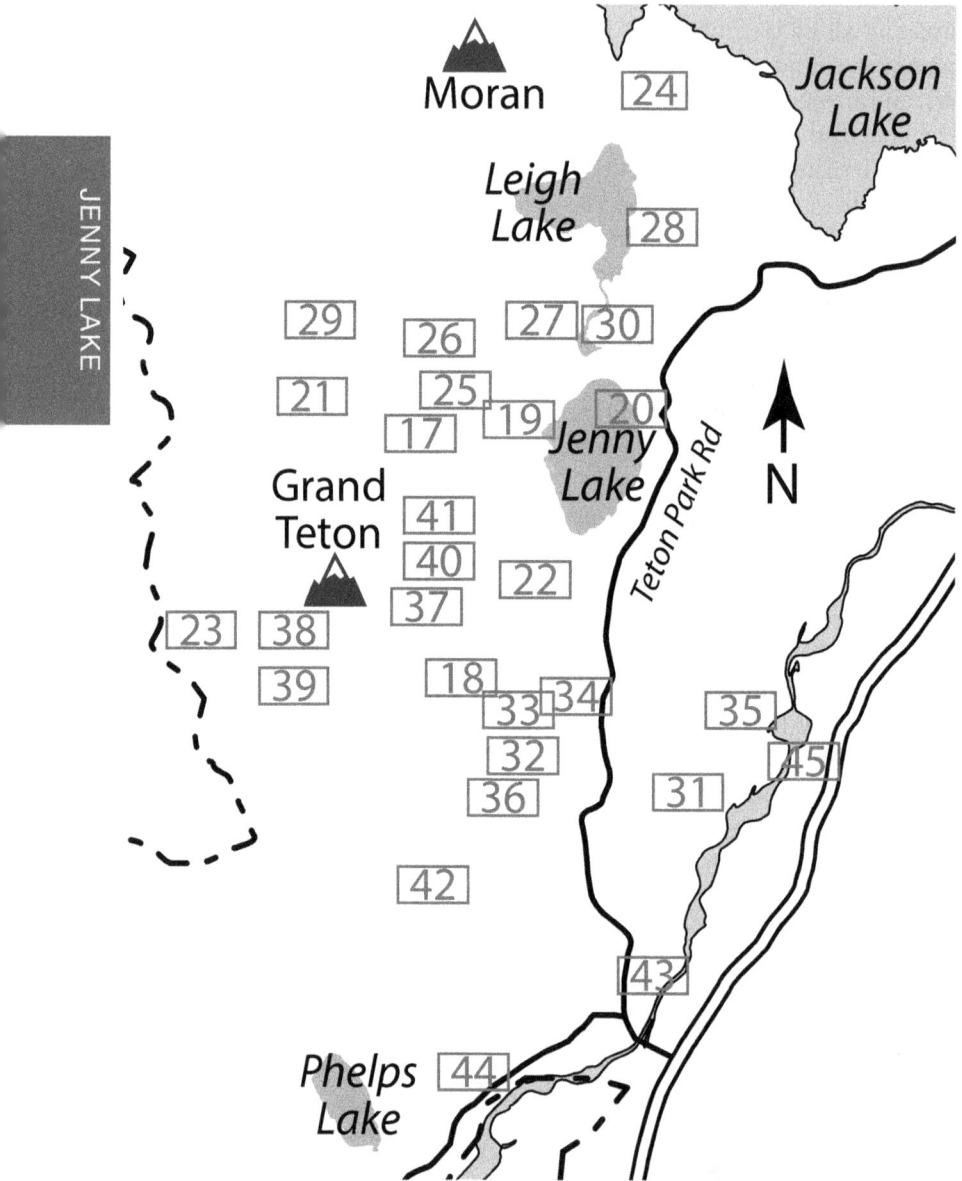

JENNY LAKE

Moran

24

Jackson
Lake

Leigh
Lake

28

29

26

27 30

21

25

19

20

17

Jenny
Lake

Grand
Teton

41

40

22

37

23

38

Teton Park Rd

N

39

18

33 34

35

32

45

36

31

42

43

Phelps
Lake

44

JENNY LAKE AREA HIKES

Jenny Lake

17. Cascade Canyon Fork
18. Grand Teton Loop
19. Hidden Falls and Inspiration Point
20. Jenny Lake Loop
21. Lake Solitude
22. Moose Ponds
23. Schoolroom Glacier

String Lake

24. Bearpaw and Trapper Lakes
25. Hanging Canyon and The Jaw
26. Holly Lake
27. Laurel Lake
28. Leigh Lake
29. Paintbrush Divide to Cascade Canyon
30. String Lake Loop

Taggart Lake

31. Bar BC Ranch
32. Bradley Lake
33. Burned Wagon Gulch
34. Lucas-Fabian Homestead
35. River Road
36. Taggart Lake

Lupine Meadows

37. Garnet Canyon
38. Lower Saddle Grand Teton
39. Middle and South Teton
40. Surprise, Amphitheater, and Delta Lakes
41. Teewinot Apex and Glacier
42. Valley Trail

Moose Entrance

43. Menors Ferry
44. Sawmill Bench
45. Schwabacher Landing

JENNY LAKE

Flowers at Laurel Lake.

Jenny Lake

Jenny Lake (6,786 feet / 2,068 m) is the crown jewel of Grand Teton National Park. Its shorelines provide a graceful base for the mountains that tower thousands of feet (meters) above this glacier-carved lake. The lake is 256 feet (78 m) deep and is cold year-round.

The park service provides a boat shuttle at the south end of the lake. This shuttle travels from the south boat dock to the west boat dock. It enables hikers to take a quick walk up to Hidden Falls and Inspiration Point. It also allows for one-way travel, ferrying tired hikers across Jenny Lake after exiting any number of hikes from Cascade Canyon.

The one-way road that travels from String Lake past Jenny Lake Lodge has one of the most spectacular viewpoints in the entire park. The turnout along this road provides visitors with a perfectly aligned view into Cascade Canyon, a dramatic glacially carved canyon that drains Lake Solitude, Schoolroom Glacier, Icefloe Lake, and other unnamed bodies of water in the north and south forks of the stunning central canyon.

The trail around Jenny Lake provides hikers with continuous views of the lake, mountains, and the valley around the entire path. The eastern part of this route is lightly hiked compared to the north, west, and south routes around the lake. The eastern shoreline views are perpetually stunning along the entire length of this relatively flat section.

Parking at the South Jenny Lake parking area and visitor center is extremely challenging in the high season. Often, the parking lot fills up before 8 a.m. with visitors excited for their day in the park. Should you plan a full day based out of this lot, leave Jackson early to avoid waiting for a parking space to open.

The south Jenny Lake complex has restrooms, a general store, a visitor center, the climbing ranger cabin, and historic buildings. The paved pathway through the area leads hikers to the boat dock. Signs along the path help visitors better understand the animals, geology, history, weather, and geography of the area.

Cascade Canyon, Jenny Lake.

17 CASCADE CANYON FORK
(11 mi / 17.7 km / Stren)

Overview: A spectacular glacial canyon with highlight views.

Trip style: Out and back

Distance: 5.5 miles (8.9 km) one way, 11 miles (17.7 km) round trip

Elevation gain: 1,038 feet (316 m)

Max. Elevation: 7,838 feet (2,389 m)

Difficulty: Moderate to strenuous

Trailhead: String Lake South
43.7842°N, -110.7274°W / 43°47'03"N, -110°43'38"W
12T 0521938E 4847940N

Traffic: Heavy

Maps: Jenny Lake, Mount Moran 7.5' USGS Topos

Notes: The trail is highly popular and may be snowbound.

Trailhead Directions

Drive north from Jackson on US 191 for 12.3 miles (19.8 km) to Moose Junction and turn left on Teton Park Road. Continue past the entrance station for a total of 10.7 miles (17.2 km) to the North Jenny Lake Junction. Turn left and continue 1.5 miles (2.4 km), then turn right and park in the first String Lake parking lot.

Trailhead Facilities

Restrooms, bike rack, trash cans, bear boxes for food storage, fuel/gas canister disposal.

Hike Description

Begin the hike at the String Lake Trailhead at the first parking lot at String Lake. Cross the large wooden bridge over the String Lake outlet. Hike 0.3 mile (0.5 km) to the first trail junction and follow the sign toward Hidden Falls and Jenny Lake Outlet.

Hike along the nearly level trail along the northwest section of Jenny Lake across a series of short wooden bridges and one large bridge crossing a large creek for a total of 1.2 miles (1.9 km). There is a signed trail junction for Cascade Canyon and Lake Solitude.

Take the fork leading away west, then climb a switchback trail for 0.7 mile (1.1 km) to the junction at the mouth of the canyon. Take the trail toward Lake Solitude.

This section of the trail gradually gains 521 feet (159 m) over 3.3 miles (5.3 km) to the main junction of the Cascade Canyon Trail. This is one of the gentlest grades covering substantial distances in Grand Teton National Park.

The trail follows Cascade Creek and stays on the north side of the creek for the entire length of this section. The trail crosses several unnamed tributaries along the way. There is a bridge 850 feet (260 m) prior to the junction to Lake Solitude Trail and the South Fork Cascade Canyon Trail.

From here, return along the same trail. Alternatively, hike to Lake Solitude or to Schoolroom Glacier as an extension of this trip.

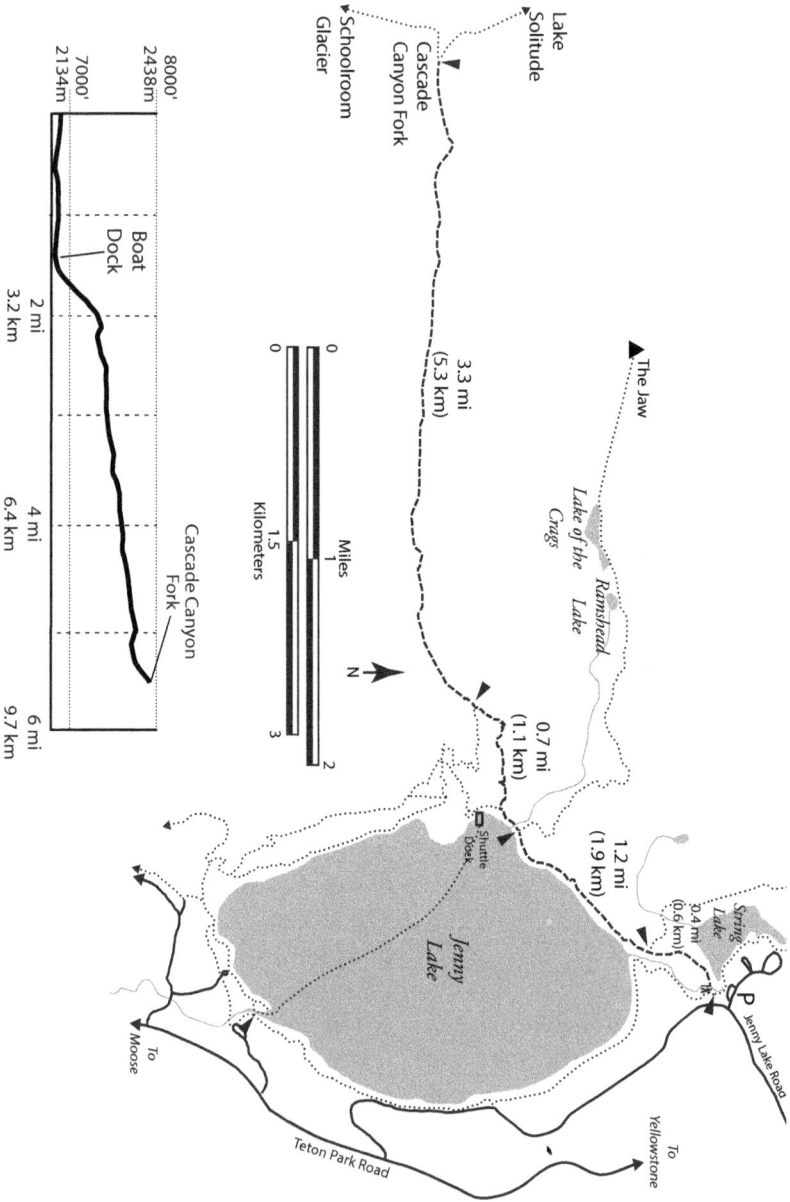

JENNY LAKE

18 GRAND TETON LOOP (32.7 mi / 52.6 km / Stren)

Overview: A multi-day tour of the highlights of Grand Teton.

Trip style: Loop

Distance: 32.7 miles (52.6 km)

Elevation gain: 6,928 feet (2,112 m) total gain/loss

Max. Elevation: 10,790 feet (3,289 m)

Difficulty: Strenuous

Trailhead: Jenny Lake South
43.7516°N, -110.7253°W / 43°45'06"N, -110°43'31"W
12T 0522113E 4844317N

Traffic: Heavy

Maps: Jenny Lake, Mount Moran, Grand Teton, Moose
7.5' USGS Topos

Notes: Be prepared for weather changes over this longer hike.

Trailhead Directions

Drive north from Jackson on US 191 for 12.3 miles (19.8 km) to Moose Junction and turn left on Teton Park Road. Continue past the entrance station for a total of 7.9 miles (12.7 km) to the Jenny Lake Junction, turn left, and park at the end of the lot.

Trailhead Facilities

Restrooms, bike rack, trash cans, fuel bottle disposal, general store, ranger station, information kiosk.

Hike Description

Begin hiking at the trailhead toward the shuttle dock. Cross the bridge and continue on the lake trail to the Valley Trail junction at 0.7 mile (1.1 km). The trail begins gaining elevation, passes the Moose Ponds junction, then loses elevation and encounters a junction in the trail.

Note that the upper and lower trails have been under construction in past years, so mind the official park signs for which to take.

Follow the trail 1.1 mile (1.8 km) to a signed junction leading to Hidden Falls. Continue 0.25 mile (0.4 km) to another junction, then climb the steep trail to Inspiration Point. Then, continue for 0.6 mile (1 km) to the next junction. Take the left (W) trail toward Lake Solitude.

Hike 3.3 miles (5.3 km) up a gradual slope to the Cascade Canyon junction. Take the left (S) fork and continue hiking upward into the South Fork of Cascade Canyon for another 3.5 miles (5.6 km) along a steepening trail. From approximately 0.5 mile (0.8 km) past the Cascade Canyon junction to the Avalanche Divide junction is the South Fork Camping Zone. A side diversion hike up Avalanche

JENNY LAKE

Divide is worth the effort for the fine views of the Cathedral Group.

This section of trail dips in and out of trees as it climbs, revealing the western side of the Cathedral Group, high above the trail. The trees begin thinning out as the trail climbs higher, turning into a more open landscape.

Hike another 0.6 mile (1 km) to the jade-green pond at the base of Schoolroom Glacier. From the ring of crumbly dirt surrounding the pond at the base of the glacier, the trail works its way up a series of steep switchbacks on an exposed cliff toward Hurricane Pass.

The trail reaches a ridge and proceeds toward the flat and often windy pass. As the trail continues south, it begins losing elevation toward Alaska Basin. At 12.6 miles (20.3 km) total distance, the trail passes by Sunset Lake. It is possible to camp without a permit outside of the park boundary in this area.

Continue past Sunset Lake for 0.3 mile (0.5 km) to the first junction toward Buck Mountain Pass. It's possible to continue farther into Alaska Basin and take the second fork toward Buck Mountain. The second option adds some distance and is a tougher climb. The reward for the effort is an extended exploration of the alpine area of Alaska Basin.

As the trail exits out of the basin and climbs toward Buck Mountain, the trees thin out, giving way to a rough and rocky landscape. Parts of this section are somewhat exposed, especially at Static Peak Divide. The exposure rewards hikers with an unobstructed view of south Jackson Hole. Note that the divide can be choked with snow, requiring an ice axe for safe travel.

The climb from Sunset Lake to Static Peak Divide gains 1,139 feet (348 m). Static Peak can be hiked from the trail with no technical gear when clear of snow. Several thin trails lead to the summit, rewarding the adventurous with a near-vertical view down to Timberline Lake.

From the divide, the trail drops 2,937 feet (895 m) over 3.5 miles (5.6 km) to Death Canyon Trail, intersecting at the Death Canyon patrol cabin.

Turn left (SE) and continue descending out of Death Canyon. A short distance past the cabin is a grassy spot with placid water pools that is a perfect place for a meal break. As the trail descends toward Phelps Lake, the views open up as the trail departs the canyon.

Continue past the junction to Phelps Lake and climb the 400 feet (122 m) up this short section to the Phelps Lake overlook. The trail continues east, reaching the Death Canyon Trailhead 1.5 miles (2.4 km) from Phelps Lake junction.

From here, the trail turns north, traveling an easy, relatively flat 3.9 miles (6.3 km) toward Taggart Lake. The trail gains a modest 240 feet (73 m) from the junction of Beaver Creek Trail and the Valley

Trail up to Taggart Lake. The trail crosses a long wooden bridge and follows the eastern lakeshore.

Continue north for 1.8 miles (2.9 km) over a minor hill to Bradley Lake. The trail curves around the eastern lakeshore, then curves northwest and crosses over a wooden bridge.

The trail continues toward Garnet Canyon for 1.5 miles (2.4 km) and climbs 300 feet (91 m) to the last hill on the trail, connecting with the Garnet Canyon Trail. Turn right at the junction. This section of the trail is busy with hikers. Hike down the ridge and hill to the Lupine Meadows parking lot.

Reconnect with the Valley Trail as it runs along the western edge of the Lupine Meadows parking lot. The trail roughly follows the edge of the road. Often hikers walk the road for speed. In 0.5 mile (0.8 km), the trail can be seen to the left (W) of the dirt road. Walk to the trail and continue the remaining 0.4 mile (0.7 km) to the Jenny Lake loop trail.

Turn right (E) at the junction and hike the last 0.7 mile (1.1 km) to the Jenny Lake parking lot.

Options

This hike is usually done as a multi-day trip. Better views of the Cathedral Group can be enjoyed by hiking the trail clockwise. However, scheduling campgrounds this way can be a challenge. Also, the climb up to Static Peak Divide is significant and challenging with a backpack.

Areas in Alaska Basin outside of the park allow dispersed camping in the national forest areas. Be aware that marmots are notorious for stealing boots and chewing into packs and tents.

Contact the park service for the latest information on campsites. Securing a site can be a challenge during the summer season. Plan well ahead and prepare to change plans to suit the circumstances.

If time allows, side trips into Avalanche Canyon and Death Canyon are worth the effort. Exploring the Jedediah Smith Wilderness in the Alaska Basin area is also enjoyable. Camping is not allowed near the shoreline of Sunset Lake.

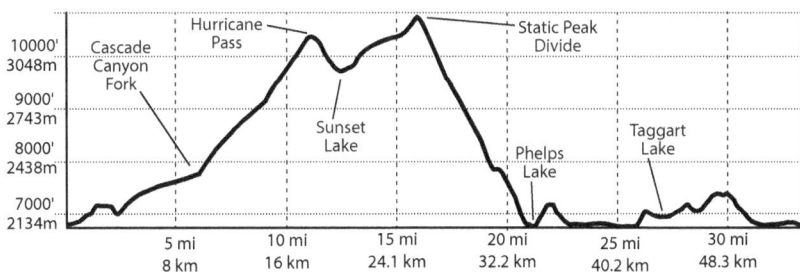

mi	km	Waypoints	mi	km	Waypoints (continued)
0.0	0.0	Jenny Lake South	19.5	31.1	Death Canyon trail junction
1.0	1.6	Valley Trail junction	21.3	34.1	Phelps Lake junction
2.4	3.8	Hidden Falls	22.8	36.5	Death Canyon TH junction
6.3	10.1	Cascade Canyon Fork	26.7	42.8	Taggart Lake
11.0	17.6	Hurricane Pass	28.5	45.7	Bradley Lake
13.0	20.8	Avalanche Canyon junction	30.0	48.1	Garnet Canyon junction
15.1	24.2	Buck Mountain Pass	31.7	50.8	Lupine Meadows Trailhead
16.0	25.6	Static Peak Divide	32.7	52.4	Jenny Lake South

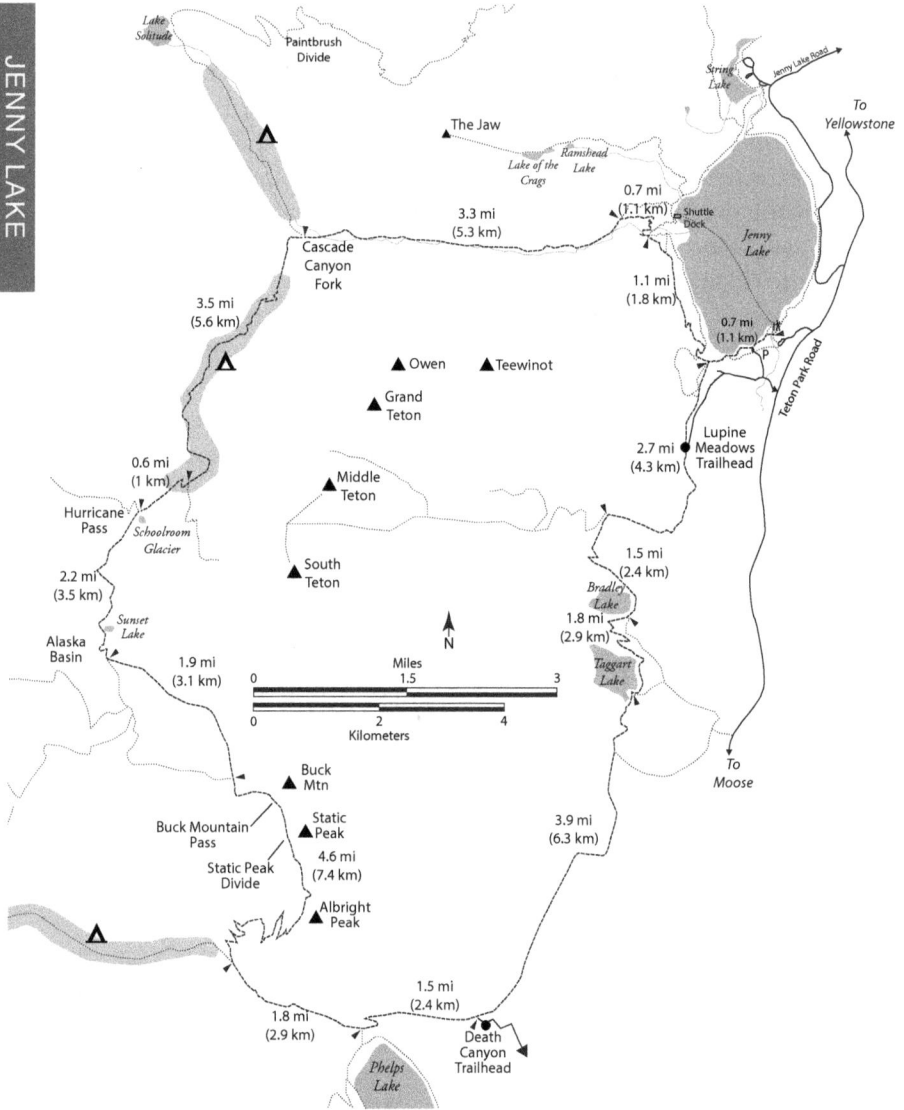

JENNY LAKE

19 HIDDEN FALLS AND INSPIRATION POINT (5.6 mi / 9 km / Mod)

JENNY LAKE

Overview: A popular hike to a falls and overlook of Jenny Lake.

Trip style: Out and back

Distance: 2.8 miles (4.5 km) one way, 5.6 miles (9 km) round trip

Elevation gain: 453 feet (138 m)

Max. Elevation: 7,238 feet (2,206 m)

Difficulty: Easy to moderate

Trailhead: Jenny Lake South
43.7516°N, -110.7253°W / 43°45'06"N, -110°43'31"W
12T 0522113E 4844317N

Traffic: Heavy

Maps: Jenny Lake, Moose 7.5' USGS topos

Notes: Busy trail with climbers and hikers.

Trailhead Directions

Drive north from Jackson on US 191 for 12.3 miles (19.8 km) to Moose Junction and turn left on Teton Park Road. Continue past the entrance station for a total of 7.9 miles (12.7 km) to the Jenny Lake Junction, turn left, and park at the end of the lot.

Trailhead Facilities

Restrooms, bike rack, trash cans, fuel bottle disposal, general store, ranger station, information kiosk.

Hike Description

Begin hiking at the trailhead toward the shuttle dock. Cross the bridge and continue on the lake trail to the Valley Trail junction at 0.7 mile (1.1 km). The trail begins gaining elevation, passes the Moose Ponds junction, then loses elevation and comes to another junction.

Note that the upper and lower trails have been under construction in past years, so mind the park signs.

Follow the trail 1 mile (1.6 km) to a signed junction toward Hidden Falls, then continue 0.25 mile (0.4 km) to another junction, turn left (W), and proceed to Hidden Falls. The falls are hidden by the trees until you reach a clearing.

To reach Inspiration Point, backtrack 200 feet (61 m) to the signed junction, then climb the steep trail 0.3 mile (0.5 km) to the overlook.

To return to the Jenny Lake, the shuttle boat can be used for a small fee payable at the dock. Check with the park service for hours of operation and costs. The boat dock is on the lakeshore along a steep trail.

HIDDEN FALLS AND INSPIRATION POINT

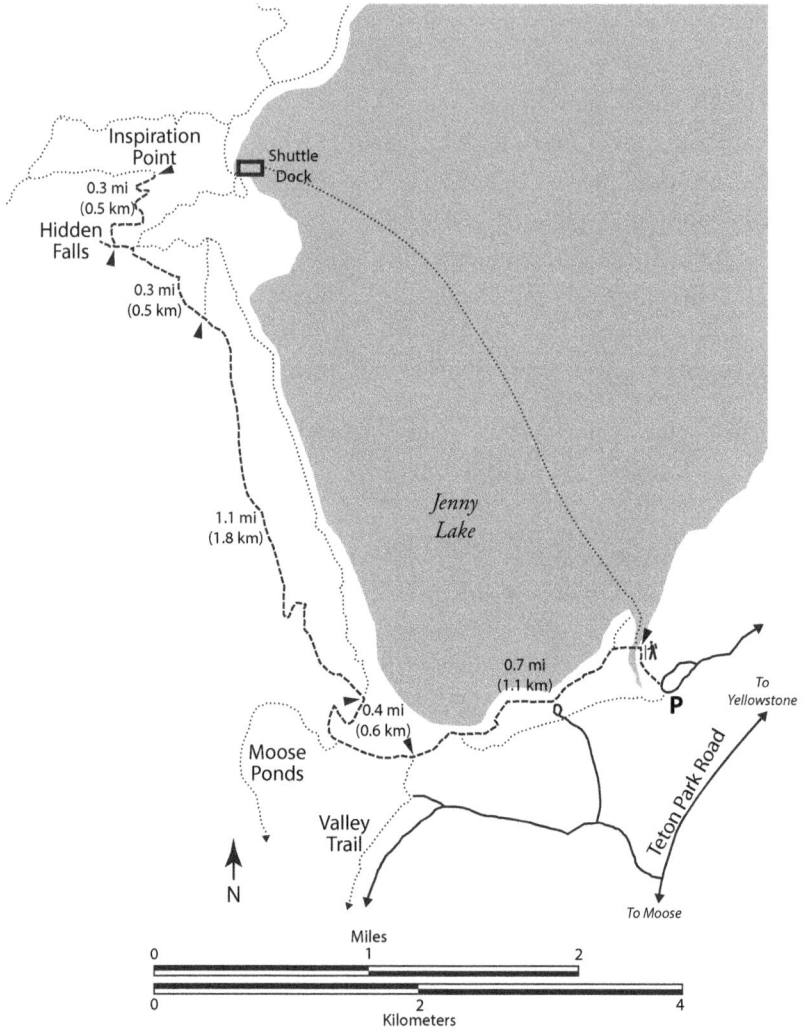

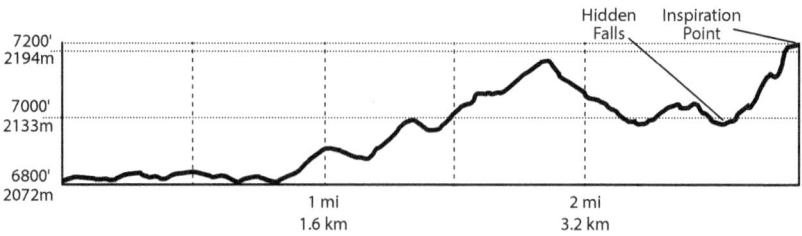

JENNY LAKE

20 JENNY LAKE LOOP (7.5 mi / 12 km / Mod)

Overview: A fine lakeside hike at the crown jewel lake of the park.

Trip style: Loop

Distance: 7.5 miles (12 km)

Elevation gain: 1,038 feet (316 m) gain/loss

Max. Elevation: 7,180 feet (2,188 m)

Difficulty: Moderate

Trailhead: String Lake South
43.7842°N, -110.7274°W / 43°47'03"N, -110°43'38"W
12T 0521938E 4847940N

Traffic: Moderate

Maps: Jenny Lake, Moose 7.5' USGS Topos

Notes: Parking can be challenging during the summer season.

Trailhead Directions

Drive north from Jackson on US 191 for 12.3 miles (19.8 km) to Moose Junction and turn left on Teton Park Road. Continue past the entrance station for a total of 10.7 miles (17.2 km) to the North Jenny Lake Junction. Turn left and continue 1.5 miles (2.4 km), then turn right and park in the first String Lake parking lot.

Trailhead Facilities

Restrooms, bike rack, trash cans, bear boxes for food storage, fuel/gas canister disposal.

Hike Description

Begin the hike at the String Lake Trailhead at the first parking lot at String Lake. Cross the large wooden bridge over the String Lake outlet. Hike 0.4 mile (0.6 km) to the first trail junction and follow the sign toward Hidden Falls and the Jenny Lake outlet.

Hike along the nearly level trail along the northwest section of Jenny Lake across a series of short wooden bridges for a total of 1.4 miles (2.3 km) to the boat dock.

Climb the short hill for 0.4 mile (0.6 km) to reach the junction to Hidden Falls, then continue southeast for another 1.1 miles (1.8 km) to the horse trail junction.

Continue another 0.4 mile (0.6 km) to the Valley Trail junction. In another 0.7 mile (1.1 km) the trail crosses a bridge at the boat launch. Take the trail through the South Jenny Lake area and follow the lakeshore for 1.4 miles (2.3 km) to the Jenny Lake Overlook parking lot.

From there, the trail follows the lakeshore to the String Lake outlet. It turns north and stays on the east side of the creek, ending at the trailhead at String Lake.

JENNY LAKE LOOP

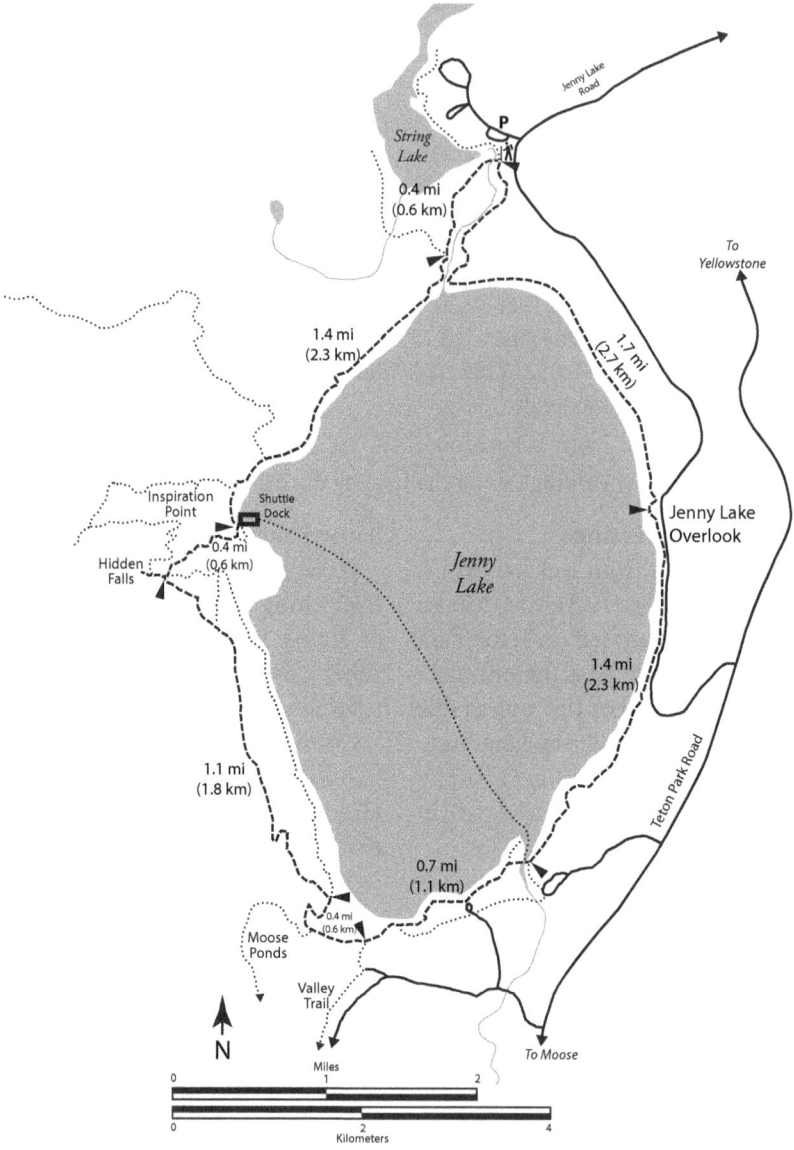

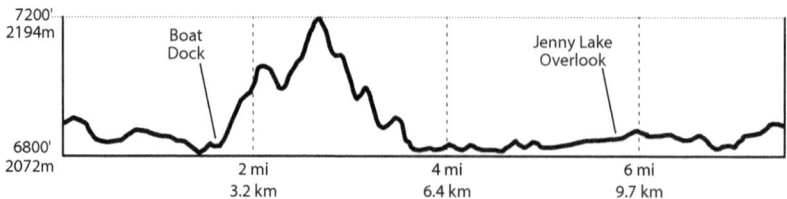

JENNY LAKE

21 LAKE SOLITUDE (16 mi / 25.8 km / Stren)

Overview: A spectacular back country lake with top park highlights.
Trip style: Out and back
Distance: 8 miles (12.9 km) one way, 16 miles (25.8 km) round trip
Elevation gain: 2,556 feet (779 m)
Max. Elevation: 9,053 feet (2,759 m)
Difficulty: Strenuous
Trailhead: String Lake South
43.7842°N, -110.7274°W / 43°47'03"N, -110°43'38"W
12T 0521938E 4847940N
Traffic: Heavy
Maps: Jenny Lake, Mount Moran 7.5' USGS Topos
Notes: The trail is highly popular and may be snowbound in July.

JENNY LAKE

Trailhead Directions

Drive north from Jackson on US 191 for 12.3 miles (19.8 km) to Moose Junction and turn left on Teton Park Road. Continue past the entrance station for a total of 10.7 miles (17.2 km) to the North Jenny Lake Junction. Turn left and continue 1.5 miles (2.4 km), then turn right and park in the first String Lake parking lot.

Trailhead Facilities

Restrooms, bike rack, trash cans, bear boxes for food storage, fuel/gas canister disposal.

Hike Description

Begin the hike at the String Lake Trailhead at the first parking lot at String Lake. Cross the large wooden bridge over the String Lake outlet. Hike 0.4 mile (0.6 km) to the first trail junction and follow the sign toward Hid-den Falls and Jenny Lake Outlet.

Hike along the nearly level trail along the northwest section of Jenny Lake across a series of short wooden bridges and one large bridge crossing a large creek for a total of 1.2 miles (1.9 km) to a signed trail junction for Cascade Canyon and Lake Solitude.

Take the trail leading away west, climb a switchback trail for 0.7 mile (1.1 km) to the junction at the mouth of the canyon. Take the trail toward Lake Solitude.

This section of trail gradually gains 521 feet (159 m) over 3.3 miles (5.3 km) to the main junction of the Cascade Canyon Trail. At this junction, take the right (NW) fork toward Lake Solitude and continue 2.5 miles (4 km) to Lake Solitude.

Return on the same trail. Paint-brush Divide is a 2.3-mile (3.7 km) climb to 10,700 feet (3,261 m). This is a steep climb with no water and southern sun exposure. The climb can be hot and grueling in the summer. There is no shelter from weather above 9,500 feet (2,896 m).

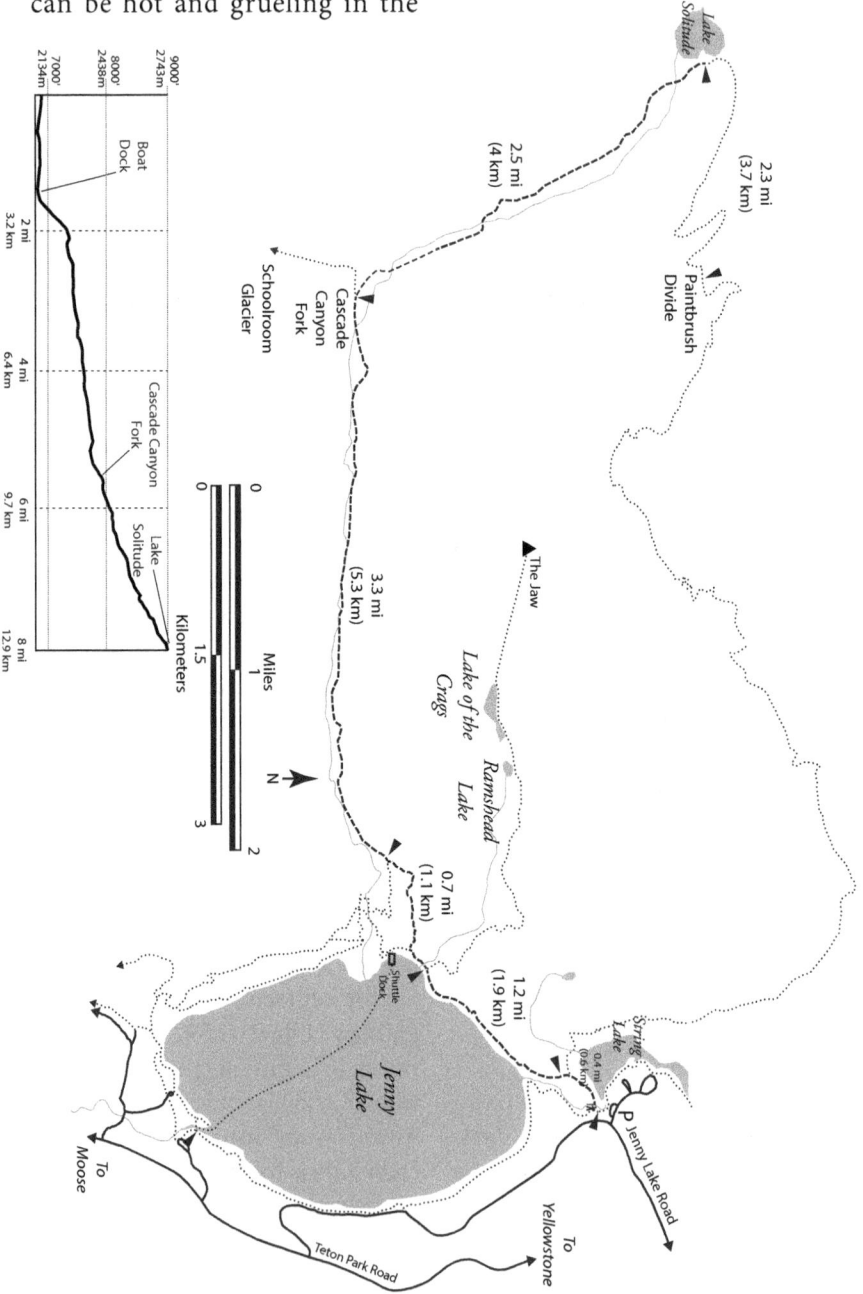

JENNY LAKE

22 MOOSE PONDS (3.6 mi / 5.8 km / Easy)

Overview: A lightly-hiked trail to hidden ponds with wildlife.

Trip style: Loop

Distance: 3.6 miles (5.8 km)

Elevation gain: 379 feet (116 m)

Max. Elevation: 6,844 feet (2,086 m)

Difficulty: Easy

Trailhead: String Lake South
43.7842°N, -110.7274°W / 43°47'03"N, -110°43'38"W
12T 0521938E 4847940N

Traffic: Light

Maps: Jenny Lake, Moose 7.5' USGS topos

Notes: Be mindful of keeping proper distance from wildlife.

JENNY LAKE

Trailhead Directions

Drive north from Jackson on US 191 for 12.3 miles (19.8 km) to Moose Junction and turn left on Teton Park Road. Continue past the entrance station for a total of 7.9 miles (12.7 km) to the Jenny Lake Junction, turn left, and park at the end of the lot.

Trailhead Facilities

Restrooms, bike rack, trash cans, fuel bottle disposal, general store, ranger station, information kiosk.

Hike Description

Begin hiking at the trailhead toward the shuttle boat dock. Cross the bridge and continue on the lake trail to the Valley Trail junction at 0.7 mile (1.1 km). The trail begins gaining elevation and connects with Moose Ponds junction in 0.2 mile (0.3 km). Turn left (SW) and follow the trail over the hill and down to the first pond.

The trail continues northwest toward the second pond, then curves counterclockwise over a plank bridge, then turns south. In a short distance, the trail crosses a creek over two logs, then delves into a heavy forest canopy. This mixed forest cover provides protection from the summer sun.

At 1.8 miles (2.9 km) total, the forest opens up and the swampy Moose Pond can be seen to the east. The trail weaves in and out of tree cover for 0.3 mile (0.5 km) before turning sharply north at the intersecting Valley Trail.

Follow the Valley Trail north, past a parking area, to the Jenny Lake Loop Trail at 3 miles (4.8 km). Turn right (W) and finish the remaining 0.7-mile (1.1 km) hike to the shuttle boat dock where the trail began.

MOOSE PONDS

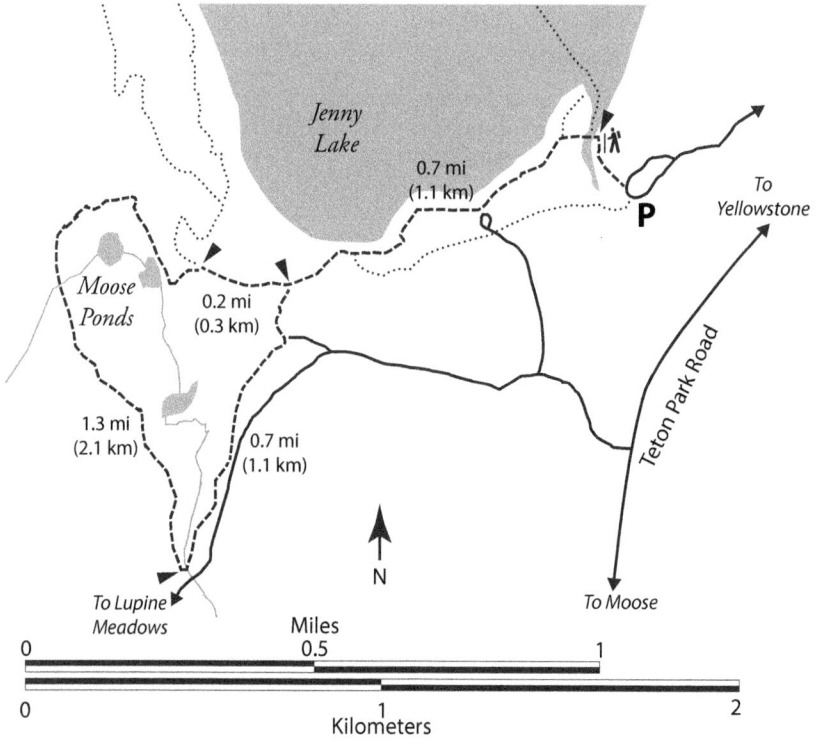

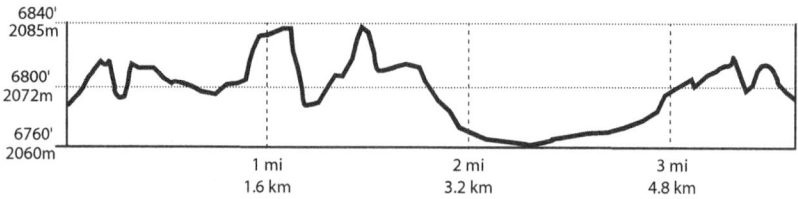

23 SCHOOLROOM GLACIER
(21.2 mi / 34 km / Stren)

Overview: A classic glacier with a jade green glacial pond.

Trip style: Out and back

Distance: 10.6 miles (17 km) one way, 21.2 miles (34 km) round trip

Elevation gain: 3,874 feet (1,181 m)

Max. Elevation: 10,038 feet (3,060 m)

Difficulty: Strenuous

Trailhead: String Lake South
43.7842°N, -110.7274°W / 43°47'03"N, -110°43'38"W
12T 0521938E 4847940N

Traffic: Heavy to Cascade Canyon junction, moderate to the glacier

Maps: Jenny Lake, Mount Moran, Grand Teton 7.5' USGS Topos

Notes: Permits are required for camping along this route.

Trailhead Directions

Drive north from Jackson on US 191 for 12.3 miles (19.8 km) to Moose Junction and turn left on Teton Park Road. Continue past the entrance station for a total of 7.9 miles (12.7 km) to the Jenny Lake Junction, turn left, and park at the end of the lot.

Trailhead Facilities

Restrooms, bike rack, trash cans, fuel bottle disposal, general store, ranger station, information kiosk.

Hike Description

Begin hiking at the trailhead toward the shuttle dock. Cross the bridge and continue on the lake trail to the Valley Trail junction at 0.7 mile (1.1 km). The trail begins gaining elevation, passes the Moose Ponds junction, then loses elevation and comes to another split in the trail.

Note the upper and lower trails have been under construction in past years, so mind the official park signs.

Follow the trail 1 mile (1.6 km) to a signed junction toward Hidden Falls, then continue 0.25 mile (0.4 km) to another junction, then climb the steep trail to Inspiration Point, then continue to the junction for 0.7 mile (1.1 km). Take the left (W) fork toward Lake Solitude.

Hike 3.3 miles (5.3 km) up a gradual slope to the Cascade Canyon junction. Take the left (S) fork and continue for another 3.5 miles (5.6 km) along a steepening trail to the junction to Icefloe Lake and The Wall. This section of trail dips in and out of trees as it climbs, revealing the western side of the Cathedral Group.

Hike another 0.6 mile (1 km) to the jade green pond at the base of

Schoolroom Glacier. It is possible to climb the small ring around the pond for a better look, though the dirt is crumbly on the steep slope.

Optionally, climb the trail to gain 500 feet (152 m) over 0.6 mile (1 km) to Hurricane Pass for the captivating view down the length of Death Canyon. This pass is famously windy.

Travel along the same trail to return to the trailhead.

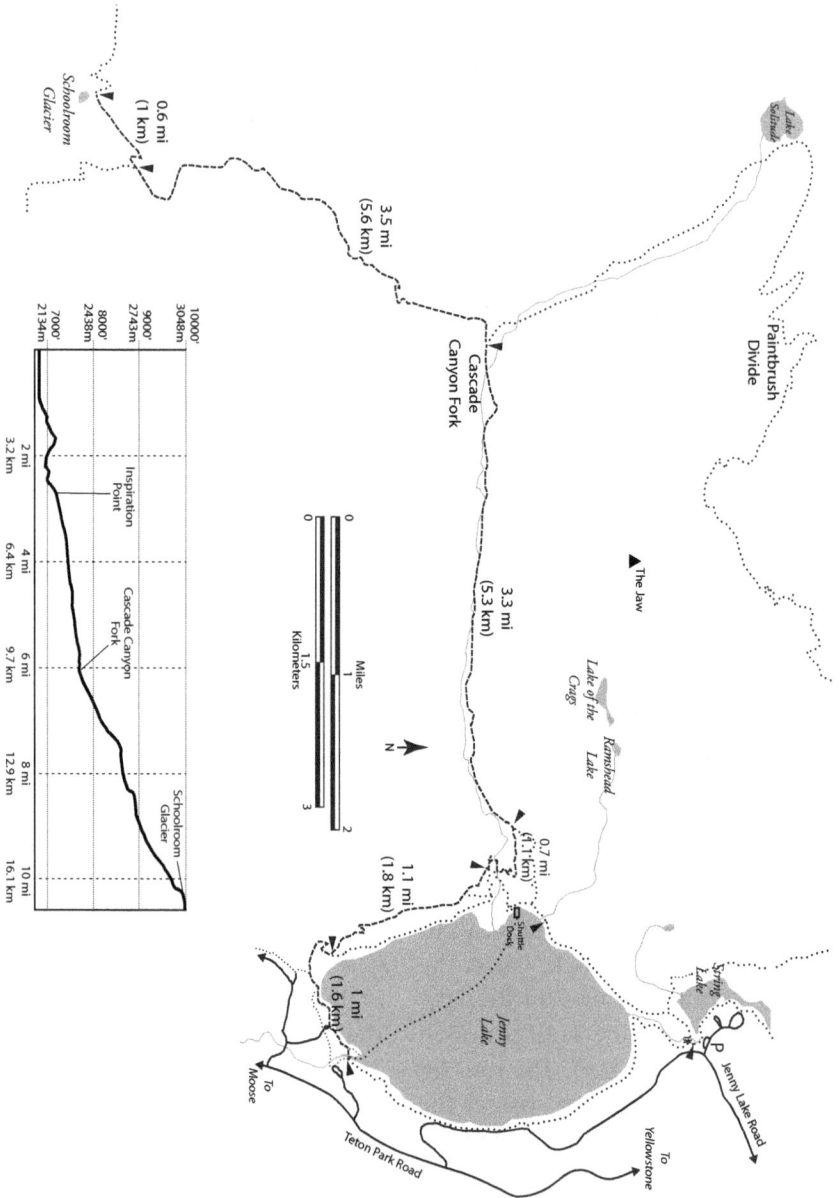

JENNY LAKE

String Lake

String Lake (6,870 feet / 2,094 m) is a highly-popular starting point to access many of Grand Teton's major sights. It is also the end (or beginning) of the Teton Crest Trail, the long-distance trail that runs the north-south length of the main part of the park's mountain range.

The lake is popular with hikers, boaters, those enjoying a picnic, and many other outdoor activities. The lake is essentially a wide connection between Leigh and Jenny lakes. It is shallow (approx. 10 feet / 3 m), allowing it to warm up compared to its sister lakes.

Footbridges span in the inlet and outlet of the lake. These long wooden spans allow hikers access to some of the prettiest landscapes in the park system. The trail that circles the lake is easy to walk and provides nearly endless views of the lakes and mountains.

Hikes originating from String Lake range from easy (Leigh Lake) to strenuous overnight backpacks (Paintbrush Canyon to Cascade Canyon). The lake's eastern shoreline is easy to walk and is easily accessible to families and adventurers alike.

Deer, elk, and other smaller wildlife can be frequently found in the tree cover around the lake. Make sure to bring bear spray, as food and trash cans attract bears.

Parking is challenging in the high season. Often, the parking lot fills up by mid-morning and then begins clearing out in the early evening. The parking lots around String Lake are also used by overnight backpackers, increasing the difficulty of finding day parking. Roadside parking is restricted in the area to reduce the impact on the ground and on plants.

Kayaking on String Lake.

STRING LAKE

24 BEARPAW AND TRAPPER LAKES
(9 mi / 14.4 km / Easy)

Overview: Enjoy four backcountry lakes with no road access.

Trip style: Out and back

Distance: 4.5 miles (7.2 km) one way, 9 miles (14.4 km) round trip

Elevation gain: 322 feet (98 m)

Max. Elevation: 6,927 feet (2,111 m)

Difficulty: Easy

Trailhead: Leigh Lake
43.7886°N, -110.7305°W / 43°47'19"N, -110°43'50"W
12T 0521683E 4848429N

Traffic: Moderate to heavy with stock animal traffic

Maps: Jenny Lake 7.5' USGS Topo

Notes: Permits required to camp at Trapper and Bearpaw lakes.

Trailhead Directions

Drive north from Jackson on US 191 for 12.3 miles (19.8 km) to Moose Junction and turn left on Teton Park Road. Continue past the entrance station for a total of 10.7 miles (17.2 km) to the North Jenny Lake Junction. Turn left and continue 1.5 miles (2.4 km), then turn right and park at the last (N) parking lot.

Trailhead Facilities

Restrooms, bike rack, trash cans, bear boxes for food storage, fuel/gas canister disposal.

Hike Description

Begin the hike at the Leigh Lake Trailhead at the last parking lot (N) at String Lake. The trailhead begins near the restroom. Walk 300 feet (91 m) on the trail toward the lake. Turn right (NW) along the shore of String Lake for 0.4 mile (0.6 km) to a junction with a trail leading off to the southeast. Continue along the trail along String Lake as the trail turns northwest.

At the trail junction with trails that lead across the creek between north String Lake and south Leigh Lake, take the right (NE) fork and continue toward Leigh Lake.

The trail along Leigh Lake follows the lakeshore for 2.8 miles (4.5 km), gaining little elevation along the route. At 2.7 miles (4.3 km), the trail breaks out of the forest and stays to the east of the thin forested strip along the lakeshore.

At the junction to Leigh, Trapper, and Bearpaw lakes, continue straight (W) to reach Trapper Lake in another 0.9 mile (1.4 km). The trail curves around counterclockwise toward Trapper Lake to circumnavigate a large swampy area to the east of Trapper Lake.

At the junction of Bearpaw and Trapper lakes, a trail continues north for 1 mile (1.6 km) to Jackson Lake. The lakeshore at this section of Jackson Lake can be quite muddy near the dead tree stumps.

There are multiple campsites in this area and there are some unofficial trails that wander through the area between Trapper and Bearpaw lakes.

It is possible to take the unofficial trail across the creek between the two sections of Bearpaw Lake. This eliminates walking around the west side of Bearpaw Lake on the return trip.

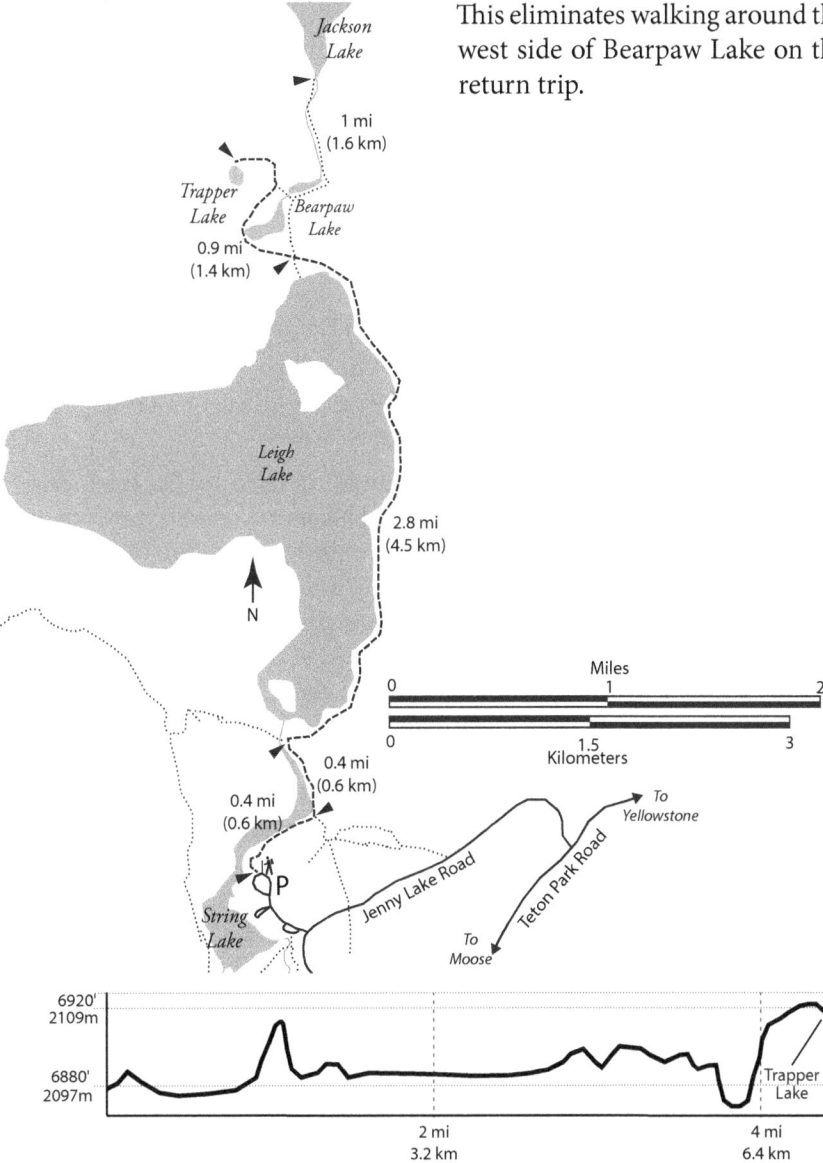

Jackson
Lake

1 mi
(1.6 km)

Trapper
Lake

Bearpaw
Lake

0.9 mi
(1.4 km)

Leigh
Lake

2.8 mi
(4.5 km)

N

Miles
0   1   2

0   1.5   3
Kilometers

0.4 mi
(0.6 km)

0.4 mi
(0.6 km)

To
Yellowstone

Jenny Lake Road

Teton Park Road

To
Moose

String
Lake

P

6920'
2109m

6880'
2097m

Trapper
Lake

2 mi
3.2 km

4 mi
6.4 km

STRING LAKE

25 HANGING CANYON AND THE JAW

(6.6 mi / 10.6 km / Stren)

JENNY LAKE

Overview: Lightly traveled hike up Hanging Canyon to Ramshead Lake, Lake of the Crags, and a bonus summit of The Jaw

Trip style: Out and back.

Distance: 3.3 miles (5.3 km) to Lake of the Crags, 4.3 miles (6.9 km) to The Jaw, 8.6 miles (13.8 km) round trip from The Jaw

Elevation gain: 2,690 feet (819 m) to Lake of the Crags, 4,531 feet (1,510 m) to The Jaw

Max. Elevation: 9,560 feet (3,187 m) Lake of the Crags, 11,401 feet (3800 m) The Jaw

Difficulty: Strenuous

Trailhead: String Lake South
43.7842°N, -110.7274°W / 43°47'03"N, -110°43'38"W
12T 0521938E 4847940N

Traffic: Heavy on Jenny Lake, light on Hanging Canyon

Maps: Moose, Mount Moran 7.5' USGS Topo

Notes: Rough, rocky, steep climber's trail with minor route finding and rock scrambling. Water available.

Trailhead Directions

Drive north from Jackson on US 191 for 12.3 miles (19.8 km) to Moose Junction and turn left on Teton Park Road. Continue past the entrance station for a total of 10.7 miles (17.2 km) to the North Jenny Lake Junction. Turn left and continue 1.5 miles (2.4 km), then turn right and park in the first String Lake parking lot.

Trailhead Facilities

Restrooms, bike rack, trash cans, bear boxes for food storage, fuel/gas canister disposal.

Hike Description

The trail up Hanging Canyon is steep, rough, and rocky. It requires minor route finding skills and scrambling over rocks. Inexperienced hikers are not recommended due to the tough nature of this unofficial trail.

Begin the hike at the String Lake Trailhead at the first parking lot at String Lake. Cross the large wooden bridge over the String Lake outlet. Hike 0.4 mile (0.6 km) to the first trail junction and follow the sign toward Hidden Falls and Jenny Lake Outlet. Hike along the nearly level trail along the northwest section of Jenny Lake across a series of three short wooden bridges.

At 1.5 miles (2.4 km), past the third wooden bridge and before the fourth, you will see an arc of large, flat rocks and a fallen dead tree lined up on a bearing of 68°

NE. Beyond the rocks, between the dead tree and its rotten stump, you will see an unsigned trail that leads you into heavy undergrowth. This is the Hanging Canyon Trail.

The overgrowth is intense at times. There are many fallen trees and hidden rocks along this heavily overgrown section of trail.

At 1.7 miles (2.7 km) and at 7,313 feet (2,229 m), you will encounter an open flat spot for a rest. Ribbon Falls is visible above you. Should you lose the trail, keep the falls to your left and do not cross the creek.

At 2 miles (3.2 km), a slight trail to the left leads to a small cliff with a waterfall. Continue on the main trail into thinning brush cover. Above this point, the trail switchbacks toward the ridge with conifer cover but does not cross the ridge. Find a good spot to top the ridge for a great view north. This is the last substantial shady spot. The trail follows the edge of the rocky cliff.

After a short distance, you will encounter a rock face. Look to your right to find the trail. If you cannot identify it, ascend the rock face, then look to the right. You will see the dirt trail to the right of the rock face. Return to the trail for faster and easier travel.

Once you encounter the first rock fall, scramble straight up the rock field. Once you crest the top of the rock field, travel toward the dirt trail to the right of the thin falls. As you ascend, look to your left (south) to see Arrowhead Pool.

At this point, avoid the ravine with vertical rock faces to your left with the creek that drains Ramshead Lake. Stay to the right and climb up a vague, steep rocky trail (chute) on the tan rock face.

At the top of the crest after 3.1 miles (5 km), Ramshead Lake will be visible beyond a wall of scraggly conifers. East of the lakeshore, the monolithic Rock of Ages is visible.

Continue around the northern edge of the lake along the trail to the rockfall. Scramble directly up the rocks until Lake of the Crags becomes visible. Travel over the rocks to 3.3 miles (5.3 km) to reach a grassy spot on the northeast edge of the lake. Return along the same trail.

The Jaw Summit Climb

Continue from the northeast corner of Lake of the Crags on a slight trail along the northern edge of the lake. Gain elevation over a large rock face, then return to the lake level to continue to the western edge of the lake. About 200 yards (182 m) west of the lake are a couple of flat, gravel campsites.

From the edge of the lake, the climb to the summit is 0.7 mile (1.1 km) with an elevation gain of 1,841 feet (561 m). Expect the climb to the summit from the lake to take 2 hours at a moderate pace.

Stay to the center of the climb through the first half of the climb, then work your way to the right (north) side of the path for the easiest, most direct climb. The climbing is second to third class with avoidable fourth class options. You must be comfortable climbing and scrambling with hands above Lake of the Crags.

The lower glaciers are at 20° slope while the upper are 30°, making uncontrolled fatal slides into boulders a possibility. There are multiple options for routes. Do not continue on if it is late in the day or weather and lightning threatens. There is no shelter from weather above Lake of the Crags.

There are two summit blocks, with the south summit appearing to be slightly higher than the north. The rock saddle between the summits is dangerous. It is corniced, with rubble and overhanging rock above a fatal fall.

Expect the travel time from the String Lake parking lot to the summit and back to be up to 11 hours under ideal conditions at a moderate pace with rest stops and route finding.

Rock of Ages over Lake of the Crags, Hanging Canyon.

Summit of The Jaw, looking at Grand Teton, 2.6 miles (4.2 km) away.

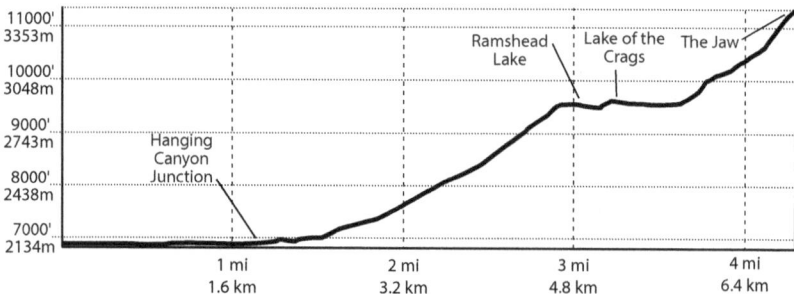

STRING LAKE

HANGING CANYON AND THE JAW

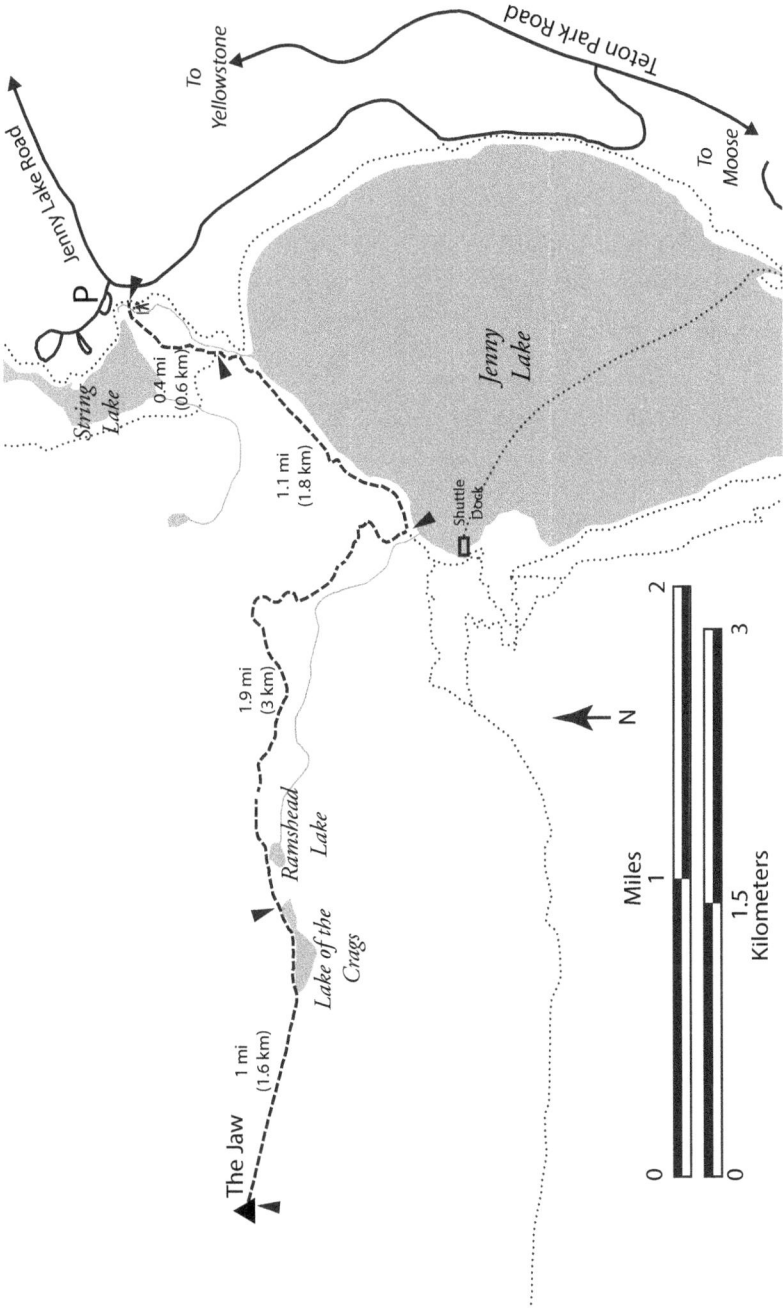

To Yellowstone

Teton Park Road

To Moose

Jenny Lake Road

JENNY LAKE

P

String Lake

0.4 mi (0.6 km)

1.1 mi (1.8 km)

Jenny Lake

Shuttle Dock

1.9 mi (3 km)

N

Miles
Kilometers

Ramshead Lake

Lake of the Crags

1 mi (1.6 km)

The Jaw

STRING LAKE

26 HOLLY LAKE (12.8 mi / 20.6 km / Stren)

JENNY LAKE

Overview: A canyon hike to a spectacular small backcountry lake with an optional longer loop hike over Paintbrush Divide.

Trip style: Out and back, loop optional

Distance: 6.4 miles (10.3 km) one way, 12.8 miles (20.6 km) round trip

Elevation gain: 2,764 feet (842 m)

Max. Elevation: 9,430 feet (2,874 m)

Difficulty: Strenuous, moderate overnighter

Trailhead: Leigh Lake
43.7886°N, -110.7305°W / 43°47'19"N, -110°43'50"W
12T 0521683E 4848429N

Traffic: Moderate to heavy

Maps: Jenny Lake 7.5' USGS Topo

Notes: Permits required to camp in Paintbrush Canyon.

Trailhead Directions

Drive north from Jackson on US 191 for 12.3 miles (19.8 km) to Moose Junction and turn left on Teton Park Road. Continue past the entrance station for a total of 10.7 miles (17.2 km) to the North Jenny Lake Junction. Turn left and continue 1.5 miles (2.4 km), then turn right and park at the last (N) parking lot.

Trailhead Facilities

Restrooms, bike rack, trash cans, bear boxes for food storage, fuel/gas canister disposal.

Hike Description

Begin the hike at the Leigh Lake Trailhead at the last parking lot at String Lake. The trailhead begins near the restroom and heads northwest along the shore of String Lake for 0.4 mile (0.6 km) to a junction with a trail leading off to the southeast. Continue along the trail along String Lake as the trail turns northwest.

At the trail junction that splits across the creek between north String Lake and south Leigh Lake, take the left (W) fork and continue across the bridge that spans the inlet to String Lake.

Continue for another 0.6 mile (1 km) to the trail junction that splits between west String Lake and Paintbrush Divide. Take the right trail fork toward Paintbrush Divide.

As the trail curves counterclockwise (NW to SW) around Rockchuck Peak, it enters Paintbrush Canyon. It approaches the creek from the south which flows down the middle of the canyon.

The trail crosses over the creek, sometimes a raging torrent in the early season, at 3.8 miles (6.1 km). Often, the trail is covered in snow well into early summer if not later, depending on the depth of the winter snow pack. Once the trail crosses to the north side of the canyon, it escapes from the heavy forest cover and is much more open to the sky.

From the junction at 1.5 miles (2.4 km), the trail rises 2,200 feet (671 m) over 4.4 miles (7.1 km) through the spectacular Paintbrush Canyon.

Between 4.3 to 4.7 miles (6.9 to 7.6 km), the trail crosses over the creek several more times over wooden bridges, then works its way up several steep switchbacks to the Holly Lake junction at 5.9 miles (9.5 km). Take the right fork toward Holly Lake.

The trail passes to the east of a small, unnamed pond and then splits to Holly Lake in 0.55 mile (0.9 km).

It is possible to return along the same path or, alternatively, to continue over Paintbrush Divide in a steep 1.3-mile (2.2 km) climb to the saddle. Ice axes are recommended for the ascent well into midsummer.

The trail then drops down to Lake Solitude and continues down Cascade Canyon to Jenny Lake. See the Lake Solitude hike in this book for detailed directions.

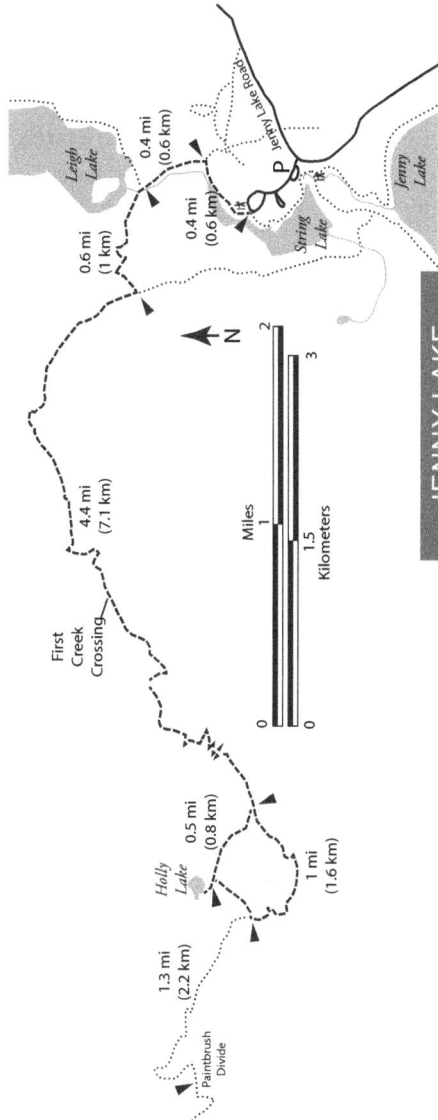

JENNY LAKE

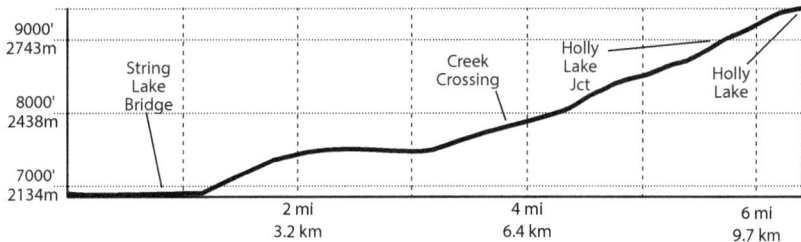

STRING LAKE

27 LAUREL LAKE (2.8 mi / 4.6 km / Mod)

Overview: A hike to a rarely visited lake overlooking String Lake.

Trip style: Out and back

Distance: 1.4 miles (2.3 km) one way, 2.8 miles (4.6 km) round trip

Elevation gain: 959 feet (292 m)

Max. Elevation: 7,620 feet (2,323 m)

Difficulty: Moderate, minor route finding

Trailhead: String Lake South
43.7842°N, -110.7274°W / 43°47'03"N, -110°43'38"W
12T 0521938E 4847940N

Traffic: Heavy, light past the Laurel Lake junction

Maps: Jenny Lake 7.5' USGS Topo

Notes: Minor route finding from the trail to the edge of the lake.

JENNY LAKE

Trailhead Directions

Drive north from Jackson on US 191 for 12.3 miles (19.8 km) to Moose Junction and turn left on Teton Park Road. Continue past the entrance station for a total of 10.7 miles (17.2 km) to the North Jenny Lake Junction. Turn left and continue 1.5 miles (2.4 km), then turn right and park in the first String Lake parking lot.

Trailhead Facilities

Restrooms, bike rack, trash cans, bear boxes for food storage, fuel/gas canister disposal.

Hike Description

Begin the hike at the String Lake Trailhead at the first parking lot at String Lake. Cross the large wooden bridge over the String Lake outlet. Follow the rocky trail away from String Lake through thin forest cover for 0.4 mile (0.6 km) to the first trail junction.

Take the right fork northwest along String Lake. Hike for another short distance of 0.2 mile (0.3 km) to a footbridge and seasonal creek. String Lake will come into view as the trail travels north and uphill.

Hike another 0.1 mile (0.2 km) from the creek to an unmarked junction with the unofficial trail on the left (W). It is well-worn though it is somewhat hidden by a shrub on the trail.

Hike directly up this steep, rocky trail. The trail is partially overgrown and eroded. In a dense tree patch, the trail turns right, then curves counterclockwise over a hill as Laurel Lake becomes visible. The trail appears to continue traveling around the rock field but disappears into the shrubbery near the feeder creek.

Instead, keep an eye out for a trail

that runs on the eastern edge of the rock field. If it is not apparent, walk over the rock field toward the lake. A trail will appear 57 feet (17 m) above the northeastern lakeshore that makes walking easier.

Follow this trail around the east shore of Laurel Lake to the drop-off. At the end of the trail, walk through the shrubs and fallen trees to the high point. A spectacular view of String, Leigh, and Jenny lakes rewards hikers from this high vantage point.

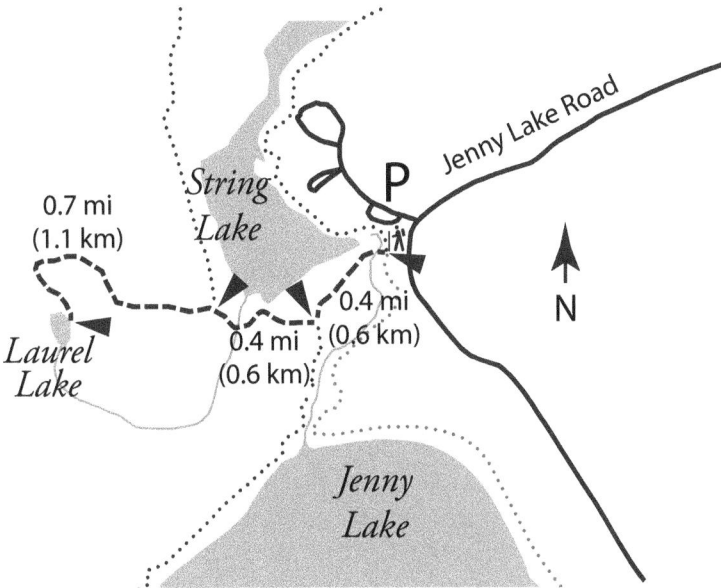

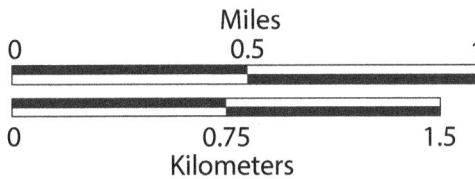

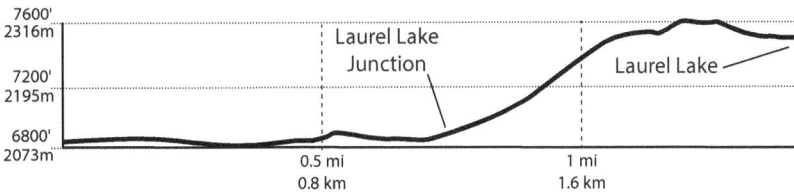

JENNY LAKE

String Lake

Laurel Lake

Jenny Lake Road

P

0.7 mi (1.1 km)

0.4 mi (0.6 km)

0.4 mi (0.6 km)

N

Miles
0   0.5   1

0   0.75   1.5
Kilometers

7600'
2316m

7200'
2195m

6800'
2073m

Laurel Lake Junction

Laurel Lake

0.5 mi
0.8 km

1 mi
1.6 km

STRING LAKE

28 LEIGH LAKE (7.2 mi / 11.6 km / Easy)

Overview: Enjoy a large backcountry lake with no road access.

Trip style: Out and back

Distance: 3.6 miles (5.8 km) one way, 7.2 miles (11.6 km) round trip

Elevation gain: 42 feet (13 feet)

Max. Elevation: 6,915 feet (2,108 m)

Difficulty: Easy

Trailhead: Leigh Lake
43.7886°N, -110.7305°W / 43°47'19"N, -110°43'50"W
12T 0521683E 4848429N

Traffic: Moderate to heavy with stock animal traffic

Maps: Jenny Lake 7.5' USGS Topo

Notes: Permits required to camp at Trapper and Bearpaw lakes.

Trailhead Directions

Drive north from Jackson on US 191 for 12.3 miles (19.8 km) to Moose Junction and turn left on Teton Park Road. Continue past the entrance station for a total of 10.7 miles (17.2 km) to the North Jenny Lake Junction. Turn left and continue 1.5 miles (2.4 km), then turn right and park at the last (N) parking lot.

Trailhead Facilities

Restrooms, bike rack, trash cans, bear boxes for food storage, fuel/gas canister disposal.

Hike Description

Begin the hike at the Leigh Lake Trailhead at the last (N) parking lot at String Lake. The trailhead begins near the restroom. Walk 300 feet (91 m) on the trail toward the lake. Turn right (NW) along the shore of String Lake for 0.4 mile (0.6 km) to a junction with a trail leading off to the southeast. Continue along the trail along String Lake as the trail turns northwest.

At the trail junction near the north inlet of String Lake and the creek connecting to Leigh Lake, take the right (NE) fork and continue toward Leigh Lake.

The trail along Leigh Lake follows the lakeshore for 2.8 miles (4.5 km), gaining little elevation along the route. At 2.7 miles (4.3 km), the trail breaks out of the forest and stays to the east of the thin forested strip along the lakeshore. This section of trail is easy to travel since there is little elevation change.

Shortly after exiting the forest, the trail connects with the Leigh, Trapper, Bearpaw, and Jackson lakes trail intersection. Travel along the same route to return to the trailhead and parking lot.

LEIGH LAKE

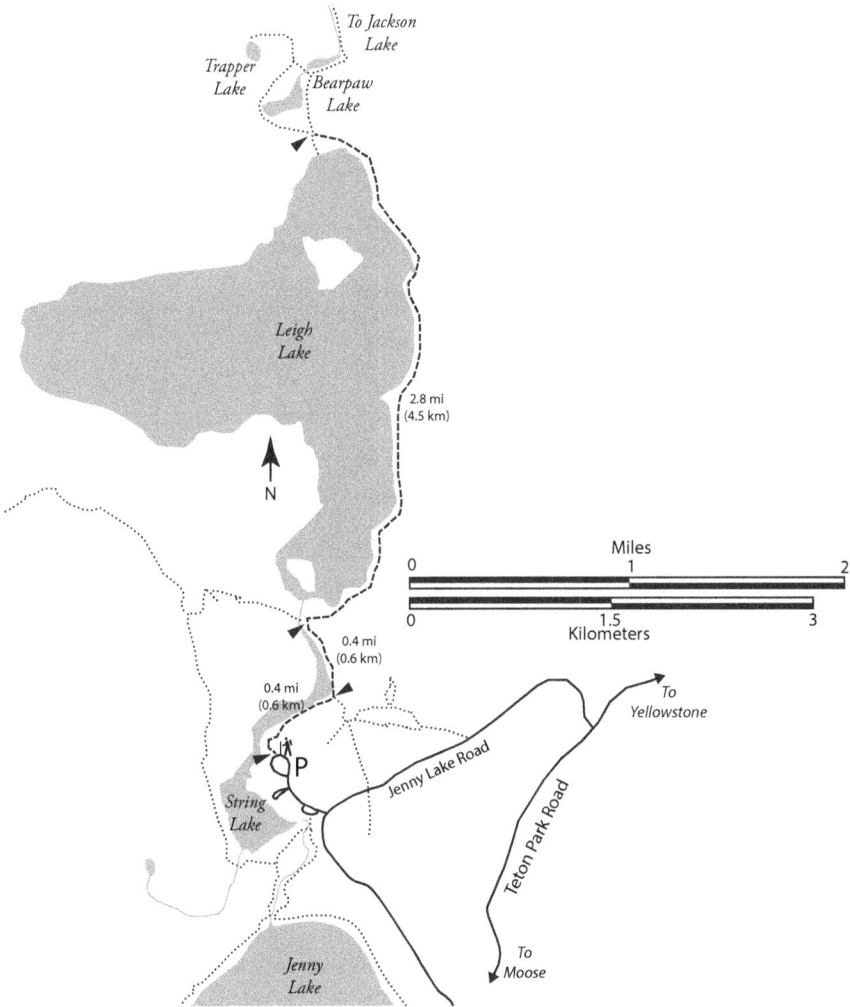

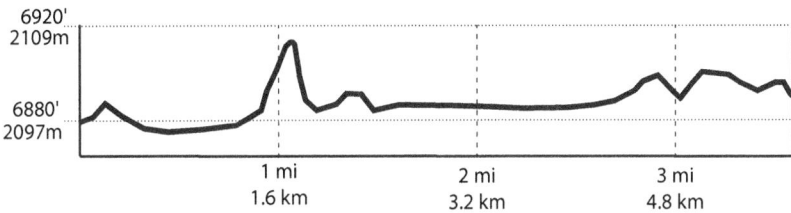

STRING LAKE

29 PAINTBRUSH DIVIDE TO CASCADE CANYON (19.2 mi / 30.8 km / Ex Stren)

JENNY LAKE

Overview: A tour of Grand Teton's most spectacular canyons.

Trip style: Loop

Distance: 19.2 miles (30.8 km)

Elevation gain: 4,293 feet (1,309 m) total gain

Max. Elevation: 10,708 feet (3,264 m)

Difficulty: Extremely Strenuous day hike, strenuous overnighter

Trailhead: Leigh Lake
43.7886°N, -110.7305°W / 43°47'19"N, -110°43'50"W
12T 0521683E 4848429N

Traffic: Moderate to heavy

Maps: Jenny Lake, Mount Moran 7.5' USGS Topo

Notes: Camping permits required along this route. Ice axe may be required on the north side of Paintbrush Divide.

Trailhead Directions

Drive north from Jackson on US 191 for 12.3 miles (19.8 km) to Moose Junction and turn left on Teton Park Road. Continue past the entrance station for a total of 10.7 miles (17.2 km) to the North Jenny Lake Junction. Turn left and continue 1.5 miles (2.4 km), then turn right and park at the last (N) parking lot.

Trailhead Facilities

Restrooms, bike rack, trash cans, bear boxes for food storage, fuel/gas canister disposal.

Hike Description

Begin the hike at the Leigh Lake Trailhead at the last parking lot at String Lake. The trailhead begins near the restroom and heads northwest along the shore of String Lake for 0.4 mile (0.6 km) to a junction with a trail leading off to the southeast. Continue on the trail along String Lake as the trail turns northwest.

At the trail junction that leads across the creek between north String Lake and south Leigh Lake, take the left (W) fork and continue across the bridge that spans the inlet to String Lake.

Continue for another 0.6 mile (1 km) to the trail junction that splits between west String Lake and Paintbrush Divide. Take the right trail fork toward Paintbrush Divide.

As the trail curves counterclockwise (NW to SW) around Rockchuck Peak, it enters Paintbrush Canyon. It approaches the creek from the south which flows down the middle of the canyon.

The trail crosses over the creek, sometimes a raging torrent in the early season, at 3.8 miles (6.1 km). Often, the trail is covered in snow well into early summer if not later, depending on the depth of the winter snow pack. Once the trail crosses to the north side of the canyon, it escapes from the heavy forest cover and is much more open to the sky.

From the junction at 1.5 miles (2.4 km), the trail rises 2,200 feet (671 m) over 4.4 miles (7.1 km) through the spectacular Paintbrush Canyon.

Between 4.3 to 4.7 miles (6.9 to 7.6 km), the trail crosses over the creek several more times over wooden bridges, then works its way up several steep switchbacks to the Holly Lake junction at 5.9 miles (9.5 km). Holly Lake is an excellent diversion if time allows or continue for 1 mile (1.6 km) curving clockwise toward the upper Holly Lake junction.

Continue on toward Paintbrush Divide. The trail breaks free of the thinning forest and begins a climb up a bowl in a steep 1.3-mile (2.2 km) climb to the saddle. Ice axes are recommended for the ascent well into summer. There is often a permanent snow pack into September when snow begins falling again in earnest. Hikers have been injured and rescued from falls in this section.

The summit and pass of Paintbrush Divide can be shrouded in clouds, making following the trail difficult. Keep a watchful eye, as casual hikers have made several routes through the delicate landscape above the tree line.

On the south side of the divide, a spectacular scene opens up. Part of the Grand Teton Cathedral Group comes into view as well as the trail to Lake Solitude, the lake itself, and a large portion of Cascade Canyon.

The 2.3-mile (3.7 km) hike down to Lake Solitude can be a bit rocky and is often busy in summer months. Be mindful to yield to hikers traveling uphill. They have the right of way.

Light grasses and a few stands of trees dot the alpine landscape around Lake Solitude. Continue on the trail around the eastern shore. The next 2.5 miles (4 km) into Cascade Canyon can be snowbound as well but does not required an ice axe.

At the Cascade Canyon junction, take the left (E) fork toward Jenny Lake. Continue east on the trail for 3.3 miles (5.3 km) to the junction for String Lake and Jenny Lake. The shortest route back is via the left (NE) fork toward String Lake.

The next 0.7-mile (1.1 km) of trail passes down a steep section of switchbacks in heavier forest cover. The trail breaks onto the main Jenny Lake Loop Trail. Take the left (N) trail fork toward String Lake.

This next 1.2-mile (1.9 km) section of trail is nearly flat with views of Jenny Lake along the entire length. Be mindful of wildlife in this section, as there are no practical escape routes along the trail.

JENNY LAKE

STRING LAKE

At the String Lake Loop junction, continue straight (NE) toward the String Lake parking lot. This 0.8 mile (1.3 km) section passes over a packed, mildly rocky trail to the bridge over the String Lake outlet.

Take the trail heading west and northwest along the lakeshore at the information kiosk. It passes parking lots and is easy to follow toward the north String Lake parking lot to the original trailhead.

Options

This trip can be done in reverse. No camping is allowed near Lake Solitude, making for a long second day over Paintbrush Divide. The views are better traveling in the counterclockwise direction.

#1 The South Fork of Cascade Canyon continues to Schoolroom Glacier. This diversion will add 8.2 miles (13.2 km) round trip distance to this hike.

#2 A pleasant diversion, adding 0.5 mile (0.8 km), takes you to Inspiration Point and Hidden Falls as well as the Jenny Lake shuttle boat dock. The view is well worth the extra effort, as it has some of the best open views of Jenny Lake.

#3 The trail can be started at the south String Lake parking lot and travel the west side of the Lake. This approach adds no difficulty.

mi	km	Waypoints
0.1	0.16	String Lake Loop
0.8	1.3	String Lake inlet bridge
5.9	9.5	Holly Lake junction
8.2	13.2	Paintbrush Divide
10.4	16.7	Lake Solitude
13.1	21.1	Cascade Canyon Fork
16.4	26.4	Inspiration Point junction
17.1	27.5	Jenny Lake loop
18.5	29.8	String Lake outlet bridge

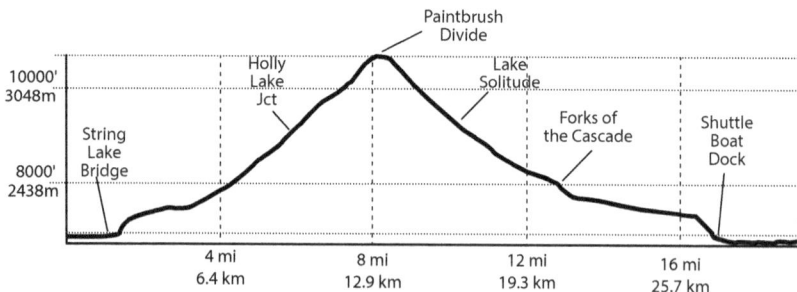

STRING LAKE

PAINTBRUSH DIVIDE TO CASCADE CANYON

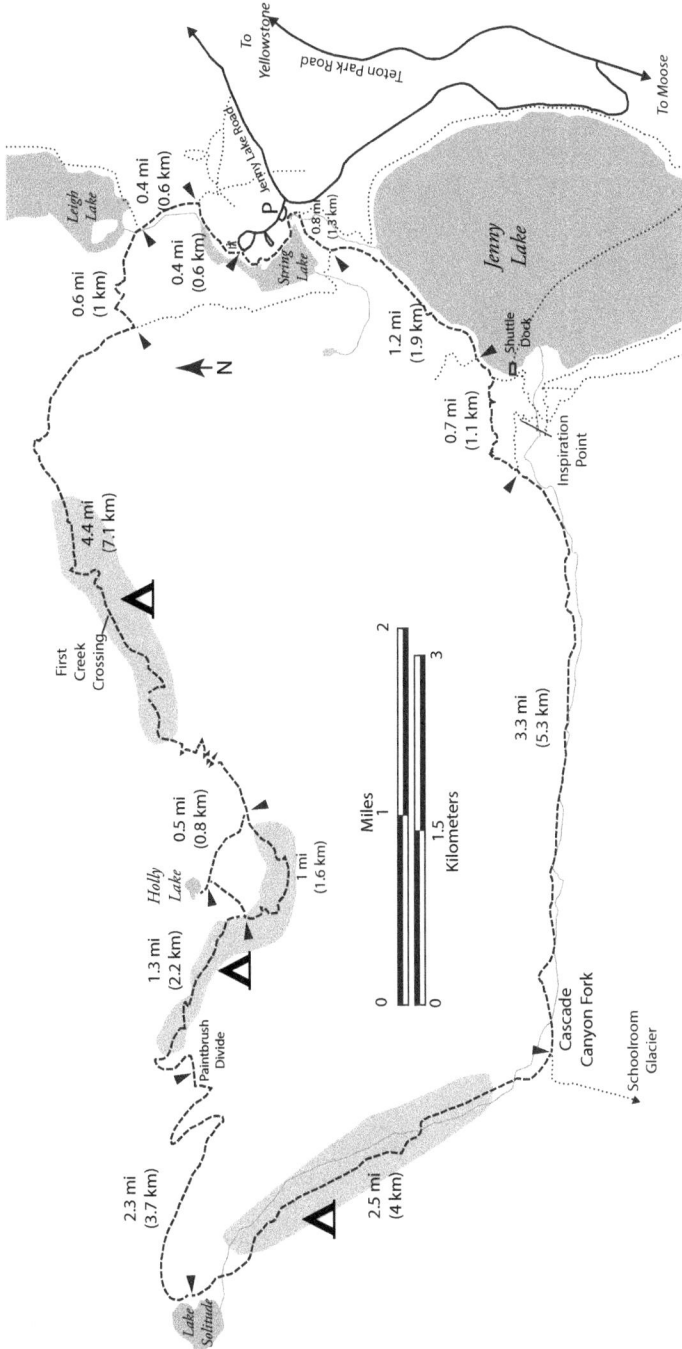

To Yellowstone

Teton Park Road

To Moose

Jenny Lake Road

Leigh Lake

String Lake

Jenny Lake

0.4 mi (0.6 km)

0.4 mi (0.6 km)

0.6 mi (1 km)

Lift

0.8 mi (1.3 km)

1.2 mi (1.9 km)

Shuttle Dock

N

0.7 mi (1.1 km)

Inspiration Point

4.4 mi (7.1 km)

First Creek Crossing

Miles

Kilometers

3.3 mi (5.3 km)

0.5 mi (0.8 km)

Holly Lake

1 mi (1.6 km)

1.3 mi (2.2 km)

Paintbrush Divide

Cascade Canyon Fork

Schoolroom Glacier

2.3 mi (3.7 km)

2.5 mi (4 km)

Lake Solitude

STRING LAKE

JENNY LAKE

30 STRING LAKE LOOP (3.8 mi / 6.1 km / Easy)

Overview: Hike a loop around a popular recreation lake.

Trip style: Loop

Distance: 3.8 miles (6.1 km)

Elevation gain: 491 feet (150 m) gain/loss

Max. Elevation: 7,162 feet (2,183 m)

Difficulty: Easy

Trailhead: Leigh Lake
43.7886°N, -110.7305°W / 43°47'19"N, -110°43'50"W
12T 0521683E 4848429N

Traffic: Heavy

Maps: Jenny Lake 7.5' USGS Topo

Notes: Arrive early, as parking is a challenge in summer.

JENNY LAKE

Trailhead Directions

Drive north from Jackson on US 191 for 12.3 miles (19.8 km) to Moose Junction and turn left on Teton Park Road. Continue past the entrance station for a total of 10.7 miles (17.2 km) to the North Jenny Lake Junction. Turn left and continue 1.5 miles (2.4 km), then turn right and park at the last (N) parking lot.

Trailhead Facilities

Restrooms, bike rack, trash cans, bear boxes for food storage, fuel/gas canister disposal.

Hike Description

Begin the hike at the Leigh Lake Trailhead at the last (N) parking lot at String Lake. The trailhead begins near the restroom. Walk 300 feet (91 m) on the trail toward the lake. Turn right (NE) along the shore of String Lake for 0.4 mile (0.6 km) to a junction with a trail leading off to the southeast. Continue along the trail along String Lake as the trail turns northwest.

At the next junction, take the left (W) fork and continue toward Paintbrush Canyon. This trail crosses the large bridge spanning the creek emptying Leigh Lake into String Lake.

Follow the trail for 0.7 mile (1.1 km) along a series of switchbacks for the only climb along this loop. The cutoff trail intersects the Paintbrush Divide Trail at the apex of this portion of the trail.

Turn left (S) at the junction. Continue hiking for 1.4 miles (2.3 km) toward and along the shoreline of String Lake. The trail curves left (E) and follows the south end of the lake until encountering a junction.

Take the left fork and hike the 0.3 mile (0.5 km) to the wooden bridge that spans the outlet of the lake and leads to the first parking lot.

Turn left (N) and hike along the well-traveled trail in and out of tree cover. The trail passes the dirt boat ramp and continues for a short distance to the northern parking lot at the trailhead.

There are several meandering trails in the area. Any of them connects to the parking lot and road, making navigation simple.

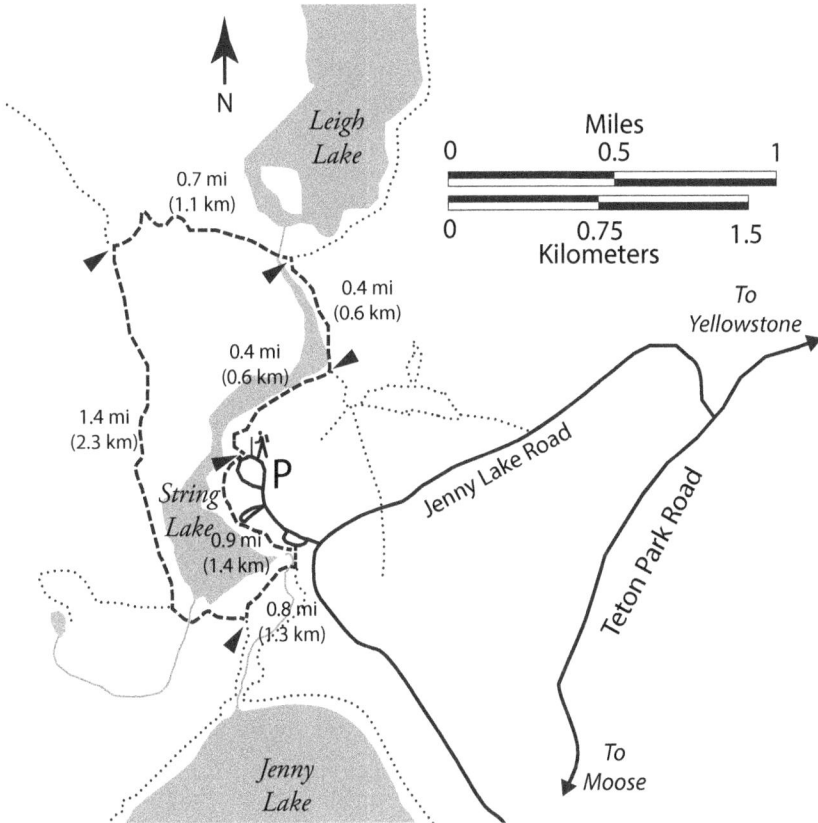

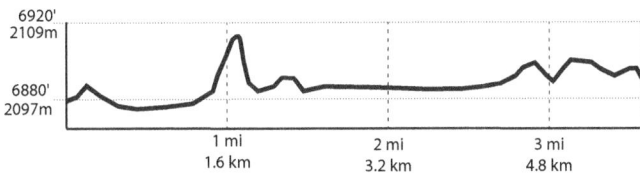

STRING LAKE

Taggart Lake

The Taggart Lake Trailhead and area is the perfect starting point to explore backcountry lakes without a big commitment. Both Taggart and Bradley are short hikes to beautiful lakes with the Tetons as a backdrop.

The parking lot at the Taggart Lake Trailhead can be incredibly busy by late morning. Plan to visit early to avoid the crowds and parking challenges. The trails in the area are easy to walk along and are easy for beginning hikers.

This area also contains several historic and important landmarks that help define Grand Teton National Park as it is known today. These homesteads, historic cabins, and famous buildings are well worth exploring. The views from these cabins are unmatched in all of the United States.

The American Alpine Club's Climber's Ranch is also located in the Taggart Lake area. Visit their website to learn more about this unique facility. It is focused on providing affordable lodging for people who dedicate a significant amount of time trying to climb some of the more challenging routes in the Teton Range.

Should you find yourself curious about mountaineering and climbing, this ranch is well worth the visit. You may just encounter some of the most famous climbers in the world enjoying their summers in Grand Teton. It is free to stop in and take a look around.

The story of Geraldine Lucas is also worth learning about when visiting this area. She was an enterprising pioneer in a harsh environment. In her era, it was rare for women to strike out by themselves, let alone establish a homestead in one of the most difficult weather locations in the continental United States. Read the park brochures for more information.

Should you have the ability to fly fish, Cottonwood Creek is an excellent choice for local trout. The original homestead fishing locations are pleasant and easy to access.

JENNY LAKE

Courtesy of Randy Isaacson

Taggart Lake Trail and Grand Teton.

31 BAR BC RANCH (0.9 mi / 1.4 km / Easy)

Overview: Easy hike through an original Jackson dude ranch.

Trip style: Lollipop loop

Distance: 0.9 mile (1.4 km) round trip

Elev. gain/loss: 57 ft. (12 m)

Max. Elevation: 6,572 ft. (2,003 m)

Difficulty: Easy

Trailhead: Bar BC Gate
43.6976°N, -110.6954°W / 43°41'51"N, -110°41'43"W
12T 0524549E 4838334N

Traffic: Light

Maps: Moose 7.5' USGS

Notes: Family-friendly. High-clearance vehicles recommended.

Trailhead Directions

Drive north from Jackson on US 191 for 12.3 miles (19.8 km) to Moose Junction and turn left on Teton Park Road. Continue for 4 miles (6.4 km) and turn right on the unmarked rough dirt road (River Road). This turn is 1,000 feet (304 m) north of the Cottonwood Creek Picnic Area. From the steel gate, drive 1.7 miles (2.7 km) to the parking area at the wooden gate.

Trailhead Facilities

No facilities available.

Hike Description

Walk around the wooden gate and proceed down the rocky road to the information sign. Turn right and continue on the overgrown road, passing the corral on the right (W) and several dude cabins on the left (E).

Walk 0.2 mile (0.3 km) to the

remnants of the main cabin and observe the dance hall to your left across the dried up swimming holes.

Continue south along the deteriorating road until it forks to the right, then begin looping to the right (W) toward the larger cabins. The road is indistinct but the area is easy to navigate.

Reconnect with the dirt road at the main cabin. Return to the parking lot along the same path.

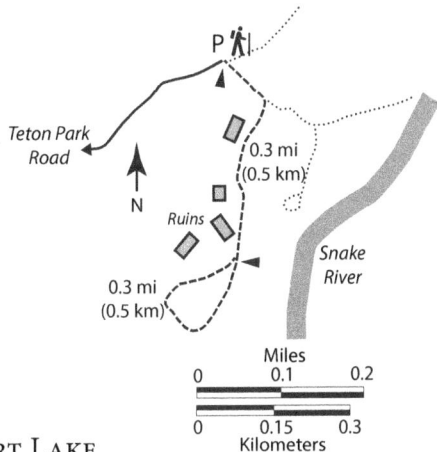

TAGGART LAKE

32 BRADLEY LAKE (4 mi / 5.2 km / Easy)

Overview: An easily accessible backcountry lake.

Trip style: Lollipop loop

Distance: 2 miles (3.6 km) one way, 4 miles (5.2 km) round trip

Elevation gain: 511 feet (156 m)

Max. Elevation: 7,142 feet (2,177 m)

Difficulty: Easy

Trailhead: Taggart Lake Trailhead
43.6932°N, -110.7329°W / 43°41'35"N, -110°43'58"W
12T 0521524E 4837828N

Traffic: Heavy

Maps: Grand Teton, Moose 7.5' USGS Topo

Notes: This is a family-friendly lake accessible only by trail.

JENNY LAKE

Trailhead Directions

Drive north from Jackson on US 191 for 12.3 miles (19.8 km) to Moose Junction and turn left on Teton Park Road. Continue past the entrance station for a total of 3.6 miles (5.7 km) to the Taggart Lake Trailhead parking lot.

Trailhead Facilities

Restrooms, bike rack, trash cans, information kiosk.

Hike Description

Start the hike near the concrete restroom building at the information and map kiosk. The wide trail leads through an open field toward the mountain and a tree-covered hill.

Take the first right (N) trail fork toward Bradley and Taggart lakes in 0.1 mile (0.2 km) from the trail-head. In 0.2 mile (0.3 km), the trail merges with the Beaver Creek Trail and curves northeast toward the horse corrals. It then curves left (NW) and gains elevation through a stand of trees.

The Bradley Lake cutoff trail is 0.7 mile (1.1 km) from the horse corrals. Take this fork and travel northwest for 0.9 mile (1.4 km) over a slight hill to reach Bradley Lake. This trail is easy to follow and travels through a lightly forested section before the thick stand of trees surrounding Bradley Lake.

It is possible to visit Taggart Lake on this hike to make a loop by re-turning via the Taggart Lake Trail. This option adds 1.2 miles (0.3 km) to the hike and gains you another backcountry lake. Taggart Lake is heavily visited and the trail back is easy to follow.

BRADLEY LAKE

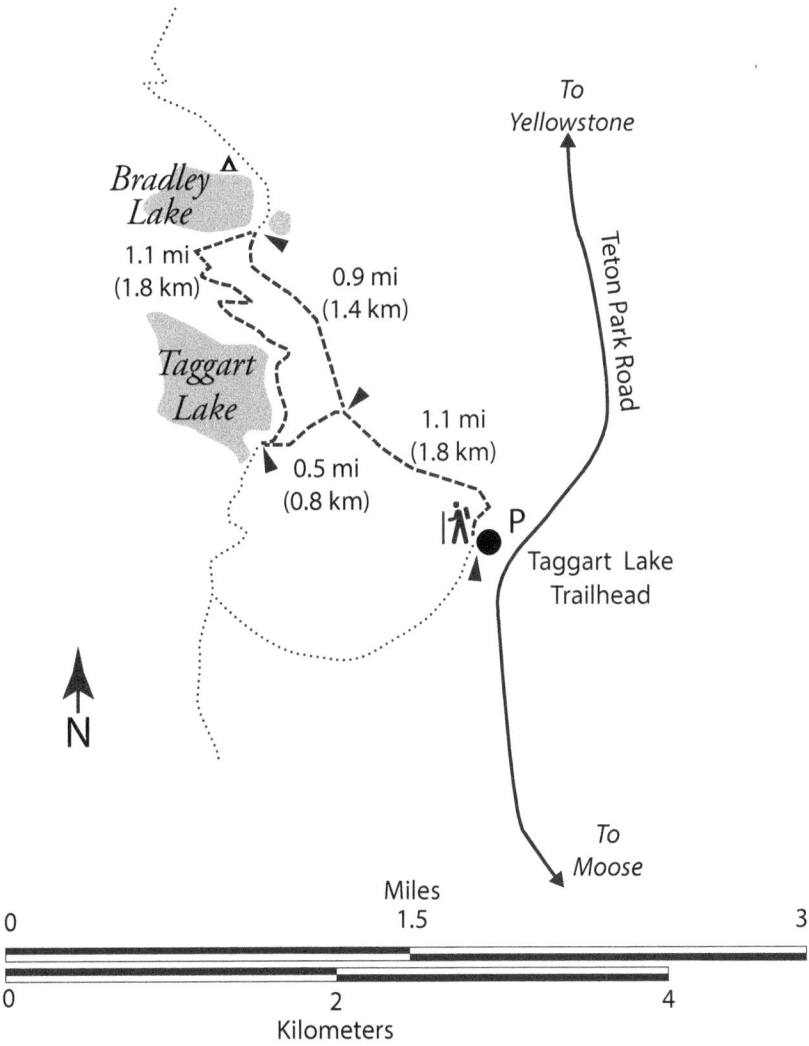

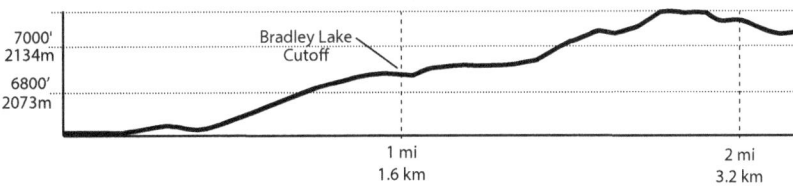

TAGGART LAKE

33 BURNED WAGON GULCH (4 mi / 7.2 km / Mod)

Overview: A lightly-hiked alternate trail to access the Cathedral Group.
Trip style: Out and back
Distance: 2 miles (3.6 km) one way, 4 miles (7.2 km) round trip
Elevation gain: 731 feet (223 m)
Max. Elevation: 7,413 feet (2,259 m)
Difficulty: Easy to moderate
Trailhead: Climbers Ranch Road
43.7095°N, -110.7315°W / 43°42'34"N, -110°43'53"W
12T 0521629E 4839644N
Traffic: Light
Maps: Moose, Grand Teton 7.5' USGS Topos
Notes: If the roadside parking is full, park at the Climbers Ranch.

JENNY LAKE

Trailhead Directions

Drive north from Jackson on US 191 for 12.3 miles (19.8 km) to Moose Junction and turn left on Teton Park Road. Continue past the entrance station for a total of 4.8 miles (7.7 km) to the Climbers Ranch turnoff. Turn left (W), proceed past the park housing and over the Cottonwood Creek Bridge, then park on the right (N) side of the road before reaching the Climbers Ranch.

Trailhead Facilities

None

Hike Description

The trailhead for this hike is unmarked. It immediately leads off into a mixed cottonwood and aspen forested area and crosses a tributary of Cottonwood Creek in 0.2 mile (0.3 km).

The trail continues into a large open area as it slowly curves northwest. At 0.5 mile (0.8 km), there is a junction with a trail leading north to the Lucas-Fabian Homestead. It is visible in the distance.

Continue following the trail toward the mountains between two stands of trees. At 0.8 mile (1.3 km), the trail passes by a large boulder with a plaque dedicated to Geraldine Lucas, the second woman to climb the Grand Teton. Past the rock, the trail enters Burned Wagon Gulch. It travels up the south face of the gulch.

At 1.6 miles (2.6 km), the trail enters an open area below the Garnet Canyon Trail. It continues climbing until it enters a stand of trees with some dead fall. It passes through shrubs and connects over a few logs with the Garnet Canyon Trail, 80 feet (24 m) east of the Valley Trail junction.

BURNED WAGON GULCH

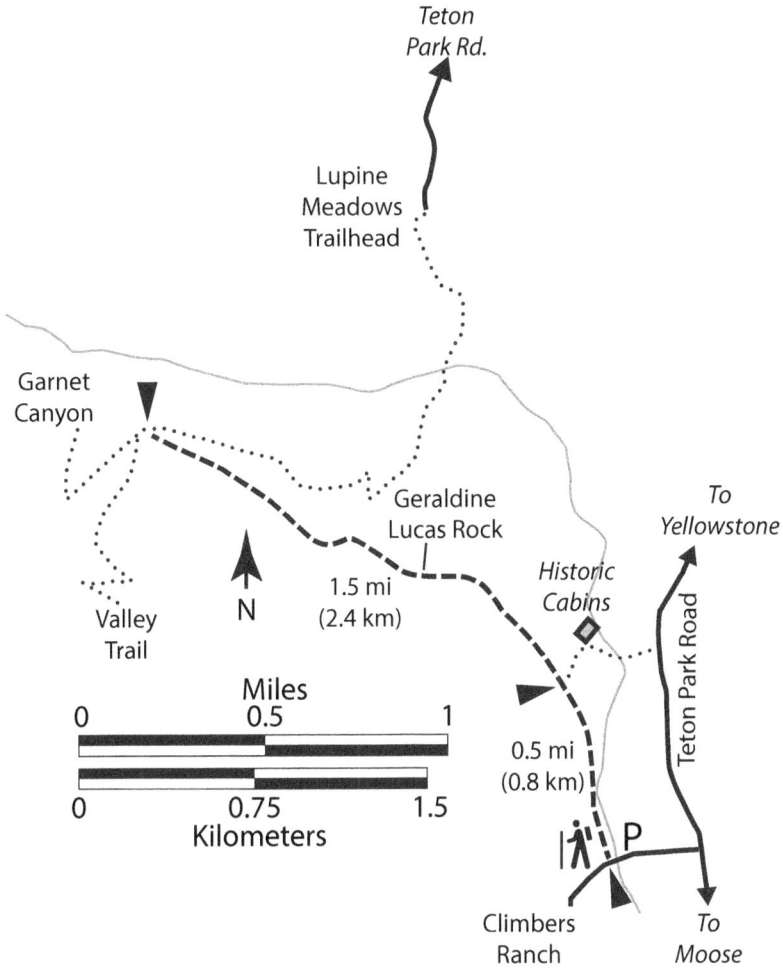

Teton Park Rd.

Lupine Meadows Trailhead

Garnet Canyon

Geraldine Lucas Rock

To Yellowstone

Historic Cabins

1.5 mi (2.4 km)

Valley Trail

N

Teton Park Road

Miles

0   0.5   1

Kilometers

0   0.75   1.5

0.5 mi (0.8 km)

P

Climbers Ranch

To Moose

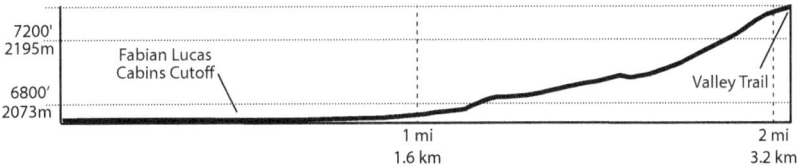

7200' 2195m

Fabian Lucas Cabins Cutoff

6800' 2073m

Valley Trail

1 mi 1.6 km

2 mi 3.2 km

34 LUCAS-FABIAN HOMESTEAD
(0.6 mi / 1 km / Easy)

Overview: A short hike to well-preserved historic cabins.

Trip style: Out and back

Distance: 0.3 mile (0.5 km) one way, 0.6 mile (1 km) round trip

Elevation gain: 11 feet (3 m)

Max. Elevation: 6,708 feet (2,045 m)

Difficulty: Easy

Trailhead: Lucas-Fabian access road
43.7174°N, -110.7291°W / 43°43'03"N, -110°43'45"W
12T 0521825E 4840523N

Traffic: Light

Maps: Moose 7.5' USGS Topo

JENNY LAKE

Trailhead Directions

Drive north from Jackson on US 191 for 12.3 miles (19.8 km) to Moose Junction and turn left on Teton Park Road. Continue past the entrance station for a total of 5.3 miles (8.6 km) to a small, unmarked dirt lot on the west side of the road. A wooden gate and sign reading "SERVICE ROAD ONLY" marks the lot. It is easy to miss, as the turnoff is on a slope not easily visible from the road when driving north.

Trailhead Facilities

None.

Hike Description

Start at the dirt lot, walk around the wooden gate and continue on the old dirt two-track road. At 0.1 mile (0.2 km), the path crosses a wooden bridge over Cottonwood Creek. It then turns slightly right (W) and continues over a small wooden bridge toward the visible structures.

There are several information signs explaining the historical significance of these cabins. They are registered with the National Historic Register of Historic Places. All of the cabins are boarded up but it's possible to enjoy the view from the porches on the larger buildings.

The Geraldine Lucas rock with the commemorative plaque is 0.5 mile (0.8 km) northwest of the cabins on the Burned Wagon Gulch Trail.

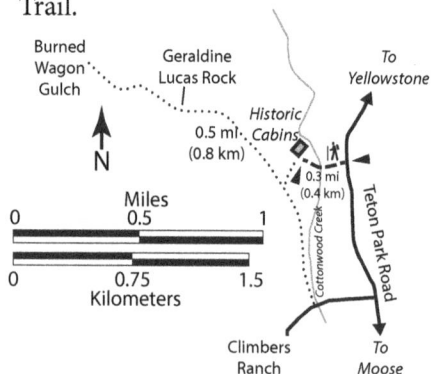

35 RIVER ROAD (13.9 mi / 22.3 km / Easy)

Overview: Easy hike along the western bank of the Snake River.

Trip style: Out and back

Distance: 13.9 miles (22.3 km) one way, shuttle recommended

Elev. gain/loss: 323 feet (98 m)

Max. Elevation: 6,893 feet (2,101 m)

Difficulty: Easy

Trailhead: Bar BC Gate
43.6976°N, -110.6954°W / 43°41'51"N, -110°41'43"W
12T 0524549E 4838334N

Traffic: Light

Maps: Moose, Jenny Lake 7.5' USGS Topos

Notes: High-clearance vehicles are recommended.

JENNY LAKE

Trailhead Directions

Drive north from Jackson on US 191 for 12.3 miles (19.8 km) to Moose Junction and turn left on Teton Park Road. Continue for 4 miles (6.4 km) and turn right on the unmarked rough dirt road (River Road). This turn is 1,000 feet (304 m) past the Cottonwood Creek Picnic Area. From the steel gate, drive 1.7 miles (2.7 km) to the parking area at the wooden gate.

Trailhead Facilities

No facilities available.

Hike Description

Start at the parking lot at the wooden gate to the Bar BC Ranch. Follow the road north along the western bank of the Snake River along the old two-track road.

The path slowly gains elevation as it works its way north along the Snake River. At 3.9 miles (6.3 km), the road turns northwest and travels up the river bench on a hill. At 5.3 miles (8.5 km), the road drops down to the lower river bench.

As the road continues northeast, it overlooks the many strands of the Snake River. Rafters and kayakers are often visible along this whole trip. At 11.7 miles (18.8 km), the road reaches the R.K.O. Road. Turn left (W) and continue for another 2.2 miles (3.5 km) to reach the Teton Park Road.

It is possible to take the River Road from either direction and have no change in difficulty. The views are equivalent in beauty in either direction.

After high water damaged the road, the park service blocked driving access to the River Road north of the Bar BC Ranch. The future of the path is uncertain.

RIVER ROAD

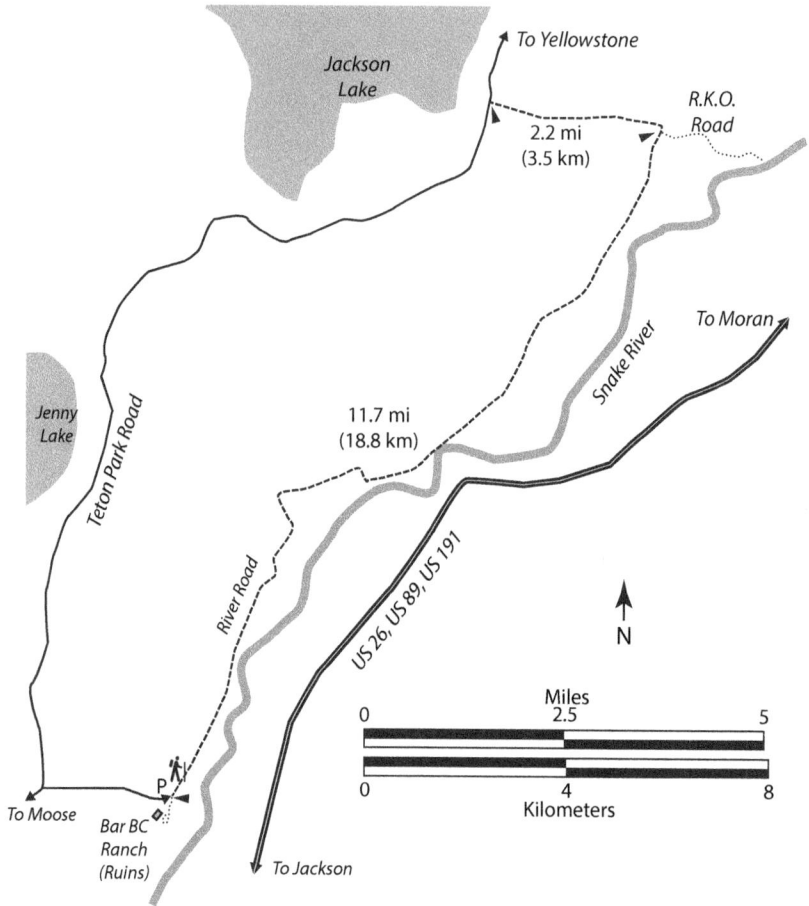

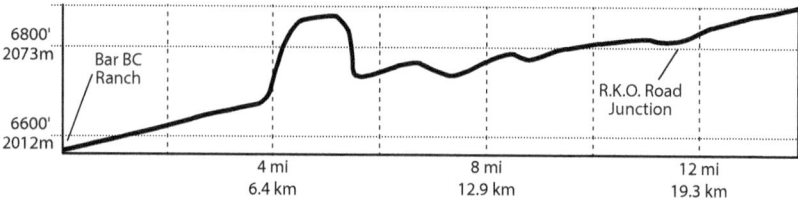

TAGGART LAKE

36 TAGGART LAKE (3.6 mi / 5.8 km / Easy)

Overview: A popular backcountry lake for all skill levels.

Trip style: Lollipop loop

Distance: 3.6 miles (5.8 km) loop

Elevation gain: 511 feet (156 m)

Max. Elevation: 7,142 feet (2,177 m)

Difficulty: Easy

Trailhead: Taggart Lake Trailhead
43.6932°N, -110.7329°W / 43°41'35"N, -110°43'58"W
12T 0521524E 4837828N

Traffic: Heavy

Maps: Grand Teton, Moose 7.5' USGS Topos

Notes: This gentle trail offers family-friendly hiking.

Trailhead Directions

Drive north from Jackson on US 191 for 12.3 miles (19.8 km) to Moose Junction and turn left on Teton Park Road. Continue past the entrance station for a total of 3.6 miles (5.7 km) to the Taggart Lake Trailhead parking lot.

Trailhead Facilities

Restrooms, bike rack, trash cans, information kiosk.

Hike Description

Start the hike near the concrete restroom building at the information and map kiosk. The wide trail leads through an open field toward the mountains and a tree-covered hill.

Take the first right (N) trail fork toward Bradley and Taggart lakes in 0.1 mile (0.2 km) from the trailhead. In 0.2 mile (0.3 km), the trail merges with the Beaver Creek Trail and curves northeast toward the horse corrals. It then curves left (NW) and gains elevation through a stand of trees.

The Bradley Lake cutoff trail is 0.7 mile (1.1 km) from the horse corrals. Take the left fork and continue another 0.5 mile (0.8 km) to Taggart Lake to explore the shoreline. From the junction, turn left (S), cross the long wooden bridge, and lose elevation to the Valley Trail and Beaver Creek connector. Turn left (SE) and continue counterclockwise back to the Taggart Lake Trailhead.

The out and back trip on the northern part of the loop is shorter and has more foot traffic. The southern part of the loop explores a marsh along Beaver Creek.

TAGGART LAKE

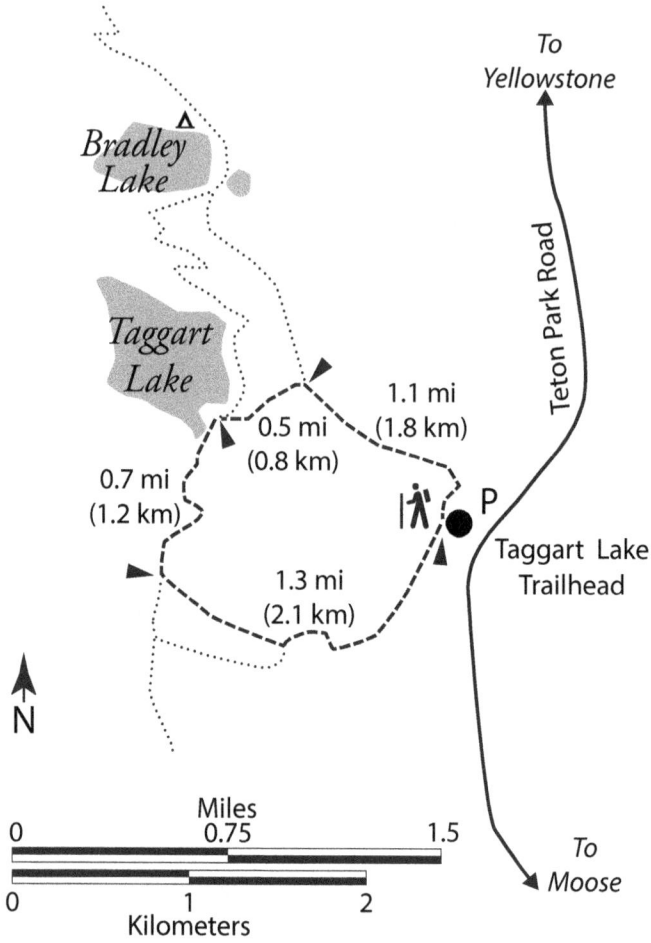

To
Yellowstone

Bradley
Lake

Teton Park Road

Taggart
Lake

1.1 mi
(1.8 km)

0.5 mi
(0.8 km)

0.7 mi
(1.2 km)

P

Taggart Lake
Trailhead

1.3 mi
(2.1 km)

N

Miles
0   0.75   1.5

0   1   2
Kilometers

To
Moose

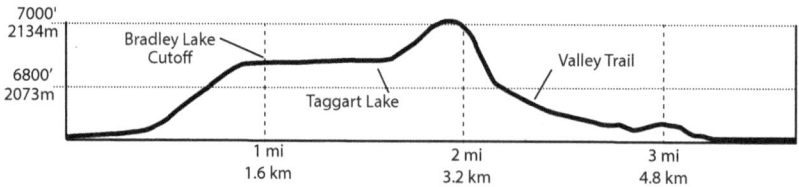

7000'
2134m

Bradley Lake
Cutoff

Valley Trail

6800'
2073m

Taggart Lake

1 mi
1.6 km

2 mi
3.2 km

3 mi
4.8 km

TAGGART LAKE

Lupine Meadows

Lupine Meadows is the starting point for many of the major climbs in the Teton Range. The trailhead is the beginning of the trail to visit the highly-popular Amphitheater, Surprise, and Delta lakes.

During the fall, visitors come to watch and listen for elk walking into the area for the mating rut. The call of an elk bugle is mysterious and haunting, though not dangerous at all. Hearing the sound of this majestic animal making its ancient call for mates is an experience you will never forget.

All of the trails leading out of this area, with the exception of the Valley Trail, seem to climb straight up the flanks of the mountains. For the most part, they do. Though there are plenty of switchbacks to reduce the intensity of the climb, expect a long, tough day of hiking.

The trails out of Lupine Meadows will test your stamina and preparation more than most of the other hikes contained in this book. Be prepared for an adventure here.

Climbing the upper reaches of many of the summits from this trailhead is beyond the scope of this book. Many of the climbs require technical experience and climbing equipment.

Make sure you are well-prepared for weather and tough, exposed climbing on the higher reaches of the Grand Teton, Teewinot, Middle Teton, and their sister summits.

The parking lot at Lupine Meadows is always busy during the entire year when it's possible to arrive by vehicle. Once the park closes the road due to snow, the parking lot becomes empty and it's easy to enjoy solitude on foot or on skis.

Grand Teton summit marker.

Delta Lake below Grand Teton.

JENNY LAKE

37 GARNET CANYON MEADOWS AND SPALDING FALLS (8.6 mi / 13.8 km / Stren)

Overview: Hike the base camp area for climbing the Cathedral Group.

Trip style: Out and back

Distance: 4.3 miles (6.9 km) one way, 8.6 miles (13.8 km) round trip

Elevation gain: 2,464 feet (751 m)

Max. Elevation: 9,200 feet (2,804 m)

Difficulty: Strenuous

Trailhead: Lupine Meadows
43.7348°N, -110.7415°W / 43°44'05"N, -110°44'29"W
12T 0520820E 4842447N

Traffic: Heavy

Maps: Moose, Grand Teton 7.5' USGS Topos

Notes: Permits are required to camp in the Meadows.

JENNY LAKE

Trailhead Directions

Drive north from Jackson on US 191 for 12.3 miles (19.8 km) to Moose Junction and turn left on Teton Park Road. Continue for 7.2 miles (11.6 km) to the Lupine Meadows Trailhead turnoff. Turn left onto the road. Cross the wooden bridge over Cottonwood Creek, then continue on the main dirt road for 1.5 miles (2.3 km) to reach the trailhead.

Trailhead Facilities

Restrooms, bike rack, trash cans, bear boxes for food storage, fuel/gas canister disposal.

Hike Description

Begin at the trailhead at the end of the parking lot. The trail starts off flat, then starts uphill, curving around a hill. In 0.6 mile (1 km), cross the wooden bridge over the creek that drains Delta Lake.

The trail turns west and works its way up a ridge to the Valley Trail junction at 1.7 miles (2.7 km). Continue straight, following the sign toward Garnet Canyon.

The path gains elevation through several switchbacks to the Amphitheater Lake junction in 1.2 miles (1.9 km). Take the left (S) fork toward Garnet Canyon.

The trail turns south and continues gaining elevation on the SE facing slope for 0.4 mile (0.6 km) before turning west and gently climbing into Garnet Canyon.

In 0.6 mile (1 km), the trail terminates at a boulder field near Cleft Falls. Make your way west over the boulders into the canyon. There are occasional sections of trail intermixed with the boulders.

Once you clear the boulders, you will catch the trail through shrubs and into the Meadows, noted by a park sign with camping and use rules for the area.

To continue on to Spalding Falls, keep an eye out for a junction to the right at the creek crossing just as you enter the open area of the Meadows near the Meadows sign. It is easy to walk right by the junction. Look to your right (N) for Spalding Falls. You will see a trail switchbacking up the steep face. Continue hiking 0.5 mile (0.8 km) up the switchbacks to the last creek crossing slightly above Spalding Falls.

Camping permits are required for this area.

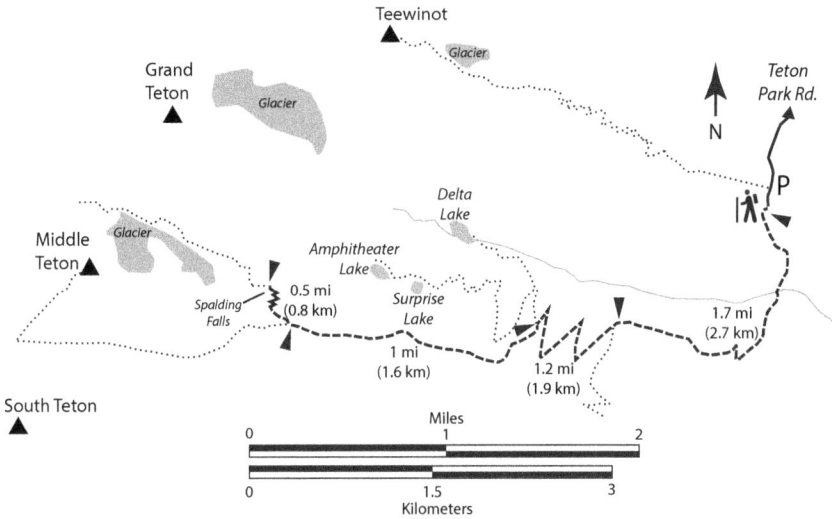

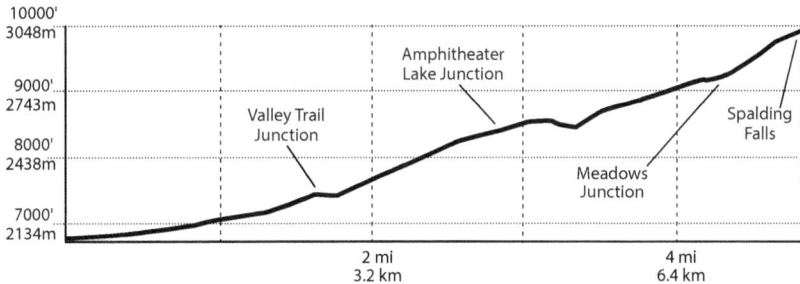

LUPINE MEADOWS

38 LOWER SADDLE GRAND TETON
(12 mi / 19.4 km / Ex Stren)

Overview: The access point for climbing the Grand Teton.

Trip style: Out and back

Distance: 6 miles (9.7 km) one way, 12 miles (19.4 km) round trip

Elevation gain: 4,905 feet (1,495 m)

Max. Elevation: 11,641 feet (3,548 m)

Difficulty: Extremely strenuous

Trailhead: Lupine Meadows
43.7348°N, -110.7415°W / 43°44'05"N, -110°44'29"W
12T 0520820E 4842447N

Traffic: Heavy

Maps: Moose, Grand Teton 7.5' USGS Topos

Notes: Involves rock climbing or glacier travel to reach the saddle.

Trailhead Directions

Drive north from Jackson on US 191 for 12.3 miles (19.8 km) to Moose Junction and turn left on Teton Park Road. Continue for 7.2 miles (11.6 km) to the Lupine Meadows Trailhead turnoff. Turn left onto the road. Cross the wooden bridge over Cottonwood Creek, then continue on the main dirt road for 1.5 miles (2.3 km) to reach the trailhead.

Trailhead Facilities

Restrooms, bike rack, trash cans, bear boxes for food storage, fuel/gas canister disposal.

Hike Description

Begin at the trailhead at the end of the parking lot. The trail starts off flat, then starts uphill, curving around a hill. At 0.6 mile (1 km), cross the wooden bridge over the creek that drains Delta Lake.

The trail turns west and works its way up a ridge to the Valley Trail junction at 1.7 miles (2.7 km). Continue straight, following the sign toward Garnet Canyon.

The path gains elevation through several switchbacks to the Amphitheater Lake junction in 1.2 miles (1.9 km). Take the left (S) fork toward Garnet Canyon.

The trail turns south and continues gaining elevation on the SE facing slope for 0.4 mile (0.6 km) before turning west and gently climbing into Garnet Canyon.

In 0.6 mile (1 km), the trail terminates at a boulder field near Cleft Falls. Make your way west over the boulders into the canyon. There are occasional sections of trail intermixed with the boulders.

JENNY LAKE

Once you clear the boulders, you will catch the trail through shrubs and into the Meadows, noted by a park sign with camping and use rules for the area.

Keep an eye out for a junction to the right at the creek crossing just as you enter the open area of the Meadows near the Meadows sign. It is easy to walk right by the junction. Look to your right (N) for Spalding Falls. You will see a trail switchbacking up the steep face. Follow the creek to the right of a large mass of shrubs as the trail begins following a sequence of switchbacks up the cliff towards Spalding Falls.

The trail travels west for 0.1 mile (0.2 km) as it crosses the creek that feeds the falls. Past there, it begins ascending another series of steep switchbacks. There are no trees beyond this point of the trail.

Follow the trail through the rocky terrain covered in boulders. The Jackson Hole Mountain Guides camp is above this trail and may be visible as you climb this steep area. The trail is well traveled but is easy to depart from over this next 0.7 mile (1.1 km) of steep climbing.

It passes several tent pads as it ascends towards the headwall. The trail terminates at a large rock cliff to the right (N) of the glacier. The park maintains a large rope to aid in ascending this cliff along a large flake of rock. This is fourth class climbing. A fall will be serious or possibly fatal. If the rope is frozen in, you will need an ice axe and crampons to ascend the steep glacier. The rock route is often wet from runoff.

At the top of the headwall, follow the vague trail straight up toward the saddle. Avoid stepping on the delicate vegetation. There is a potable water spring (with a hose) in the rocks a short distance before the Exum Guides and National Park camp on the top of the saddle.

The view from the saddle is stunning and worth the effort to reach it. Above here, the route to climb higher on the Grand Teton is technical, though countless reach the summit wearing nothing but running shoes and shorts. Note that a fall will be serious or fatal.

Do not underestimate the climbing time from the saddle to the summit if you continue on. There is another 2,100 feet (640 m) of tough climbing. Inexperienced climbers often go off route and end up trapped in the Owens-Spalding Couloir, a steep ravine to the left (W) of the classic Owens-Spalding route. Routes above the Lower Saddle are serious and may require gear. The route is icy most of the year.

There is no shelter in case of adverse weather or lightning above the saddle. Many climbers have been killed by fast-moving lightning storms.

LOWER SADDLE GRAND TETON

JENNY LAKE

South Teton

Middle Teton

Lower Saddle

Grand Teton

Glacier

Glacier

1.1 mi (1.8 km)

Spalding Falls

Dissapointment Peak

0.5 mi (0.8 km)

Amphitheater Lake

1 mi (1.6 km)

Surprise Lake

Delta Lake

Teewinot

Glacier

1.2 mi (1.9 km)

1.7 mi (2.7 km)

0   1.5   3
Kilometers

0   1   2
Miles

N

P

Teton Park Rd.

11000' 3353m			
10000' 3048m		Amphitheater Lake Junction	
9000' 2743m	Valley Trail Junction		
8000' 2438m			Spalding Falls
7000'		Meadows Junction	
2134m	2 mi 3.2 km	4 mi 6.4 km	

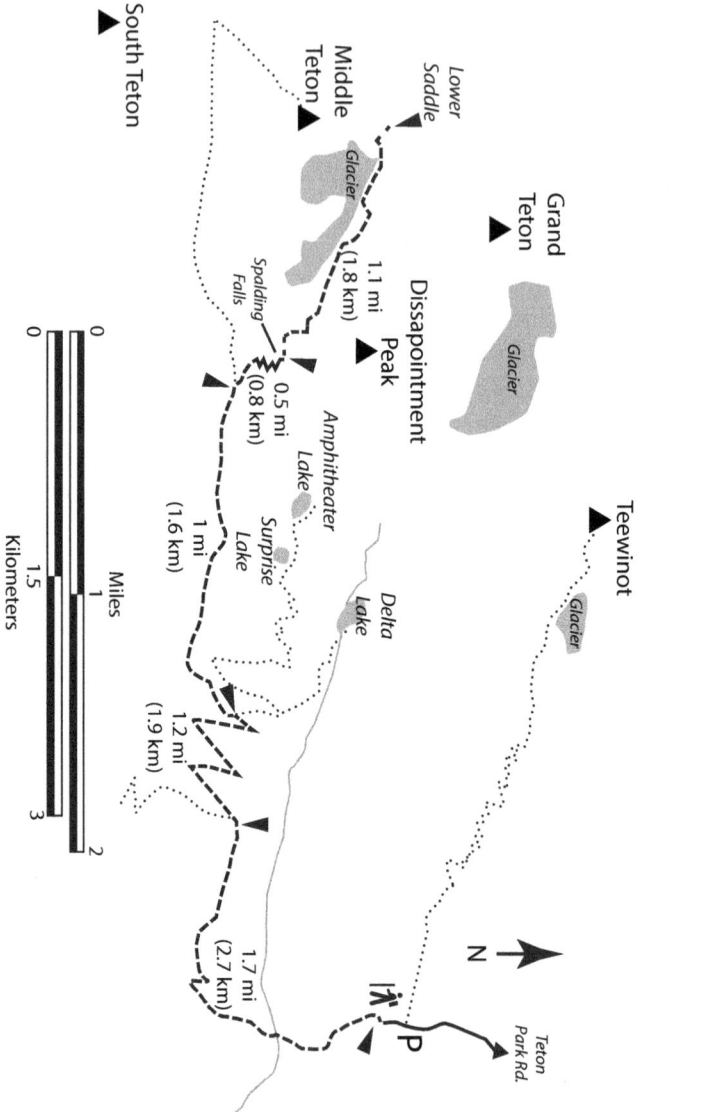

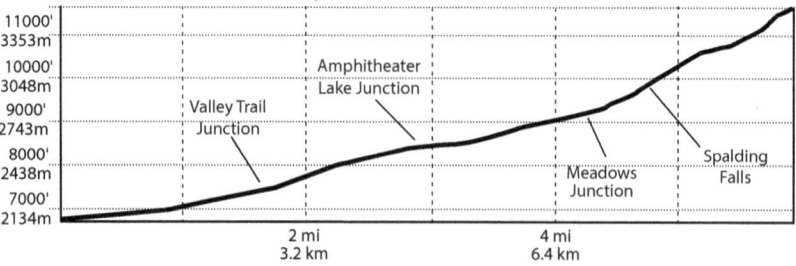

LUPINE MEADOWS

39 MIDDLE AND SOUTH TETON
(12.8 mi / 20.6 km / Ex Stren)

Overview: Two popular summits for skilled climbers and hikers.

Trip style: Out and back

Distance: 6.4 miles (10.3 km) one way, 12.8 miles (20.6 km) round trip

Elevation gain: 6,069 feet (1,850 m)

Max. Elevation: 12,805 feet (3,903 m) Middle Teton

Difficulty: Extremely strenuous

Trailhead: Lupine Meadows
43.7348°N, -110.7415°W / 43°44'05"N, -110°44'29"W
12T 0520820E 4842447N

Traffic: Heavy

Maps: Moose, Grand Teton 7.5' USGS Topos

Notes: Middle Teton requires climbing. South Teton requires scrambling.

Trailhead Directions

Drive north from Jackson on US 191 for 12.3 miles (19.8 km) to Moose Junction and turn left on Teton Park Road. Continue for 7.2 miles (11.6 km) to the Lupine Meadows Trailhead turnoff. Turn left onto the road. Cross the wooden bridge over Cottonwood Creek, then continue on the main dirt road for 1.5 miles (2.3 km) to reach the trailhead.

Trailhead Facilities

Restrooms, bike rack, trash cans, bear boxes for food storage, fuel/gas canister disposal.

Hike Description

Begin at the trailhead at the end of the parking lot. The trail starts off flat, then starts uphill, curving around a hill. At 0.6 mile (1 km), cross the wooden bridge over the creek that drains Delta Lake.

The trail turns west and works its way up a ridge to the Valley Trail junction at 1.7 miles (2.7 km). Continue straight, following the sign toward Garnet Canyon.

The path gains elevation through several switchbacks to the Amphitheater Lake junction in 1.2 miles (1.9 km). Take the left (S) fork toward Garnet Canyon.

The trail turns south and continues gaining elevation on the SE facing slope for 0.4 mile (0.6 km) before turning west and gently climbing into Garnet Canyon.

In 0.6 mile (1 km), the trail terminates at a boulder field near Cleft Falls. Make your way west over the boulders into the canyon.

JENNY LAKE

There are occasional sections of trail intermixed with the boulders. Once you clear the boulders, you will catch the trail through shrubs and into the Meadows, noted by a park sign with camping and use rules for the area.

Keep an eye out for a junction to the right at the creek crossing just as you enter the open area of the Meadows near the Meadows sign. Continue straight into the Meadows along the path toward Middle Teton. The trail disappears halfway into the Meadows.

Hike toward the south end of the meadows toward a massive boulder to the left (S) of the Middle Teton glacier. It is far larger than any others. Target this boulder and hike to the left (S) of it, scrambling up scree slope. Boulder hop the first saddle as you ascend. Avoid climbing the glacier without crampons or an ice axe, as it is steep at the top.

Continue over a series of rises and saddles toward the main saddle between South and Middle Teton. There is no trail. Do not rely on following the few cairns. Boulder hopping in this area requires care and time.

At the saddle between the summits, you can either turn around or continue climbing either if time and conditions allow.

To climb Middle Teton via the Southwest Couloir, follow the saddle straight (N) toward the summit. Soon you will find yourself in a slight couloir (gully) climbing over loose rocks and rough terrain. A helmet is highly recommended, as there is rockfall. This is class 3-4 climbing with no trail. It will take some time to reach the summit.

To climb South Teton, follow the ridge of the saddle (S) toward the mountain. There is a faint climber's trail leading to an open dirt area to the west of the summit. Ascend to the ridge, then turn left (E) and proceed toward the summit. The path passes through a few large rock notches. Note these, as they are easy to miss on the descent. Taking the wrong route puts you on steep terrain toward the Meadows or Snowdrift Lake.

It is possible to climb both summits in a single, long day from Lupine Meadows. The effort to travel over the boulder field past the Meadows is substantial and many underestimate the energy and stamina required.

Start your hike in the early morning hours, as hikers often take 8–15 hours for the round trip up both mountains. Make sure to bring a headlamp and the other hiking essentials listed in the back of this book.

There is no protection from weather or lightning past the Meadows. There is substantial rockfall danger on both mountains, especially with climbers above you. The later in the day you climb, the more rockfall there will be. Wear a helmet to protect yourself from falling rocks.

MIDDLE AND SOUTH TETON

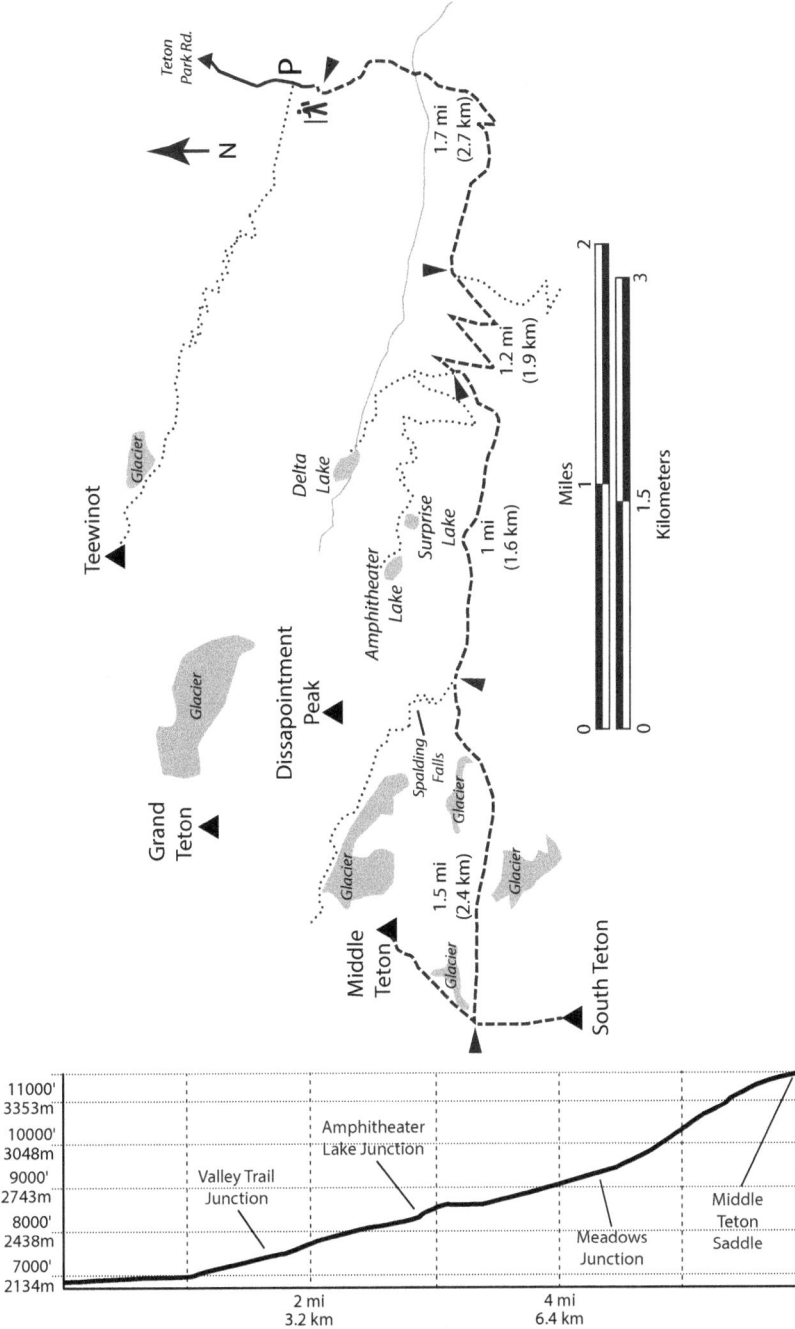

Teton
Park Rd.

P

1.7 mi
(2.7 km)

N

1.2 mi
(1.9 km)

Glacier

Teewinot

Delta
Lake

Surprise
Lake

1 mi
(1.6 km)

Amphitheater
Lake

2

Miles

1

Kilometers

1.5

3

0

0

Dissapointment
Peak

Spalding
Falls

Glacier

Glacier

Grand
Teton

Glacier

Glacier

1.5 mi
(2.4 km)

Middle
Teton

Glacier

South Teton

11000'
3353m

10000'
3048m

9000'
2743m

8000'
2438m

7000'
2134m

Amphitheater
Lake Junction

Valley Trail
Junction

Meadows
Junction

Middle
Teton
Saddle

2 mi
3.2 km

4 mi
6.4 km

LUPINE MEADOWS

40 SURPRISE, AMPHITHEATER, AND DELTA LAKES (9.6 mi / 15.4 km / Stren)

Overview:	Popular hike to lakes with stunning views with Grand Teton as a backdrop.
Trip style:	Out and back
Distance:	4.8 miles (7.7 km) one way, 9.6 miles (15.4 km) round trip
Elevation gain:	2,982 feet (909 m)
Max. Elevation:	9,708 feet (2,959 m)
Difficulty:	Strenuous
Trailhead:	Lupine Meadows
	43.7348°N, -110.7415°W / 43°44'05"N, -110°44'29"W
	12T 0520820E 4842447N
Traffic:	Heavy
Maps:	Moose, Grand Teton 7.5' USGS Topos
Notes:	Busy trail with climbers and hikers. Water available.

JENNY LAKE

Trailhead Directions

Drive north from Jackson on US 191 for 12.3 miles (19.8 km) to Moose Junction and turn left on Teton Park Road. Continue for 7.2 miles (11.6 km) to the Lupine Meadows Trailhead turnoff. Turn left onto the road. Cross the wooden bridge over Cottonwood Creek, then continue on the main dirt road for 1.5 miles (2.3 km) to reach the trailhead.

Trailhead Facilities

Restrooms, bike rack, trash cans, bear boxes for food storage, fuel/gas canister disposal.

Hike Description

Begin at the trailhead at the end of the parking lot. The trail starts off flat, then starts uphill, curving around a hill. At 0.6 mile (1 km), cross the wooden bridge over the creek that drains Delta Lake.

The trail turns west and works its way up a ridge to the Valley Trail junction at 1.7 miles (2.7 km). The switchbacks provide expansive views of Taggart and Bradley lakes. Continue on the trail for another 1.2 miles (1.9 km) to reach the Garnet Canyon junction.

Turn right and continue up a series of steepening switchbacks for another 1.6 miles (2.6 km) to reach Surprise Lake. Follow the west trail partially around the lake to observe a spectacular view down the steep ravine created by Inspiration Peak.

From Surprise Lake, continue on the trail another 0.2 mile (0.3 km) to reach Amphitheater Lake. Check with the park service for regulations on the few scattered campgrounds in the area. Return along the same trail. The southern slope of Amphitheater is the access point to continue climbing toward Disappointment Peak.

Delta Lake Hike Description

After departing the Garnet Canyon junction, travel 1,000 feet (363 m) to the end of this switchback. Steep wooden stairs will be visible leading down a ravine on a 0.8-mile (1.4 km) trail to Delta Lake.

Delta Lake cutoff:

43.7284°N, -110.7652°W
43°43'42"N, -110°45'55"W
12T 0518913E 4841737N

Work your way along the rough trail across several rockfalls. When crossing the rockfalls, maintain a constant elevation to reconnect with the dirt trail. Look across the rock field to identify the trail to guide yourself. Avoid climbing directly up the rocks.

The last 500 feet (169 m) is extremely steep and rocky. Avoid dislodging rocks that will fall on other hikers below you. Once you reach the flat area, Delta Lake will become visible. Return along the same trail.

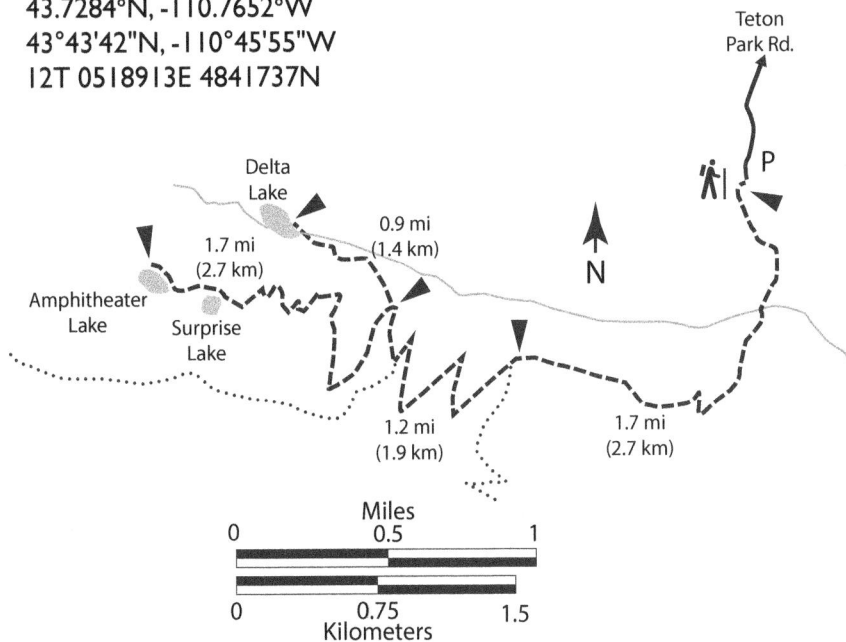

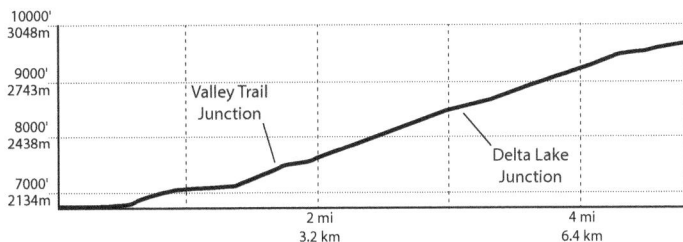

JENNY LAKE

LUPINE MEADOWS

41 TEEWINOT APEX AND GLACIER
(5 mi / 8 km / Ex Stren)

Overview: A classic Grand Teton peak hike with endless views.

Trip style: Out and back

Distance: 2.5 miles (4 km) one way, 5 miles (8 km) round trip

Elevation gain: 3,809 feet (1,161 m)

Max. Elevation: 10,540 feet (3,213 m)

Difficulty: Extremely strenuous

Trailhead: Lupine Meadows
43.7348°N, -110.7415°W / 43°44'05"N, -110°44'29"W
12T 0520820E 4842447N

Traffic: Light

Maps: Grand Teton 7.5' USGS Topo

Notes: Bring an ice axe and crampons to climb on the glacier.

JENNY LAKE

Trailhead Directions

Drive north from Jackson on US 191 for 12.3 miles (19.8 km) to Moose Junction and turn left on Teton Park Road. Continue for 7.2 miles (11.6 km) to the Lupine Meadows Trailhead turnoff. Turn left onto the road. Cross the wooden bridge over Cottonwood Creek, then continue on the main dirt road for 1.5 miles (2.3 km) to reach the trailhead.

Trailhead Facilities

Restrooms, bike rack, trash cans, bear boxes for food storage, fuel/gas canister disposal.

Hike Description

There are two trails that lead away from the north end of the parking lot. The two trails are unmarked but clearly visible, worn in the grass and dirt. They both lead toward Teewinot and merge in 300 feet (93 m).

In a short distance past the merge, the trail disappears into a small pile of boulders. Proceed straight across and reconnect with the path. Soon, the trail enters an area of aspens smashed by an avalanche.

In 0.5 mile (0.8 km), the trail passes near the falls streaming down the eastern face of Teewinot. The trail turns north and works its way around and then onto a rock face. It then follows the creek and waterfalls.

Cutting north, the path then begins making its way up a series of seemingly endless switchbacks to 1.9 miles (3.1 km). The trail will seem to disappear approaching the apex as it wanders through small boulders. Walk up a few feet (meters) and look back to find your way. It is easier to find the main trail looking down if you lose it. The trail then works its way along the ridge with expansive views along the top of the Apex.

At 2.14 miles (3.9 km), the trail dramatically steepens. Many hikers turn around at this point. To continue on, follow the climbers trail that rapidly gains elevation. Mind your footing and be aware of dislodging rocks on hikers below you.

At 2.5 miles (4 km), the path goes over a large rock face. It then levels out and curves northwest, terminating at a glacier and a rock field.

Depending on the time of year, the Teewinot glacier may be farther up above Idol and Worshiper, the rock spires towering over the glacier.

Avoid crossing the steep glacier without crampons and an ice axe. A fall on the glacier without the ability to arrest your slide will result in **serious injury or death**. There have been multiple fatalities from unprotected falls on the glacier.

Climbing onto and beyond the glacier is dangerous. It is easy to become lost near the summit. Approaching lightning cannot be seen until it is on top of you. Check the forecast before hiking Teewinot.

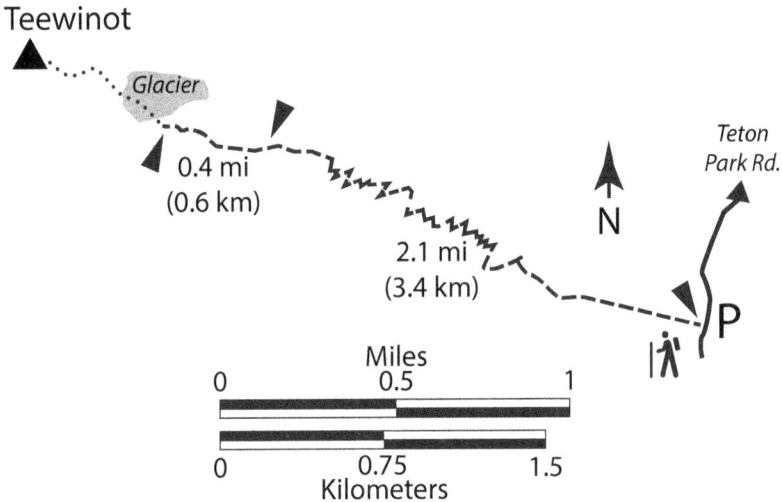

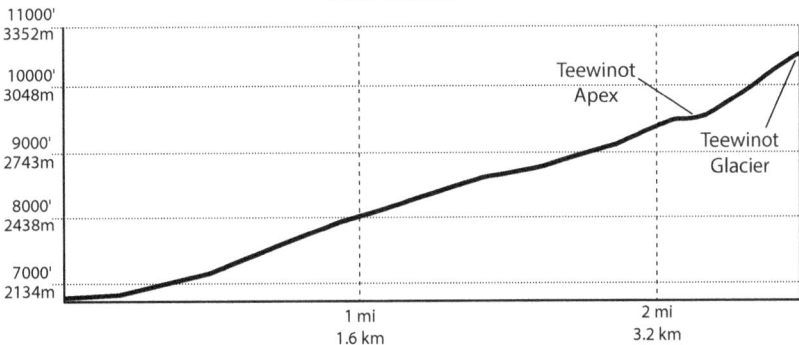

Teewinot

Glacier

0.4 mi
(0.6 km)

2.1 mi
(3.4 km)

N

Teton
Park Rd.

P

Miles
0   0.5   1

0   0.75   1.5
Kilometers

11000'
3352m

10000'
3048m

9000'
2743m

8000'
2438m

7000'
2134m

Teewinot
Apex

Teewinot
Glacier

1 mi
1.6 km

2 mi
3.2 km

LUPINE MEADOWS

42 VALLEY TRAIL (15.7 mi / 25.3 km / Stren)

Overview: A tour of the eastern slope of the Teton Range.

Trip style: One way / shuttle

Distance: 15.7 miles (25.3 km) one way

Elevation gain: 969 feet (295 m), 2,649 feet (807 m) gain/loss

Max. Elevation: 7,427 feet (2,264 m)

Difficulty: Strenuous, moderate overnighter where possible

Trailhead: Lupine Meadows
43.7348°N, -110.7415°W / 43°44'05"N, -110°44'29"W
12T 0520820E 4842447N

Traffic: Moderate to heavy, horse traffic near Teton Village

Maps: Moose, Grand Teton, Teton Village 7.5' USGS Topos

Notes: This hike is best done as a shuttle.

Trailhead Directions

Drive north from Jackson on US 191 for 12.3 miles (19.8 km) to Moose Junction and turn left on Teton Park Road. Continue for 7.2 miles (11.6 km) to the Lupine Meadows Trailhead turnoff. Turn left onto the road. Cross the wooden bridge over Cottonwood Creek, then continue on the main dirt road for 1.5 miles (2.3 km) to reach the trailhead.

Trailhead Facilities

Restrooms, bike rack, trash cans, bear boxes for food storage, fuel/gas canister disposal.

Hike Description

Begin at the trailhead at the end of the parking lot. The trail starts off flat, then starts uphill, curving around a hill. At 0.6 mile (1 km), cross the wooden bridge over the creek that drains Delta Lake.

The trail turns west and works its way up a ridge to the Valley Trail junction at 1.7 miles (2.7 km). Turn left (S) and begin losing elevation over the next 1.2 miles (1.9 km) until it reaches Bradley Lake over a large wooden bridge.

Curving around the eastern edge of Bradley Lake, the trail again turns south toward Taggart Lake. Continue past the junction to the Taggart Lake Trailhead parking lot. Cross another long wooden bridge in 2.1 miles (3.4 km) at the south end of Taggart Lake.

The trail climbs over a short hill before dropping down to the Beaver Creek Trail. Follow the sign for the Valley Trail to the south for 3.9 miles (6.3 km) to the Death Canyon trailhead junction. The trailhead is 0.1 mile (0.2 km) from the junction.

Continue for 1.5 miles (2.4 km) toward Phelps Lake. At the high point of this section of the trail, a signed and fine overlook of Phelps Lake can be enjoyed. There are a few switchbacks on this relatively steep section of trail to moderate the slope.

Take the trail toward Phelps Lake (away from Death Canyon), connect with Phelps Lake, then turn right (SW) and follow along the Phelps Lake Loop Trail. Bypass the first and second junctions into Open Canyon and the tough Mount Hunt Divide.

The next section of trail drops 450 feet (137 m) over 2 miles (3.2 km) to Granite Canyon junc-tion. Continue hiking south past the junction for 1.8 miles (2.9 km) along the edge of the mountain range toward Teton Village (Jackson Hole Mountain Resort). This section may have horse traffic.

The last section of trail leading into Teton Village is a lacework of confusing trails. Continue focusing on the tram car and Teton Village buildings to find your way to the parking lot and the end of the Valley Trail.

Options

It is possible to begin this hike at south Jenny Lake or even the Leigh Lake Trailhead. The Leigh Lake start is the longest version of the Valley Trail. It covers nearly every highlight of the park's lower elevations.

mi	km	Waypoints
0.0	0.0	Lupine Meadows Trailhead
1.7	2.7	Valley Trail and Garnet Trail junction
2.9	4.7	Bradley Lake
4.3	6.9	Taggart Lake
8.9	14.3	Death Canyon Trailhead
10.6	17.0	Phelps Lake
11.4	18.3	Open Canyon junction
15.7	25.3	Teton Village

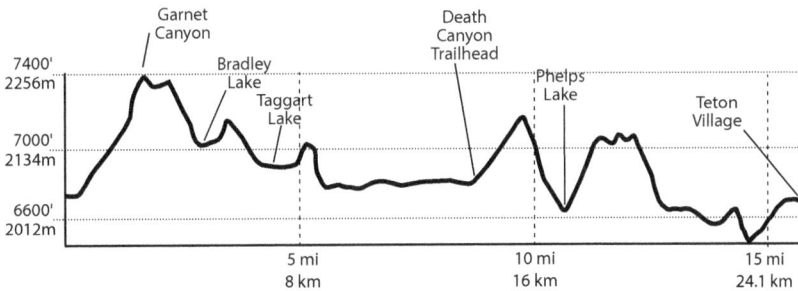

LUPINE MEADOWS

VALLEY TRAIL

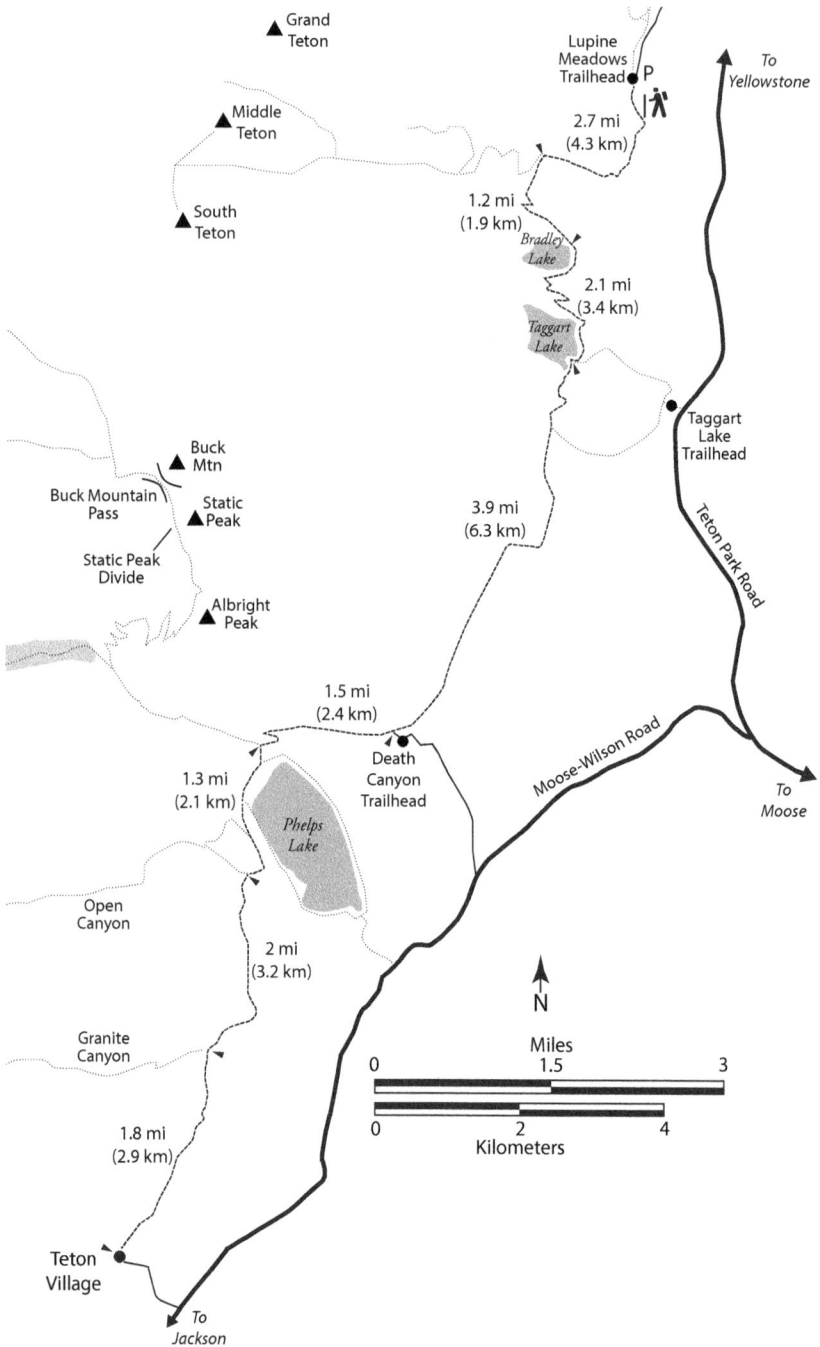

Grand Teton

Middle Teton

South Teton

Buck Mtn

Buck Mountain Pass

Static Peak

Static Peak Divide

Albright Peak

Open Canyon

Granite Canyon

Teton Village

JENNY LAKE

Lupine Meadows Trailhead P

To Yellowstone

2.7 mi (4.3 km)

1.2 mi (1.9 km)

Bradley Lake

2.1 mi (3.4 km)

Taggart Lake

Taggart Lake Trailhead

3.9 mi (6.3 km)

Teton Park Road

Moose-Wilson Road

To Moose

1.5 mi (2.4 km)

Death Canyon Trailhead

1.3 mi (2.1 km)

Phelps Lake

2 mi (3.2 km)

N

Miles
0   1.5   3

0   2   4
Kilometers

1.8 mi (2.9 km)

To Jackson

LUPINE MEADOWS

Moose Entrance

The Moose entrance to Grand Teton National Park is likely the busiest of the several entrances to this national park. There are convenience stores, gas stations, visitor centers, outdoor equipment rentals, and restaurants at Dornans.

A little farther to the west is the Craig Thomas Discovery & Visitor Center, the official park visitor center. This magnificent building is well worth stopping in to learn more about the park, its history, heritage, wildlife, and geography. Here, you can acquire a backcountry permit for overnight camping.

The hiking areas near the Moose entrance are spread out and are not as busy as other areas of the park. Rarely, if ever, is a parking lot so full that you cannot find a space.

Should you wish to try your hand at fly fishing, the Snake River traverses through the Moose area.

Moose are also common at the Moose entrance along the Snake River, hence the name. The willows and marshy areas created by the river are prime habitat for this magnificent and powerful animal. Although they look tame and ungainly, they are anything but. They can easily outrun you, bounding terrific distances with only a few steps. Although they are fun and exciting to watch, give moose a wide berth to avoid pressuring them. They need plenty of space to feel comfortable and unthreatened by the crowds that can form while viewing them in their natural summer water habitat.

Schwabacher Landing looking toward the Cathedral Group.

MOOSE ENTRANCE

43 MENORS FERRY (0.4 mi / 0.6 km / Easy)

Overview: An easy walk to famous Grand Teton historic sites.

Trip style: Loop

Distance: 0.4 mile (0.6 km) round trip

Elev. gain/loss: 39 ft. (12 m)

Max. Elevation: 6,467 ft. (1,971 m)

Difficulty: Easy, disabled-friendly

Trailhead: Chapel of the Transfiguration parking lot
43.6595°N, -110.7143°W / 43°39'34"N, -110°42'52"W
12T 0523033E 4834096N

Traffic: Heavy

Maps: Moose 7.5' USGS Topo

Trailhead Directions

Drive north from Jackson on US 191 for 12.3 miles (19.8 km) to Moose Junction and turn left on Teton Park Road. Continue for 1.2 miles (2 km), turn right on Menors Ferry Rd, and drive 0.4 mile (0.6 km) to the Chapel of the Transfiguration parking lot.

Trailhead Facilities

Restrooms, bike rack, trash cans, information signs.

Hike Description

The path begins at the southeast corner of the parking lot at the map kiosk. Walk west for 0.1 mile (0.2 km) on the wide dirt path, crossing a dirt road, to the replica ferry and Menor's cabin and country store.

Turn right and walk down a slight slope along the dirt path to the Snake River. Visit the Menors Ferry General Store, well, storage shed, and ferry system.

Continue southwest on the path, past the transportation barn, to the historic Maud Noble Cabin for another 0.1 mile (0.2 km).

Face away from the cabin entrance and follow the dirt path to the buck rail fence. Turn right, and continue along the dirt path to the restrooms. Turn left and return to the parking lot.

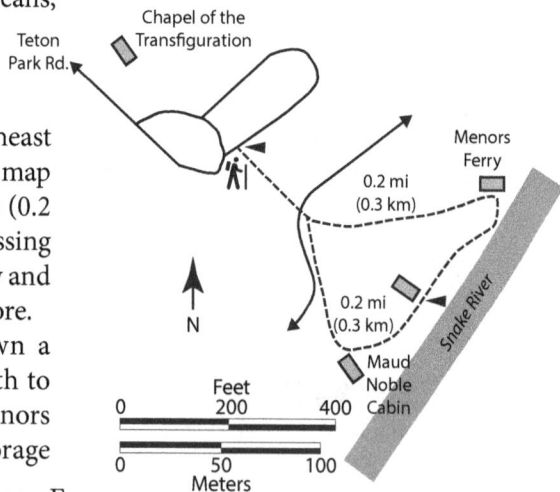

MOOSE ENTRANCE

44 SAWMILL BENCH (2.4 mi / 3.8 km / Easy)

Overview: An easy walk to a rare sawmill ruin in Grand Teton.

Trip style: Out and back

Distance: 1.2 miles (1.9 km) one way, 2.4 miles (3.8 km) round trip

Elev. gain/loss: 30 feet (9 m)

Max. Elevation: 6,483 feet (1,976 m)

Difficulty: Easy

Trailhead: Moose Ponds Overlook
43.6540°N, -110.7381°W / 43°39'14"N, -110°44'17"W
12T 0521120E 4833474N

Traffic: Light

Maps: Moose 7.5' USGS Topo

Notes: The trailhead and trail are not signed or marked.

Trailhead Directions

Drive north from Jackson on US 191 for 12.3 miles (19.8 km) to Moose Junction and turn left on Teton Park Road. Drive for 0.7 mile (1.1 km) and turn left on the Moose Wilson Road (signed as Wilson Road). Continue another 1.2 miles (2 km) and park in the large turnoff at the Moose Ponds overlook.

Trailhead Facilities

Wildlife information signs for Moose Ponds area.

Hike Description

The hike begins at the south end of the dirt parking lot. A single, wide trail leads away through a stand of cottonwood trees. As it passes through, it follows into an open sagebrush area with patchy cottonwood trees.

The path follows along the top of the river bench for 0.3 mile (0.5 km) to a power line. At 0.5 mile (0.8 km), the trail passes by concrete ruins on the east (river) side.

The trail passes by a vague northwest trail fork at 0.6 mile (1 km) that leads to an old overgrown airstrip. As the trail continues, it fades into the sage. Keep an eye out for the old sawmill, a wooden structure hidden in the shrubs.

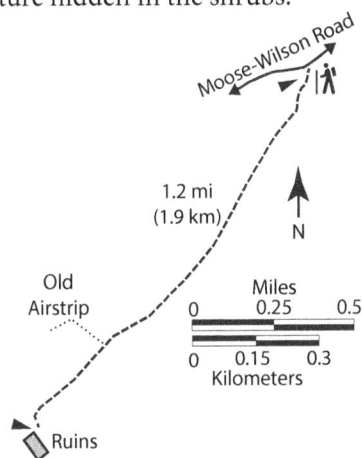

MOOSE ENTRANCE

45 SCHWABACHER LANDING
(3.2 mi / 5.2 km / Easy)

JENNY LAKE

Overview: Walk from a famous photography spot in Grand Teton along a beaver pond and river bed to a fly fishing spot.

Trip style: Out and back with loop option

Distance: 1.6 miles (2.6 km) one way, 3.2 miles (5.2 km) round trip

Elevation gain: 19 feet (5.7 m)

Max. Elevation: 6,558 feet (1,999 m)

Difficulty: Easy

Trailhead: Schwabacher Landing North parking lot
43.7116°N, -110.6704°W / 43°42'42"N, -110°40'13"W
12T 0526553E 4839891N

Traffic: Moderate

Maps: Moose 7.5' USGS Topo

Notes: Few hikers travel past the main beaver pond and lodge.

Trailhead Directions

Drive north from Jackson on US 191 for 16.4 miles (26.3 km) and turn left at the Schwabacher Landing sign. Continue for 1 mile (1.6 km) to the large dirt lot.

Trailhead Facilities

Information signs, restrooms.

Hike Description

Begin the hike at the southwest corner of the parking lot near the kiosk that leads down to the water. Follow the trail 80 feet (25 m), then turn north (right) and continue along the stream. A small beaver dam is at 0.1 mile (0.16 km). The second larger dam is at 0.2 mile (0.32 km). This dam created a beaver pond with several beaver lodges on the far side of the pond.

There are cut log benches shortly after the lodges at a dirt clearing on the edge of the pond. They are an excellent spot to try and observe beaver activity.

Past the wooden benches, the trail reduces to a thinner path, occasionally encroached upon by sagebrush. Most people who go beyond here are anglers headed for the Snake River.

At 0.5 mile (0.8 km), the trail splits. The left path heads west through tall grass toward the Snake River. Continuing north adds a 0.4 mile (0.6 km) U-shaped loop that reconnects to the grassy trail at 0.6 mile (1 km).

At 1 mile (1.6 km), there is a minor rocky creek crossing. At 1.2 miles (1.9 km), there is another wider creek crossing. The bank of the Snake River is 150 feet (43 m) west of the crossing.

Traveling 500 feet (157 m) south of this point will bring you to a rocky bank in the late season that is a potentially good fishing spot. Return along the same trail to the parking lot.

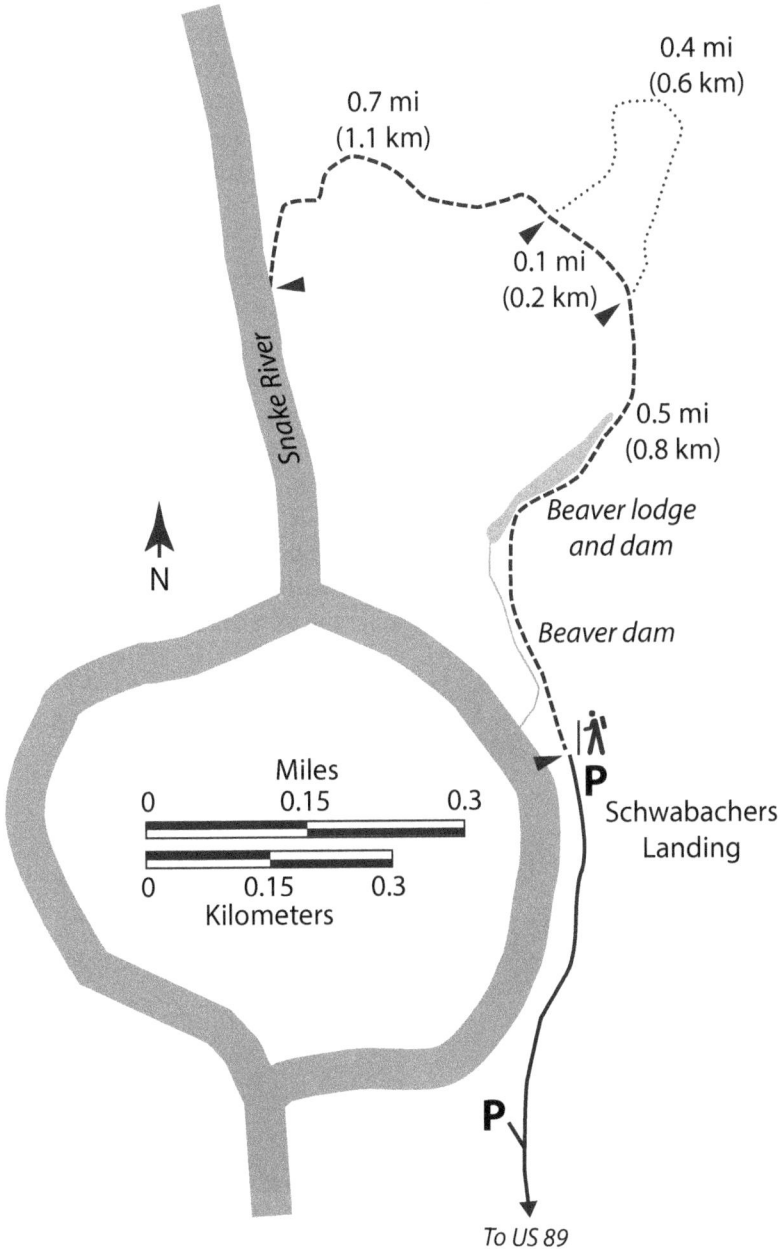

0.4 mi
(0.6 km)

0.7 mi
(1.1 km)

Snake River

0.1 mi
(0.2 km)

0.5 mi
(0.8 km)

Beaver lodge
and dam

Beaver dam

N

Miles
0   0.15   0.3

0   0.15   0.3
Kilometers

P
Schwabachers
Landing

P
To US 89

MOOSE ENTRANCE

PHELPS LAKE

The Phelps Lake area of Jackson Hole contains the largest lake in the southern part of Grand Teton National Park. This hiking area contains both easy and strenuous hikes for every skill level.

The aspens abound in this area, making it a prime area for leaf viewing in the fall. The gentle rustle of these leafy trees in the fall makes for enjoyable, calming hikes. The Valley Trail passes through the Phelps Lake area as it makes its way from Jenny Lake to Teton Village. Up to the base of the mountains, most of the hikes in this area are moderate. However, once you enter the canyons, the difficulty skyrockets and makes the heartiest hikers breathe heavily.

Static Peak is a good choice for those wanting to try their hand at climbing a named summit that requires no technical climbing skill or equipment. Although the peak is simply a hike, it is anything but easy. The grade is relentless and takes hikers to a spectacular overview of Timberline Lake, well over 1,000 feet (304 m) below.

Open Canyon is one of the lesser-visited canyons of Grand Teton. Although it isn't nearly as popular as Cascade Canyon, a long hike into this canyon is well worth the excursion. The ability to enjoy the grandeur of the park without the crowds makes this trek enjoyable even with the effort as it crosses over the tough Mount Hunt Divide.

Trail bridge near Phelps Lake.

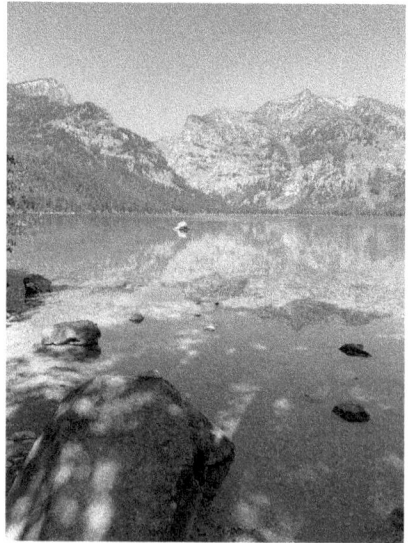

Enjoying a secluded beach at Phelps Lake.

PHELPS LAKE AREA HIKES

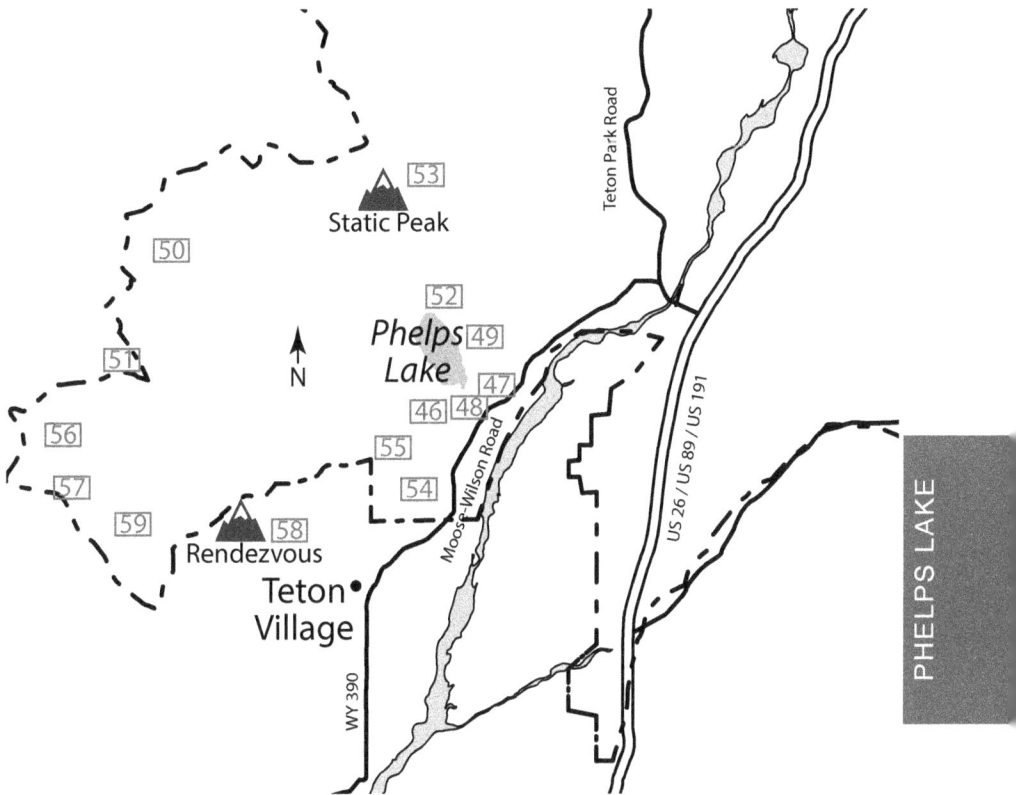

LSR and Phelps
46. Aspen Ridge
47. Boulder Ridge
48. Lake Creek and Woodland Loop
49. Phelps Lake and Jumping Rock

Death Canyon
50. Death Canyon Shelf to Alaska Basin
51. Fox Creek Pass

52. Phelps Lake Overlook
53. Static Peak and Static Peak Divide
54. Granite Canyon to Death Canyon
55. Granite Canyon to Open Canyon
56. Marion Lake
57. Teton Crest Trail
58. Rendezvous Mountain
59. Rendezvous Mountain to Granite Canyon

LSR and Phelps

The Laurance S. Rockefeller Preserve Center (LSR) in the southern zone of Grand Teton National Park is a hidden gem in an otherwise constantly busy landscape. Parking is limited and can be challenging at peak hours. The wait is worth it, though.

Should you have the time, the audio room at the LSR Center is worth sitting in. Here, you will enjoy an auditory landscape like no other. Should the weather be poor for hiking, this is a perfect second option to avoid rain and lightning.

Many of the hikes leading away from the LSR Center are easy and gentle. They lead hikers through woodlands and along creeks that feel altogether different than many other parts of Grand Teton. The awe-inspiring views of Phelps Lake with Death Canyon as a backdrop are well worth the effort to reach.

Located along the Moose-Wilson Road, this area is constantly busy with drivers looking for moose, bears, and beavers along its path. The entrance to Death Canyon is somewhat deceiving, as it does not look like it leads anywhere interesting. The actual fact is quite to the contrary.

This area is popular with photographers and videographers as well. There are many gorgeous scenes that are more accessible than most other areas of the park. With the creeks running through the area, more wildlife are visible here, too.

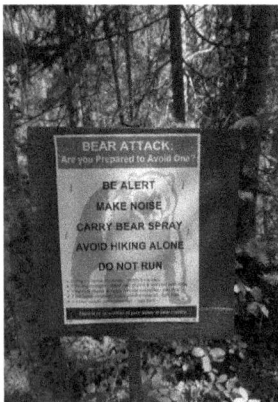

Grizzly bear warning sign near Phelps Lake.

The Laurance S. Rockefeller Preserve Center.

46 ASPEN RIDGE (4.6 mi / 7.3 km / Mod)

Overview: A pleasant hike overlooking Phelps Lake.

Trip style: Lollipop loop

Distance: 4.6 miles (7.3 km)

Elev. gain/loss: 413 feet (126 m)

Max. Elevation: 6,814 feet (2,077 m)

Difficulty: Moderate

Trailhead: LSR Center parking lot
43.6266°N, -110.7735°W / 43°37'36"N, -110°46'24"W
12T 0518277E 4830427N

Traffic: Heavy

Maps: Grand Teton 7.5' USGS Topo

Trailhead Directions

Drive north from Jackson on US 191 for 12.3 miles (19.8 km) to Moose Junction and turn left on Teton Park Road. Continue for 0.7 mile (1.1 km) and turn left on the Moose-Wilson Road. Drive south for 3.7 miles (5.9 km) and turn left at the Laurance S. Rockefeller Center turnoff. Drive south 0.3 mile (0.5 km) to the parking area.

Trailhead Facilities

Restrooms, trash cans, information kiosks, visitor center.

Hike Description

Walk west from the parking lot toward the LSR Center building. At the west end of the building, continue on the trail for 0.1 mile (0.2 km) to the junction near the waterfall.

Take the left fork on the Lake Creek Trail and continue for 0.5 mile (0.8 km) to the Aspen Ridge trail junction. Turn left (SW) and continue through the patchy forest. At 1.4 miles (2.3 km), the trail turns northwest and begins climbing up the ridge to the top at 2.3 miles (3.7 km).

From here, the trail drops down towards Phelps Lake, reaching the shoreline at 3 miles (4.8 km). Explore the overlooks and beaches in the area.

There are multiple options to return to the parking area. The most immediate option is the Lake Creek Trail that passes over a wooden plank bridge and continues south through a tall grass meadow along Lake Creek.

The trail passes the Aspen Ridge and Woodland Trail cutoff junction at 3.8 miles (6.1 km). Follow the reversed route along the Lake Creek Trail back to the visitor center to complete the loop hike.

ASPEN RIDGE TRAIL

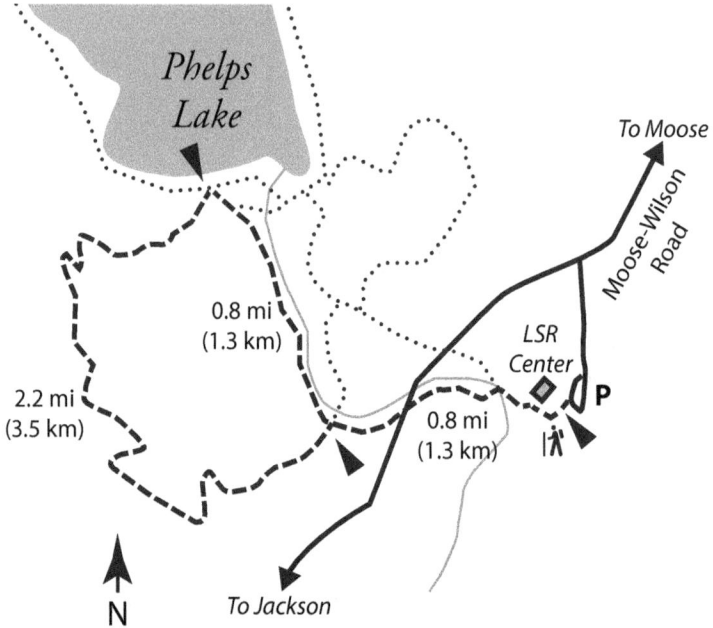

PHELPS LAKE

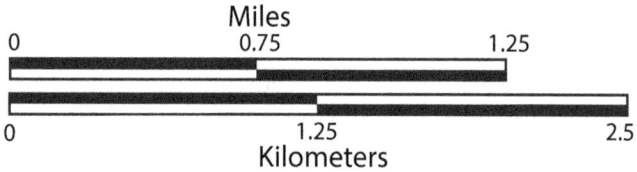

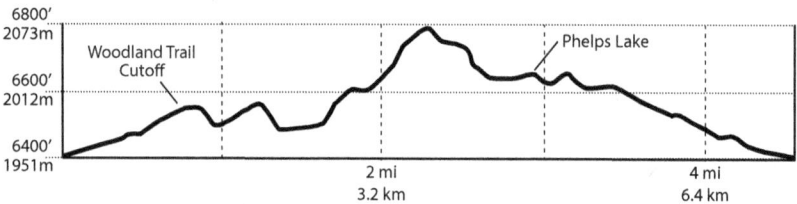

LSR AND PHELPS

47 BOULDER RIDGE LOOP (3.4 mi / 5.5 km / Mod)

Overview: Explore a unique geologic feature of unexpected boulders.
Trip style: Lollipop loop
Distance: 3.4 miles (5.5 km)
Elev. gain/loss: 337 feet (103 m) total gain/loss
Max. Elevation: 6,738 feet (2,054 m)
Difficulty: Moderate
Trailhead: LSR Center parking lot
43.6266°N, -110.7735°W / 43°37'36"N, -110°46'24"W
12T 0518277E 4830427N
Traffic: Heavy
Maps: Grand Teton 7.5' USGS Topo

Trailhead Directions

Drive north from Jackson on US 191 for 12.3 miles (19.8 km) to Moose Junction and turn left on Teton Park Road. Continue for 0.7 mile (1.1 km) and turn left on the Moose-Wilson Road. Drive south for 3.7 miles (5.9 km) and turn left at the Laurance S. Rockefeller Center turnoff. Drive south 0.3 mile (0.5 km) to the parking area.

Trailhead Facilities

Restrooms, trash cans, information kiosks, visitor center.

Hike Description

Walk west from the parking lot toward the LSR Center building. At the west end of the building, continue on the trail for 0.1 mile (0.2 km) to the junction near the waterfall. Continue along the Woodland Trail, staying to the right (NE) of Lake Creek.

At 0.6 mile (1 km) farther, the trail intersects the Woodland and Aspen Ridge Cutoff Trail as well as the Boulder Ridge Trail junction. Take the right (NE) fork and continue up the hill.

In 0.1 mile (0.2 km), there is a small rise off the trail where a fine view of Sheep Mountain (Sleeping Indian) can be enjoyed. In 0.7 mile (1.1 km) farther, the trail splits. Take the left fork to hike through the unique boulder field where glacial erratic rocks were deposited across the lumpy landscape. The trail climbs along the ridge, then rapidly drops to Phelps Lake.

Turn left (SW) at the trail junction, then in 0.1 mile (0.2 km), turn left (S) on the Woodland Trail to begin working back toward the LSR Preserve. In 0.4 mile (0.6 km), the trail passes the Boulder Ridge Trail junction. Continue on the Woodland Trail to finish the hike.

BOULDER RIDGE TRAIL

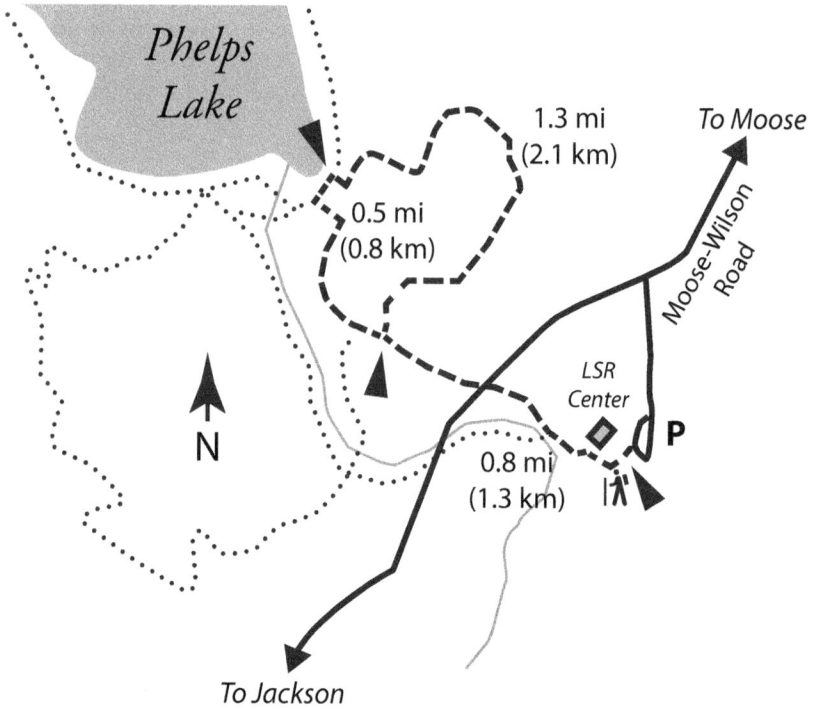

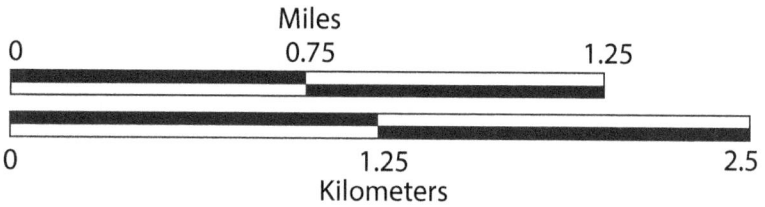

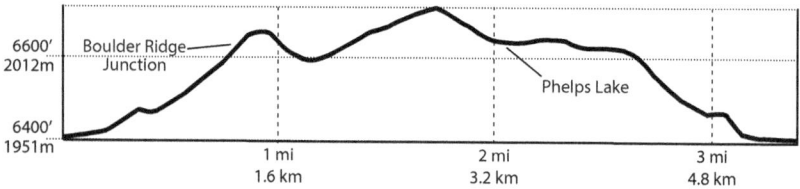

Phelps Lake

1.3 mi
(2.1 km)

To Moose

0.5 mi
(0.8 km)

Moose-Wilson Road

LSR Center

P

N

0.8 mi
(1.3 km)

To Jackson

Miles

| 0 | 0.75 | 1.25 |

| 0 | 1.25 | 2.5 |

Kilometers

6600'
2012m

Boulder Ridge
Junction

Phelps Lake

6400'
1951m

1 mi
1.6 km

2 mi
3.2 km

3 mi
4.8 km

PHELPS LAKE

LSR AND PHELPS

48 LAKE CREEK AND WOODLAND LOOP
(3 mi / 4.8 km / Easy)

Overview: The most popular family-friendly route to Phelps Lake.

Trip style: Lollipop loop

Distance: 3 miles (4.8 km)

Elev. gain/loss: 262 feet (80 m) total gain/loss

Max. Elevation: 6,663 feet (2,031 m)

Difficulty: Easy

Trailhead: LSR Center parking lot
43.6266°N, -110.7735°W / 43°37'36"N, -110°46'24"W
12T 0518277E 4830427N

Traffic: Heavy

Maps: Grand Teton 7.5' USGS Topo

Trailhead Directions

Drive north from Jackson on US 191 for 12.3 miles (19.8 km) to Moose Junction and turn left on Teton Park Road. Continue for 0.7 mile (1.1 km) and turn left on the Moose-Wilson Road. Drive south for 3.7 miles (5.9 km) and turn left at the Laurance S. Rockefeller Center turnoff. Drive south 0.3 mile (0.5 km) to the parking area.

Trailhead Facilities

Restrooms, trash cans, information kiosks, visitor center.

Hike Description

Walk west from the parking lot toward the LSR Center building. At the west end of the building, continue on the trail for 0.1 mile (0.2 km) to the junction near the waterfall. Take the left fork on the Lake Creek Trail over the creek. Follow the pathway 0.5 mile (0.8 km) to the Aspen Ridge Trail and Woodland Cutoff Trail junction and continue north on the Lake Creek Trail.

The trail passes through an open area with tall grasses and mostly open woodland for 0.7 mile (1.1 km). Then, it passes over a wooden bridge and intersects Phelps Lake. There is a restroom 130 feet (40 m) east of the trail. Along this section of lakeshore, there are overlooks with benches as well as secluded beaches to enjoy.

Continue east along Phelps Lake until you reach the Woodland Trail junction. Turn right (S) and continue on the Woodland Trail. Turn left (N) to take the hike to Jumping Rock in 1.1 miles (1.8 km).

Follow this trail 0.4 mile (0.6 km) to the cutoff trail. Continue on the Woodland Trail 0.5 mile (0.8 km) to the waterfall and then to the LSR Preserve building and on to the parking lot.

LAKE CREEK AND WOODLAND LOOP

PHELPS LAKE

Phelps Lake

Phelps Lake

To Moose

Moose-Wilson Road

0.7 mi
(1.1 km)

0.8 mi
(1.3 km)

LSR
Center

P

1.5 mi
(2.4 km)

To Jackson

N

Miles

| 0 | 0.75 | 1.25 |

| 0 | 1.25 | 2.5 |

Kilometers

6600'
2012m

Phelps Lake

6400'
1951m

| 1 mi | 2 mi | 3 mi |
| 1.6 km | 3.2 km | 4.8 km |

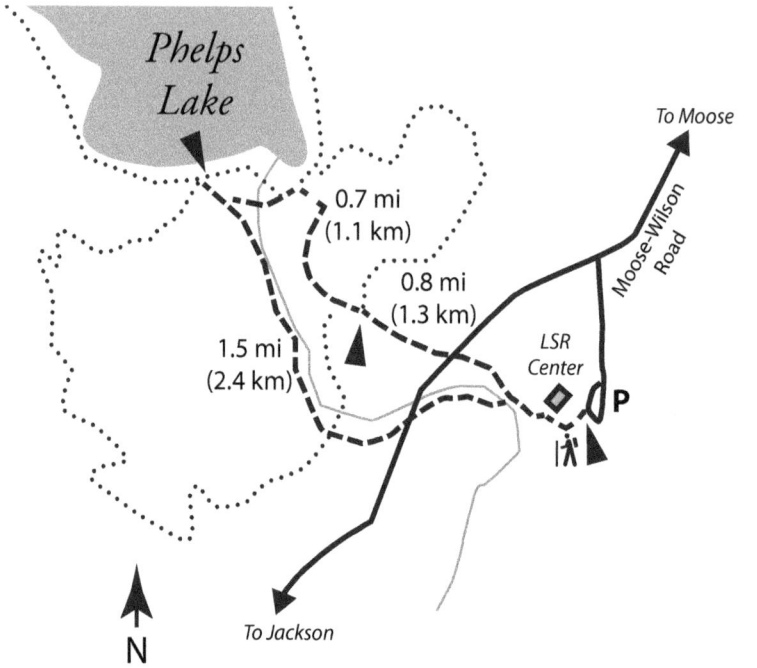

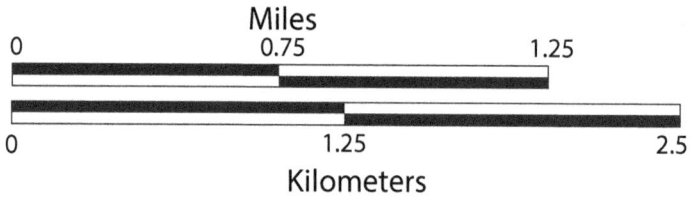

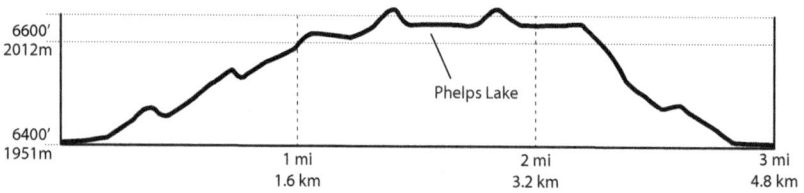

LSR and Phelps

49 PHELPS LAKE AND JUMPING ROCK
(6.6 mi / 10.6 km / Easy)

Overview: The most popular family-friendly route to Phelps Lake.

Trip style: Lollipop loop

Distance: 6.6 miles (10.6 km)

Elev. gain/loss: 368 feet (112 m) total gain/loss

Max. Elevation: 6,769 feet (2,063 m)

Difficulty: Easy

Trailhead: LSR Center parking lot
43.6266°N, -110.7735°W / 43°37'36"N, -110°46'24"W
12T 0518277E 4830427N

Traffic: Heavy

Maps: Grand Teton 7.5' USGS Topo

Trailhead Directions

Drive north from Jackson on US 191 for 12.3 miles (19.8 km) to Moose Junction and turn left on Teton Park Road. Continue for 0.7 mile (1.1 km) and turn left on the Moose-Wilson Road. Drive south for 3.7 miles (5.9 km) and turn left at the Laurance S. Rockefeller Center turnoff. Drive south 0.3 mile (0.5 km) to the parking area.

Trailhead Facilities

Restrooms, trash cans, information kiosks, visitor center.

Hike Description

Walk west from the parking lot toward the LSR Center building. At the west end of the building, continue on the trail for 0.1 mile (0.2 km) to the junction near the waterfall. Continue along the Woodland Trail, staying to the right (E) of Lake Creek.

At 0.6 mile (1 km) farther, the trail intersects the Woodland and Aspen Ridge Cutoff Trail as well as the Boulder Ridge Trail junction. Continue on the Woodland Trail north.

Hike for 0.7 mile (1.1 km) to Phelps Lake, then turn right (NE) and begin circling clockwise around the lake. In 1.1 miles (1.8 km), you will pass by the large and popular Jumping Rock, a favorite hotspot for jumping off a massive (25 feet / 7.6 m) boulder into the chilly water.

In another 0.8 mile (1.3 km), the trail curves southwest and intersects the cutoff to the Death Canyon Trail. Continue hiking up a short hill for another 0.4 mile (0.6 km) to the Valley Trail junction. From this junction, continue following the western side of Phelps Lake for another 1.5 miles (2.4 km) as you make your way around on a nearly level trail back toward the southern end of the lake.

At the junction with the Aspen Ridge Trail, continue straight toward the Lake Creek Trail. Follow this trail through mixed woodlands and tall grasslands for another 1.5 miles (2.4 km) to the southern junction with the Aspen Ridge Trail. Stay on the Lake Creek Trail as it works its way back to the waterfall where the trail rejoins the Woodland Trail.

Continue walking past the small waterfall and the LSR Preserve. Finish the hike by walking through the open sagebrush space back to the trailhead at the parking lot.

PHELPS LAKE

Death Canyon

0.4 mi (0.6 km)

0.8 mi (1.3 km)

Death Canyon Trailhead

Jumping Rock

Phelps Lake

1.1 mi (1.8 km)

N

To Moose

1.5 mi (2.4 km)

Valley Trail

0.7 mi (1.1 km)

0.8 mi (1.3 km)

Moose-Wilson Road

LSR Center

P

1.5 mi (2.4 km)

To Jackson

Miles
0   0.75   1.25

0   1.25   2.5
Kilometers

6600'
2012m

Jumping Rock

Death Canyon Junction

6400'
1951m

2 mi
3.2 km

4 mi
6.4 km

6 mi
9.7 km

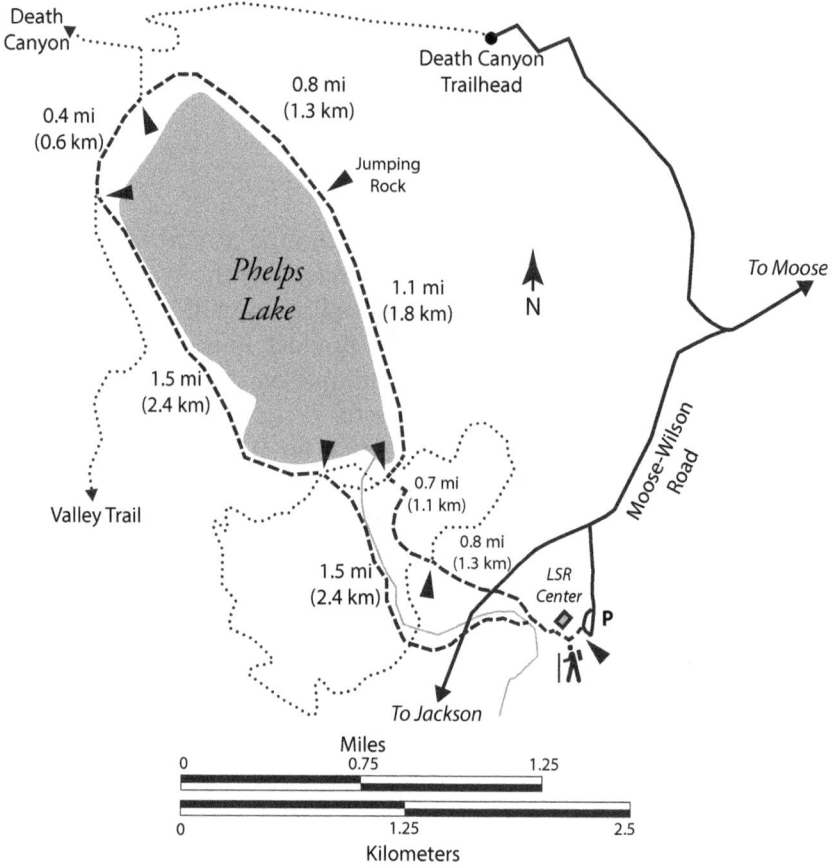

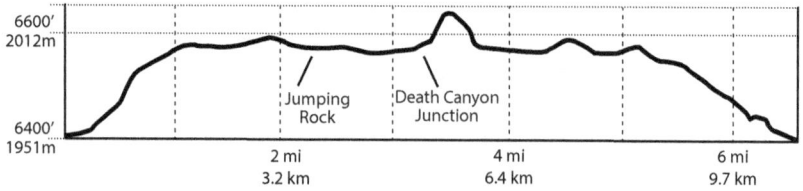

LSR AND PHELPS

Death Canyon

A hike into Death Canyon is well worth the effort. Though it has a forbidding name, this canyon provides hikers access to some of the most dramatic landscapes in Jackson Hole. This area gives visitors a sense that they have departed the busy thoroughfares and have entered a different world.

Nearly all of the hikes in this area are challenging if not downright difficult. The only relatively easy hike in this area is the Phelps Lake overlook. This short hike is enjoyable and mildly difficult if you only have a little time available. The lake overlook is not visible until the very few last steps to the sign. The surprise of the view is enjoyable and worthy of a photograph.

Most of the hikes take all day to complete and many are best enjoyed as an overnight trip. As this area is in Grand Teton, permits are required for overnight camping.

One advantage of the Death Canyon Trailhead is the opportunity to enjoy several loop hikes rather than out and back trips. These trails allow you to enjoy a continuously changing landscape along the entire path of the trail. Be prepared for significant elevation changes.

The road to the Death Canyon Trailhead can be rough. A high-clearance vehicle is generally not needed when the road is dry. Simply drive slowly and with some caution. Should the drive prove too difficult for your vehicle, park in one of the pullouts along the dirt track and finish the short walk to the trailhead.

The other hikes from this zone depart from trailheads other than Death Canyon. This area is also the best starting point to enjoy the famous Teton Crest Trail. By hiking this route rather than using the Teton Village tram, you can extend your acclimatization time, reducing the likelihood of developing debilitating altitude sickness.

Hiking Static Peak during a breezy summer day.

DEATH CANYON

50 DEATH CANYON SHELF TO ALASKA BASIN LOOP (23.6 mi / 38 km / Stren)

Overview: A hike featuring multiple Grand Teton highlight areas.

Trip style: Loop, tough single day, moderate overnighter

Distance: 23.6 miles (38 km)

Elevation gain: 4,079 feet (1,243 m)

Max. Elevation: 10,790 feet (3,289 m)

Difficulty: Strenuous

Trailhead: Death Canyon Trailhead
43.6558°N, -110.7811°W / 43°39'21"N, -110°46'52"W
12T 0517653E 4833669N

Traffic: Moderate

Maps: Grand Teton, Mount Bannon 7.5' USGS Topos

Notes: Camping permits are required on this route inside GTNP.

PHELPS LAKE

Trailhead Directions

Drive north from Jackson on US 191 for 12.3 miles (19.8 km) to Moose Junction and turn left on Teton Park Road. Continue for 0.7 mile (1.1 km) and turn left on the Moose-Wilson Road. Drive south for 3.1 miles (5 km) and turn right at the Death Canyon Trailhead junction. Drive 1.6 miles (2.6 km) to the trailhead parking area.

Trailhead Facilities

Restrooms, trash cans.

Hike Description

Begin hiking at the information sign at the edge of the parking lot. Hike 400 feet (122 m) to the junction with the Valley Trail. Turn left and continue hiking 1.5 miles (2.4 km) west toward Death Canyon, passing Phelps Lake overlook at the hill, then drop down to the Phelps Lake cutoff trail.

Begin climbing in earnest into Death Canyon for 1.7 miles (2.7 km) on a fairly steep climb, switchbacking several times before reaching a level, grassy spot for a rest. Continue 0.1 mile (0.2 km) to the Death Canyon patrol cabin and the Static Peak junction.

The hike into and up Death Canyon for 5.2 miles (8.4 km) is long and scenic. The view of the wall holding up Death Shelf is in view for much of the hike. Shortly past the patrol cabin is the Death Canyon camping zone (permits required).

At 5.5 miles (8.9 km), the trail curves left (SW) and continues climbing up toward Death Shelf and Fox Creek Pass. The last 0.7 mile (1.1 km) to reach the southern end of Death Shelf is a steep hike up an exposed, rocky section of trail, connecting with the Teton Crest Trail. Turn right (N) and continue onto Death Shelf.

The trail continues for a relatively flat 3.8 miles (6.1 km) along the scenic Death Shelf camping zone. The view into Death Canyon is stunning and continuous. Hike to Mt. Meek Divide where the Crest Trail connects to the Teton Shelf Trail at a junction.

The trail passes over Mt. Meek Divide, then drops 2 miles (3.2 km) into Alaska Basin and connects to the Alaska Basin Trail. A short distance west of the Teton Crest Trail is the Jedediah Smith Wilderness. It is outside of the Grand Teton boundary where dispersed camping is allowed. Follow the signs to ensure the proper campsite placement.

To continue with the loop, take the first trail toward Buck Mountain Pass and Static Peak Divide. This is the most direct route.

It's possible to continue farther into Alaska Basin and take the second fork at the junction with the trail to Buck Mountain. This option adds some distance and is a tougher climb but it rewards hikers with an extended exploration of the alpine area of Alaska Basin. Hiking around this area is worth the time.

As the trail exits out of the basin and climbs toward Buck Mountain, the trees thin out, giving way to a rough and rocky landscape. Parts

of this section are somewhat exposed, especially at Static Peak Divide. The exposure rewards hikers with an unobstructed view of south Jackson Hole. Note that the divide can be packed with snow, requiring an ice axe for safe travel.

The climb from the first junction in Alaska Basin to Static Peak Divide climbs an exposed 1,310 feet (399 m) over 2.7 miles (4.3 km). Static Peak can be hiked from the trail with no technical gear when it is clear of snow. There are several thin trails leading to the summit, rewarding the adventurous with a near-vertical view down to Timberline Lake.

From the divide, the trail drops 2,937 feet (895 m) over 3.5 miles (5.6 km) to Death Canyon Trail, intersecting at the Death Canyon patrol cabin.

Turn left (SE) and continue descending out of Death Canyon. A short distance past the cabin is a grassy spot with placid water pools. It is a perfect place for a final break. As the trail descends toward Phelps Lake, the views open up as the trail departs the canyon.

Continue straight, bypassing the junction to Phelps Lake and climb the 400 feet (122 m) up this short section to the Phelps Lake overlook. The trail continues east, reaching the Death Canyon Trailhead cutoff 1.5 miles (2.4 km) from the Phelps Lake junction cutoff. Hike the 400 feet (122 m) to the Death Canyon Trailhead parking lot.

DEATH CANYON

DEATH CANYON TO ALASKA BASIN LOOP

mi	km	Waypoints
0.0	0.0	Death Canyon Trailhead
1.5	2.4	Phelps Lake cutoff
3.2	5.1	Death Canyon patrol cabin
8.5	13.7	Teton Crest junction
11.7	18.8	Mount Meek Divide
13.8	22.2	Alaska Basin
15.7	25.3	Buck Mountain Pass
16.7	26.9	Static Peak Divide
20.3	32.7	Death Canyon patrol cabin
22.0	35.4	Phelps Lake cutoff
23.6	38.0	Granite Canyon Trailhead

PHELPS LAKE

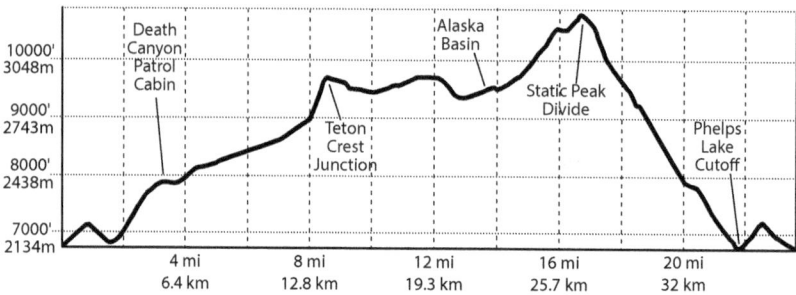

The junction of the Valley Trail and the Death Canyon Trail.

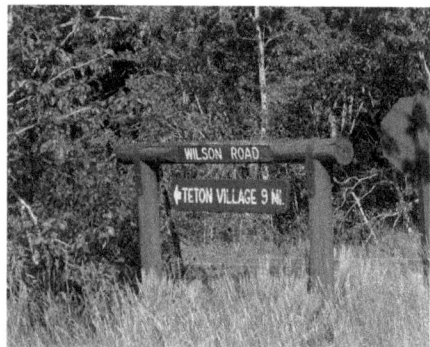

The Moose-Wilson Road sign at Moose.

DEATH CANYON

DEATH CANYON TO ALASKA BASIN LOOP

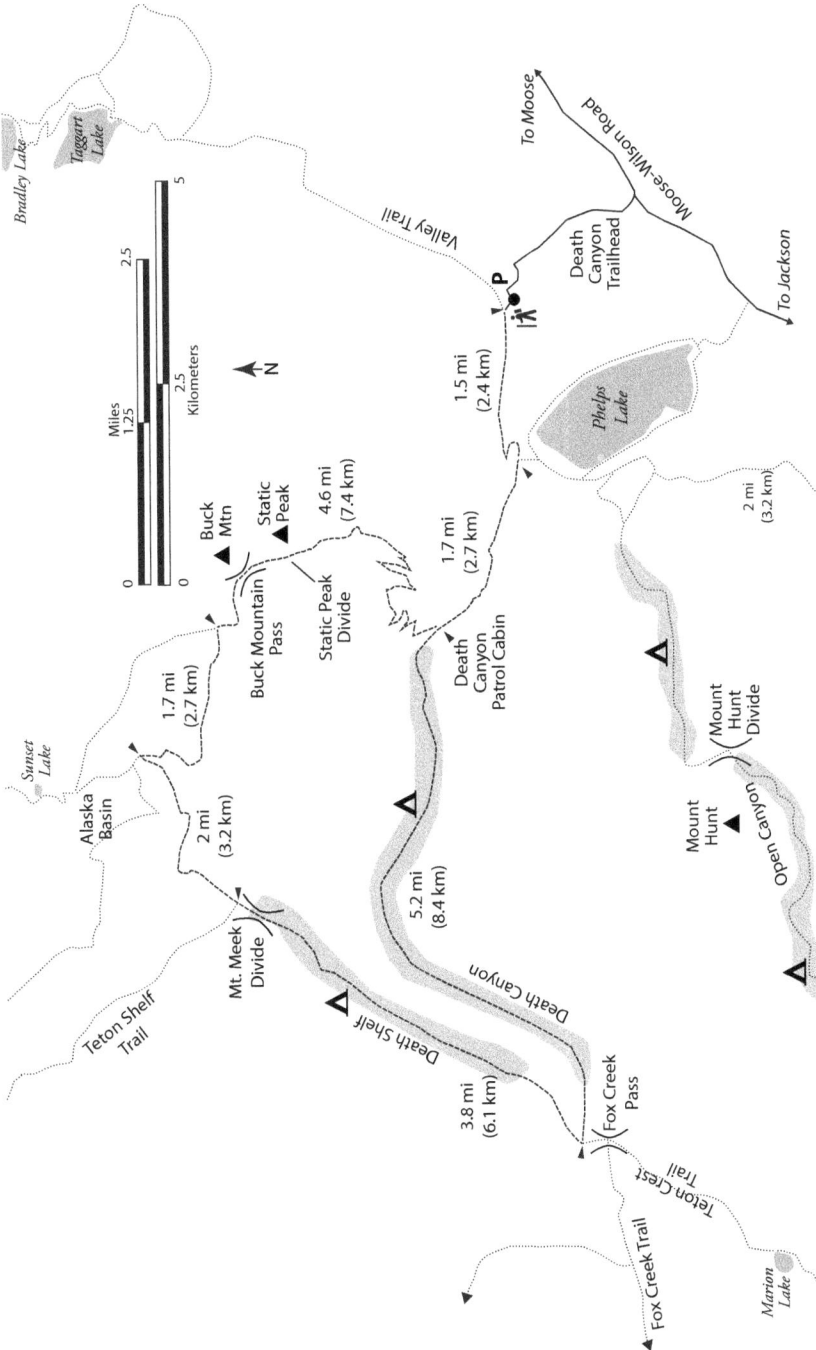

To Moose

Moose-Wilson Road

To Jackson

Death Canyon Trailhead

Valley Trail

P

1.5 mi (2.4 km)

Bradley Lake

Taggart Lake

Phelps Lake

2 mi (3.2 km)

Buck Mtn

Static Peak

4.6 mi (7.4 km)

Buck Mountain Pass

Static Peak Divide

1.7 mi (2.7 km)

Death Canyon Patrol Cabin

Mount Hunt Divide

Mount Hunt

Open Canyon

Sunset Lake

Alaska Basin

1.7 mi (2.7 km)

2 mi (3.2 km)

5.2 mi (8.4 km)

Death Canyon

Teton Shelf Trail

Mt. Meek Divide

Death Shelf

3.8 mi (6.1 km)

Fox Creek Pass

Teton Crest Trail

Fox Creek Trail

Marion Lake

DEATH CANYON

Miles
0   1.25   2.5

Kilometers
0   2.5   5

N

PHELPS LAKE

51 FOX CREEK PASS (17.2 mi / 27.6 km / Stren)

Overview: A hike featuring the highlights of the Death Canyon area.

Trip style: Out and back

Distance: 8.6 miles (13.8 km) one way, 17.2 miles (27.6 km) round trip

Elevation gain: 2,750 feet (838 m)

Max. Elevation: 9,570 feet (2,917 m)

Difficulty: Strenuous

Trailhead: Death Canyon Trailhead
43.6558°N, -110.7811°W / 43°39'21"N, -110°46'52"W
12T 0517653E 4833669N

Traffic: Light to moderate

Maps: Grand Teton, Mount Bannon 7.5' USGS Topos

Notes: Camping permits are required on this route.

Trailhead Directions

Drive north from Jackson on US 191 for 12.3 miles (19.8 km) to Moose Junction and turn left on Teton Park Road. Continue for 0.7 mile (1.1 km) and turn left on the Moose-Wilson Road. Drive south for 3.1 miles (5 km) and turn right at the Death Canyon Trailhead Junction. Drive 1.6 miles (2.6 km) to the trailhead parking area.

Trailhead Facilities

Restrooms, trash cans.

Hike Description

Begin hiking at the information sign at the edge of the parking lot. Hike 400 feet (122 m) to the junction with the Valley Trail and turn left (W). Continue hiking 1.5 miles (2.4 km) west toward Death Canyon, passing Phelps Lake overlook at the hill, then drop down to the Phelps Lake cutoff trail.

Begin climbing in earnest into Death Canyon for 1.7 miles (2.7 km) on a fairly steep climb, switch-backing several times before reaching a level, grassy spot for a rest. Continue 0.1 mile (0.2 km) to the Death Canyon patrol cabin and the Static Peak junction.

The hike up and into Death Canyon for 5.2 miles (8.4 km) is long and scenic. The view of the wall that makes up Death Shelf is in view for much of the hike. Shortly past the patrol cabin is the Death Canyon camping zone (permits required).

At 5.5 miles (8.9 km), the trail curves left (SW) and continues climbing up toward Death Shelf and Fox Creek Pass. Continue below the ancient rock face. The last 0.7 mile (1.1 km) to reach the southern end of Death Shelf is a

PHELPS LAKE

steep hike up an exposed, rocky section of trail, connecting with the Teton Crest Trail near the pass.

Turn left (S) and continue for 0.15 mile (0.25 km) to Fox Creek Pass. Visit Pass Lake which is 0.18 mile (0.29 km) southeast of Fox Creek Pass. It is possible to see Rendezvous Peak, Granite Canyon, and much of the rest of the southern Teton Range along the Teton Crest Trail from here.

Turn around and retrace your steps through Death Canyon to return to the trailhead by way of Phelps Lake.

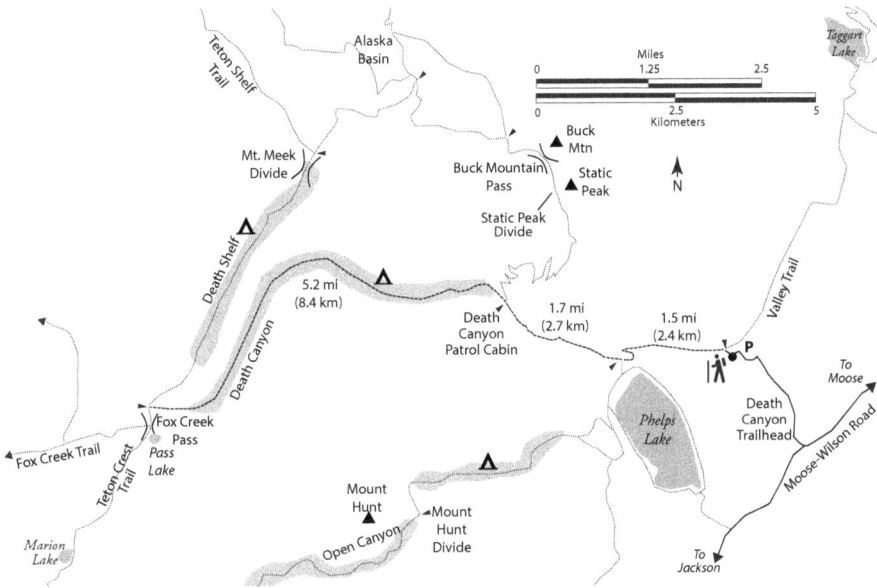

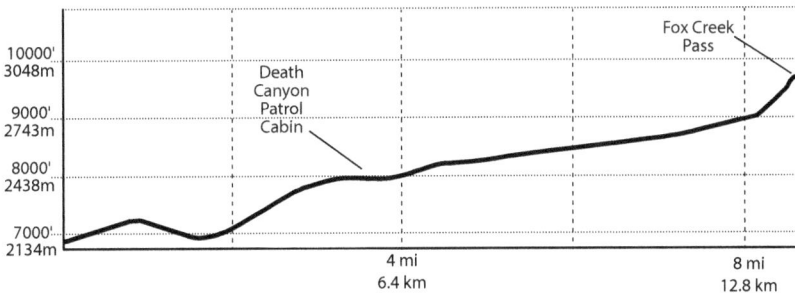

DEATH CANYON

52 PHELPS LAKE OVERLOOK (2 mi / 3.2 km / Mod)

Overview: A short, popular hike to a spectacular lake lookout.

Trip style: Out and back

Distance: 1 mile (1.6 km) one way, 2 miles (3.2 km) round trip

Elevation gain: 332 feet (101 m)

Max. Elevation: 7,200 feet (2,195 m)

Difficulty: Moderate

Trailhead: Death Canyon Trailhead
43.6558°N, -110.7811°W / 43°39'21"N, -110°46'52"W
12T 0517653E 4833669N

Traffic: Heavy

Maps: Grand Teton 7.5' USGS Topo

Trailhead Directions

Drive north from Jackson on US 191 for 12.3 miles (19.8 km) to Moose Junction and turn left on Teton Park Road. Continue for 0.7 mile (1.1 km) and turn left on the Moose-Wilson Road. Drive south for 3.1 miles (5 km) and turn right at the Death Canyon Trailhead Junction. Drive 1.6 miles (2.6 km) to the trailhead parking area.

Trailhead Facilities

Restroom, trash cans.

Hike Description

Begin hiking at the information sign at the edge of the parking lot. Hike 0.1 mile (0.2 km) north to the Death Canyon and Valley Trail junction. Turn left (W) and begin climbing up the tree-covered slope. At 0.5 mile (0.8 km), the trail breaks into an open area. At 0.8 mile (1.3 km), it returns to a thinly forested area as it approaches the Phelps Lake overlook. The trail leads directly to the Phelps Lake overlook sign with the elevation noted. The lake appears a few steps prior to reaching the sign.

The lakeshore is 0.8 mile (1.3 km) further along the trail. Return to the trailhead by reversing the route. This trail is popular and well-traveled.

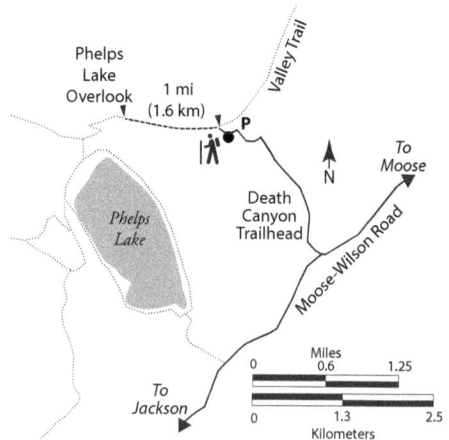

53 STATIC PEAK AND STATIC PEAK DIVIDE (14 mi / 22.6 km / Ex Stren)

Overview: A hike to a prominent peak above 11,000 feet (3,353 m).

Trip style: Out and back

Distance: 7 miles (11.3 km) one way, 14 miles (22.6 km) round trip

Elevation gain: 4,496 feet (1,370 m)

Max. Elevation: 11,302 feet (3,445 m)

Difficulty: Extremely strenuous

Trailhead: Death Canyon Trailhead
43.6558°N, -110.7811°W / 43°39'21"N, -110°46'52"W
12T 0517653E 4833669N

Traffic: Light to moderate

Maps: Grand Teton, Mount Bannon 7.5' USGS Topos

Notes: Be mindful of bears, moose, and cougars along the trail.

Trailhead Directions

Drive north from Jackson on US 191 for 12.3 miles (19.8 km) to Moose Junction and turn left on Teton Park Road. Continue for 0.7 mile (1.1 km) and turn left on the Moose-Wilson Road. Drive south for 3.1 miles (5 km) and turn right at the Death Canyon Trailhead Junction. Drive 1.6 miles (2.6 km) to the trailhead parking area.

Trailhead Facilities

Restrooms, trash cans.

Hike Description

Begin hiking at the information sign at the edge of the parking lot. Hike 400 feet (122 m) to the junction with the Valley Trail. Continue hiking 1.5 miles (2.4 km) west toward Death Canyon, passing Phelps Lake overlook at the hill, then drop down to the Phelps Lake cutoff trail.

Begin climbing in earnest into Death Canyon for 1.7 miles (2.7 km) on a fairly steep climb, switchbacking several times before reaching a level, grassy spot for a rest. Continue 0.1 mile (0.2 km) to the Death Canyon patrol cabin and the Static Peak junction. Turn right and continue toward Static Peak.

The steep trail from the patrol cabin to the summit climbs 3,459 feet (1,054 m) over 3.7 miles (6 km). There are several excellent views of Jackson Hole.

From a short distance west of Static Peak Divide, turn north toward Static Peak. There is no official trail but many social trails leading to the summit. At the summit is a dizzying view down to Timberline Lake. Return on the same trail.

STATIC PEAK AND STATIC PEAK DIVIDE

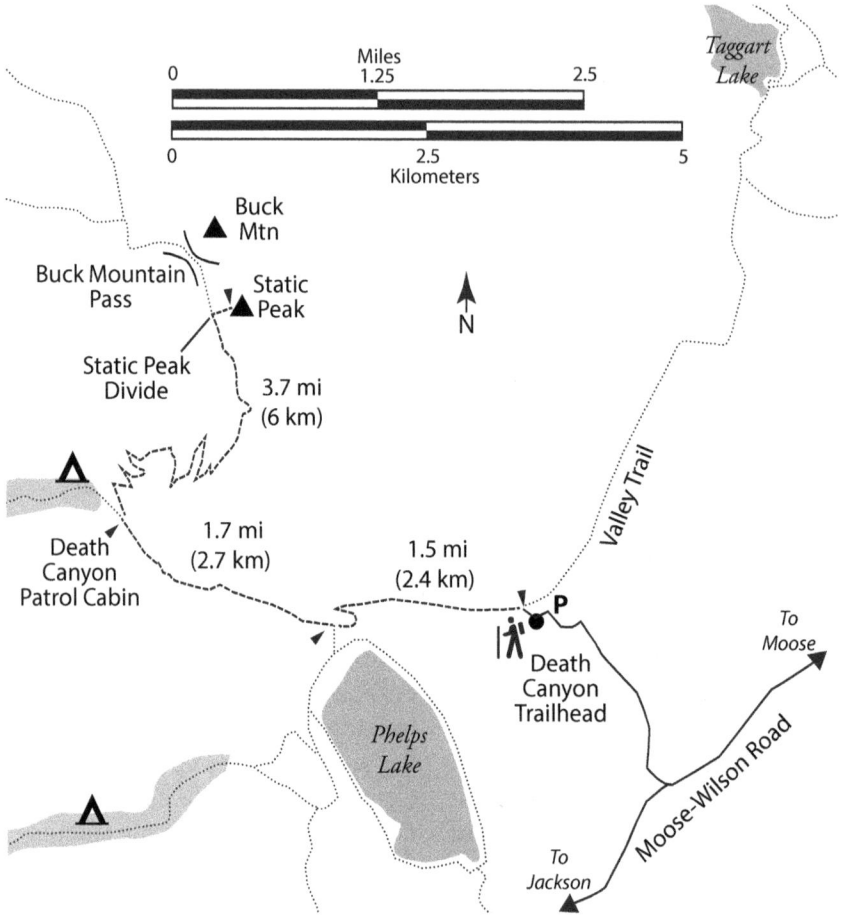

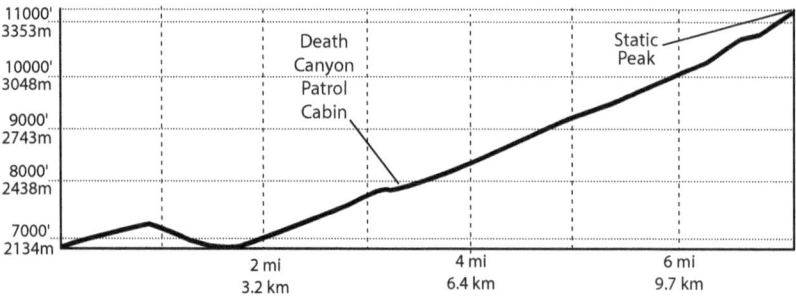

Miles
0   1.25   2.5

0   2.5   5
Kilometers

Taggart Lake

Buck Mtn

Buck Mountain Pass

Static Peak

Static Peak Divide

3.7 mi (6 km)

N

Valley Trail

1.7 mi (2.7 km)

Death Canyon Patrol Cabin

1.5 mi (2.4 km)

PHELPS LAKE

Death Canyon Trailhead

P

To Moose

Phelps Lake

To Jackson

Moose-Wilson Road

11000' 3353m
10000' 3048m
9000' 2743m
8000' 2438m
7000' 2134m

Death Canyon Patrol Cabin

Static Peak

2 mi 3.2 km
4 mi 6.4 km
6 mi 9.7 km

DEATH CANYON

54 GRANITE CANYON TO DEATH CANYON

(23.4 mi / 37.7 km / Stren)

Overview: A loop tour of two dramatic Grand Teton canyons.
Trip style: Loop
Distance: 23.4 miles (37.7 km)
Elevation gain: 3,299 feet (1,006 m) net, 4,343 feet (1,324 m) total gain
Max. Elevation: 9,677 feet (2,950 m)
Difficulty: Strenuous single day, moderate overnighter
Trailhead: Granite Canyon
43.6074°N, -110.7929°W / 43°36'27"N, -110°47'35"W
12T 0516711E 4828288N
Traffic: Moderate
Maps: Teton Village, Rendezvous Peak, Mount Bannon, Grand Teton 7.5' USGS Topos
Notes: There can be snow on Fox Creek Pass in the summer.

Trailhead Directions

Drive west from Jackson on Broadway (US 191) 1.5 miles (2.4 km) and turn right (N) on Wyoming 22 (Wilson / Teton Village). Drive 4.1 miles (6.6 km) and turn right (N) on WY 390 (Teton Village). Continue north for 8.7 miles (14 km) past the park entrance to the Granite Canyon Trailhead.

Trailhead Facilities

Information kiosk. The dirt parking area often overflows during the summer season.

Hike Description

Begin hiking west and northwest at the Granite Canyon Trailhead. In 0.6 mile (1 km), the trail crosses the Bear Paw Trail. Continue west and north for 1 mile (1.6 km) to the Valley Trail junction. Walk 0.1 mile (0.2 km) north along the Valley Trail to the next junction with Granite Canyon. These trail junctions are well signed.

Continue hiking up the gentle grade into Granite Canyon for 4.9 miles (7.9 km). Aspen and cottonwood fill the canyon creek area, making it prime moose habitat. Keep a safe distance from these powerful animals.

Pass the first junction to Teton Village and Rendezvous Mountain. In 0.8 mile (1.3 km), the trail connects with Open Canyon. Stay on the Granite Canyon Trail. Continue 1.2 miles (1.9 km) to the Teton Crest Trail junction. Turn right (N) and climb this steep, short 0.6-mile (1 km) section over a lip to Marion Lake.

From Marion Lake, the trail works its way north for 2.3 miles

(3.7 km) up to Fox Creek Pass at 9,570 feet (2,917 m), 0.2 mile (0.3 km) south of the junction to Death Canyon. Continue to the Death Canyon junction and take a right (E) into the canyon.

The trail rapidly loses elevation into Death Canyon, passing along the limestone cliff face, riddled with holes and ridges. It is visible from the park road.

Follow the trail into Death Canyon for 5.2 miles (8.4 km) through the Death Canyon camping zone. The trail travels northeast, then gently curves to the east and continues to the Death Canyon patrol cabin. This signed junction connects to Static Peak. A short 0.2 mile (0.3 km) east of the patrol cabin is a pleasant grassy area for a welcome rest break.

The trail rapidly loses elevation from this point for 1.7 miles (2.7 km) to the Phelps Lake cutoff junction. Take the right (S) fork towards Phelps Lake. Turn right (SW) at the Phelps Lake loop junction and continue around the lake.

Follow the Valley Trail for a total of 3.4 miles (5.5 km) from the Phelps Lake junction to the Granite Canyon Trail. Follow the short split along the Valley Trail, then turn left (S-SE) along the Granite Canyon Trail toward the trailhead. Hike the last 1.6 miles (2.6 km) to return to the Granite Canyon Trailhead.

PHELPS LAKE

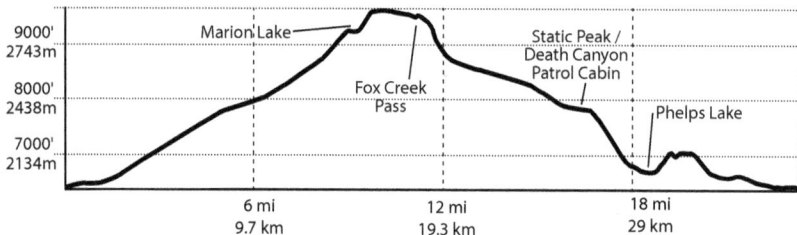

mi	km	Waypoints
0.0	0.0	Granite Canyon Trailhead
1.6	2.6	Valley Trail junction
8.5	13.7	Teton Crest Trail junction
9.1	14.6	Marion Lake
11.4	18.3	Death Canyon junction
16.6	26.7	Static Peak junction / Death Canyon patrol cabin
18.3	29.5	Phelps Lake junction
18.9	30.4	Valley Trail / Phelps Lake loop junction
19.7	31.7	Open Canyon cutoff trail
21.7	34.9	Granite Canyon junction
23.4	37.7	Granite Canyon Trailhead

GRANITE CANYON

GRANITE CANYON TO DEATH CANYON

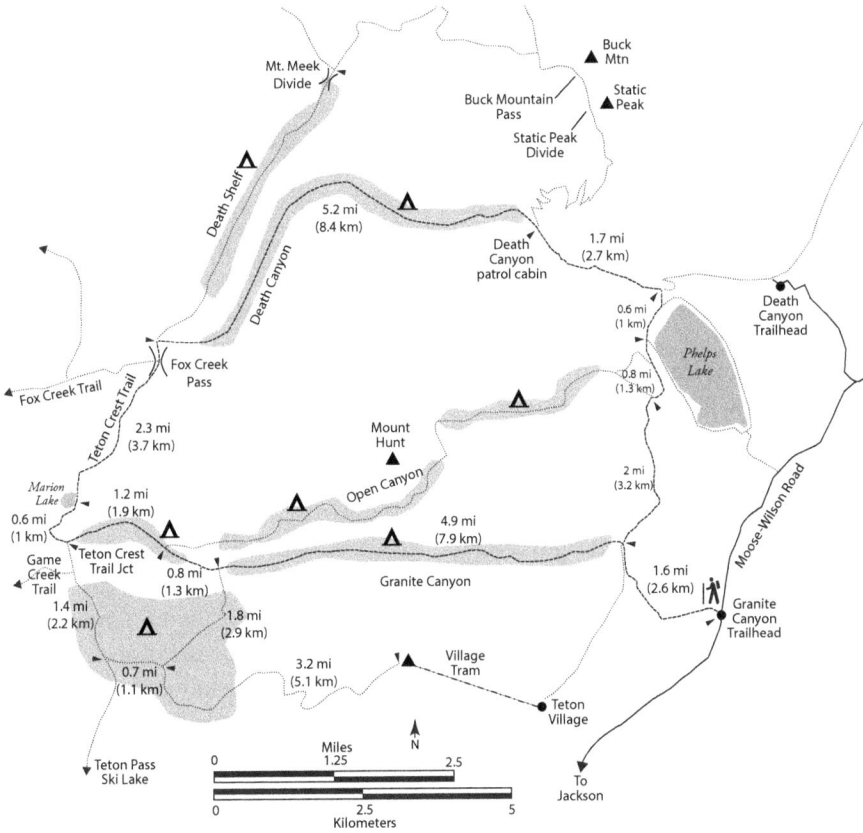

Buck
Mtn

Mt. Meek
Divide

Buck Mountain
Pass

Static
Peak

Static Peak
Divide

Death Shelf

5.2 mi
(8.4 km)

Death Canyon

Death
Canyon
patrol cabin

1.7 mi
(2.7 km)

Death
Canyon
Trailhead

0.6 mi
(1 km)

Phelps
Lake

Fox Creek
Pass

Fox Creek Trail

0.8 mi
(1.3 km)

Teton Crest Trail

2.3 mi
(3.7 km)

Mount
Hunt

Open Canyon

2 mi
(3.2 km)

Marion
Lake

1.2 mi
(1.9 km)

0.6 mi
(1 km)

Teton Crest
Trail Jct

4.9 mi
(7.9 km)

Moose-Wilson Road

Game
Creek
Trail

0.8 mi
(1.3 km)

Granite Canyon

1.6 mi
(2.6 km)

Granite
Canyon
Trailhead

1.4 mi
(2.2 km)

1.8 mi
(2.9 km)

0.7 mi
(1.1 km)

3.2 mi
(5.1 km)

Village
Tram

Teton
Village

Teton Pass
Ski Lake

Miles

N

To
Jackson

0   1.25   2.5

0   2.5   5
Kilometers

PHELPS LAKE

55 GRANITE CANYON TO OPEN CANYON
(18.8 mi / 30.3 km / Stren)

Overview: A canyon loop tour with less hiker traffic but all the views.

Trip style: Loop

Distance: 18.8 miles (30.3 km)

Elevation gain: 3,314 feet (1,010 m) net, 3,969 feet (1,210 m) net gain

Max. Elevation: 9,686 feet (2,952 m)

Difficulty: Strenuous single day, moderate overnighter

Trailhead: Granite Canyon
43.6074°N, -110.7929°W / 43°36'27"N, -110°47'35"W
12T 0516711E 4828288N

Traffic: Moderate in Granite Canyon, light in Open Canyon

Maps: Teton Village, Rendezvous Peak, Mount Bannon, Grand Teton 7.5' USGS Topos

Notes: There can be snow on the Mount Hunt Divide in summer.

PHELPS LAKE

Trailhead Directions

Drive west from Jackson on Broadway (US 191) 1.5 miles (2.4 km) and turn right (N) on Wyoming 22 (Wilson / Teton Village). Drive 4.1 miles (6.6 km) and turn right (N) on WY 390 (Teton Village). Continue north for 8.7 miles (14 km) past the park entrance to the Granite Canyon Trailhead.

Trailhead Facilities

Information kiosk. The dirt parking area often overflows during the summer season.

Hike Description

Begin hiking west and northwest at the Granite Canyon Trailhead. In 0.6 mile (1 km), the trail crosses the Bear Paw Trail. Continue west and north for 1 mile (1.6 km) to the Valley Trail junction. Walk 0.1 mile (0.2 km) north along the Valley Trail to the next junction with Granite Canyon. These trail junctions are well signed.

Continue hiking up the gentle grade into Granite Canyon for 4.9 miles (7.9 km). Aspen and cottonwood fill the canyon along the creek, making it prime moose habitat. Keep a safe distance from these powerful animals.

Pass the first junction to Teton Village and Rendezvous Mountain. In 0.8 mile (1.3 km), the trail connects with Open Canyon. Turn right (N-NE) onto the Open Canyon trail toward Mount Hunt Divide.

The trail continues to rise as it climbs up the north slope of Granite Canyon. The path follows the contours of the canyon, changing direction several times. The trail crosses a creek at 9.4 miles (15.1 km) into the trip in a relatively flat area before entering a stand of trees.

From here, the trail curves counterclockwise east then northeast as it continues following the undulating path. This is where the grade becomes steep, gaining over 1,000 feet in 1.6 miles (305 m in 2.6 km) to Mount Hunt Divide.

From here, the southern Teton Range becomes visible and the grade changes sharply. The trail continues north, working its way down a series of switchbacks as it approaches a creek. The path then turns abruptly east and continues on a switchback path in trees on the south side of a ravine to 14.1 miles (22.7 km). The trail then crosses the creek and continues in open terrain toward Phelps Lake.

Continue on the Open Canyon cutoff trail to the junction with the Valley Trail. Turn right (S) on the Valley Trail. Follow the Valley Trail for 2 miles (3.2 km). This section is mostly in the open.

Follow the short split along the Valley Trail, then turn left (S-SE) along the Granite Canyon Trail toward the trailhead. Hike the last 1.6 miles (2.6 km) to return to the Granite Canyon Trailhead.

mi	km	Waypoints
0.0	0.0	Granite Canyon Trailhead
1.6	2.6	Valley Trail junction
6.6	10.6	Rendezvous Mountain junction
7.4	11.9	Open Canyon junction
11.2	18.0	Mount Hunt Divide
14.8	23.8	Open Canyon cutoff trail junction
15.2	24.4	Valley Trail junction
17.2	27.7	Granite Canyon junction
18.8	30.3	Granite Canyon Trailhead

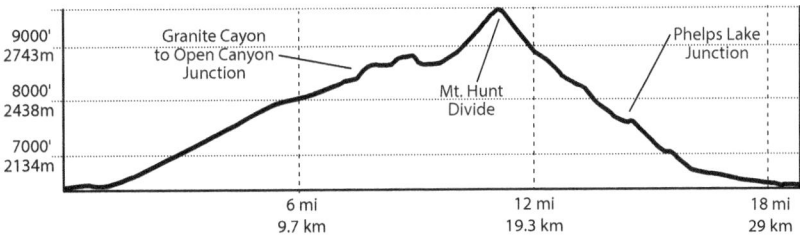

GRANITE CANYON

GRANITE CANYON TO OPEN CANYON

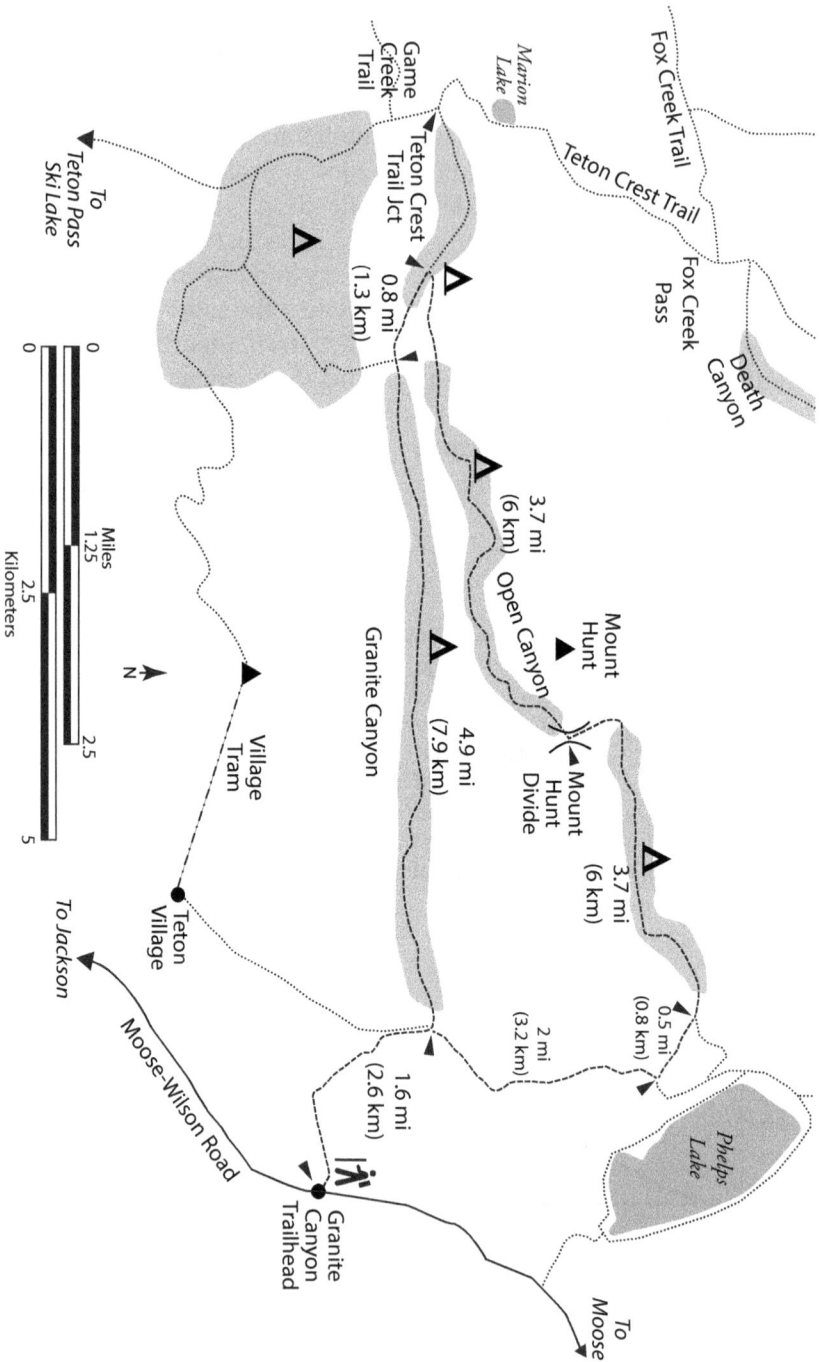

Fox Creek Trail

Game Creek Trail

Marion Lake

Teton Crest Trail

Teton Crest Trail Jct

To Teton Pass Ski Lake

Fox Creek Pass

Death Canyon

0.8 mi (1.3 km)

3.7 mi (6 km)

Open Canyon

Mount Hunt

PHELPS LAKE

Miles
1.25

Kilometers
2.5

N

2.5

Granite Canyon

4.9 mi (7.9 km)

Mount Hunt Divide

3.7 mi (6 km)

Village Tram

Teton Village

To Jackson

Moose-Wilson Road

0.5 mi (0.8 km)

2 mi (3.2 km)

1.6 mi (2.6 km)

Phelps Lake

Granite Canyon Trailhead

To Moose

GRANITE CANYON

56 MARION LAKE (18.2 mi / 29.2 km / Stren)

Overview: A pleasant canyon hike with a high-altitude picturesque lake.

Trip style: Out and back

Distance: 9.1 miles (14.6 km) one way, 18.2 miles (29.2 km) round trip

Elevation gain: 2,880 feet (878 m)

Max. Elevation: 9,239 feet (2,816 m)

Difficulty: Strenuous single day, moderate overnighter

Trailhead: Granite Canyon
43.6074°N, -110.7929°W / 43°36'27"N, -110°47'35"W
12T 0516711E 4828288N

Traffic: Moderate

Maps: Teton Village, Rendezvous Peak, Mount Bannon 7.5' USGS Topos

Notes: Multiple starting points are possible.

Trailhead Directions

Drive west from Jackson on Broadway (US 191) 1.5 miles (2.4 km) and turn right (N) on Wyoming 22 (Wilson / Teton Village). Drive 4.1 miles (6.6 km) and turn right (N) on WY 390 (Teton Village). Continue north for 8.7 miles (14 km) past the park entrance to the Granite Canyon Trailhead.

Trailhead Facilities

Information kiosk. The dirt parking area often overflows during the summer season.

Hike Description

Begin hiking west and northwest at the Granite Canyon Trailhead. In 0.6 mile (1 km), the trail crosses the Bear Paw Trail. Continue west and north for 1 mile (1.6 km) to the Valley Trail junction. Walk 0.1 mile (0.2 km) north along the Valley Trail to the next junction with Granite Canyon. These trail junctions are well signed.

Continue hiking up the gentle grade into Granite Canyon for 4.9 miles (7.9 km). Cottonwood and aspen fill the canyon along the creek, making it prime moose habitat. Keep a safe distance from these powerful animals.

Pass the first junction to Teton Village and Rendezvous Mountain. In 0.8 mile (1.3 km), the trail connects with Open Canyon. Stay on the Granite Canyon Trail. Continue 1.2 miles (1.9 km) to the Teton Crest Trail junction. Turn right (N) and climb this steep, short 0.6-mile (1 km) section over a lip to Marion Lake.

From the lake, return along the same trail to reach the trailhead.

Alternative Trail Starts

It is possible to use the Teton Village (JHMR) tram to cut significant distance off the hike to Marion Lake. Be mindful of the dramatic elevation gain to prevent altitude sickness (AMS).

Also note the tram's hours and the weather. The tram will stop in dangerous weather, necessitating a long walk back to Teton Village.

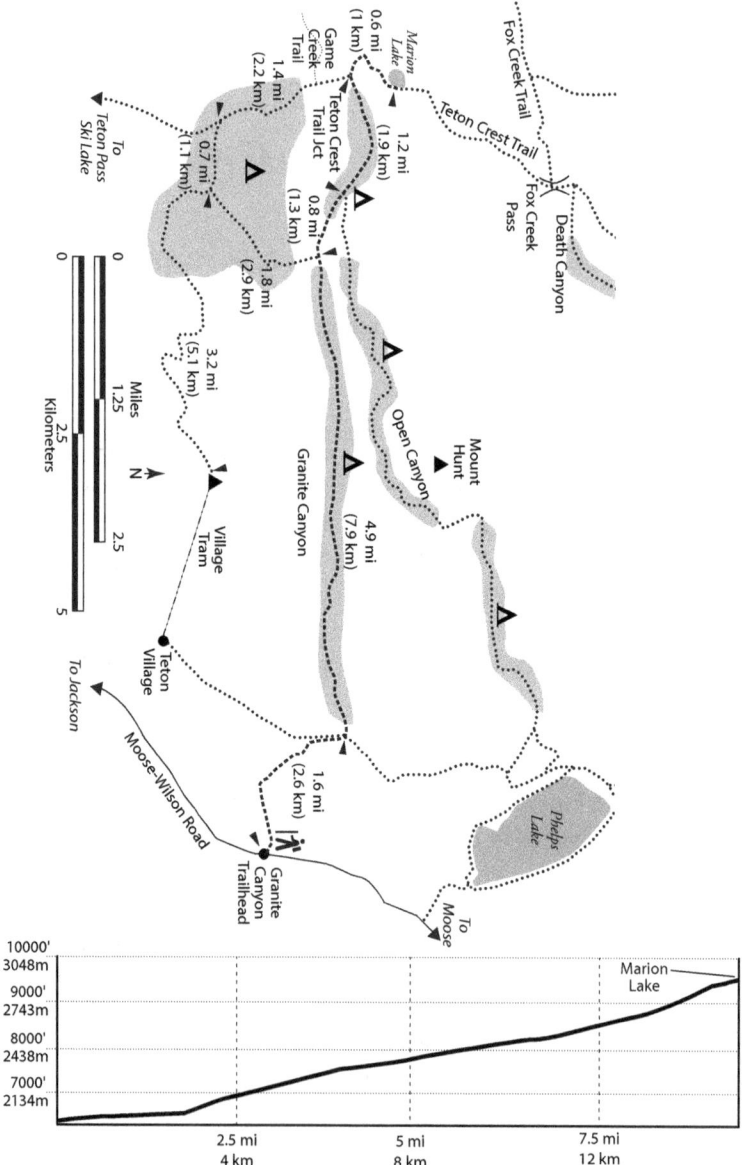

GRANITE CANYON

57 TETON CREST TRAIL (37.5 mi / 60.4 km / Stren)

Overview: This is an epic hike covering the highlights of Grand Teton.

Trip style: One way shuttle

Distance: 37.5 miles (60.4 km) one way

Elevation gain: 4,317 feet (1,332 m), 8,295 feet (2,528 m) total gain/loss

Max. Elevation: 10,700 feet (3,261 m)

Difficulty: Strenuous, multi-day

Trailhead: Granite Canyon
43.6074°N, -110.7929°W / 43°36'27"N, -110°47'35"W
12T 0516711E 4828288N

Traffic: Heavy to light

Maps: Jenny Lake, Mount Moran, Moose, Grand Teton, Mount Bannon, Teton Village, Rendezvous Peak, Teton Pass 7.5' USGS Topos

Notes: Busy trail with climbers and hikers. Water available. An ice axe may be required to cross Paintbrush Divide.

Trailhead Directions

Drive west from Jackson on Broadway (US 191) 1.5 miles (2.4 km) and turn right (N) on Wyoming 22 (Wilson / Teton Village). Drive 4.1 miles (6.6 km) and turn right (N) on WY 390 (Teton Village). Continue north for 8.7 miles (14 km) past the park entrance to the Granite Canyon Trailhead.

Trailhead Facilities

Information kiosk. The dirt parking area often overflows during the summer season.

Starting Points

The Teton Crest Trail has several popular starting points that deliver a different schedule and experience. The hike presented here provides an easier shuttle experience and a more controlled altitude gain to reduce the chance of altitude sickness. Other popular options are presented at the end of this hike description.

Hike Description

Begin hiking west and northwest at the Granite Canyon Trailhead. In 0.6 mile (1 km), the trail crosses the Bear Paw Trail. Continue west and north for 1 mile (1.6 km) to the Valley Trail junction. Walk 0.1 mile (0.2 km) north along the Valley Trail to the next junction with Granite Canyon. These trail junctions are well signed.

Continue hiking up the gentle grade into Granite Canyon for 4.9 miles (7.9 km). Cottonwood and aspen fill the canyon along the creek, making it prime moose habitat. Keep a safe distance from these powerful animals.

Pass the first junction to Teton Village and Rendezvous Mountain. In 0.8 mile (1.3 km), the trail connects with Open Canyon. Stay on the Granite Canyon Trail. Continue 1.2 miles (1.9 km) to the Teton Crest Trail junction. Turn right (N) and climb this steep, short 0.6-mile (1 km) section over a lip to Marion Lake.

From Marion Lake, the trail works its way north for 2.3 miles (3.7 km) up to Fox Creek Pass at 9,570 feet (2,917 m), 0.2 mile (0.3 km) south of the junction to Death Canyon.

The trail continues for a relatively flat 3.8 miles (6.1 km) along the scenic Death Shelf camping zone. The view into Death Canyon is stunning and continuous to Mt. Meek Divide where the Crest Trail connects to the Teton Shelf Trail.

The trail drops into Alaska Basin and connects to the Alaska Basin Trail. A short distance west of the Teton Crest Trail is the Jedediah Smith Wilderness area outside of the Grand Teton boundary where dispersed camping is allowed. Follow the signs to ensure the proper campsite placement.

Follow the trail signs for Hurricane Pass from Alaska Basin. Begin the climb toward Sunset Lake, 1.3 miles (2 km) north of Alaska Basin. Note that camping is not allowed near the shoreline. The climb from Sunset Lake to Hurricane Pass gains 880 feet (268 m) over this 1.5-mile (2.4 km) section. The southern view of the Cathedral Group is visible in its full glory at this stunning viewpoint.

Follow the exposed, steep switchback trail for 0.7 mile (1.1 km) into the South Fork of Cascade Canyon, dropping down to the jade green pond at the bottom of Schoolroom Glacier. From here, the trail continues north, losing 2,190 feet (668 m) over the 4.2-mile (6.8 km) hike through this busy camping zone.

At the Cascade Canyon junction, take the left (NW) fork toward Lake Solitude and continue 2.5 miles (4 km) to Lake Solitude. Camping is not allowed in the vicinity of this busy lake.

Paintbrush Divide is a 2.3-mile (3.7 km) climb to 10,700 feet (3,261 m). This is a steep climb with no water and southern exposure. The climb can be hot in the summer and there is no shelter from weather above 9,500 feet (2,896 m). At the high point of this hike, 10,700 feet (3,261 m) at Paintbrush Divide, the trail can be confusing to follow. There are multiple social trails across the ridge. Look for the sign which will indicate the trail over the north side of the divide.

From here, the trail drops precipitously into Paintbrush Canyon. Be aware that an ice axe may be required, as the slope is steep and is often snowbound the entire year. Multiple accidents have occurred on this section of trail.

PHELPS LAKE

GRANITE CANYON

From the divide, the trail drops 1.3 miles (2.2 km) to the first junction of Holly Lake, a nice diversion from the main trail which adds negligible distance to the hike. From the second junction to Holly Lake, the trail continues to lose elevation through a series of switchbacks and creek crossings for the next 4.4 miles (7.1 km) to the String Lake Loop junction.

Take the left (E) fork across the long wooden bridge across the String Lake inlet and finish the last 1.5 miles (2.4 km) of this epic hike. Ride or shuttle back to the trailhead.

Alternative Trail Starts

It is possible to hike the true entire length of the Teton Crest Trail from the Phillips Canyon/Ski Lake Trailhead. Alternatively, start at Teton Pass and hike directly up to Mt. Glory for the complete Teton Crest experience.

Note that these options are substantially more difficult, as there is no water for a long distance along these routes.

Some hikers use the Teton Village tram to bypass the first segment of the trail. This does save time by bypassing the hike up Granite Canyon.

Be wary of this approach. Hikers have fallen ill due to altitude sickness (AMS). Starting a strenuous hike from 10,000 feet (3,048 m) after flying into Jackson from sea level the day prior is not recommended. It can necessitate a hazardous and expensive rescue. In some circumstances, AMS can be life-threatening.

Trail Notes

It is possible to complete this entire hike in less than twenty-four hours. The author has hiked this route in 16 hours from the Granite Canyon Trailhead to String Lake, traveling through the night. He then rode a bike from String Lake to Granite Canyon to complete the loop in 22 hours. This approach is not for the faint of heart.

The trail can be backpacked in 3 days (2 nights) without too much difficulty, assuming no side trips are taken. If weather allows, use the time to visit the different canyons and shelves. The Grand Teton hiking season is short and it is well worth planning for an extra day or three for the full backcountry experience.

For a human powered loop adventure, secure a bike at the Leigh Lake Trailhead. Then, drive to Granite Canyon. From there, complete the Teton Crest hike to String Lake. Pick up the bike, then ride back to the Granite Canyon Trailhead along the park road connecting to the Moose-Wilson Road to make this a trip into one of epic proportions.

Ripe trailside huckleberries ready for eating.

GRANITE CANYON

TETON CREST TRAIL

mi	km	Waypoints
0.0	0.0	Granite Canyon Trailhead
1.6	2.6	Valley Trail junction
8.5	13.7	Teton Crest Trail junction
9.1	14.6	Marion Lake
11.4	18.3	Death Canyon junction
15.0	24.1	Teton Shelf junction
16.6	26.7	Alaska Basin
18.1	29.1	Sunset Lake
19.6	31.5	Hurricane Pass
20.3	32.7	Schoolroom Glacier
24.4	39.3	Cascade Canyon Fork
26.9	43.3	Lake Solitude
29.1	46.8	Paintbrush Divide
30.6	49.2	Holly Lake junction
35.9	57.8	String Lake Loop junction
37.5	60.4	String Lake parking lot

PHELPS LAKE

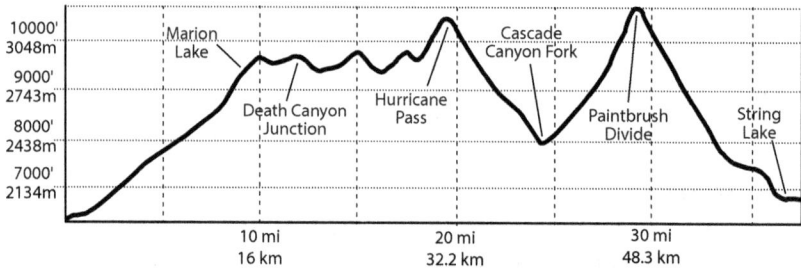

Backpackers preparing to descend Paintbrush Divide in October during heavy snowfall.

GRANITE CANYON

TETON CREST TRAIL

Miles
0 2.5 5

0 5 10
Kilometers

Leigh Lake

2.3 mi (3.7 km) 1.3 mi (2.2 km) Holly Lake 4.4 mi (7.1 km) 1.5 mi (2.4 km)

Lake Solitude

Paintbrush Divide

Jenny Lake Road

1 mi (1.6 km)

String Lake

To Yellowstone

The Jaw

2.5 mi (4 km)

Lake of the Crags Ramshead Lake

Shuttle Dock Jenny Lake

Cascade Canyon Fork

N

Teton Canyon

Table Mountain

4.6 mi (7.4 km)

Owen Teewinot

Grand Teton

Lupine Meadows Trailhead

Hurricane Pass

Schoolroom Glacier

Middle Teton

South Teton

Bradley Lake

Teton Park Road

1.4 mi (2.2 km)

Sunset Lake

Alaska Basin Trail

Alaska Basin

Taggart Lake

3.2 mi (5.1 km)

Buck Mtn

PHELPS LAKE

Teton Shelf Trail

Mt. Meek Divide

Buck Mountain Pass

Static Peak

3.8 mi (6.1 km)

Static Peak Divide

Death Canyon

Death Shelf

Death Canyon Trailhead

To Moose

Fox Creek Pass

Phelps Lake

Moose-Wilson Road

Fox Creek Trail

2.3 mi (3.7 km)

Mount Hunt

Marion Lake

0.6 mi (1 km)

Open Canyon

6.8 mi (10.9 km)

Teton Crest Trail Jct

Granite Canyon

1.6 mi (2.6 km)

Granite Canyon Trailhead

Game Creek Trail

Village Tram

Teton Village

Teton Pass Ski Lake

To Jackson

GRANITE CANYON

58 RENDEZVOUS MOUNTAIN
(14.2 mi / 23 km / Ex Stren)

Overview: A steep hike with endless Jackson Hole views.

Trip style: Out and back

Distance: 7.1 miles (11.5 km) one way, 14.2 miles (23 km) round trip

Elevation gain: 4,139 feet (1,262 m)

Max. Elevation: 10,450 feet (3,185 m)

Difficulty: Extremely strenuous

Trailhead: Teton Village
43.5964°N, -110.8270°W / 43°35'47"N, -110°49'37"W
12T 0513963E 4827061N

Traffic: Moderate

Maps: Teton Village, Rendezvous Peak 7.5' USGS Topos

Notes: Multiple starting points possible. Watch for downhill bikes.

Trailhead Directions

Drive west from Jackson on Broadway (US 191) 1.5 miles (2.4 km) and turn right (N) on Wyoming 22 (Wilson / Teton Village). Drive 4.1 miles (6.6 km) and turn right (N) on WY 390 (Teton Village). Continue north for 6.4 miles (10.3 km) and turn left at the Teton Village sign. Drive to the main parking lot.

Trailhead Facilities

Restrooms, bike rack, trash cans, shops, restaurants, resort facilities.

Solitude Trail Starting Point

Walk toward Gondola and follow the trail to the right (N) along the buildings toward the Solitude Trail.

Once past the buildings, the Solitude Trail enters a mixed forest cover of aspen and conifer trees. It traverses the face of the mountain over several switchbacks, covering 2.8 miles (4.5 km) until it connects with the Wildflower Trail at 7,580 feet (2,310 m). Continue with the upper mountain description.

Wildflower Trail Starting Point

Walk under the tram and connect with the trail that leads straight up the mountain. This trail has over a dozen switchbacks as it makes its way up the mountain face between the tram and gondola. The trail gains 1,300 feet (396 m) over 1.8 miles (2.9 km) until it connects with the Solitude Trail.

Upper Mountain

Once the Wildflower and Solitude Trails merge near the Casper chair lift, continue climbing for 1.1 miles (1.8 km) until the trail connects with the summit road. Two options are available: use the road or continue toward the Gondola

PHELPS LAKE

Summit for the first return option.

The road ascends the rest of the way to the tram summit over a steep, dusty 3.2 miles (5.1 km). There are several spur access roads along this path.

The second option is to follow the Wildflower Trail to the Gondola Summit, then continue on the steep Cirque Trail to reach the summit in 2.7 miles (4.3 km).

Hikers can either take the tram down or return along the same route. Watch out for vehicle traffic on the upper mountain.

Either option has little to no tree cover above 9,000 feet (2,743 m). Be aware that western thunderstorms are invisible, hidden by the mountain, until they appear seemingly out of nowhere. Check the weather forecast before setting out on this hike.

Check with the resort for current tram prices and operating hours.

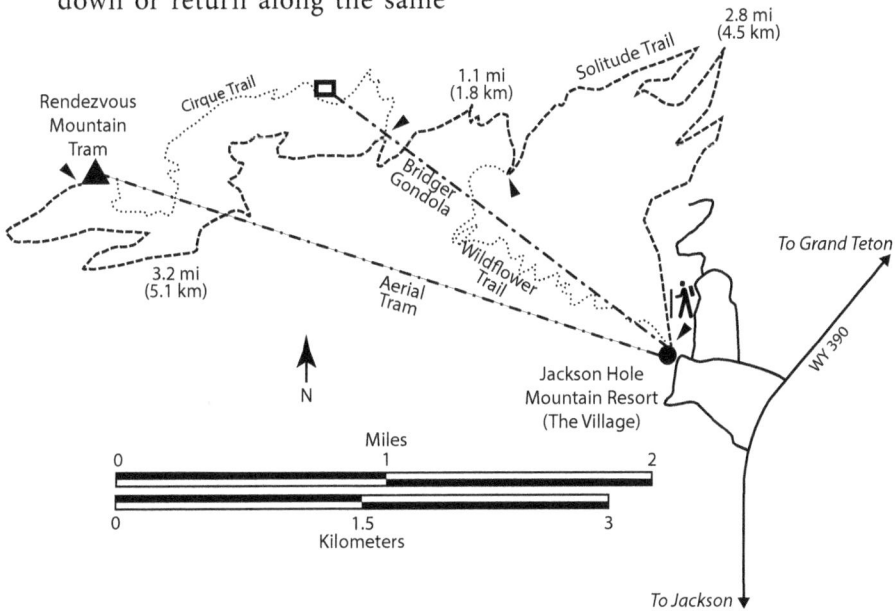

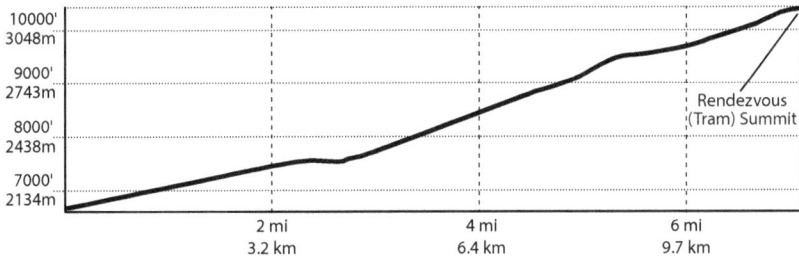

TETON VILLAGE

59 RENDEZVOUS MOUNTAIN TO GRANITE CANYON LOOP (18.1 mi / 29.1 km / Ex Stren)

Overview: A steep hike with stunning views of Jackson Hole.

Trip style: Out and back

Distance: 18.1 miles (29.1 km) loop

Elevation gain: 3,691 feet (1,125 m)

Max. Elevation: 10,450 feet (3,185 m)

Difficulty: Extremely strenuous day hike, strenuous overnighter

Trailhead: Teton Village
43.5964°N, -110.8270°W / 43°35'47"N, -110°49'37"W
12T 0513963E 4827061N

Traffic: Moderate

Maps: Teton Village, Rendezvous Peak 7.5' USGS Topos

Notes: Multiple starting points possible. Watch for downhill bikes.

PHELPS LAKE

Trailhead Directions

Drive west from Jackson on Broadway (US 191) 1.5 miles (2.4 km) and turn right (N) on Wyoming 22 (Wilson / Teton Village). Drive 4.1 miles (6.6 km) and turn right (N) on WY 390 (Teton Village). Continue north for 6.4 miles (10.3 km) and turn left at the Teton Village sign. Drive to the main parking lot.

Trailhead Facilities

Restrooms, bike rack, trash cans, shops, restaurants, resort facilities.

Solitude Trail Starting Point

Walk toward Gondola and follow the trail to the right (N) along the buildings toward the Solitude Trail.

Once past the buildings, the Solitude Trail drops into a mixed forest cover of aspen and conifer trees. It traverses the face of the mountain over several switchbacks, covering 2.8 miles (4.5 km) until it connects with the Wildflower Trail at 7,580 feet (2,310 m). Continue with the upper mountain description.

Wildflower Trail Starting Point

Walk under the tram and connect with the trail that leads straight up the mountain. This trail has over a dozen switchbacks as it makes its way up the mountain face between the tram and gondola. The trail gains 1,300 feet (396 m) over 1.8 miles (2.9 km) until it connects with the Solitude Trail.

Upper Mountain

Once the Wildflower and Solitude Trails merge near the Casper chair lift, continue climbing for 1.1 miles (1.8 km) until the trail connects with the summit road. Two options are available: use the road or continue toward the Gondola Summit.

The road ascends the rest of the way to the tram summit over a steep, dusty 3.2 miles (5.1 km). There are several spur access roads along this path.

The second option is to follow the Wildflower Trail to the Gondola Summit, then continue on the steep Cirque Trail to reach the summit in 2.7 miles (4.3 km). Should weather be approaching, seek shelter.

Once at the tram, hike back down the summit road 0.4 mile (0.6 km) to the junction, then continue southwest 0.3 mile (0.5 km) to the Rendezvous Mountain Trail junction. Turn right (NE) and begin descending the western face of the mountain.

This 2.6-mile (4.2 km) section of trail works its way north then abruptly turns southwest, working its way around a large ridge. The trail grade lessens as it crosses the South Fork of Granite Creek and connects with the South Fork Cutoff Granite Canyon Trail.

Continue north and then northwest on the South Fork Granite Canyon Trail for 1.8 miles (2.9 km) through a partly forested area until entering deeper forest cover around the Middle Fork of Granite Creek where the trail connects with the main Granite Canyon Trail. Turn right (E) at the junction and travel toward the Granite Canyon Trailhead parking lot.

Hike 4.9 miles (7.9 km) in Granite Canyon to the Valley Trail junction. Turn right (S) on the Valley Trail and continue south for 2.5 miles (4 km) to Jackson Hole Mountain Resort (Teton Village) to complete the hike.

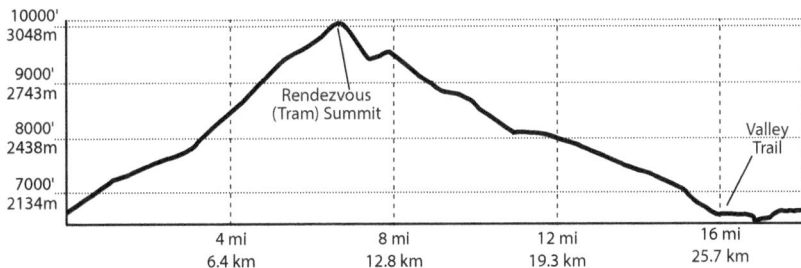

TETON VILLAGE

RENDEZVOUS MOUNTAIN GRANITE CANYON

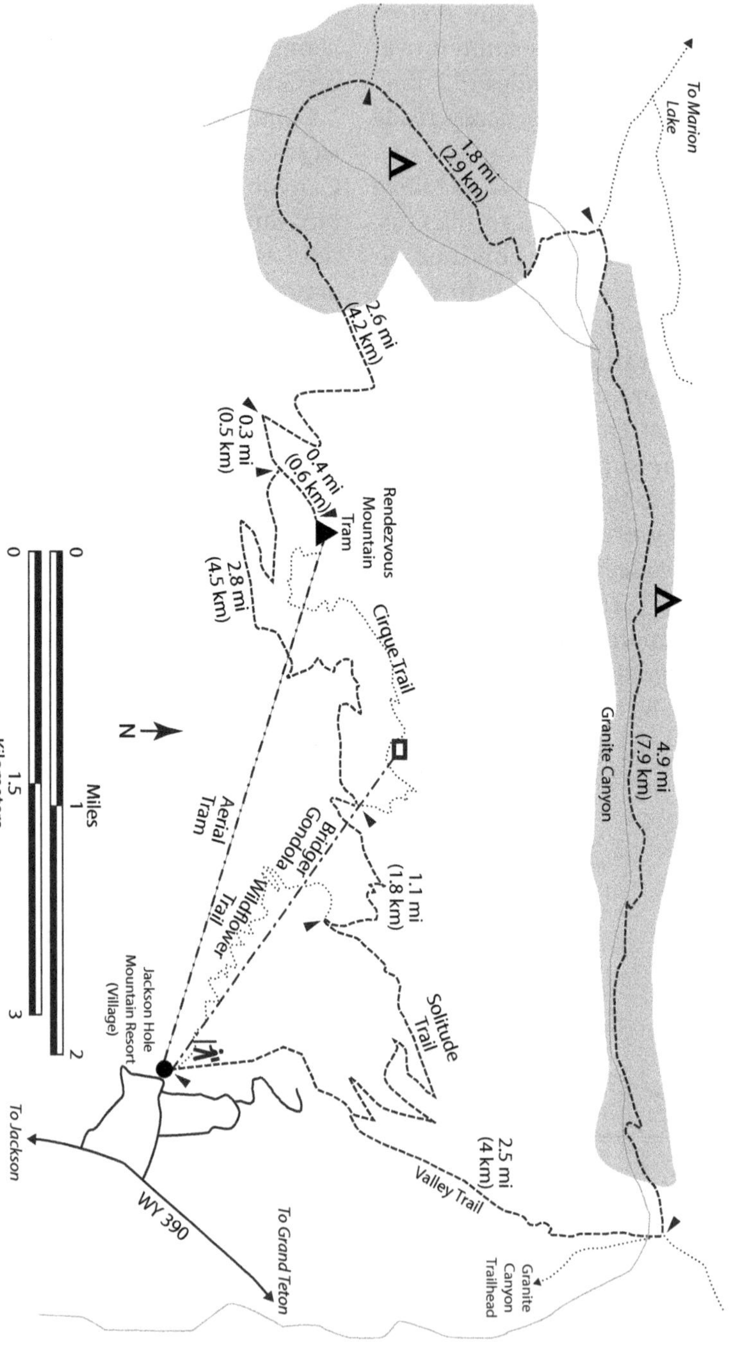

To Marion Lake

1.8 mi (2.9 km)

2.6 mi (4.2 km)

0.3 mi (0.5 km)

0.4 km (0.6 km)

Rendezvous Mountain Tram

2.8 mi (4.5 km)

Cirque Trail

Granite Canyon

4.9 mi (7.9 km)

N

Aerial Tram

Bridger Gondola

Wildflower Trail

1.1 mi (1.8 km)

Solitude Trail

Jackson Hole Mountain Resort (Village)

0   1.5   3   Kilometers

0   1   2   Miles

2.5 mi (4 km)

Valley Trail

Granite Canyon Trailhead

To Jackson

WY 390

To Grand Teton

TETON VILLAGE

CENTRAL JH

CENTRAL JACKSON

The Central Jackson hiking area is full of short, long, easy, and challenging hikes. There is a little something for every hiker of every ability in and around the town of Jackson.

Should you find yourself with little time for a hike, the trails around the town can help hikers get the most out of their visit to the area.

There are four main hiking areas in central Jackson: Snow King, Cache Creek, the Nelson Trailhead, and South Central Jackson.

Snow King is the steep mountain that borders the southern edge of the town of Jackson. This broad mountain dominates the skyline and provides many hiking options for the beginning, as well as the advanced hiker with strong legs and lungs.

Cache Creek is the local's secret hiking area. Though, from the traffic in the area, it may not seem like a secret at all. It is popular with dog walkers and mountain bikers alike.

The Nelson Trailhead is an alternative access point to the Cache Creek area. It is a better starting point for many of the hikes in Cache Creek, as it is less busy and provides shorter approaches to some destinations. Parking is limited at this trailhead.

The South Central Jackson area is where you will find the less-traveled trails of the area. Some of these trails exist in no guidebooks or websites. They are lightly traveled trails and are offered as a chance to experience something completely different from the standard trails in other guides.

If you only have a little time to get a hike in without needing to drive to Grand Teton, this section is for you.

An elk resting in the National Wildlife Refuge at the northern edge of Jackson.

CENTRAL JH

CENTRAL JACKSON AREA HIKES

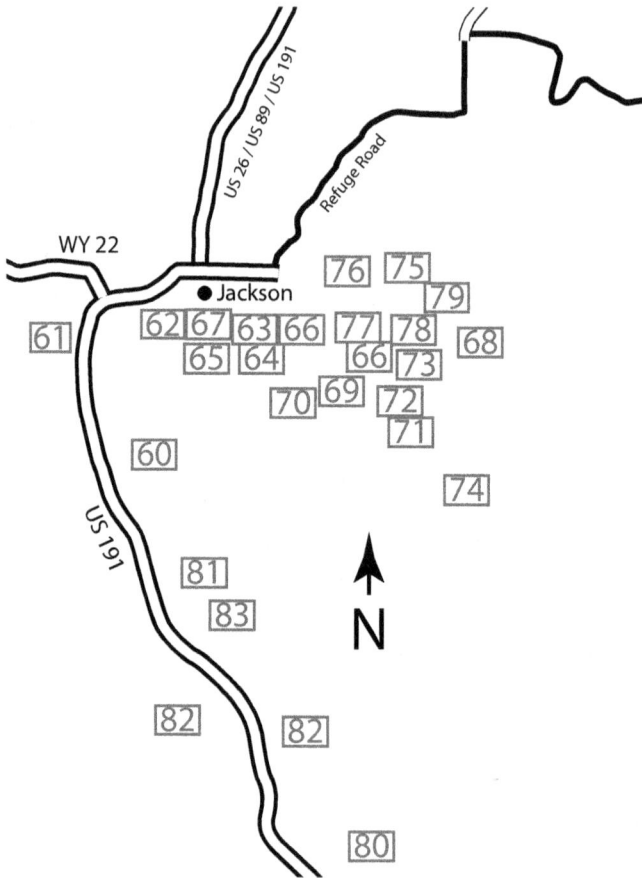

Snow King

60. Adams Canyon
61. High School Butte
62. Josie's Ridge
63. Shade Monkey
64. Sink or Swim
65. Snow King Bootpack
66. Snow King Summit
67. Wildlife Drive Network

Cache Creek

68. Cache Creek Main Trail
69. Ferrin's Trail
70. Hagen Highway
71. Hagen Trail

72. River Trail
73. Sidewalk Trail
74. Skyline Trail Loop

Nelson Trailhead

75. Crystal Butte
76. Crystal Lite
77. Nelson Knoll
78. Putt Putt and Town Overlook
79. Woods Canyon to Crystal Butte

South Central Jackson

80. Game Creek to Cache Creek
81. Lower Valley Energy Ridge
82. South Park Loop
83. Wilson Canyon to Snow King

CENTRAL JH

Snow King

Snow King dominates the southern skyline of Jackson and forms the southern edge of the town. This impressive wall of rock, dirt, and lodgepole pines is laced with a substantial trail network that connects to Cache Creek, Wilson Canyon, and Game Creek.

The mountain is one of the steepest official ski hills in the continental United States. This makes for excellent skiing in the winter and steep hikes, mountain biking, and dog walking in the summer.

There are several ski lifts that serve the mountain. If you are strong enough to reach the summit, you can pay a small fee to "download" off the mountain to save your knees as a first-time visitor. Most local hikers use Snow King as a gym, working out by climbing the mountain on the main summit trail, also known as the Slow Trail.

The ski lift summit of Snow King is not actually the mountain's highest point. The higher summit is a radio antenna array to the east of the ski lift summit. Compared to the number of people who walk up to the top of the mountain, few ever venture over to the higher summit at just above 8,000 feet (2,438 m). The official summit elevation of Snow King is 7,808 feet (2,380 m).

There are several other hikes contained in this book's Snow King hiking zone that are not actually on Snow King but are considered in the Snow King area. Though these hikes are comparatively short, they gain elevation quickly.

Hiking up High School Butte with Snow King and Cache Creek in the background.

SNOW KING

60 ADAMS CANYON (3.6 mi / 5.8 km / Stren)

Overview: A hike into a canyon overlooking south Jackson Hole.
Trip style: Out and back
Distance: 1.8 miles (2.9 km) one way, 3.6 miles (5.8 km) round trip
Elevation gain: 1,618 feet (493 m)
Max. Elevation: 7,828 feet (2,386 m)
Difficulty: Strenuous
Trailhead: Adams Canyon
43.4357°N -110.7827°W / 43°26'08"N, -110°46'58"W
12T 0517590E 4809222N
Traffic: Light to none
Maps: Jackson 7.5' USGS Topo
Notes: Respect private property boundaries and fences.

Trailhead Directions

Drive west from Jackson on Broadway (US 191) 4.5 miles (7.2 km) to Adams Canyon Drive. Turn left, drive 0.3 mile (0.5 km) past the buildings and up the hill. Park in the turnout outside the fenced area.

Trailhead Facilities

None.

Hike Description

Begin hiking up the steep hill outside the fenced area toward Adams Canyon. The trail passes south of a large concrete block and circular tanks.

There are two options to this trail. The first travels into the tree-covered area of the canyon and blocks much of the views up the trail. The second, recommended trail, travels to the southern edge of the trees up the ridge of the canyon. This 1.8-mile (2.9 km) trail travels clear of the trees above the canyon and provides better views of the southern area of Jackson Hole all the way to the top of the ridge. The trail connects to the Leeks Canyon and Wilson Canyon trails at the ridge line.

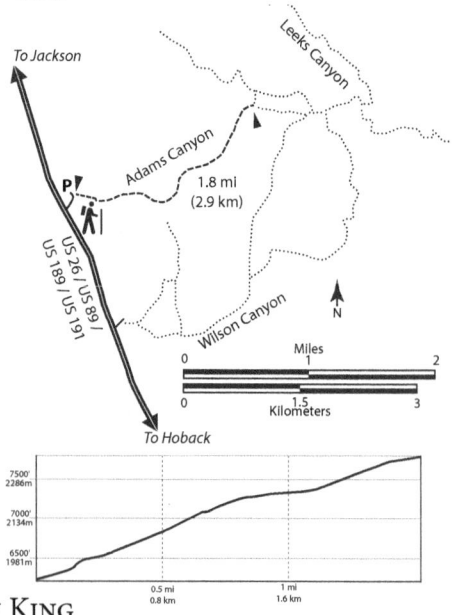

SNOW KING

61 HIGH SCHOOL BUTTE (0.8 mi / 1.2 km / Stren)

Overview: A popular hike with expansive views of south Jackson Hole.

Trip style: Out and back

Distance: 0.4 mile (0.6 km) one way, 0.8 mile (1.2 km) round trip

Elevation gain: 652 feet (199 m)

Max. Elevation: 6,787 feet (2,069 m)

Difficulty: Strenuous

Trailhead: South Park Loop / Blair Drive
43.4646°N, -110.8050°W / 43°27'53"N, -110°48'18"W
12T 0515771E 4812429N

Traffic: Heavy

Maps: Jackson 7.5' USGS Topo

Notes: Respect private property boundaries and fences.

Trailhead Directions

Drive west from Jackson on Broadway (US 191) for 2 miles (3.2 km) and turn right (W) on South Park Loop Road. Continue for 0.7 mile (1.1 km) and park near the trailhead.

Trailhead Facilities

None.

Hike Description

Begin hiking up High School Butte at the northeast corner of the intersection. The trail is heavily traveled and is easy to follow with views of south Jackson all the way up.

The trail begins a series of switchbacks in 0.1 mile (0.2 km), working its way back and forth up the hill. There is no shade along the trail, so be prepared. At 0.15 mile (0.25 km), there is a trail fork that leads north around the butte. This trail terminates at a private property fence.

Continue hiking the switchbacks until you encounter a fence, then turn right and follow the trail east. The trail splits but merges in 0.1 mile (0.2 km), terminating at a broad dirt pad. Return via the same route.

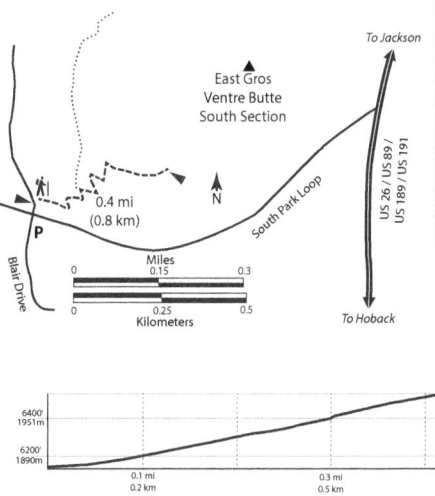

62 JOSIE'S RIDGE (2.2 mi / 3.4 km / Stren)

Overview: A popular hike and alternative to other Snow King climbs.

Trip style: Out and back

Distance: 1.1 miles (1.7 km) one way, 2.2 miles (3.4 km) round trip

Elevation gain: 1,029 feet (314 m)

Max. Elevation: 7,172 feet (2,186 m)

Difficulty: Strenuous

Trailhead: Russ Garaman Park
43.4663°N, -110.7863°W / 43°27'59"N, -110°47'11"W
12T 0517282E 4812619N

Traffic: Heavy

Maps: Jackson 7.5' USGS Topo

Notes: Respect private property boundaries and fences.

Trailhead Directions

Drive west from the Town Square on Broadway for 1.3 miles (2.1 km) and turn left (S) on Powderhorn Lane. Continue 0.5 mile (0.9 km) on Powderhorn, turn right (W) at Crabtree Lane. Park near the pathway entrance.

Trailhead Facilities

Restrooms, bike rack, trash cans, water fountains, information kiosk.

Hike Description

Walk south along the paved pathway for 400 feet (121 m) to the pathway intersection. Turn left (NE) and walk 600 feet (183 m) to the trailhead.

Begin walking up the trail. In 230 feet (70 m), the Josie's Ridge Trail intersects Kelly's Trail. Continue south and then east for 0.5 mile (0.8 km) in mostly open terrain to

the second junction with Kelly's Trail. Continue climbing 0.15 mile (0.25 km) up switchbacks to the Sink or Swim junction.

Stay on the Josie's Ridge Trail up a series of switchbacks for 0.5 mile (0.8 km) to the crest of the trail. From here, you can hike 0.4 mile (0.6 km) southwest to the end of the ridge or continue 1.1 miles (1.8 km) to the Snow King lift station.

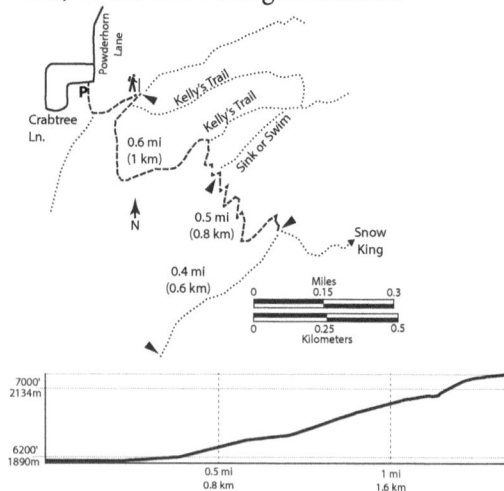

SNOW KING

63 SHADE MONKEY (1.4 mi / 2.2 km / Mod)

Overview: A popular short hike on Snow King.

Trip style: Out and back

Distance: 0.7 mile (1.1 km) one way, 1.4 miles (2.2 km) round trip

Elevation gain: 356 feet (109 m)

Max. Elevation: 6,621 feet (2,018 m)

Difficulty: Moderate

Trailhead: Snow King Exhibition Chairlift
43.4719°N, -110.7611°W / 43°28'19"N, -110°45'40"W
12T 0519323E 4813246N

Traffic: Heavy

Maps: Jackson 7.5' USGS Topo

Notes: Respect private property boundaries and fences.

Trailhead Directions

Drive south on South Cache from the Town Square for 0.4 mile (0.6 km) and turn left (E) on E. Snow King Avenue. Park in the parking lot at Phil Baux Park.

Trailhead Facilities

Restrooms, bike rack, trash cans, information kiosks.

Hike Description

Begin hiking to the southwest from the Snow King Trailhead. The trail initially starts as a series of switchbacks that works its way up the right (W) side of the open face of the ski run.

At 0.4 mile (0.6 km), the trail enters the conifer forest 200 feet (61 m) above the private residences on Pine Glade Drive uphill of the vehicle access tunnel.

From here, continue hiking 0.3 mile (0.5 km) in the heavily forested area as the trail gains elevation and merges with the Sink or Swim Trail which traverses the main face of Snow King. At 0.6 mile (1 km), the trail enters the Bridger-Teton National Forest. Be aware of mountain bikers and trail runners, as this section of trail has limited visibility.

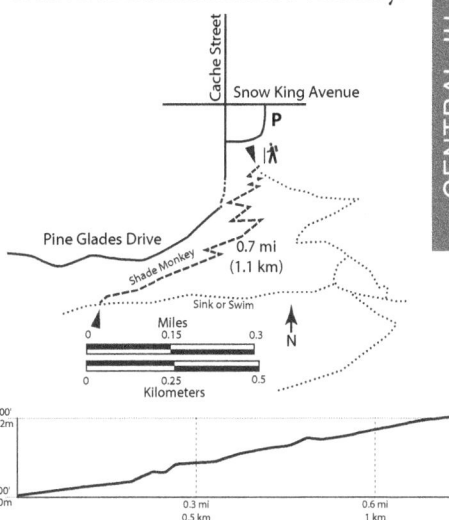

SNOW KING

64 SINK OR SWIM (5.6 mi / 9 km / Mod)

Overview: A highly popular trail that traverses Snow King.

Trip style: Out and back or shuttle

Distance: 2.8 miles (4.5 km) one way, 5.6 miles (9 km) round trip

Elevation gain: 672 feet (205 m)

Max. Elevation: 6,842 feet (2,085 m)

Difficulty: Moderate

Trailhead: Russ Garaman Park
43.4663°N, -110.7863°W / 43°27'59"W, -110°47'11"W
12T 0517282E 4812619N

Traffic: Heavy, mountain bikes

Maps: Jackson, Cache Cr. 7.5' USGS Topo

Notes: Respect private property boundaries and fences.

CENTRAL JH

Trailhead Directions

Drive west from the Town Square on Broadway for 1.3 miles (2.1 km) and turn left (S) on Powderhorn Lane. Continue 0.5 mile (0.9 km) on Powderhorn, turn right (W) at Crabtree Lane. Park near the pathway entrance. Note there are multiple entry and exit points for this trail.

Trailhead Facilities

Restrooms, bike rack, trash cans, water fountains, information kiosk.

Hike Description

Walk south along the paved pathway for 400 feet (121 m) to the pathway intersection. Turn left (NE) and walk 600 feet (183 m) to the trailhead.

Begin walking up the trail. In 230 feet (70 m), the Josie's Ridge Trail intersects Kelly's Trail. Continue south and then east for 0.5 mile (0.8 km) in mostly open terrain to the second junction with Kelly's Trail. Continue climbing 0.15 mile (0.25 km) up switchbacks to the Sink or Swim junction. Turn left (E) and begin the traverse.

At 1.8 miles (2.9 km), the trail breaks out of the heavy tree cover and passes under the Snow King chairlifts on the open ski slope. It then passes above Snow King Resort and the Rafferty lift. It then enters an area of heavy tree cover, passes the Tanager Trail junction and scissor-crosses the Hagen Highway. In another 0.3 mile (0.5 km), the trail terminates at Ferrin's Trail.

Hike via the same route or drop to Cache Creek to return.

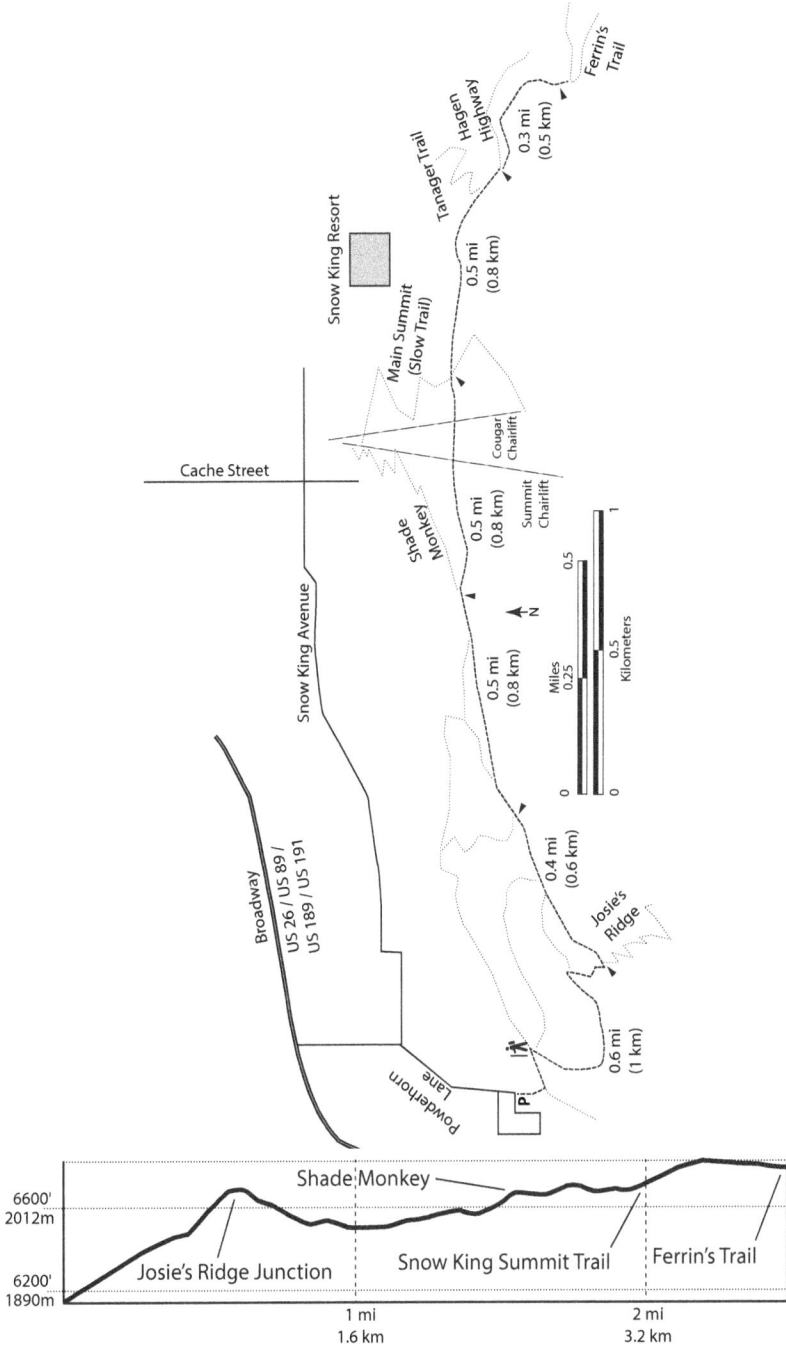

SINK OR SWIM

Ferrin's Trail

Hagen Highway

Tanager Trail

0.3 mi (0.5 km)

0.5 mi (0.8 km)

Snow King Resort

Main Summit (Slow Trail)

Cache Street

Cougar Chairlift

Summit Chairlift

Shade Monkey

0.5 mi (0.8 km)

Snow King Avenue

0.5 mi (0.8 km)

N

Miles

Kilometers

0.4 mi (0.6 km)

Broadway

US 26 / US 89 / US 189 / US 191

Josie's Ridge

0.6 mi (1 km)

P

Powderhorn Lane

CENTRAL JH

6600' 2012m

Shade Monkey

Josie's Ridge Junction

Snow King Summit Trail

Ferrin's Trail

6200' 1890m

1 mi
1.6 km

2 mi
3.2 km

SNOW KING

65 SNOW KING BOOTPACK (1.4 mi / 2.2 km / Ex Stren)

Overview: A tough direct climb up Snow King.

Trip style: Out and back

Distance: 0.7 mile (1.1 km) one way, 1.4 miles (2.2 km) round trip

Elevation gain: 1,571 feet (479 m)

Max. Elevation: 7,808 feet (2,380 m)

Difficulty: Extremely strenuous

Trailhead: Snow King Exhibition Chairlift
43.4719°N, -110.7611°W / 43°28'19"N, -110°45'40"W
12T 0519323E 4813246N

Traffic: Light

Maps: Jackson 7.5' USGS Topo

Notes: Respect private property boundaries and fences.

Trailhead Directions

Drive south on South Cache from the Town Square for 0.4 mile (0.6 km) and turn left (E) on E. Snow King Avenue. Park in the parking lot at Phil Baux Park.

Trailhead Facilities

Restrooms, bike rack, trash cans, information kiosks.

Hike Description

Begin hiking to the southwest from the Snow King Trailhead. Head directly toward the right side (W) of the ski slope toward the condominiums.

The start of the bootpack is above the condominiums. The Shade Monkey Trail is a viable option to help reduce erosion on the lower slopes.

The main portion of the boot-pack trail begins climbing along the western edge of the ski slope along the tree line. The trail becomes steeper the higher you climb, reaching a 50° incline at the top. At 0.5 mile (0.8 km), there are a series of switchbacks to the summit.

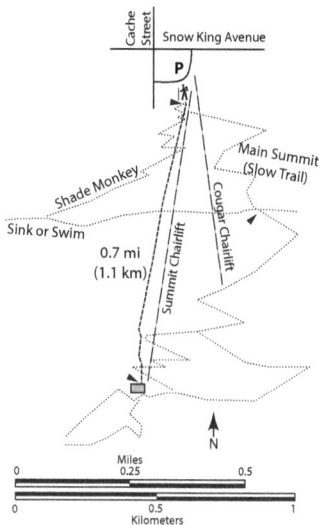

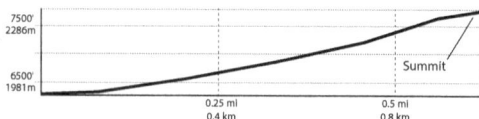

SNOW KING

66 SNOW KING SUMMIT (3.6 mi / 5.8 km / Stren)

Overview: A classic and popular climb up Snow King.

Trip style: Out and back

Distance: 1.8 miles (2.9 km) one way, 3.6 miles (5.8 km) round trip

Elevation gain: 1,571 feet (479 m)

Max. Elevation: 7,808 feet (2,380 m)

Difficulty: Strenuous

Trailhead: Snow King Exhibition Chairlift
43.4719°N, -110.7611°W / 43°28'19"N, -110°45'40"W
12T 0519323E 4813246N

Traffic: Heavy

Maps: Jackson 7.5' USGS Topo

Notes: Respect private property boundaries and fences.

Trailhead Directions

Drive south on South Cache from the Town Square for 0.4 mile (0.6 km) and turn left (E) on E. Snow King Avenue. Park in the parking lot at Phil Baux Park.

Trailhead Facilities

Restrooms, bike rack, trash cans, information kiosks.

Hike Description

Begin hiking on the southeast trail that starts under the summit lift. It travels above the Snow King Events Center and into the trees, then shortly passes by the cemetery and switches back toward the open ski slope.

At 0.5 mile (0.8 km), the trail passes over the Sink or Swim Trail and continues up the wide trail. It switchbacks several times, traveling steeply up to the top of the

Cougar Chairlift.

The trail then continues a series of steep switchbacks, making its way through tree cover. The final switchback climbs up an exposed slope, topping out on the ridge. Hike the last 0.2 mile (0.3 km) toward the top of the summit lift to reach the town overlook deck.

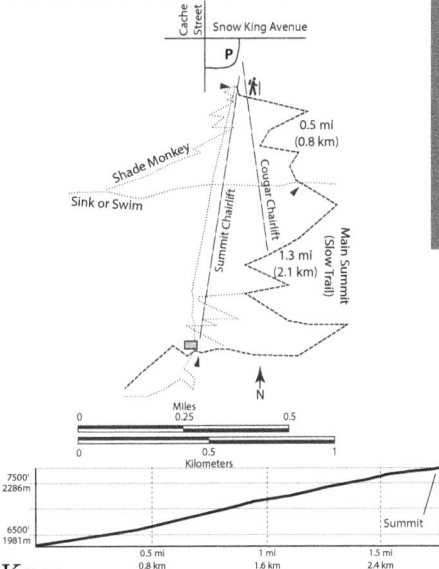

SNOW KING

67 WILDLIFE DRIVE NETWORK (Varies / Mod)

Overview: An extensive network of short trails for a quick hike.

Trip style: Out and back

Distance: Varies

Elevation gain: Varies

Max. Elevation: Varies

Difficulty: Easy to moderate

Trailhead: Wildlife Drive Trailhead
43.4710°N, -110.7763°W / 43°28'15"N, -110°46'35"W
12T 0518093E 4813142N

Traffic: Heavy

Maps: Jackson 7.5' USGS Topo

Notes: Respect private property boundaries and fences.

Trailhead Directions

Drive south on South Cache from the Town Square for 0.4 mile (0.6 km) and turn right (W) on W. Snow King Avenue. Drive 0.7 mile (1.1 km) and turn left at Wildlife Drive, then park at the trailhead.

Trailhead Facilities

Information kiosks.

Hike Description

The Wildlife Drive trail network is extensive. There are multiple options for shorter hikes with mild elevation gains. It is possible to string together several trails for more distance without adding too much vertical gain as well.

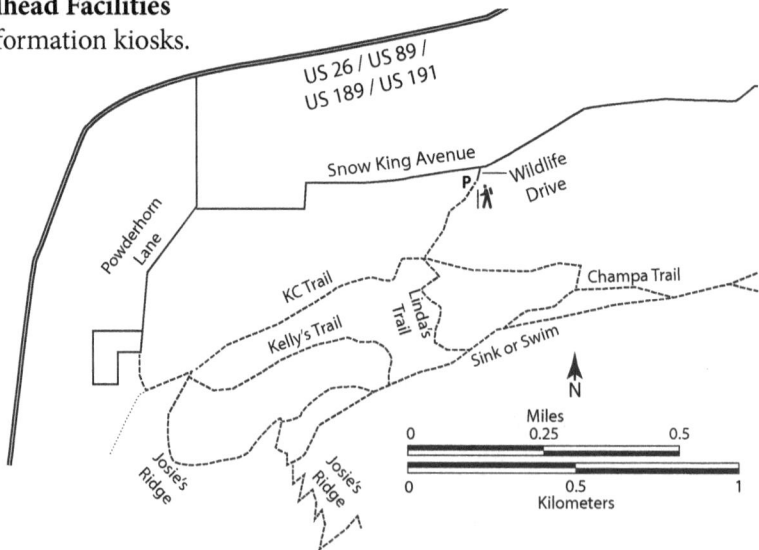

SNOW KING

Cache Creek

Cache Creek is the local's favorite hiking spot. Although well-known to townsfolk, it isn't nearly as visited as neighboring Snow King and certainly not Grand Teton.

Cache Creek covers a single drainage yet has two distinctive climates. The south-facing side of the canyon is dry. The north-facing side of the canyon is completely different, being moist and full of flowers in the lower elevations near Cache Creek.

Much of Cache Creek runs underground through Jackson, as development has slowly taken over this once-magnificent small creek. This area has a few tough, steep hikes. Most, however, are easy and accessible to nearly every skill level.

In the Cache Creek section of this part of the book, certain trails have been omitted from maps for clarity. This particular area has a high density of trails. It is difficult to print a map to scale, covering large areas, with multiple trails that are separated by a short distance.

A complete map of Cache Creek covering the first 6 miles (9.6 km) of the area, printed in a book format, looks like an unintelligible mass of lines. For the reader's convenience, only relevant connections and main trails are shown in each individual trail map.

For more detailed historical, flora, and fauna information about Cache Creek, seek out Susan Marsh's book, *Cache Creek: A Trailside Guide to Jackson Hole's Backyard Wilderness*, available from Sastrugi Press. It can be found at local bookstores and online.

Looking toward Jackson on the Hagen Trail.

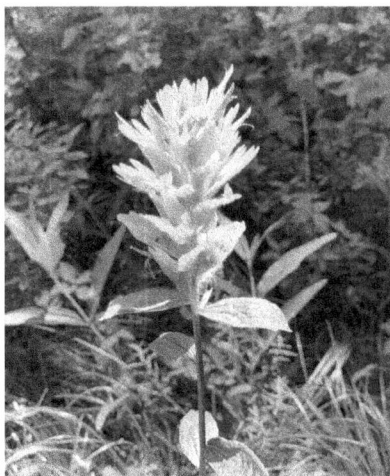

Indian Paintbrush, the Wyoming state flower, on the River Trail.

CENTRAL JH

68 CACHE CREEK MAIN TRAIL
(11.2 mi / 18 km / Easy)

Overview: A popular and easily accessible Jackson Hole trail.

Trip style: Out and back

Distance: 5.6 miles (9 km) one way, 11.2 miles (18 km) round trip

Elevation gain: 1,201 feet (366 m)

Max. Elevation: 7,661 feet (2,335 m)

Difficulty: Easy

Trailhead: Cache Creek Trailhead
43.46511°N, -110.7299°W / 43°27'54"N, -110°43'48"W
12T 0521845E 4812496N

Traffic: Heavy

Maps: Cache Cr. 7.5' USGS Topo

Notes: Respect private property boundaries and fences.

Trailhead Directions

Drive 0.6 mile (1 km) west from the Town Square on Broadway to Redmond Street. Turn right and drive 0.5 mile (0.8 km) and turn left on Cache Creek Drive. Continue 1.2 miles (2 km) on a partial dirt road to reach the main Cache Creek Trailhead.

Trailhead Facilities

Restrooms, bike rack, trash cans, picnic tables, grills, information kiosks.

Hike Description

Begin hiking at the end of the parking lot at the metal gate. The trail follows Cache Creek. It stays north of the creek for the entire distance to the Gros Ventre Wilderness Boundary.

For the first 0.4 mile (0.6 km), the trail only gains a slight amount of elevation as it moves through a lightly covered area. As the trail begins climbing, it crosses several intersecting access points with the Putt Putt, Hagen, and River Trails.

At 2.2 miles (3.5 km), the final intersection of the Putt Putt and Hagen Trail crosses the trail. At this point, the trail thins out, transforming from a wide road to a grass-lined two-track and finally winnowing down to a single-track trail. There are excellent trail markers with maps to help with navigation and distance measurements.

The Cache Creek Trail intersects the Game Creek Trail at 3.8 miles (6.1 km), continuing to gain elevation. For the next 1.8 miles (2.9 km), the trail begins slowly curving southeast as it encounters the marked Gros Ventre Wilderness Boundary with special regulations.

Follow the main Cache Creek Trail to return to the trailhead.

CACHE CREEK TRAIL

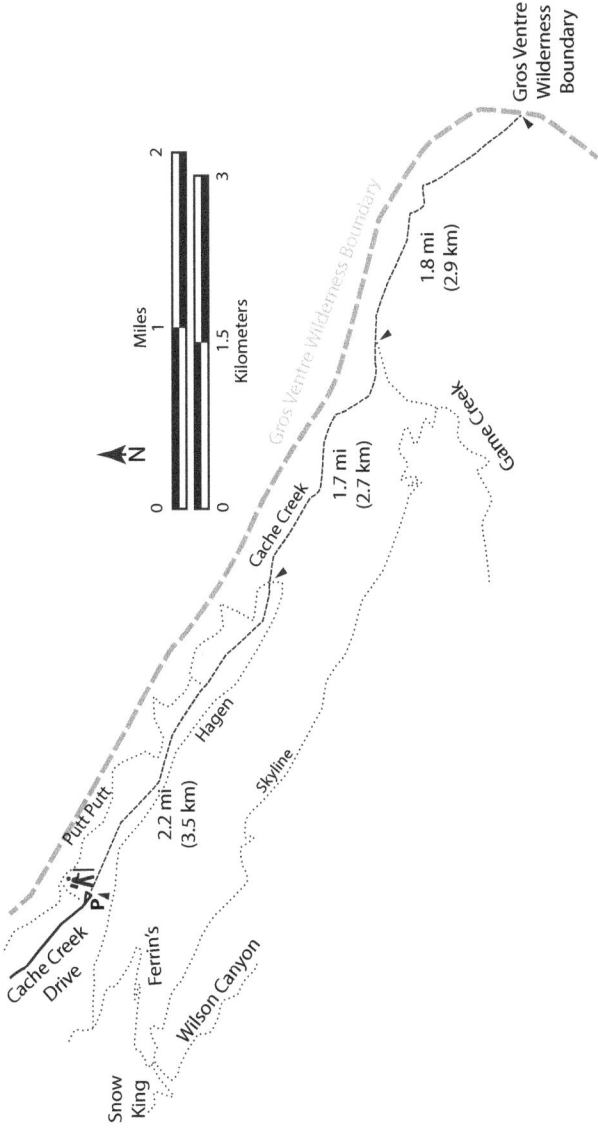

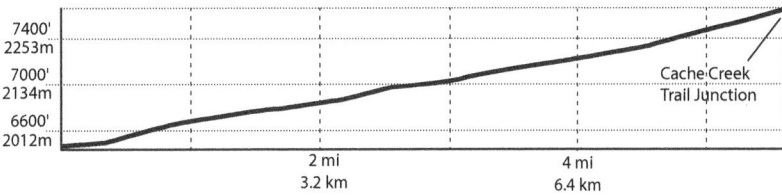

Gros Ventre Wilderness Boundary

1.8 mi (2.9 km)

Game Creek

Gros Ventre Wilderness Boundary

Cache Creek

1.7 mi (2.7 km)

Miles

Kilometers

N

Hagen

Skyline

Putt Putt

2.2 mi (3.5 km)

Cache Creek Drive

Ferrin's

Wilson Canyon

Snow King

CENTRAL JH

7400'
2253m

7000'
2134m

6600'
2012m

Cache Creek Trail Junction

2 mi
3.2 km

4 mi
6.4 km

CACHE CREEK

69 FERRIN'S TRAIL (6.2 mi / 10 km / Stren)

Overview: A quick access path to the Skyline Trail.

Trip style: Out and back

Distance: 3.1 miles (5 km) one way, 6.2 miles (10 km) round trip

Elevation gain: 1,224 feet (373 m)

Max. Elevation: 7,664 feet (2,336 m)

Difficulty: Moderate to strenuous

Trailhead: Cache Creek Trailhead
43.4651°N, -110.7299°W / 43°27'54"N, -110°43'48"W
12T 0521845E 4812496N

Traffic: Moderate

Maps: Cache Cr. 7.5' USGS Topo

Notes: Respect private property boundaries and fences.

Trailhead Directions

Drive 0.6 mile (1 km) west from the Town Square on Broadway to Redmond Street. Turn right and drive 0.5 mile (0.8 km) and turn left on Cache Creek Drive. Continue 1.2 miles (2 km) on a partial dirt road to reach the main Cache Creek Trailhead.

Trailhead Facilities

Restrooms, bike rack, trash cans, picnic tables, grills, information kiosks.

Hike Description

Walk 180 feet (54 m) west of the main parking lot and begin hiking south down a short slope to a wooden bridge over Cache Creek. This area is well-signed, so it's easy to navigate the labyrinth of trails.

Follow the sign toward the Hagen Trail and Ferrin's Trail. In 370 feet (113 m), the trail splits again.

In 0.25 mile (0.4 km), the trail splits once more with the River Trail. Follow the sign toward the Ferrin's Trail. From here, the trail begins climbing laterally up the mountain. At 1.3 miles (2.1 km), there is a junction with the Sink or Swim Trail. Turn left and continue on the Ferrin's Trail.

The trail continues southeast and then proceeds through a series of switchbacks for 1.9 miles (3 km). The forest canopy is heavy in this section and provides shade from the sun. Near the top, it breaks out into an open area at 2.8 miles (4.5 km). Shortly after, the trail tops out at the crest of the mountain on a wide ridge. This is a major junction with the Snow King Summit, Skyline, and Wilson Canyon Trails.

Proceed back down the Ferrin's Trail to return to the trailhead parking area.

FERRIN'S TRAIL

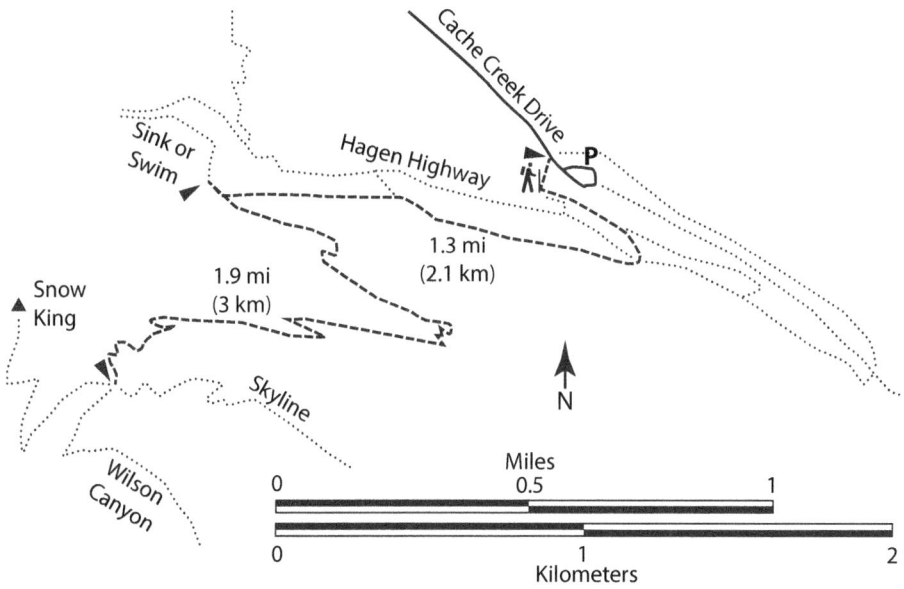

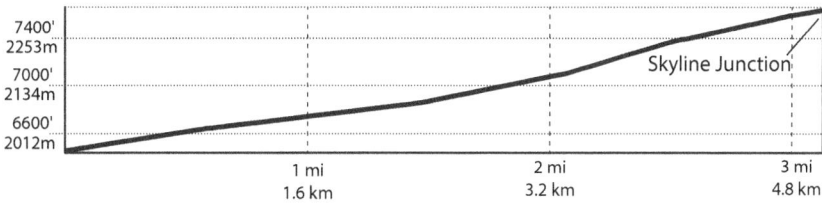

Cache Creek Drive

Sink or Swim

Hagen Highway

P

1.3 mi
(2.1 km)

1.9 mi
(3 km)

Snow
King

Skyline

N

Wilson
Canyon

Miles
0   0.5   1

0   1   2
Kilometers

CENTRAL JH

7400'
2253m

7000'
2134m   Skyline Junction

6600'
2012m

1 mi   2 mi   3 mi
1.6 km   3.2 km   4.8 km

CACHE CREEK

70 HAGEN HIGHWAY (3 mi / 4.8 km / Mod)

Overview: A popular route to the top of Snow King resort.
Trip style: Out and back
Distance: 1.5 miles (2.4 km) one way, 3 miles (4.8 km) round trip
Elevation gain: 450 feet (137 m)
Max. Elevation: 6,889 feet (2,100 m)
Difficulty: Moderate
Trailhead: Cache Creek Trailhead
43.46651°N, -110.7299°W / 43°27'54"N, -110°43'48"W
12T 0521845E 4812496N
Traffic: Moderate to heavy
Maps: Cache Cr. 7.5' USGS Topo
Notes: Watch for mountain bikes and trail runners.

Trailhead Directions

Drive 0.6 mile (1 km) west from the Town Square on Broadway to Redmond Street. Turn right and drive 0.5 mile (0.8 km) and turn left on Cache Creek Drive. Continue 1.2 miles (2 km) on a partial dirt road to reach the main Cache Creek Trailhead.

Trailhead Facilities

Restrooms, bike rack, trash cans, picnic tables, grills, information kiosks.

Hike Description

Walk 180 feet (54 m) west of the main parking lot and begin hiking south down a short slope to a wooden bridge over Cache Creek. This area is well-signed, so it's easy to navigate the labyrinth of trails.

Follow the sign toward the Hagen Trail and Ferrin's Trail. In 370 feet (113 m), the trail passes the River Trail. Walk another 470 feet (145 m) and turn right at the intersection of the Hagen Highway and the Hagen Trail. Continue on the Hagen Highway Trail.

The trail begins working its way up the face of the mountain toward Snow King Resort. The trail stays in moderate to thick tree cover for nearly the entire distance. It passes Lloyd's Cut which leads to Ferrin's Trail, then continues on to the junction of Jack's Trail.

After that, the trail does a scissor crossing with the Sink or Swim Trail and begins to travel in more open terrain. It runs parallel to Sink or Swim for 0.2 mile (0.3 km) before breaking away and heading for the top of the Rafferty Chairlift.

From here, you can return via the Hagen Highway, drop down to the Snow King Resort, or use any of the other trail crossings to return.

HAGEN HIGHWAY

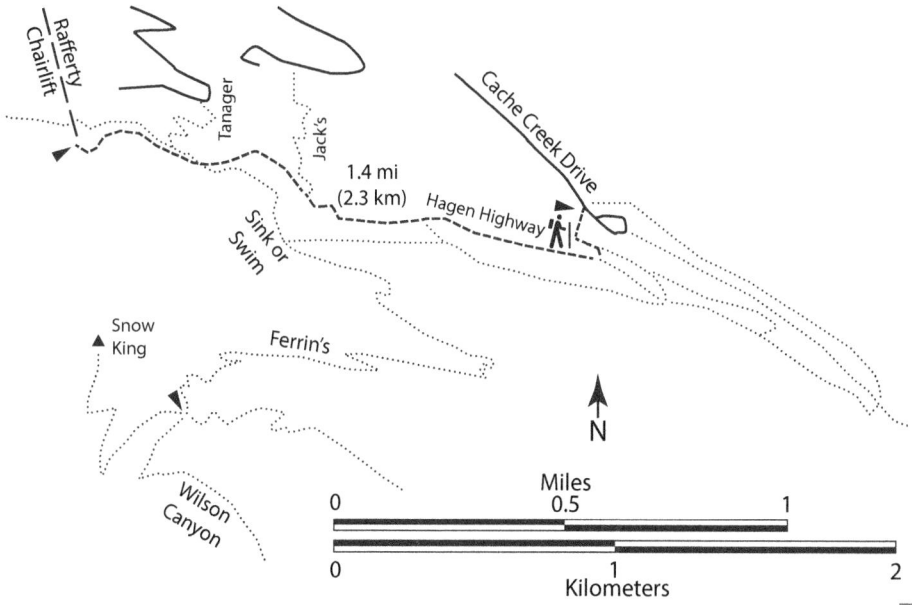

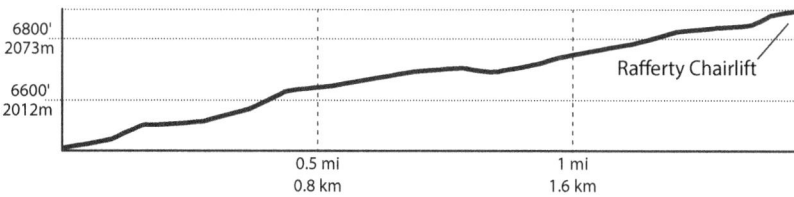

Rafferty Chairlift

Tanager

Jack's

Cache Creek Drive

1.4 mi
(2.3 km)

Hagen Highway

Sink or Swim

Snow King

Ferrin's

Wilson Canyon

N

Miles
0   0.5   1

0   1   2
Kilometers

6800'
2073m

6600'
2012m

Rafferty Chairlift

0.5 mi
0.8 km

1 mi
1.6 km

CENTRAL JH

CACHE CREEK

71 HAGEN TRAIL (5.2 mi / 8.4 km / Mod)

Overview: A popular route on the southern side of Cache Creek.

Trip style: Out and back

Distance: 2.6 miles (4.2 km) one way, 5.2 miles (8.4 km) round trip

Elevation gain: 470 feet (143 m)

Max. Elevation: 6,909 feet (2,106 m)

Difficulty: Moderate

Trailhead: Cache Creek Trailhead
43.46651°N, -110.7299°W / 43°27'54"N, -110°43'48"W
12T 0521845E 4812496N

Traffic: Heavy

Maps: Cache Cr. 7.5' USGS Topo

Notes: Watch for mountain bikes and trail runners.

Trailhead Directions

Drive 0.6 mile (1 km) west from the Town Square on Broadway to Redmond Street. Turn right and drive 0.5 mile (0.8 km) and turn left on Cache Creek Drive. Continue 1.2 miles (2 km) on a partial dirt road to reach the main Cache Creek Trailhead.

Trailhead Facilities

Restrooms, bike rack, trash cans, picnic tables, grills, information kiosks.

Hike Description

Walk 180 feet (54 m) west of the main parking lot and begin hiking south down a short slope to a wooden bridge over Cache Creek. This area is well-signed, so it's easy to navigate the labyrinth of trails.

Follow the sign toward the Hagen Trail and Ferrin's Trail. In 370 feet (113 m), the trail passes the River Trail. Walk another 470 feet (145 m) and turn left and travel 0.2 mile (0.3 km) to the intersection of the Ferrin's Trail and continue on the Hagen Trail.

In another 0.2 mile (0.3 km), the path passes by the River Trail. At 0.9 mile (1.4 km), the trail passes the first river bridge.

At 1 mile (1.6 km), the trail rapidly ascends a steep set of stairs called the Hagen Stairs. These are supported by logs and lumber to prevent erosion and make it easier to climb this short steep section.

Past here, the trail continues gaining elevation and passes two more trail junctions that cross Cache Creek. At 2.6 miles (4.2 km), the trail drops to the main Cache Creek Trail.

From here, you can return via the Hagen Trail or take the Cache Creek Trail back to the trailhead.

CENTRAL JH

HAGEN TRAIL

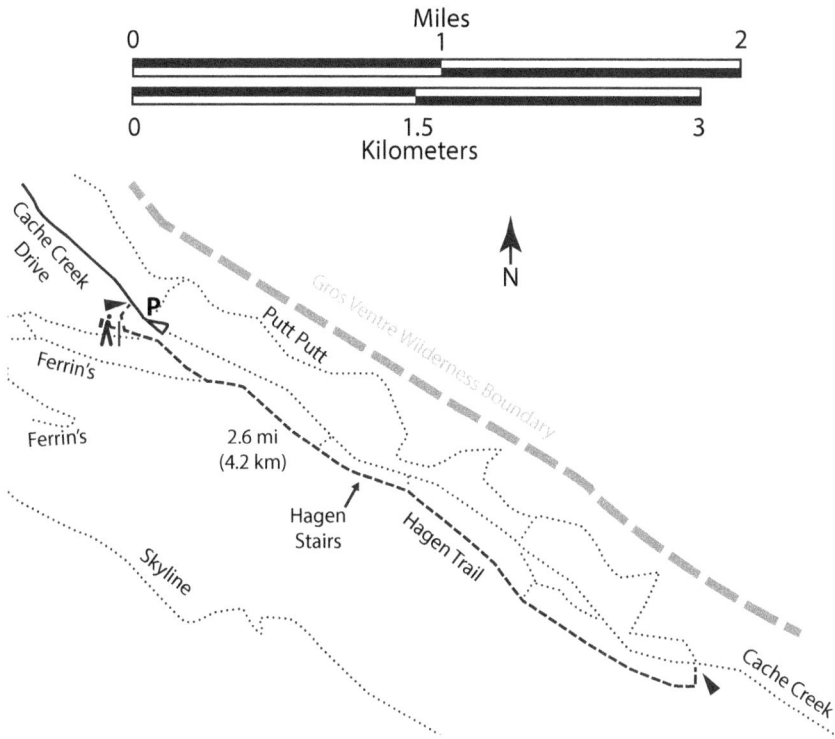

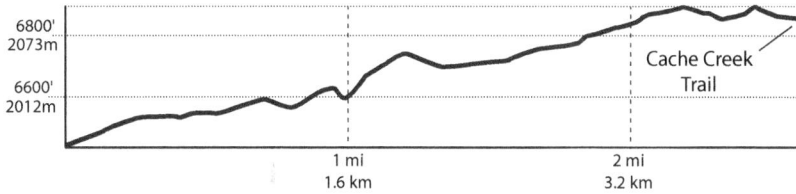

CACHE CREEK

72 RIVER TRAIL (1.4 mi / 2.2 km / Easy)

Overview: A quiet, easy route along the south bank of Cache Creek.

Trip style: Out and back

Distance: 0.7 mile (1.1 km) one way, 1.4 miles (2.2 km) round trip

Elevation gain: 117 feet (36 m)

Max. Elevation: 6,556 feet (1,998 m)

Difficulty: Easy

Trailhead: Cache Creek Trailhead
43.4651°N, -110.7299°W / 43°27'54"N, -110°43'48"W
12T 0521845E 4812496N

Traffic: Light

Maps: Cache Cr. 7.5' USGS Topo

Notes: Watch for mountain bikes and trail runners.

Trailhead Directions

Drive 0.6 mile (1 km) west from the Town Square on Broadway to Redmond Street. Turn right and drive 0.5 mile (0.8 km) and turn left on Cache Creek Drive. Continue 1.2 miles (2 km) on a partial dirt road to reach the main Cache Creek Trailhead.

Trailhead Facilities

Restrooms, bike rack, trash cans, picnic tables, grills, information kiosks.

Hike Description

Walk 180 feet (54 m) west of the main parking lot and begin hiking south down a short slope to a wooden bridge over Cache Creek. This area is well-signed, so it's easy to navigate the labyrinth of trails.

Follow the sign toward the Hagen Trail and Ferrin's Trail. In 370 feet (113 m), the trail intersects the River Trail. Turn left and continue on the trail.

At 0.2 mile (0.3 km), the River Trail intersects the Ferrin's Trail. Continue left to stay on the River Trail. The next 0.4 mile (0.6 km) continues along a shaded trail on the south edge of Cache Creek.

The trail then switches back to the west and intersects the Hagen Trail. From here, hike along the Hagen Trail to return to the trailhead and parking area.

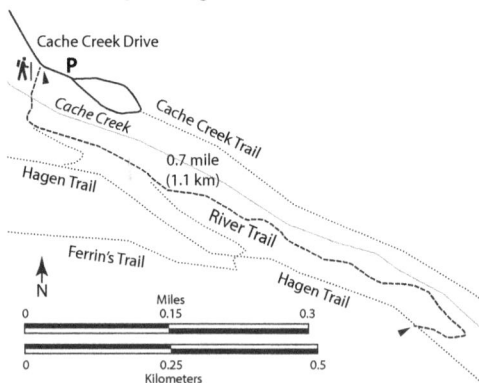

CENTRAL JH

73 SIDEWALK TRAIL (3 mi / 4.8 km / Easy)

Overview: An alternative to the Cache Creek Trail with open skies.

Trip style: Out and back

Distance: 1.5 miles (2.4 km) one way, 3 miles (4.8 km) round trip

Elevation gain: 276 feet (84 m)

Max. Elevation: 6,703 feet (2,043 feet)

Difficulty: Easy

Trailhead: Cache Creek Trailhead
43.4651°N, -110.7299°W / 43°27'54"N, -110°43'48"W
12T 0521845E 4812496N

Traffic: Heavy

Maps: Cache Cr. 7.5' USGS Topo

Notes: Watch for mountain bikes and trail runners.

Trailhead Directions

Drive 0.6 mile (1 km) west from the Town Square on Broadway to Redmond Street. Turn right and drive 0.5 mile (0.8 km) and turn left on Cache Creek Drive. Continue 1.2 miles (2 km) on a partial dirt road to reach the main Cache Creek Trailhead.

Trailhead Facilities

Restrooms, bike rack, trash cans, picnic tables, grills, information kiosks.

Hike Description

Park at the turnout prior to entering the main Cache Creek parking area. The larger turnout on the north side of the road is the primary access point for the Sidewalk Trail.

From the information kiosk, walk 190 feet (58 m) north on the path to connect with the Sidewalk Trail. Note that the trail travels west 1,000 feet (305 m) as an alternative to walking on Cache Creek Drive. Turn right and begin hiking. The trail gains elevation and begins traveling a short distance above the Cache Creek Trail as an alternative route to follow for the 1.5 miles (2.4 km) before it terminates on the Cache Creek Trail.

There are several junctions along the path to allow hikers to drop down to the main Cache Creek Trail, allowing for a variety of loops and shortcuts to be taken.

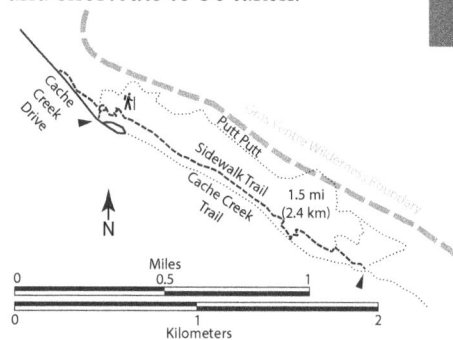

CENTRAL JH

CACHE CREEK

74 SKYLINE TRAIL LOOP (13.3 mi / 21.4 km / Stren)

Overview: A grand tour of the Cache Creek area.

Trip style: Loop

Distance: 13.3 miles (21.4 km)

Elevation gain: 1,733 feet (528 m)

Max. Elevation: 8,176 feet (2,492 m)

Difficulty: Moderate to strenuous

Trailhead: Cache Creek Trailhead
43.4651°N, -110.7299°W / 43°27'54"N, -110°43'48"W
12T 0521845E 4812496N

Traffic: Heavy on the lower trails, light on the Skyline Trail

Maps: Cache Cr. 7.5' USGS Topo

Notes: This trail has an alternative route on the ridge.

Trailhead Directions

Drive 0.6 mile (1 km) west from the Town Square on Broadway to Redmond Street. Turn right and drive 0.5 mile (0.8 km) and turn left on Cache Creek Drive. Continue 1.2 miles (2 km) on a partial dirt road to reach the main Cache Creek Trailhead.

Trailhead Facilities

Restrooms, bike rack, trash cans, picnic tables, grills, information kiosks.

Hike Description

Walk 180 feet (54 m) west of the main parking lot and begin hiking south down a short slope to a wooden bridge over Cache Creek. This area is well-signed, so it's easy to navigate the labyrinth of trails.

Follow the sign toward the Hagen Trail and Ferrin's Trail. In 370 feet (113 m), the trail splits again. In 0.25 mile (0.4 km), the trail splits once more with the River Trail. Follow the sign toward the Ferrin's Trail. From here, the trail begins to climb laterally up the mountain. At 1.3 miles (2.1 km), the trail passes the Sink or Swim Trail. Turn left and continue on the Ferrin's Trail.

The trail continues southeast and then proceeds through a series of switchbacks for 1.9 miles (3 km). The forest canopy is heavy in this section and provides shade from the sun. Near the top, it breaks out into an open area at 2.8 miles (4.5 km). Shortly after, the trail tops out at the crest of the mountain on a wide ridge at 3.2 miles (5.1 km). This is a major junction with the Snow King Summit, Skyline, and Wilson Canyon Trails.

Turn left and continue on the Skyline Trail. For the next 2 miles (3.6 km), the trail begins with a

CENTRAL JH

series of switchbacks. It then has a long, relatively straight run as it climbs the last 520 feet (173 m) to the apex of the Skyline Trail.

From this high point, several mountain ranges and prominent summits can be seen in the distance. Much of the Cache Creek drainage area, including the main trail, is visible. At this point, the main Cache Creek Trail is 0.6 mile (0.9 km) north and 1,542 feet (514 m) below the overlook.

From here, the trail continues working its way southeast, losing and then gaining elevation. At 5.8 miles (9.3 km), the trail departs the top of the ridge for the next 1.5 miles (2.4 km). The path is 0.1 mile (0.2 km) below the actual ridgeline and travels in heavy tree cover. See the Optional Skyline Route for further details on an alternate route in this section.

At 7.6 miles (12.2 km), the trail descends a series of switchbacks for 1.4 miles (2.3 km), terminating at the Game Creek Trail. Turn left (N) and hike 0.6 mile (1 km) to the main Cache Creek Trail. Turn left (W) and begin descending.

At 11.2 miles (18 km), the Cache Creek Trail intersects the Hagen and Putt Putt Trails. The trail also widens from a single trail to a double-track and then to a dirt road. Follow this path for 2.1 miles (3.3 km) to return to the Cache Creek Trailhead.

Optional Skyline Route

For the adventurous with solid off-trail navigation skills, diverting away from the trail along the section after the high point, staying on the ridgeline, is a more satisfying hike. The views are far better. This section gains an additional 330 feet (110 m) to reach the high point of 8,414 feet (2,804 m).

There is no official junction for this alternative route. The departure point is best found at 0.5 mile (0.8 km) from the high point where the trail enters heavy tree cover.

The ridgeline is surrounded by the Game Creek Trail and the Cache Creek Trail at the eastern end. The best location to reconnect is where the ridge drops to a slight saddle before rising up again at the eastern terminus of the ridgeline. The trail is visible at this point 130 feet (39 m) north of the ridgeline at the saddle. This is at 7.3 miles (11.7 km) of total travel.

CENTRAL JH

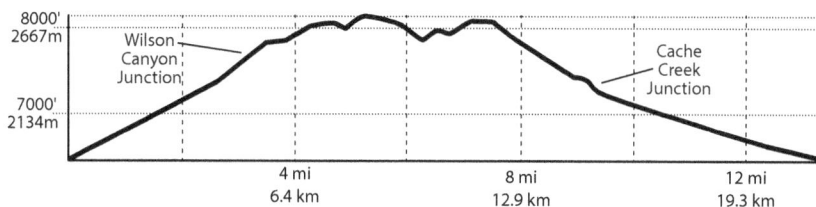

CACHE CREEK

SKYLINE TRAIL LOOP

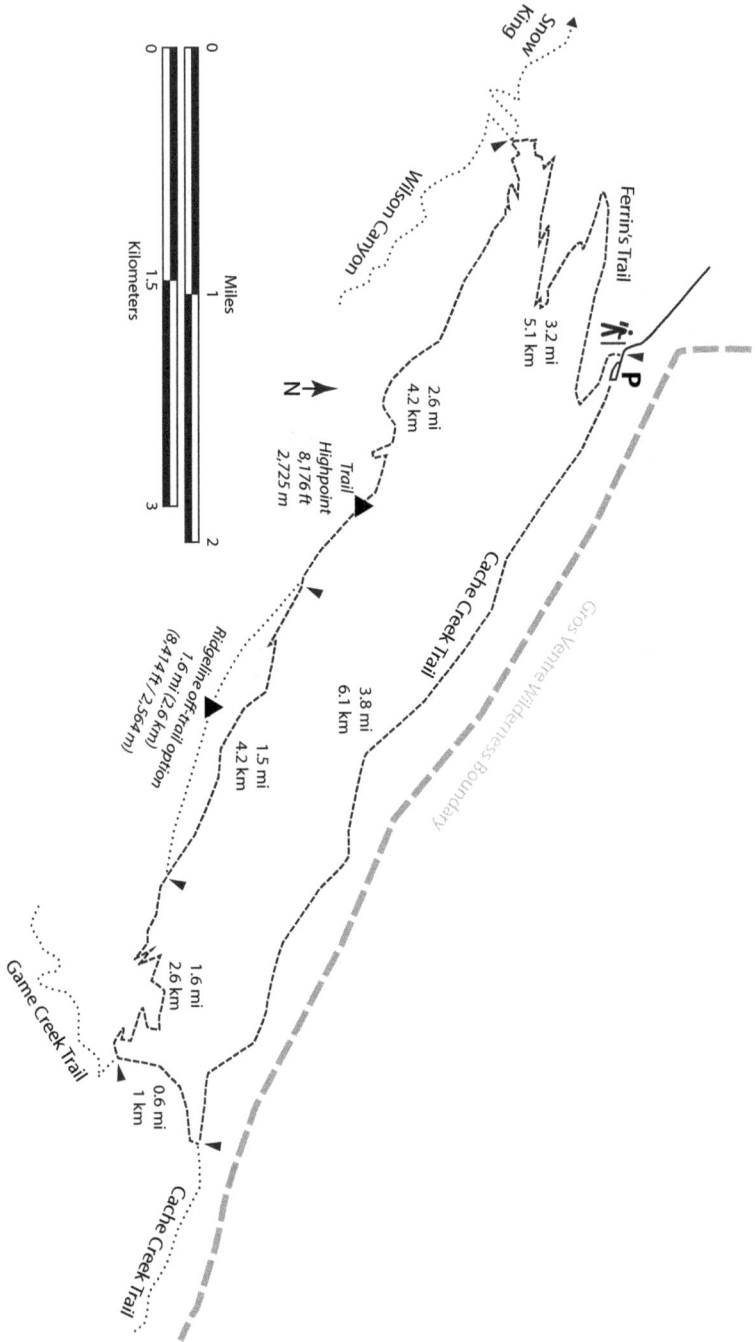

Snow King

Wilson Canyon

Ferrin's Trail

3.2 mi
5.1 km

P

2.6 mi
4.2 km

Trail
Highpoint
8,176 ft
2,725 m

Cache Creek Trail

3.8 mi
6.1 km

Ridgeline off-trail option
1.6 mi (2.6 km)
(8,414 ft / 2,564 m)

1.5 mi
4.2 km

Game Creek Trail

1.6 mi
2.6 km

Gros Ventre Wilderness Boundary

0.6 mi
1 km

Cache Creek Trail

N

0   0
Miles   1
Kilometers
1.5
3   2

CACHE CREEK

Nelson Trailhead

The Nelson Trailhead is the alternative access point to several of the Cache Creek hikes. Somewhat hidden in the east Jackson neighborhoods, this trailhead is an excellent starting point for several easy and a few extremely strenuous hikes in the area.

This is also a popular starting point for mountain bikers and dog walkers alike. If you don't have a lot of time and want a simple hike that takes hardly any effort, check out the Nelson Knoll hike. This easy short loop will gain you a quick view of east Jackson and the National Elk Refuge with little effort.

For something more serious, consider Crystal Butte or the Woods Canyon to Crystal Butte loop. These two hikes are some of the most extremely strenuous contained in this book. They are both incredibly steep and challenging for even the most seasoned hikers who want to burn their quads.

From Crystal Butte, Jackson, Snow King, and Teton Pass are visible.

NELSON TRAILHEAD

75 CRYSTAL BUTTE (5 mi / 8 km / Ex Stren)

Overview: A steep hike with expansive views of central Jackson Hole.

Trip style: Out and back

Distance: 2.5 miles (4 km) one way, 5 miles (8 km) round trip

Elevation gain: 2,228 feet (679 m)

Max. Elevation: 8,583 feet (2,616 m)

Difficulty: Extremely Strenuous

Trailhead: Nelson Trailhead
43.4765°N, -110.7408°W / 43°28'35"N, -110°44'27"W
12T 0520964E 4813761N

Traffic: Moderate

Maps: Cache Cr. 7.5' USGS Topo

Notes: Steep exposed, loose, dusty trail with no water.

Trailhead Directions

Drive 0.9 mile (1.4 km) east on Broadway from the Town Square. Turn right on Nelson Drive, then continue 0.2 mile (0.3 km) and take the left (SE) fork of the road. Drive 360 feet (109 m) to the Nelson Drive Trailhead parking lot.

Trailhead Facilities

Information kiosk.

Hike Description

Start at the south trailhead and walk south 250 feet (76 m) and take the left fork marked Woods Canyon Trail. Walk 0.2 mile (0.3 km) through a small patch of trees and mostly open terrain to the junction for the Crystal Lite Trail.

Continue past here for another 0.2 mile (0.3 km) to reach the Crystal Butte Trail. Signage has changed over the years and the trail may not be marked. Turn left and begin working your way up the Crystal Butte Trail. The trail rapidly gains elevation from here.

The first effective shade on the trail is in 0.4 mile (0.6 km) after gaining 440 feet (134 m) of steep climbing. At 0.9 mile (1.4 km), the trail switchbacks several times before a long southeast run.

At 1.5 miles (2.4 km), the trail turns northeast and continues for 0.9 mile (1.4 km) to the apex of the trail. The last short distance over the lip of the top may be difficult to follow depending on the time of year with plant cover.

The trail continues for 0.1 mile (0.2 km) before disappearing into heavy plant cover. Return down the same path to the Nelson Trailhead. Hiking poles are recommended for the steep descent, as the surface is loose and dusty.

CRYSTAL BUTTE

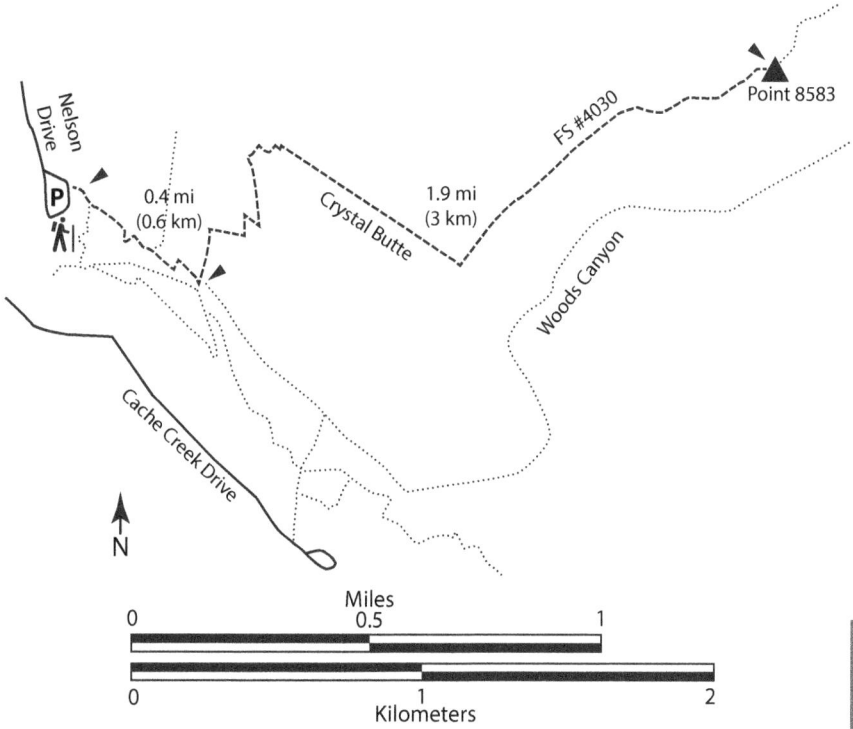

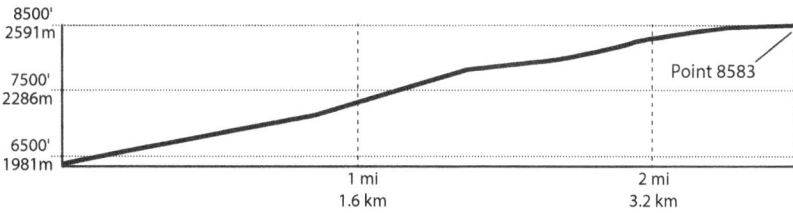

Nelson Drive

P

0.4 mi
(0.6 km)

Crystal Butte

1.9 mi
(3 km)

FS #4030

Point 8583

Woods Canyon

Cache Creek Drive

N

Miles
0   0.5   1

0   1   2
Kilometers

8500'
2591m

7500'
2286m

6500'
1981m

Point 8583

1 mi
1.6 km

2 mi
3.2 km

NELSON TRAILHEAD

76 CRYSTAL LITE (1.2 mi / 2 km / Stren)

Overview: A steep hike with views of central Jackson.

Trip style: Out and back

Distance: 0.6 mile (1 km) one way, 1.2 miles (2 km) round trip

Elevation gain: 441 feet (134 m)

Max. Elevation: 6,788 feet (2,069 m)

Difficulty: Strenuous

Trailhead: Nelson Trailhead
43.4765°N, -110.7408°W / 43°28'35"N, -110°44'27"W
12T 0520964E 4813761N

Traffic: Moderate

Maps: Cache Cr. 7.5' USGS Topo

Notes: Steep exposed, loose, dusty trail with no water.

Trailhead Directions

Drive 0.9 mile (1.4 km) east on Broadway from the Town Square. Turn right on Nelson Drive, then continue 0.2 mile (0.3 km) and take the left (SE) fork of the road. Drive 360 feet (109 m) to the Nelson Drive Trailhead parking lot.

Trailhead Facilities

Information kiosk.

Hike Description

Start at the south trailhead and walk south 250 feet (76 m) and take the left fork marked Woods Canyon Trail. Walk 0.2 mile (0.3 km) through a small patch of trees and mostly open terrain to the junction for the Crystal Lite Trail.

Continue hiking up the slight draw for 0.3 mile (0.5 km) to reach the top of the Crystal Lite Trail. There is no shade along this part of the trail. Return to the trailhead along the same path.

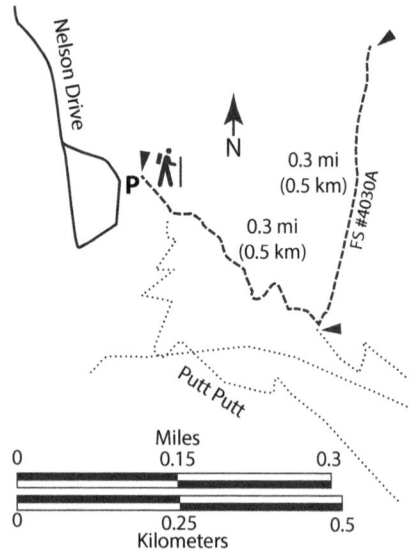

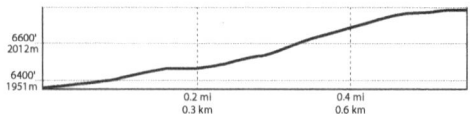

77 NELSON KNOLL (0.6 mi / 1 km / Easy)

Overview: An easy hike with a view of the Elk Refuge and Jackson.

Trip style: Loop

Distance: 0.6 mile (1 km)

Elevation gain: 121 feet (37 m)

Max. Elevation: 6,469 feet (1,972 m)

Difficulty: Easy

Trailhead: Nelson Trailhead
43.4765°N, -110.7408°W / 43°28'35"N, -110°44'27"W
12T 0520964E 4813761N

Traffic: Moderate

Maps: Cache Cr. 7.5' USGS Topo

Trailhead Directions

Drive 0.9 mile (1.4 km) east on Broadway from the Town Square. Turn right on Nelson Drive, then continue 0.2 mile (0.3 km) and take the left (SE) fork of the road. Drive 360 feet (109 m) to the Nelson Drive Trailhead parking lot.

Trailhead Facilities

Information kiosk.

Hike Description

Start at the north trailhead in the Nelson Drive parking lot and begin hiking up the trail that curves left (W) and works its way up the knoll and around in a clockwise direction. There are two main switchbacks on the way up this short, pleasant hike.

At the top lip of the knoll, hikers are presented with three options for completing the next 0.2 mile (0.3 km). The left route will take you along the path with the best views of Jackson and the Elk Refuge. Also, there are benches near the first split. At the second split, the trail switchbacks once and drops down to a dirt access road near the Elk Refuge fence. Return to the trailhead on the dirt road.

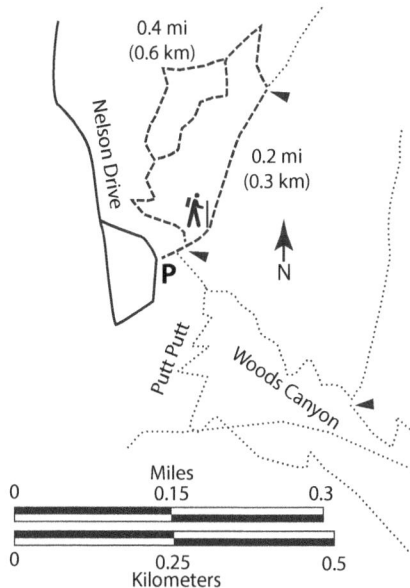

CENTRAL JH

NELSON TRAILHEAD

~~~~~~

78 PUTT PUTT AND TOWN OVERLOOK
(8.8 mi / 14.2 km / Mod)

~~~~~~

Overview: A busy multi-use path along the north side of Cache Creek.

Trip style: Out and back

Distance: 4.4 miles (7.1 km) one way, 8.8 miles (14. 2 km) round trip

Elevation gain: 717 feet (219 m)

Max. Elevation: 7,065 feet (2,153 m)

Difficulty: Moderate

Trailhead: Nelson Trailhead
43.4765°N, -110.7408°W / 43°28'35"N, -110°44'27"W
12T 0520964E 4813761N

Traffic: Heavy

Maps: Cache Cr. 7.5' USGS Topo

Notes: Bike and stock animal traffic on this route.

Trailhead Directions

Drive 0.9 mile (1.4 km) east on Broadway from the Town Square. Turn right on Nelson Drive, then continue 0.2 mile (0.3 km) and take the left (SE) fork of the road. Drive 360 feet (109 m) to the Nelson Drive trailhead parking lot.

Trailhead Facilities

Information kiosk.

Hike Description

Start at the south trailhead and walk south 250 feet (76 m) and take the right fork labeled Putt Putt. The path passes an old building then proceeds to switchback up a path covered in aspens. From here, it continues in open ground southwest, then switchbacks twice to gain elevation. At the second switchback, there is a town overlook bench. This is a good stopping point for those who want a short hike with a view.

From here, the trail travels 0.6 mile (1 km) to the first junction which leads to the Cache Creek Trailhead. The next section switchbacks through a grove of aspens as it gains elevation, then breaks out into open terrain for 1 mile (1.6 km) to the Wiggle Cutoff Trail that leads to the Sidewalk and Cache Creek Trails.

For the next 0.4 mile (0.6 km), the trail moves in and out of tree cover until it reaches the Salt Lick Cutoff Trail. It then switchbacks twice and passes a westbound trail. It then passes the Serengeti Trail Cutoff at 3.2 miles (5.1 km).

The next 1.3 miles (2.1 km) meanders up and down the hill, then crosses over a seasonal creek. The path then parallels the Cache Creek Trail and finally merges with the Cache Creek Trail at 4.2 miles (6.8 km).

From here, you can return via the Putt Putt or take the Cache Creek Trail back to the trailhead. The Cache Creek route is substantially faster and shorter. If you take this return route, travel to the Cache Creek Trailhead, then take the Woods Canyon connector trail to the Putt Putt. Then, follow the Putt Putt back to the Nelson Trailhead.

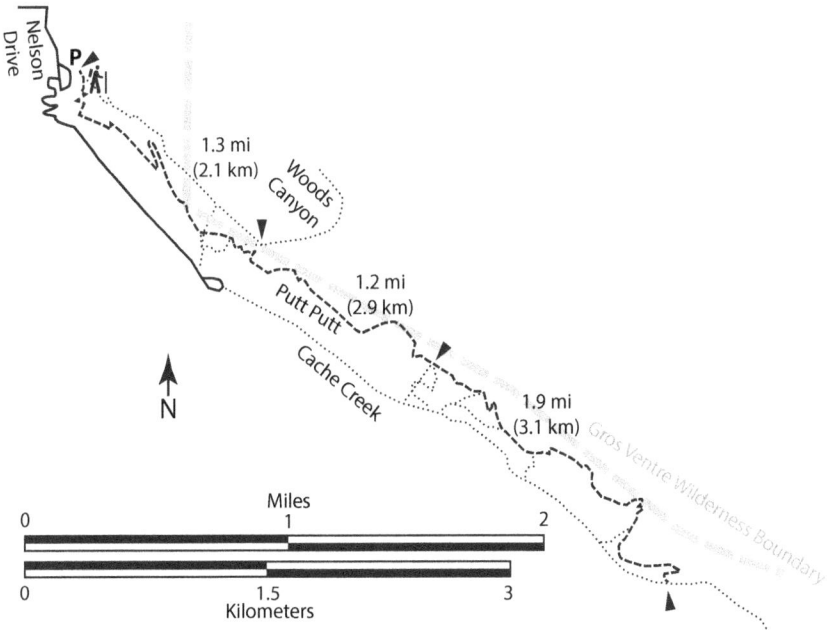

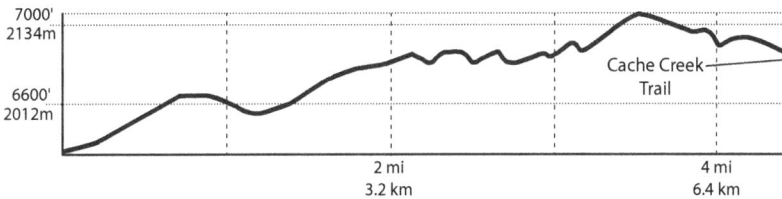

CENTRAL JH

NELSON TRAILHEAD

79 WOODS CANYON TO CRYSTAL BUTTE LOOP (5.6 mi / 9 km / Ex Stren)

Overview: A steep canyon hike with off-trail travel.

Trip style: Loop

Distance: 5.6 miles (9 km)

Elevation gain: 2,230 feet (680 m) total gain/loss

Max. Elevation: 8,583 feet (2,616 m)

Difficulty: Extremely Strenuous

Trailhead: Nelson Trailhead
43.4765°N, -110.7408°W / 43°28'35"N, -110°44'27"W
12T 0520964E 4813761N

Traffic: Light

Maps: Cache Cr. 7.5' USGS Topo

Notes: Off-trail navigation required.

Trailhead Directions

Drive 0.9 mile (1.4 km) east on Broadway from the Town Square. Turn right on Nelson Drive, then continue 0.2 mile (0.3 km) and take the left (SE) fork of the road. Drive 360 feet (109 m) to the Nelson Drive Trailhead parking lot.

Trailhead Facilities

Information kiosk.

Hike Description

Start at the south trailhead and walk south 250 feet (76 m) and take the left fork marked Woods Canyon Trail. Walk 0.2 mile (0.3 km) through a small patch of trees and mostly open terrain to the junction for the Crystal Lite Trail.

Continue past here for another 0.2 mile (0.3 km) to reach the Crystal Butte Trail. Continue on the Woods Canyon Trail for another 0.6 mile (1 km) to reach the Woods Canyon junction that splits into the canyon. Turn left, up the hill, and continue following the trail.

For the next 1.8 miles (2.9 km), the trail follows a tightly enclosed canyon with heavy tree cover and brush. This trail is lightly traveled, so parts of the trail are partly overgrown.

At the 2.6-mile (4.2 km) point, the trail begins working its way up the north side of the canyon. This section is steep, rough, and narrow. The trail does crumble in a few sections. In 0.2 mile (0.3 km), the trail fully disappears in the undergrowth.

From here, take a bearing of 280° true north and begin walking through the open field toward a stand of trees for 300 feet (91 m). At the wall of trees, continue on this bearing for 600 feet (183 m)

CENTRAL JH

through the trees into a large, open clearing. Once in the clearing, adjust your bearing to 270° true north and continue for another 600 feet (183 m) until you cross the trail. It is overgrown and is challenging to find in the plant growth. Continue following the edge of the ridge toward the lip of the butte.

Find point 8583 at these coordinates if you cannot find the trail:

43.4800°N, -110.7113°W
43°28'48"N, -110°42'41"W
12T 0523349E 4814164N

Once you connect with the trail, begin working your way down the Crystal Butte Trail. This path loses 1,930 feet (588 m) over 1.8 miles (3 km) where it reconnects with the Woods Canyon Trail. Turn right and continue for 0.4 mile (0.6 km) to reach the Nelson Trailhead.

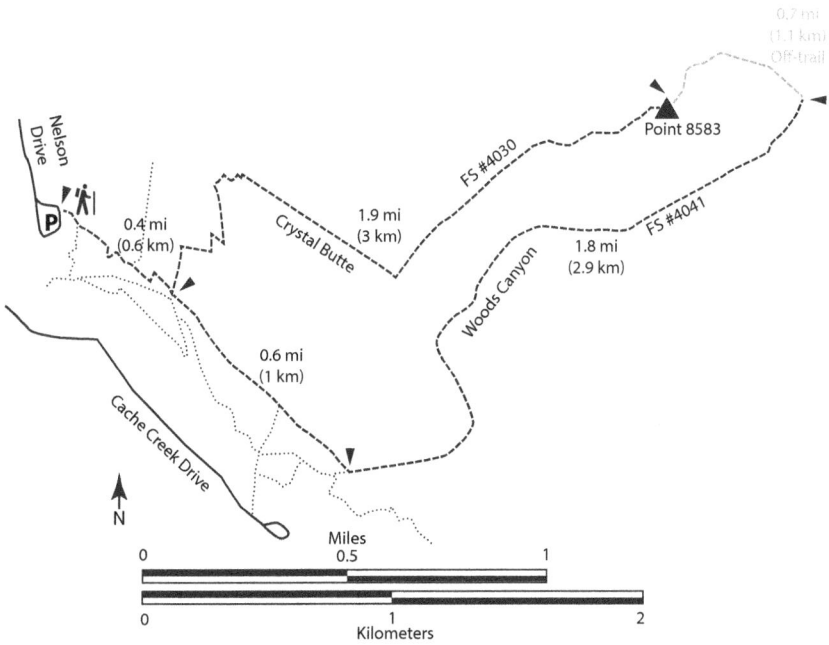

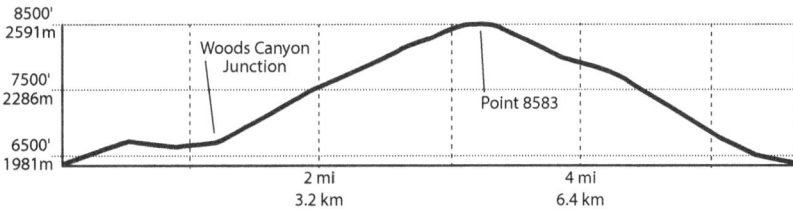

NELSON TRAILHEAD

South Central Jackson

The South Central hiking zone of Central Jackson sounds like it is a location from a big city. It is anything but that. This lightly hiked area contains several gems that only locals visit and few visitors are even aware of.

A few of the hikes in this section are quite easy and one is nearly flat. The South Park Loop can be handled by virtually anyone, as it has an elevation gain and loss of a mere 42 feet (13 m). It is a pleasant walk through the southern elk feed grounds of the town before re-entering the hills and mountains at the south end of the valley.

Contrast that hike with the Lower Valley Energy Ridge hike. This extremely strenuous hike is on few if any maps. It is not an official trail, and it will test your muscles and joints to their absolute limit. If you want to try climbing something steep to earn expansive views, this worthwhile hike is one of the toughest in this book. Hikers will earn their hiking badge on this one.

Kayaker enjoying South Park on Flat Creek.

Panoramic view from Lower Valley Energy Ridge above Wilson Canyon (center, left), with southern Jackson Hole and Munger Mountain in view (right).

CENTRAL JH

80 GAME CREEK TO CACHE CREEK SHUTTLE (9.8 mi / 15.8 km / Mod)

Overview:	A tour of two central Jackson backcountry trails.
Trip style:	Shuttle
Distance:	9.8 miles (15.8 km)
Elevation gain:	1,581 feet (482 m) / 1,256 feet (383 m) gain/loss
Max. Elevation:	7,445 feet (2,269 m)
Difficulty:	Moderate
Trailhead:	Game Creek Trailhead 43.3939°N, -110.7289°W / 43°23'38"N, -110°43'44"W 12T 0521957E 4804596N
Traffic:	Light
Maps:	Jackson, Cache Cr. 7.5' USGS Topos
Notes:	Watch for mountain bikers and stock traffic.

Trailhead Directions

Drive 7.8 miles (12.5 km) from the Town Square west on Broadway as it turns south on US 26 / US 89 / US 189 / US 191 to Game Creek. Turn left across the highway, then drive 1 mile (1.6 km) to the Game Creek Trailhead parking.

Trailhead Facilities

Information sign.

Hike Description

Start at the trailhead parking area and walk toward the northeast trailhead and start on the wide trail, often a two-track dirt road. This is an old forest service road to the beaver ponds.

Travel east on the trail for the first 0.7 mile (1.1 km). From here, the trail begins curving north. It stays to the left (W) of the large forested area, following the Game Creek drainage. The path crosses several seasonal tributaries of Game Creek. These will be dry later in the season and are not a problem to cross if water is still flowing.

At 1.5 miles (2.4 km), a trail splits from the two-track. It wiggles east and west, then reconnects in 0.2 mile (0.3 km) to the main two-track trail. The path then stays to the east of a marshy area for 0.25 mile (0.4 km) before the trail splits again.

Either route will take you 0.9 mile (1.4 km) to where the trails reconnect. The two-track (Beaver Ponds Loop) follows the west side of Game Creek and the single-track trail stays to the east of the creek. The two-track tends to have more bike traffic. A wooden bridge reconnects the end of the two-track with the trail. This is where the two-track disappears into the undergrowth.

From here, follow the trail another 0.3 mile (0.5 km) to where the West Game Creek Trail splits left (W) from the Game Creek Trail. This option will take you 3.2 miles (5.1 km) west to connect with the Wilson Canyon Trail. Otherwise, continue north.

The trail turns east and continues following Game Creek as it tracks between the ridgeline mountain to the left (W) and the forested area to the right (E). The elevation gain becomes more intense, gaining 760 feet (232 m) over the next 2.2 miles (3.6 km). At 5.4 miles (8.7 km), the Skyline Trail terminates at the Game Creek Trail. Continue working your way north over the rise. The trail then rapidly drops down to intersect with the Cache Creek Trail.

Turn left (W) and continue on the Cache Creek Trail. In 1.7 miles (2.7 km), the Hagen and Putt Putt Trails intersect the Cache Creek Trail. At this point, the trail widens substantially as it continues to lose elevation. Continue on the wide trail for 2.1 miles (3.4 km) to reach the Cache Creek Trailhead.

Completing the Shuttle

Arrange a pickup, leave a separate vehicle, or lock a bike at the Cache Creek Trailhead parking lot. You will travel from the Cache Creek Trailhead to Cache Creek Drive. Turn right on Redmond Street and then left on Broadway to reach the Town Square. From here, follow the trailhead directions section of this hike to complete the shuttle trip.

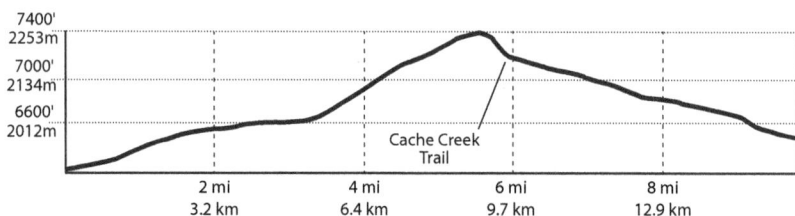

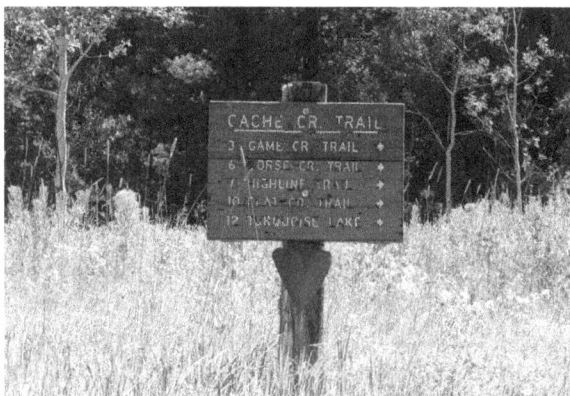

A sign along the Cache Creek Trail after departing Game Creek.

GAME CREEK TO CACHE CREEK SHUTTLE

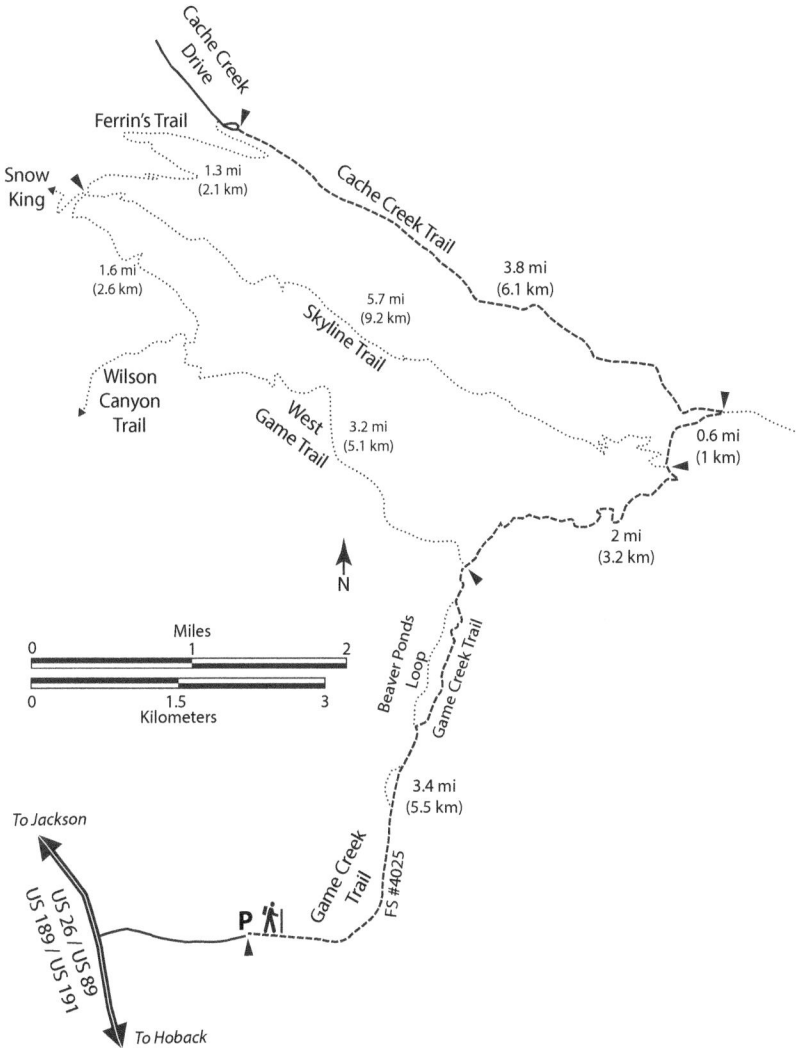

Cache Creek Drive

Ferrin's Trail

Snow King

1.3 mi (2.1 km)

Cache Creek Trail

Snow King

1.6 mi (2.6 km)

3.8 mi (6.1 km)

5.7 mi (9.2 km)

Skyline Trail

Wilson Canyon Trail

West Game Trail

3.2 mi (5.1 km)

0.6 mi (1 km)

N

2 mi (3.2 km)

Miles
0   1   2

0   1.5   3
Kilometers

Beaver Ponds Loop

Game Creek Trail

3.4 mi (5.5 km)

To Jackson

US 26 / US 89
US 189 / US 191

P

Game Creek Trail

FS #4025

To Hoback

SOUTH CENTRAL JACKSON

81 LOWER VALLEY ENERGY RIDGE
(2.4 mi / 3.9 km / Ex Stren)

Overview: A steep, tough hike with expansive views of the valley.

Trip style: Loop

Distance: 2.4 miles (3.9 km)

Elevation gain: 1,352 feet (412 m)

Max. Elevation: 7,499 feet (2,286 m)

Difficulty: Extremely strenuous

Trailhead: Wilson Canyon Trailhead at Lower Valley Energy
43.4218°N, -110.7746°W / 43°25'18"N, -110°46'29"W
12T 0518246E 4807680N

Traffic: Light to none

Maps: Jackson 7.5' USGS Topo

Notes: Steep, rugged, slippery trail. Trekking poles are helpful.

Trailhead Directions

Drive 5.3 miles (8.5 km) from the Town Square west on Broadway as it turns south on US 26 / US 89 / US 189 / US 191 to the Lower Valley Energy parking lot. Turn left across the highway, then drive straight back to the northeast corner of the parking lot.

Trailhead Facilities

None.

Hike Description

Start hiking on the trail to the north of the power substation to the trail fence with information signs. Continue for another 130 feet (40 m), then turn left (N) at the first trail junction. Follow the winding trail under the power lines at 0.15 mile (0.25 km) where the trail begins working its way up the steep face of the slope.

By 0.3 mile (0.5 km), the trail be-gins a series of steep switchbacks headed for the large rock outcrop-ping. It is easy to lose the trail, as it is steep. At 0.4 mile (0.6 km), the trail passes under and to the left (N) of the rock outcrop, then con-tinues above it, and then abruptly turns right (E).

At this point, the trail mostly dis-appears. Switchback for the next 260 feet (79 m) of elevation gain toward the ridge. Turn right (SE) to make the climb easier. The path is tough and crumbly.

At the top of the ridge, there will be a well-traveled trail. Turn left (N) and continue for 0.5 mile (0.8 km), gaining an additional 266 feet (81 M). Several limestone out-crops make for good stairs. Along this part of the route, you will lose a little elevation, only to regain it until you reach the top of the ridge. At this point, there is a trail leading

CENTRAL JH

east, down the hill which leads to the Adams Canyon Trail, the Leeks Canyon Trail, and the Wilson Canyon Trail.

From here, turn around and begin your descent along the ridge. Once you reach the point you originally connected to the ridge, you will see an obvious trail carved into the top of the ridge heading south. Follow this path for an easier hike to the lower elevation.

The trail works its way steeply down the ridge to a rock outcropping and cluster of trees, then turns slightly to the right as the next section of trail becomes visible. The path slowly curves to the right (W) as it begins working its way toward the Wilson Canyon Trail on the slight rise above the wide grassy area.

Turn right and follow the Wilson Canyon Trail. This will lead you 0.3 mile (0.5 km) back to the trailhead fence and the parking lot.

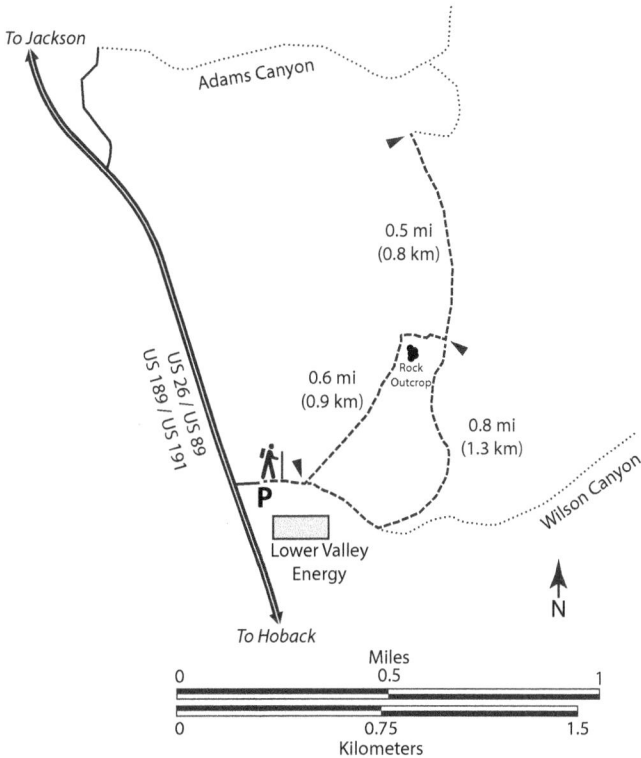

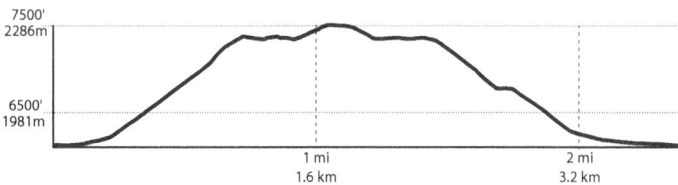

SOUTH CENTRAL JACKSON

82 SOUTH PARK LOOP (1.4 mi / 2.3 km / Easy)

Overview: A pleasant stroll through the southern elk feedgrounds.
Trip style: Loop
Distance: 1.4 miles (2.3 km)
Elevation gain: +/- 42 feet (13 m)
Max. Elevation: 5,984 feet (1,824 m)
Difficulty: Easy
Trailhead: South Park West Trailhead
43.3990°N, -110.7707°W / 43°23'57"N, -110°46'14"W
12T 0518569E 4805155N
Traffic: Light
Maps: Jackson 7.5' USGS Topo

Trailhead Directions

Drive 7.2 miles (11.6 km) from the Town Square west on Broadway as it turns south on US 26 / US 89 / US 189 / US 191 to South Park Feedgrounds Road on the west side of the highway. The turn is 380 feet (116 m) past the Teton County landfill transfer station. After turning right on the road, drive 1 mile (1.6 km) to the end of the road at the hay storage buildings.

Trailhead Facilities

Information sign.

Hike Description

Start the hike by crossing the large bridge over Flat Creek. At the junction, continue straight (S) along the path into the open field. At 0.3 mile (0.5 km), the trail enters the open grove of cottonwood trees and intersects the dirt road at 0.4 mile (0.7 km).

Turn right (W) and continue 0.4 mile (0.7 km) to a junction. Turn right and continue for 0.5 mile (0.8 km) to return to the trailhead.

CENTRAL JH

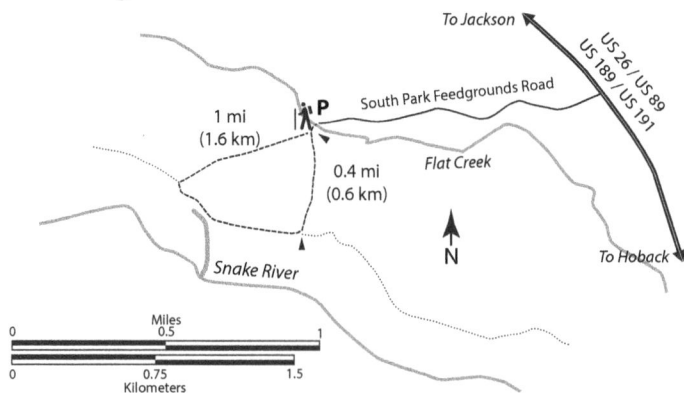

SOUTH CENTRAL JACKSON

83 WILSON CANYON TO SNOW KING SHUTTLE (7.5 mi / 12.1 km / Mod)

Overview: A tour of south Jackson Hole canyon areas.

Trip style: Shuttle

Distance: 7.5 miles (12.1 km)

Elevation gain: 1,735 feet (529 m)

Max. Elevation: 7,887 feet (2,404 m)

Difficulty: Moderate

Trailhead: Wilson Canyon Trailhead at Lower Valley Energy
43.4218°N, -110.7746°W / 43°25'18"N, -110°46'29"W
12T 0518246E 4807680N

Traffic: Light

Maps: Jackson, Cache Cr. 7.5' USGS Topo

Trailhead Directions

Drive 5.3 miles (8.5 km) from the Town Square west on Broadway as it turns south on US 26 / US 89 / US 189 / US 191 to the Lower Valley Energy parking lot. Turn left across the highway, then drive straight back to the northeast corner of the parking lot.

Trailhead Facilities

None.

Hike Description

Start hiking on the trail to the north of the power substation to the trail fence with information signs. Follow the trail as it curves toward the mouth of the canyon through the grass field. At 1 mile (1.6 km), the trail passes a large, crumbling limestone cliff.

In 600 feet (188 m) past the cliff, the trail curves left (N) and continues on, steeply gaining elevation. Cresting the hill at 1.7 miles (2.7 km), you will pass a decaying wooden dam from old Jackson Hole days.

From here, continue 1 mile (1.6 km) to an open, slightly marshy grass field as the canyon gives way to an open area. Bypass the lightly overgrown trails to the left and continue walking for another 0.6 mile (1 km).

Here, the trail intersects the West Game Trail. Turn left and continue on the Wilson Canyon Trail. This path curves north and then northwest. It continues to gently gain elevation as it works toward Snow King.

As the trail works its way toward the ridge, it maneuvers in and out of tree cover. At 4.7 miles (7.6 km), the trail turns sharply northeast, working its way up a steepening ridge to intersect the Skyline Trail.

Turn left (W) and follow a series of long switchbacks as the trail

CENTRAL JH

crests the ridge that leads to the antenna towers at the summit of Snow King. Drop northwest down the trail toward the resort chairlift.

Once the trail intersects the summit trail, turn right and begin working your way down the main, wide trail. Follow this heavily-traveled path to the base of the mountain at the parking lot. From here, catch a ride or take a bike back to the Wilson Canyon Trailhead.

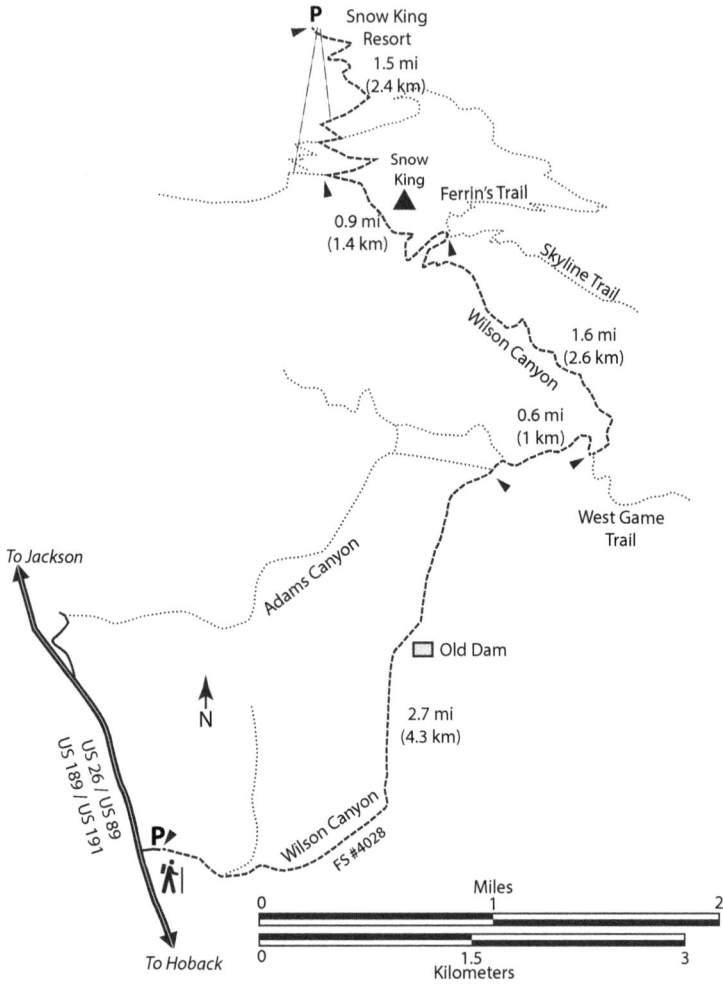

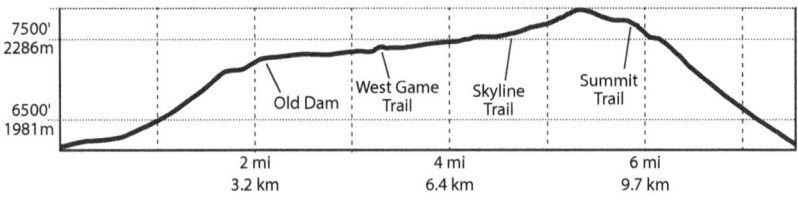

SOUTH CENTRAL JACKSON

TETON PASS

Teton Pass has defined Jackson and Jackson Hole for over a century. This hiking area contains a popular backcountry ski area as well as a destination for mountain bikers (MTB) from all over the west. MTB riders travel to the Jackson Hole area to experience the trails in and around Teton Pass.

The famously steep modern 10% grade is not nearly as steep as the Old Pass Road. Though closed to traffic, hikers, dog walkers, and bike riders can enjoy this paved roadway all the way to the pass. It was once said that the road was so curvy and steep that you could see your own tail lights as you drove over the hill.

The modern road is still notorious for inexperienced drivers burning up their brakes. The smell is unmistakable as it wafts through the air at Hungry Jacks in Wilson. Downshift when descending the road.

The Teton Pass hiking area is divided into two main hiking zones, The Pass and Wilson. The nature of the geography of the area dictates lumping together several distinct and varied hiking areas.

The Pass area contains multiple hikes on either side and on top of Teton Pass. The terrain is varied, from easy to extremely strenuous.

Wilson is at the eastern base of the pass and is home to some of the richest and most famous people in the entire world. Most of their homes are tucked away in the hills and are often referred to as cabins in the woods. These mansions are not simple log cabins nestled in the wilderness.

The sign on Teton Pass pointing the way for visitors to Jackson.

TETON PASS AREA HIKES

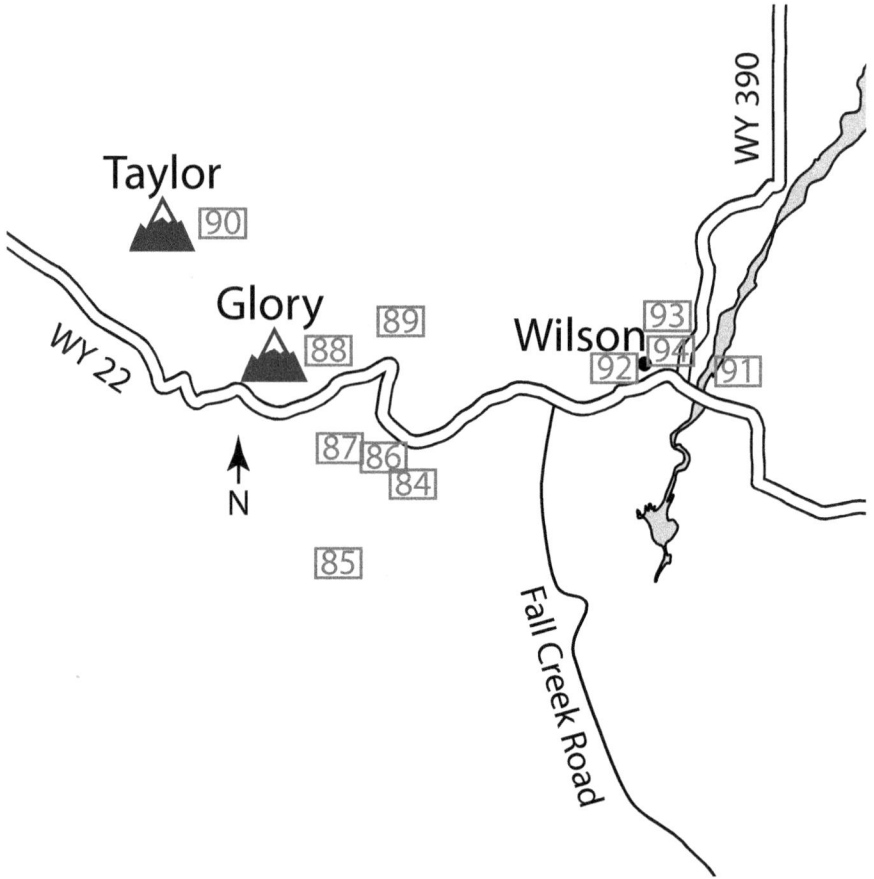

The Pass

84. Big Rocks Loop
85. Black Canyon
86. Crater Trail to Old Pass Road
87. History Trail
88. Mount Glory
89. Ski Lake
90. Taylor Mountain

Wilson

91. Dike Trail via Emily Stevens Park
92. Owen Bircher Wetland Trail
93. Rendezvous Park
94. Wilson Elementary Loop

TETON PASS

The Pass

The actual pass road, commonly called "The Pass" by locals, passes over an elevation of 8,431 feet (2,570 m) on a paved roadway. The original pass a century ago passed over this point, then diverged along the southern side of the current roadway on the eastern side of the mountain.

Eventually, a paved pass road was put in to replace the old wagon road. This reduced travel time from days between Jackson and Victor to less than an hour. However, the Old Pass Road was unpleasantly steep and curvy for vehicles longer than a passenger car.

Eventually, a new road was constructed that "only" has a grade of 10%. It is still incredibly steep by any standard. The smell of burned brakes is all too common for people unfamiliar with downshifting their vehicle on a road this steep.

The advantage of the access afforded to outdoor lovers by the pass is immediately apparent. High elevation with higher-still terrain abounds in this area. The variety of trail options is perfect for any hiker.

Courtesy of Randy Isaacson

Coal Creek near Taylor Mountain.

TETON PASS

84 BIG ROCKS LOOP (2.5 mi / 4 km / Mod)

Overview: A short hike through a hidden bouldering area for climbers.
Trip style: Loop
Distance: 2.5 miles (4 km)
Elevation gain: 613 feet (187 m)
Max. Elevation: 7,106 feet (2,166 m)
Difficulty: Easy to moderate
Trailhead: Old Pass Road
43.4919°N, -110.9081°W / 43°29'31"N, -110°54'29"W
12T 0507430E 4815446N
Traffic: Light
Maps: Teton Pass 7.5' USGS Topo

Trailhead Directions

Drive 1.5 miles (2.4 km) west from the Town Square on Broadway to Highway 22 and turn right (N). Continue 6.6 miles (10.6 km), passing through Wilson, and turn left (SW) on Old Pass Road. Drive 0.9 mile (1.4 km) to the end of the road.

Trailhead Facilities

Information kiosk.

Hike Description

Start hiking on the south trail to the left of the information kiosk. The trail crosses Trail Creek, then splits at a junction. Take the right trail fork past the old mill equipment. Then, in 160 feet (49 m), continue straight, past the History Trail junction.

The Big Rocks Trail begins gaining elevation as it continues south. It curves right (W) and travels through heavy tree cover. At 0.9 mile (1.4 km), the trail switchbacks to the left where it passes the first large rock. In 0.1 mile (0.2 km), the trail passes two substantially larger boulders. At 1.2 miles (1.9 km), the path passes the Lithium Trail, then begins losing elevation. At 1.5 miles (2.4 km) it passes by the Black Canyon overlook. This is an excellent viewpoint to rest before making your way down the trail.

The trail then proceeds down several moderate switchbacks and intersects the Black Rock Trail. Turn left and continue losing elevation for 0.6 mile (1 km) where it intersects the lower part of the Lithium Trail.

The trail then enters the open field where it reconnects with the beginning of the Big Rocks Trail at the old mill equipment. From here, continue along the same path over Trail Creek to return to the parking lot.

TETON PASS

BIG ROCKS LOOP

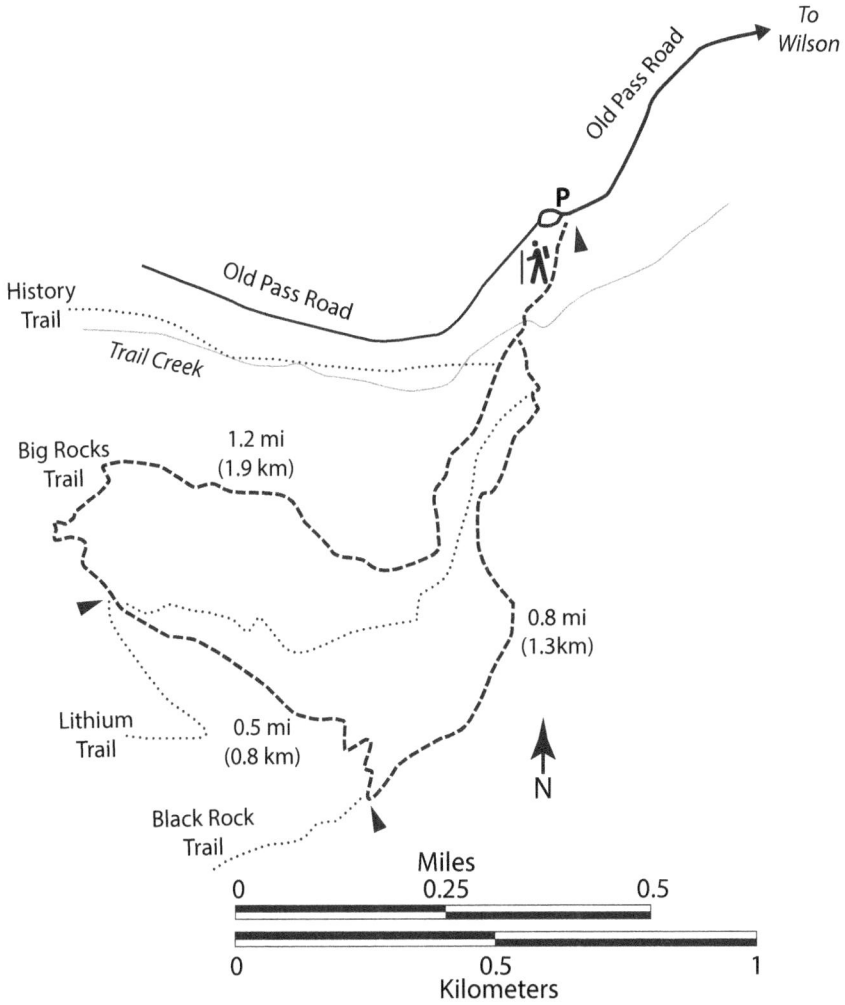

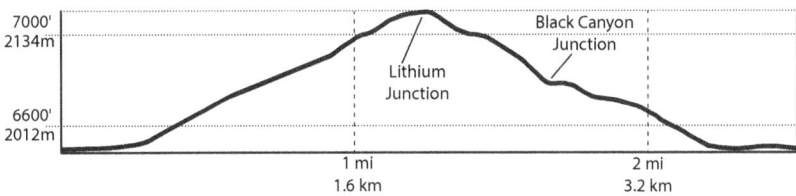

To
Wilson

Old Pass Road

P

Old Pass Road

History
Trail

Trail Creek

Big Rocks
Trail

1.2 mi
(1.9 km)

0.8 mi
(1.3km)

Lithium
Trail

0.5 mi
(0.8 km)

N

Black Rock
Trail

Miles
| 0 | 0.25 | 0.5 |

| 0 | 0.5 | 1 |
Kilometers

7000'
2134m

Black Canyon
Junction

Lithium
Junction

6600'
2012m

1 mi
1.6 km

2 mi
3.2 km

THE PASS

TETON PASS

85 BLACK CANYON (7 mi / 11.2 km / Mod)

Overview: A shuttle hike into a stunning broad canyon on Teton Pass.
Trip style: Shuttle
Distance: 7 miles (11.2 km)
Elevation gain: 742 feet (226 m) gain, 2,749 feet (838 m) loss
Max. Elevation: 9,252 feet (2,820 m)
Difficulty: Moderate
Trailhead: Teton Pass
43.4973°N, -110.9553°W / 43°29'50"N, -110°57'19"W
12T 0503610E 4816040N
Traffic: Light to moderate
Maps: Teton Pass 7.5' USGS Topo
Notes: Expect mountain bike traffic. Trekking poles are helpful.

Trailhead Directions

Drive 1.5 miles (2.4 km) west from the Town Square on Broadway to Highway 22 and turn right (N). Continue 10.7 miles (17.3 km), passing through Wilson, and up Teton Pass. Park on the left (S) in the broad parking lot.

Trailhead Facilities

Information kiosk.

Hike Description

Start hiking from the western end of the parking lot on the dirt service road and walk around the closed steel gate. The road switchbacks towards a series of antennas to a viewpoint on the edge of the ridge at 0.3 mile (0.5 km).

Alternate Start: Begin at the east parking lot trail that climbs up the exposed face of the hill. The path wanders around a slight bulge in the ridge, then turns right and heads for the antenna towers at 0.5 mile (0.8 km). This route is more scenic but more exposed and longer than the service road on the west side of the ridge.

Continue for the next 1.4 miles (2.3 km) as the trail works its way up the face of the bowl with one set of switchbacks in tree cover. At 1.5 miles (2.4 km), take a short walk on the stub trail to the expansive overlook with sweeping views of the east side of Teton Pass.

At 1.7 miles (2.7 km), the Lithium Trail (mountain bike only) branches off from the trail and heads downhill. In another short 0.1 mile (0.2 km), there is a junction to Mt. Ely, a short 0.2 mile (0.3 km) worthwhile walk to the overlook at Mt. Ely. There are remnants

TETON PASS

of a rock campfire ring and logs pulled together for hikers who enjoy the evenings.

From here, the trail enters dramatically into Black Canyon, as the trail is visible from the ridge. It drops down a series of switchbacks, rapidly descending. The trail passes through patches of trees until it enters heavy forest cover at 4 miles (6.4 km). Be mindful of your footing, as the trail has deep ruts from bike traffic at steep drop-offs and sharp switchback corners.

From here, the trail stays in tree cover as it connects with the Big Rocks Trail Loop at 6 miles (9.7 km). Continue on the path into the open grassy area with the rusting remnants of an old mill operation.

Follow the well-traveled trail over a wooden bridge over Trail Creek to the Old Pass Road parking lot. From here, take Old Pass Road to WY 22, then make your way back up to the top of Teton Pass.

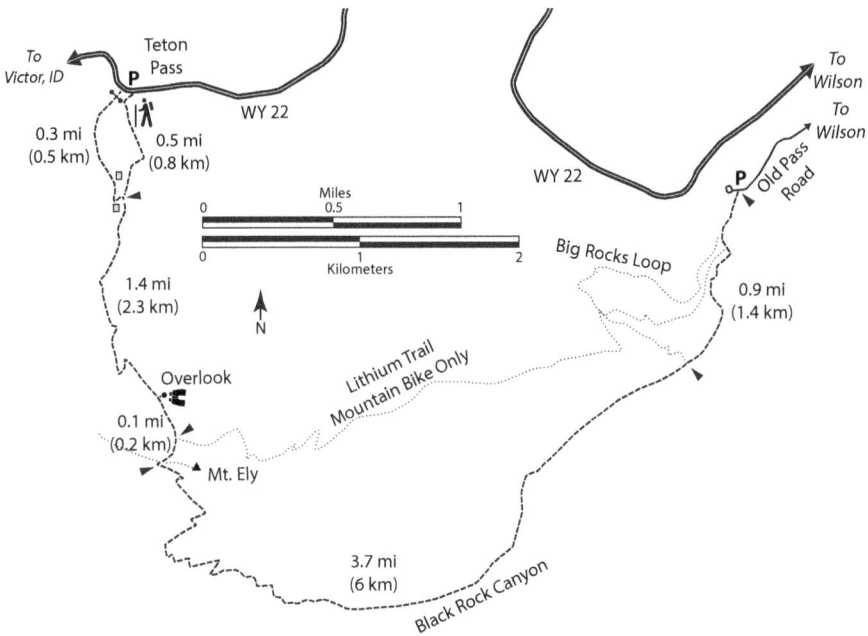

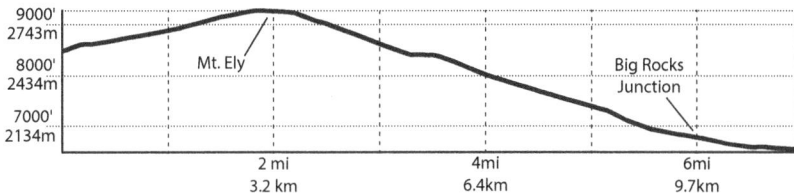

THE PASS

86 CRATER TRAIL TO OLD PASS ROAD
(3 mi / 4.8 km / Mod)

Overview: A short trail alternative to reach Crater Lake.

Trip style: Out and back

Distance: 1.5 miles (2.4 km) one way, 3 miles (4.8 km) round trip

Elevation gain: 679 feet (207 m) gain

Max. Elevation: 7,189 feet (2,191 m)

Difficulty: Moderate

Trailhead: Teton Pass
43.4973°N, -110.9553°W / 43°29'50"N, -110°57'19"W
12T 0503610E 4816040N

Traffic: Moderate

Maps: Teton Pass 7.5' USGS Topo

Trailhead Directions

Drive 1.5 miles (2.4 km) west from the Town Square on Broadway to Highway 22 and turn right (N). Continue 6.6 miles (10.6 km), passing through Wilson, and turn left (SW) on Old Pass Road. Drive 0.9 mile (1.4 km) to the end of the road.

Trailhead Facilities

Information kiosk.

Hike Description

Start hiking from the southern trailhead to the left of the information kiosk. Walk 50 feet (15 m) and take the Crater Trail junction to the right (W). The trail parallels the Old Pass Road, sometimes coming within a few feet/meters of the roadbed.

At 0.3 mile (0.5 km), the trail curves to the right (W) and turns northwest. At 1 mile (1.6 km), the trail comes within a short distance of the History Trail and crosses the North Fork of Trail Creek.

At 1.5 miles (2.4 km), the trail turns right (N) and intersects the History to Crater Trail connector. In 800 feet (244 m), the trail intersects the paved Old Pass Road. Turn right to reach Crater Lake. Return via the road for an easy walk.

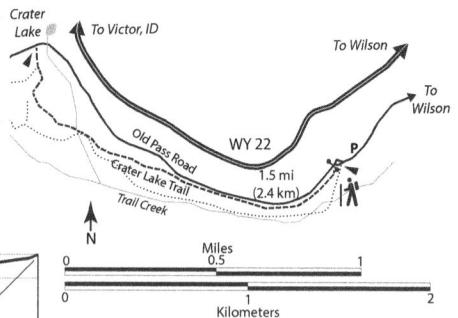

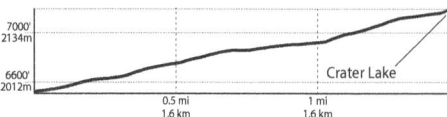

87 HISTORY TRAIL (4 mi / 6.4 km / Stren)

Overview: A hike along the historic Old Pass Route.

Trip style: Out and back

Distance: 4 miles (6.4 km)

Elevation gain: 1,916 feet (584 m)

Max. Elevation: 8,422 feet (2,567 m)

Difficulty: Strenuous

Trailhead: Old Pass Road
43.4919°N, -110.9081°W / 43°29'31"N, -110°54'29"W
12T 0507430E 4815446N

Traffic: Moderate

Maps: Teton Pass 7.5' USGS Topo

Trailhead Directions

Drive 1.5 miles (2.4 km) west from the Town Square on Broadway to Highway 22 and turn right (N). Continue 6.6 miles (10.6 km), passing through Wilson, and turn left (SW) on Old Pass Road. Drive 0.9 mile (1.4 km) to the end of the road.

Trailhead Facilities

Information kiosk.

Hike Description

Start hiking on the south trail to the left of the information kiosk. The trail crosses Trail Creek, then splits at a junction. Take the right fork past the old mill equipment. Then, in 160 feet (49 m), take the branch marked History Trail. It passes an information kiosk giving you ideas of historical points of interest.

The trail enters a thick tree and vegetation-covered area as it fol-lows Trail Creek up. At 0.5 mile (0.8 km), there is a tasty patch of raspberries when in season.

At 1 mile (1.6 km), the trail passes near the Crater Trail. At 1.3 miles (2.1 km), there is a signed junction to Crater Lake. The trail continues climbing, then abruptly turns north and intersects a short trail to the Old Pass Road.

From here, the trail curves around the landscape and works its way up into a more open area. At 2.9 miles (4.7 km), the trail begins working its way up a series of switchbacks. This continuous gain in elevation feels steeper in the exposed terrain.

The last switchback cuts across the hill below WY 22. It then intersects the Teton Pass parking lot at the eastern end with large rocks to rest on. Return via the same path or catch a ride back down to the Old Pass Road.

TETON PASS

HISTORY TRAIL

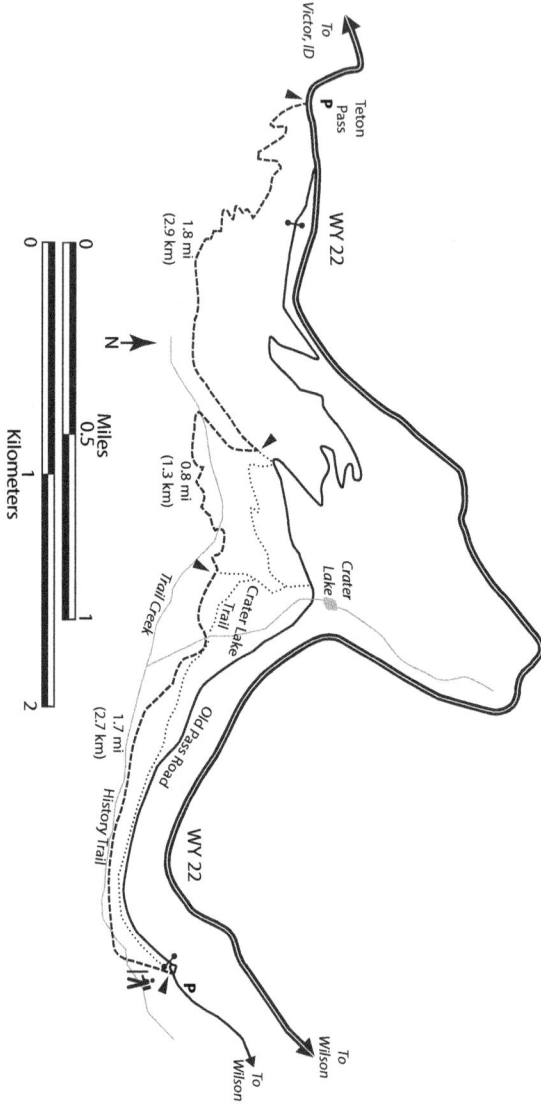

To Victor, ID

Teton Pass
P

WY 22

1.8 mi (2.9 km)

0.8 mi (1.3 km)

N

0
Miles
0.5
1
Kilometers
2

Crater Lake

Trail Creek

Crater Lake Trail

1.7 mi (2.7 km)

Old Pass Road

History Trail

WY 22

P

To Wilson

To Wilson

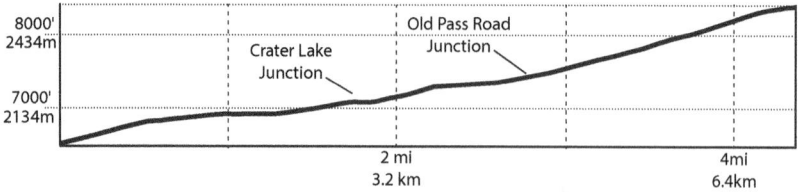

8000'
2434m

7000'
2134m

Crater Lake Junction

Old Pass Road Junction

2 mi
3.2 km

4mi
6.4km

THE PASS

TETON PASS

88 MOUNT GLORY (1.6 mi / 2.8 km / Ex Stren)

Overview: A quick, steep hike to over 10,000 feet (3,048 m) with views.
Trip style: Out and back
Distance: 0.8 mile (1.4 km) one way, 1.6 miles (2.8 km) round trip
Elevation gain: 1,649 feet (503 m)
Max. Elevation: 10,086 feet (3,074 m)
Difficulty: Extremely strenuous
Trailhead: Teton Pass
43.4973°N, -110.9553°W / 43°29'50"N, -110°57'19"W
12T 0503610E 4816040N
Traffic: Light to moderate
Maps: Teton Pass, Rendezvous Peak 7.5' USGS Topos
Notes: Trekking poles are helpful for this slippery trail.

Trailhead Directions

Drive 1.5 miles (2.4 km) west from the Town Square on Broadway to Highway 22 and turn right (N). Continue 10.7 miles (17.3 km), passing through Wilson, and up Teton Pass. Park on the left (S) in the broad parking lot.

Trailhead Facilities

None.

Hike Description

Cross the highway to the north side of the pass where the obvious trail is cut into the hillside. Pass the skier avalanche beacon safety sign and follow the trail as it rapidly ascends the mountain. There are minor switchbacks at a few of the rock outcrops on the way up.

At 0.7 mile (1.1 km), 9,844 feet (3,000 m), the large metal tower appears over the trail. From here, pass under it and ascend the trail as it continues over a slightly flat area before making the final ascent to the summit.

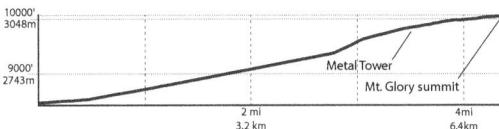

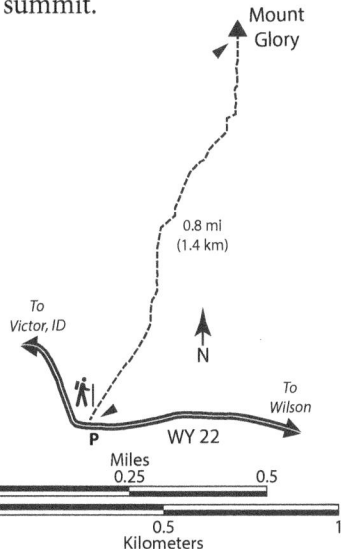

89 SKI LAKE (4.2 mi / 6.6 km / Mod)

Overview: A pleasant hike to a small lake at the base of a broad ridge.

Trip style: Out and back

Distance: 2.1 miles (3.3 km) one way, 4.2 miles (6.6 km) round trip

Elevation gain: 1,038 feet (316 m)

Max. Elevation: 8,661 feet (2,640 m)

Difficulty: Moderate

Trailhead: Phillips Canyon Trailhead
43.5052°N, -110.9273°W / 43°30'19"N, -110°55'38"W
12T 0505877E 4816926N

Traffic: Moderate

Maps: Teton Pass 7.5' USGS Topo

Trailhead Directions

Drive 1.5 miles (2.4 km) west from the Town Square on Broadway to Highway 22 and turn right (N). Continue 9.5 miles (15.3 km) and park at the Phillips Canyon parking area.

Trailhead Facilities

None.

Hike Description

Start hiking on the dirt road heading north and uphill on the two-track for 0.2 mile (0.3 km). Take the left fork to the Ski Lake Trail.

The single trail parallels the road for 0.8 mile (1.3 km) and then turns north. It enters a tree-covered area at 1 mile (1.6 km), then exits in 500 feet (152 m).

At 1.2 miles (1.9 km), the trail splits at the Phillips Pass Trail. Stay left and continue northwest, gaining elevation. In another 0.9 mile

(1.4 km), the trail reaches Ski Lake.

To reach the ridge for expansive views, hike another 1.5 miles (2.4 km), gaining another 1,000 feet (305 m). Return on the same trail.

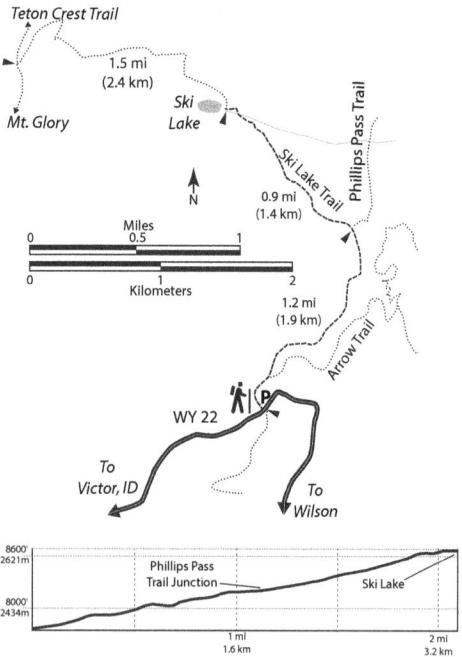

90 TAYLOR MOUNTAIN (8.8 mi / 14.2 km / Stren)

Overview A summit hike with Jackson Hole and Teton Valley views.

Trip style: Out and back

Distance: 4.4 miles (7.1 km) one way, 8.8 miles (14.2 km) round trip

Elev. gain/loss: 3,097 ft. (943 m)

Max. Elevation: 10,351 ft. (2,555 m)

Difficulty: Strenuous

Trailhead: Coal Creek Trailhead
43.5102°N, -110.9862°W / 43°30'37"N, -110°59'10"W
12T 0501117E 4817476N

Traffic: Light to moderate

Maps: Rendezvous Peak 7.5' USGS Topo

Trailhead Directions

Drive 1.5 miles (2.4 km) west from the Town Square on Broadway to Highway 22 and turn right (N). Continue 13.3 miles (21.4 km) through Wilson and over Teton Pass, then park in the large parking area to the right (N) side of WY 22 at the Coal Creek Trailhead.

Trailhead Facilities

Information kiosk.

Hike Description

The trail travels through tall vegetation with insects for the first half of the hike. Dress and protect yourself appropriately.

The hike starts at the west edge of the parking lot near the wilderness information kiosk. Walk on the trail toward the bridge over Coal Creek and cross it. The trail turns north and begins working its way through a shaded forest. You will encounter the wooden Jedediah Smith Wilderness sign in 0.5 mile (0.8 km).

After you cross the wilderness boundary, the trail curves east for 0.4 mile (0.6 km), then turns north along the east-facing slope and rapidly rises above Coal Creek. From here the trail departs the conifer tree cover and is exposed to the sun. There are a series of rises and flatter areas with tall vegetation.

At 1.2 miles (1.9 km), you reach an easy crossing of Coal Creek over a spread of logs and large branches. From there, the trail switchbacks to the west-facing slope of the valley in a mixed stand of conifers and aspen trees.

After one steep slope, you will come over a rise into a large meadow area with shorter and different plants than the previous open areas. At 2 miles (3.3 km), you will cross a dry creek. The trail will switchback

TETON PASS

through a tree-covered section. It travels up a short, steep section, leading to a second, larger, flatter meadow with short grasses and flowers in the middle of summer.

The trail crosses a small snow-melt creek. This is the last water access on the trail. At 2.5 miles (4 km), take the left fork that splits the Coal-Mesquite Trail (labeled 040) and the Taylor Mountain Trail (labeled 037).

As you work your way up a series of steep switchbacks and level areas, you will encounter one flat area with two sink holes that may be collapsed caves in the limestone. The rock piles to the south are home to pika—listen for their distinctive chirp.

At 3 miles (4.8 km), the trail switchbacks to the east for 900 feet (280 m) before turning northwest toward the summit ridge. There is a thin covering of conifers offering a few shady spots for a rest.

Above here, there is no substan-tial tree cover for protection from weather. The soil turns red from iron deposits as you reach the saddle where Teton Valley in Idaho becomes visible at 3.5 miles (6.4 km).

After the saddle, the trail deteriorates to broken rock in 1,000 feet (324 m), becoming indistinct and intermittent. Continue on the top of the ridge to a rocky false summit.

From here, the true summit is another 0.5 mile (740 m) to the southwest, approximately a 20-minute walk. Continue on the top of the ridge on the gray limestone which offers easy walking. Avoid the trail to the east of the ridge, as short sections are exposed to drop-offs.

The final rocky slope to the summit has a steep drop-off on the west side of the ridge. The summit is reached after a final, short steep climb up broken rock. Several summits are visible including Glory Mountain, Sheep Mountain, and the Grand Teton. Return down the same route.

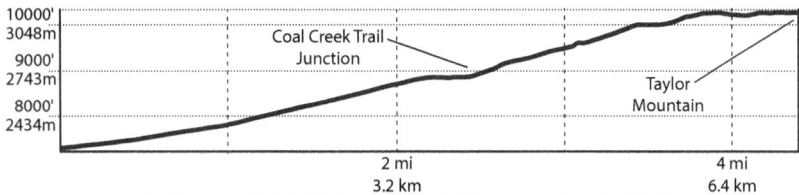

The summit of Taylor Mountain with summer rain showers passing over southern Jackson Hole.

TAYLOR MOUNTAIN

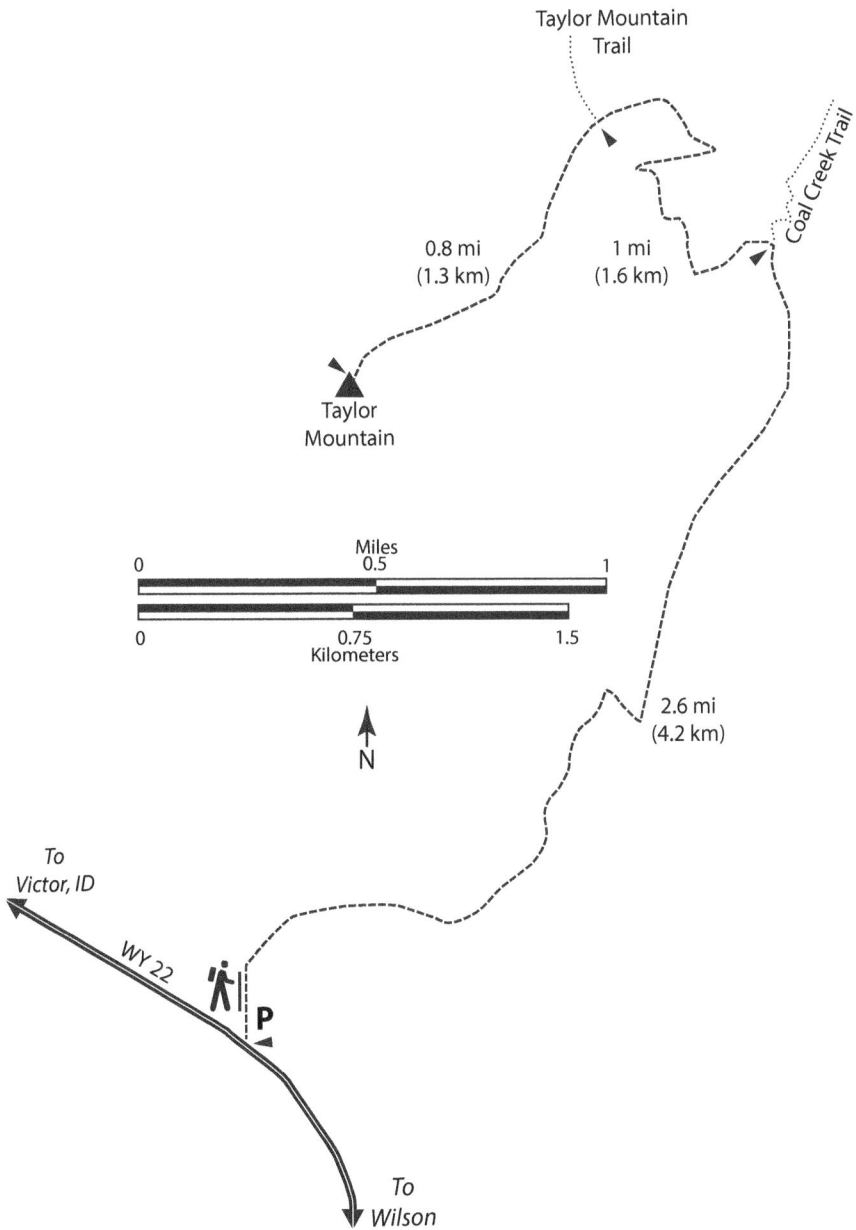

Taylor Mountain
Trail

Coal Creek Trail

0.8 mi
(1.3 km)

1 mi
(1.6 km)

Taylor
Mountain

Miles
0   0.5   1

0   0.75   1.5
Kilometers

N

2.6 mi
(4.2 km)

To
Victor, ID

WY 22

P

To
Wilson

THE PASS

Wilson

The small town of Wilson may not have a large population (1,482 as of 2010) but it makes up for it in adventure access and property prices. Some of the most famous and richest people in the world have homes in and around the town of Wilson, also referred to as the West Bank (of the Snake River).

Wilson is unique in that all of the hikes represented in this area are easy and most are disabled-friendly. All are family-friendly, even for young children. This collection of trails allows anyone to experience the outdoors without feeling like they need to conquer the Grand Teton. This hiking area also has one of the shortest hikes in this book.

The Owen Bircher Wetland Trail is unique in the area. It is the only short boardwalk trail in this book dedicated to wetland wildlife rather than the larger, more common wildlife of the region.

One unique offering is Rendezvous Park. This collection of trails is easy for anyone to follow. Becoming lost is essentially impossible. The availability of several ponds to play in is a huge draw for families, too.

Mileage marker on the dike along the Snake River, accessible from the Emily Stevens Park.

91 DIKE TRAIL VIA EMILY STEVENS PARK
(4.4 mi / 7 km / Easy)

Overview: A highly popular flat hike along the Snake River.

Trip style: Out and back

Distance: 2.2 miles (3.5 km) one way, 4.4 miles (7 km) round trip

Elevation gain: 38 feet (11.6 m)

Max. Elevation: 6,201 feet (1,890 m)

Difficulty: Easy, disabled-friendly

Trailhead: Emily Stevens Park
43.4988°N, -110.8363°W / 43°29'56"N, -110°50'11"W
12T 0513231E 4816219N

Traffic: Heavy

Maps: Jackson, Teton Village 7.5' USGS Topos

Trailhead Directions

Drive 1.5 miles (2.4 km) west from the Town Square on Broadway to Highway 22 and turn right (N). Continue 3.5 miles (5.7 km) and turn right (N) into the Emily Stevens Park parking lot to the east of the Snake River.

Trailhead Facilities

Restrooms, information kiosk.

Hike Description

Start from the parking lot at the restroom and steel gate and continue for 450 feet (137 m) to the pedestrian bridge and benches. Turn right (N) and continue on the Dike Trail.

Follow the wide trail for 1.6 miles (2.6 km) along the Snake River to the trail junction. The left path follows the river and the right path passes through cottonwoods and aspens. The trail ends at a locked gate. Return along the same path to the trailhead. The trail is wide enough for hikers, bike riders, and dog walkers to have space.

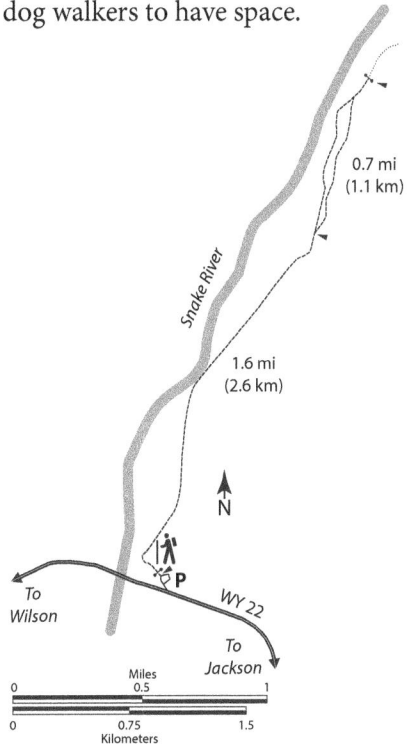

92 OWEN BIRCHER WETLAND TRAIL
(0.4 mi / 0.6 km / Easy)

Overview: A fun, short wetland trail full of birds and water animals.

Trip style: Out and back

Distance: 0.2 mile (0.3 km) one way, 0.4 mile (0.6 km) round trip

Elevation gain: 13 feet (4 m)

Max. Elevation: 6,155 feet (1,876 m)

Difficulty: Easy, disabled-friendly

Trailhead: Owen Bircher Park
43.5005°N, -110.8742°W / 43°30'02"N -110°52'27"W
12T 0510174E 4816405N

Traffic: Heavy, disabled-friendly

Maps: Teton Village, Jackson 7.5' USGS Topos

Trailhead Directions

Drive 1.5 miles (2.4 km) west from the Town Square on Broadway to Highway 22 and turn right (N). Continue 5.6 miles (9 km), then turn right on West Street in Wilson, the first right (N) turn past Fish Creek bridge. Drive 0.17 mile (0.27 km), turn right on Main Street, and in 500 feet (152 m), park in the Owen Bircher parking lot.

Trailhead Facilities

Restrooms, information kiosk, picnic tables.

Hike Description

Start from the parking lot and walk past the restroom building. Follow the concrete walkway, continue past the playground, curve past near the gazebo, and connect with the plank walk path over the Fish Creek marsh.

From here, follow the path as it wanders through the pleasant marsh with information signs along the way. The trail ends at a monument and the parking lot of Hungry Jack's. Return along the same path.

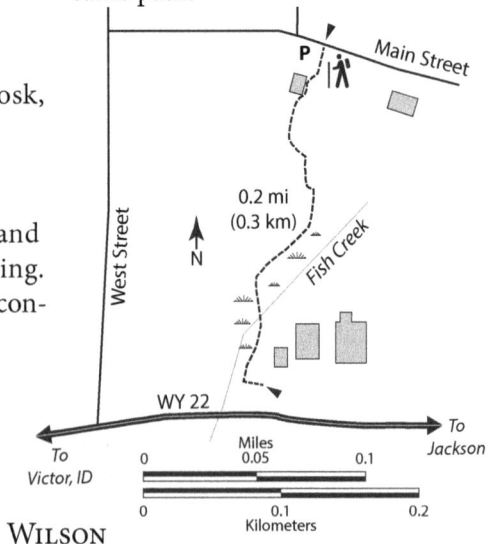

WILSON

TETON PASS

93 RENDEZVOUS PARK (Varies / Easy)

Overview: A network of easy trails with ponds.

Trip style: Loop, out and back

Distance: Variable distances

Elevation gain: Variable, minimal changes

Max. Elevation: 6,165 feet (1,879 m)

Difficulty: Easy, disabled-friendly

Trailhead: Rendezvous Park
43.5037°N, -110.8438°W / 43°30'13"N, -110°50'38"W
12T 0512631E 4816761N

Traffic: Heavy

Maps: Teton Village 7.5' USGS Topo

Trailhead Directions

Drive 1.5 miles (2.4 km) west from the Town Square on Broadway to Highway 22 and turn right (N). Continue 4 miles (6.4 km), turn right on WY 390 (Teton Village Road), then turn right in 0.25 mile (0.4 km) on River Springs Drive.

The dirt road running along the south edge of the park leads to the Snake River where rafters put in their crafts. This road is an alternative parking area when the main lot on the north end of the park is full.

Trailhead Facilities

Restrooms, information kiosk, picnic tables.

Hike Description

Rendezvous Park has an extensive network of level trails for hikers to enjoy. All of the pathways are a short distance from several ponds where water play is allowed.

See the information kiosks for the latest regulation updates.

The trail that runs along the Snake River from the boat ramp is straight, wide, and flat as well. It is a good option to enjoy the rush of the river. The trail across the eastern pond is on a series of stones placed at stepping and hopping distance.

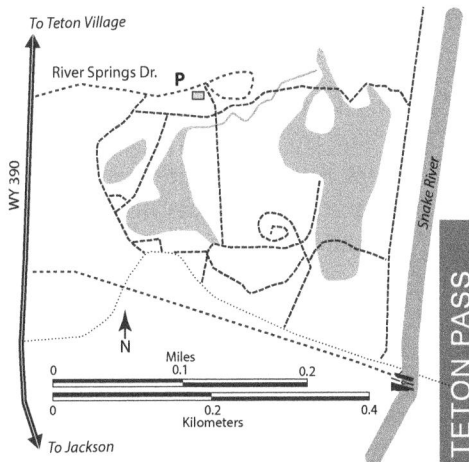

WILSON

94 WILSON ELEMENTARY LOOP
(0.3 mi / 0.4 km / Easy)

Overview: A pleasant loop stroll in an open grassland.

Trip style: Loop

Distance: 0.25 mile (0.4 km)

Elevation gain: 3 feet (1 m)

Max. Elevation: 6,158 feet (1,877 m)

Difficulty: Easy, disabled-friendly

Trailhead: Wilson Elementary parking lot
43.4995°N, -110.8655°W / 43°29'58"N, -110°51'56"W
12T 0510877E 4816297N

Traffic: Light

Maps: Jackson 7.5' USGS Topo

Trailhead Directions

Drive 1.5 miles (2.4 km) west from the Town Square on Broadway to Highway 22 and turn right (N). Continue 5.1 miles (8.2 km), turn right on HHR Ranch Road. Turn into the second loop, follow the road around the building, then park in the back parking lot.

Trailhead Facilities

Restrooms, information kiosk.

Hike Description

Start from the parking lot, walk to the restroom building and start your stroll around the winding loop in the grassy field. The views here are wide and sweeping with no substantial trees to block anything.

The ring path weaves back and forth as it makes its way around the grassy field. This easy pathway is on a hard trail with a granite over-lay to protect the path. The trail circles around and curves back to the parking lot. There is a paved path to the north of this loop which leads to the greater Jackson pathway system.

Mind the elementary school hours. Visiting on weekends or after school hours is best to avoid disturbing students and the school.

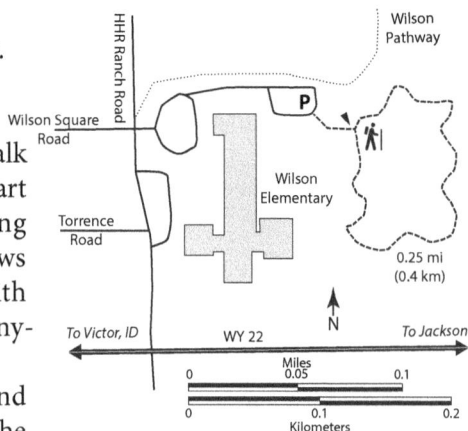

TETON PASS

TETON VALLEY

Teton Valley, located in Idaho, is now a social extension to the Jackson Hole area. The Wyoming and Idaho state line runs along the western edge of the mountain range. Some trails in the area cross over the Teton Range into Wyoming and on to Jackson Hole.

Some of the most popular trails in this book are located in Teton Valley. Specifically, Teton Canyon has one of the busiest trailheads outside of the Jenny Lake area. The popularity of trails on the Idaho side of the mountain range cannot be understated.

Uniquely, one of the trails in Darby Canyon takes hikers to a large cave system. There is a signif-icant amount of limestone in the mountain ranges in the area. Fossil Mountain and Death Shelf are limestone uplifts and shelves.

There are caves in these ranges due to the nature of the rock and the local geology. Most caves are simply inaccessible or the entrances are caved in. Do not enter any cave without proper equipment, training, and preparation.

Although geographically isolated from Jackson Hole, the towns of Victor, Driggs, and Tetonia have become part of Jackson Hole if no other way than financially. Hundreds of commuters drive over the pass every day for work. Living "over the hill" is a good option for some.

Falls in spring in South Teton Canyon.

Courtesy of Randy Isaacson

TETON VALLEY AREA HIKES

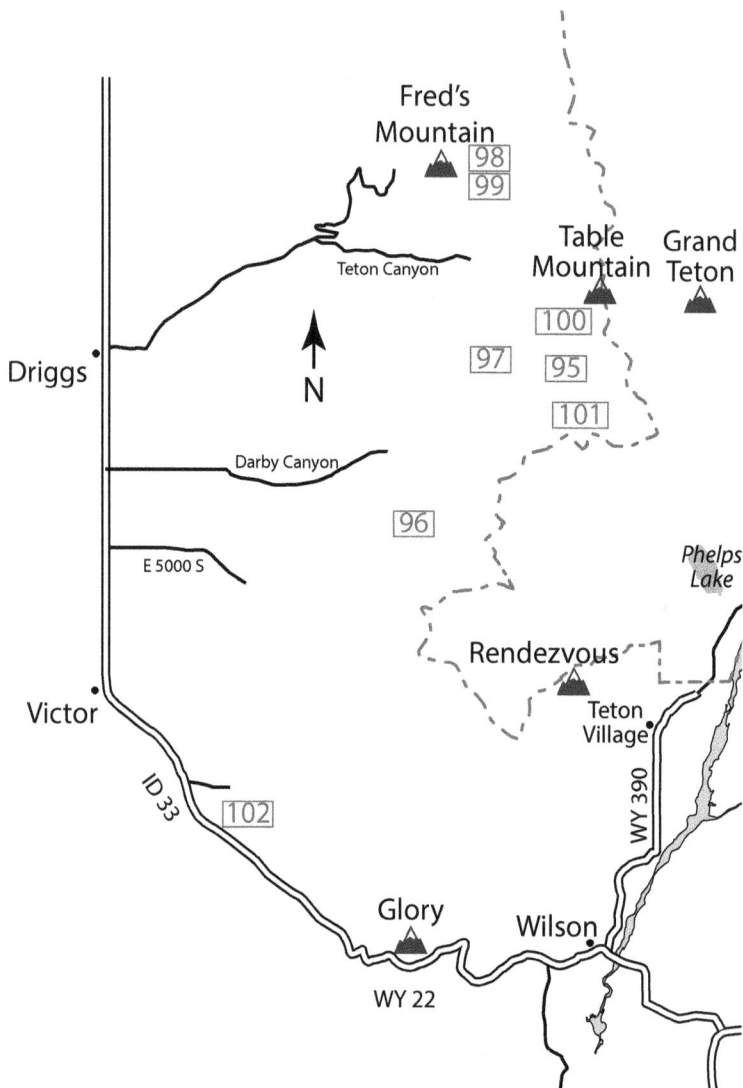

Driggs

95. Alaska Basin via Teton Canyon
96. Darby Wind Cave
97. Devils Stairs to Teton Shelf
98. Fred's Mountain

99. Grand Targhee Trail Network
100. Table Mountain
101. Teton Range Traverse

Victor

102. Rush Hour

Driggs

The town of Driggs is an excellent starting point for many of the hikes in Teton Valley. The town is large enough that it has just about anything travelers need for their adventures. The population hovers around 2,000 people.

Multiple worthwhile trails are accessible only a few miles (kilometers) from Driggs. Most are down dirt roads, making the adventure more interesting. The Teton Traverse, one of the few hiking trips across the Tetons, is also accessible from the Driggs area.

There is a popular climbing gym in Driggs, something that Jackson has struggled to compete with. The facility is large and well worth a visit if the weather is poor and you need to get your climbing fix.

Access to Grand Targhee, the world-famous ski resort, is easy from Driggs. The drive up to the resort isn't too challenging, even in deep winter. Although not as well-known as Teton Village, Grand Targhee offers some of the best powder skiing in the country. In the summer, there are many hiking options available. Some hikes have stunning views, too.

The Teton Canyon Trailhead marker with destinations and their distances carved into a plank.

95 ALASKA BASIN VIA TETON CANYON
(14.4 mi / 23.4 km / Stren)

Overview: A long, continuous climb into a famous alpine basin.

Trip style: Out and back

Distance: 7.2 miles (11.7 km) one way, 14.4 miles (23.4 km) round trip

Elevation gain: 2,570 feet (783 m)

Max. Elevation: 9,529 feet (2,904 m)

Difficulty: Strenuous

Trailhead: Teton Canyon East Trailhead
43.7569°N, -110.9175°W / 43°45'25"N, -110°55'03"W
12T 0506644E 4844872N

Traffic: Heavy

Maps: Granite Basin, Mount Bannon, Grand Teton 7.5' USGS Topos

Notes: Special regulations apply to wilderness areas.

Trailhead Directions

Drive 1.5 miles (2.4 km) west from the Town Square on Broadway to Highway 22 and turn right (N). Continue 24.4 miles (39.3 km) to Victor, Idaho. Continue north on ID-33 for 8.3 miles (13.4 km) and turn right on Ski Hill Road. Drive 6.6 miles (10.6 km) and turn on Teton Canyon Road. Continue 4.4 miles (7.1 km) on the dirt road to the east parking lot.

Trailhead Facilities

Restrooms, information kiosk.

Hike Description

Start from the parking lot on South Teton Trail 027. The start of the trail is broad and easy to follow as it immediately enters the Jedediah Smith Wilderness. It meanders the open forest until it crosses the South Fork of Teton Creek on a wooden bridge at 0.8 mile (1.3 km).

The trail continues deeper south into Teton Canyon, staying on the west side of the South Fork of Teton Creek. It cuts through small patches of trees but is mostly exposed to the sun.

At 2.8 miles (4.5 km), bypass the Teton Shelf via Devils Stairs Trail 028. The trail continues for another 1.1 miles (1.8 km) along a couple short switchbacks before encountering the end of the canyon.

From here, continue up a series of switchbacks as the trail gains elevation for 1 mile (1.6 km). The trail then continues east before encountering another series of switchbacks at 5.6 miles (9 km). It then turns south and climbs a gentle grade to 6.5 miles (10.5 km).

The trail then abruptly turns northwest and follows another set of switchbacks as it intersects the Teton Crest Trail at 7 miles (11.3

km). Turn right (S) and continue the last 0.2 mile (0.3 km) into Alaska Basin to explore the Basin Lakes.

Follow the same path back to the Teton Canyon Trailhead. No permit is required to camp east of Grand Teton National Park. No campfires are allowed in Alaska Basin. Mind special campsite regulations in the Grand Teton area.

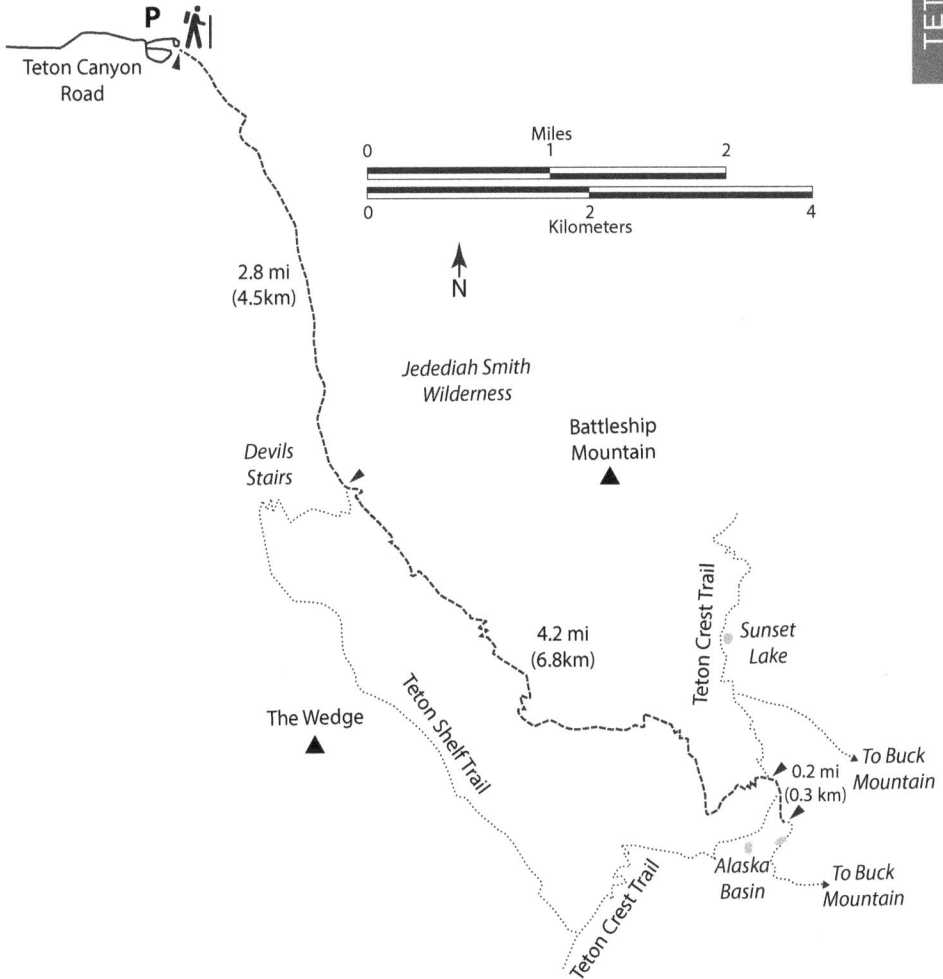

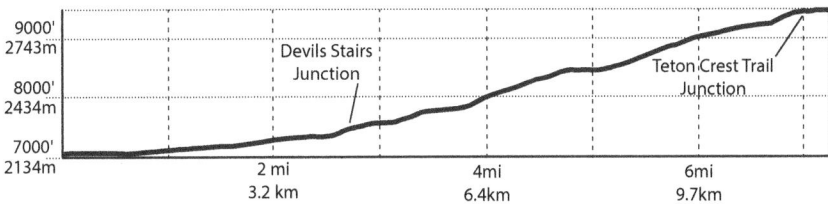

TETON VALLEY

P

Teton Canyon Road

Miles
0 1 2

0 2 4
Kilometers

N

2.8 mi
(4.5km)

Jedediah Smith Wilderness

Battleship Mountain

Devils Stairs

Teton Crest Trail

4.2 mi
(6.8km)

Sunset Lake

The Wedge

Teton Shelf Trail

To Buck Mountain
0.2 mi
(0.3 km)

Teton Crest Trail

Alaska Basin

To Buck Mountain

9000'
2743m

Devils Stairs Junction

Teton Crest Trail Junction

8000'
2434m

7000'
2134m

2 mi
3.2 km

4mi
6.4km

6mi
9.7km

96 DARBY WIND CAVE (7.2 mi / 11.6 km / Mod)

Overview: Hike to the area's most popular cave.
Trip style: Out and back
Distance: 3.6 miles (5.8 km) one way, 7.2 miles (11.6 km) round trip
Elevation gain: 1,867 feet (569 m)
Max. Elevation: 8,902 feet (2,713 m)
Difficulty: Moderate
Trailhead: Darby Canyon Trailhead
43.6866°N, -110.9687°W / 43°41'12"N, -110°58'07"W
12T 0502521E 4837061N
Traffic: Heavy
Maps: Mount Bannon 7.5' USGS Topo
Notes: Bring a headlamp, spare flashlight, and warm clothes.

Trailhead Directions

Drive 1.5 miles (2.4 km) west from the Town Square on Broadway to Highway 22 and turn right (N). Drive 22.6 miles (36.4 km) to Victor, Idaho. Continue 5.3 miles (8.5 km) and turn right on West 3000 South, then drive 3.2 miles (5.2 km) and turn right on S. Stateline Road. Continue on Darby Canyon Road for 4.3 miles (6.9 km) to the Darby Canyon Trailhead.

Trailhead Facilities

Restrooms, information kiosk.

Hike Description

From the parking lot, take the trail that travels along the canyon. At 0.4 mile (0.6 km), the trail crosses Darby Creek on a wooden bridge.

At 0.8 mile (1.3 km), the trail passes into the Jedediah Smith Wilderness. At this point, the trail begins gaining elevation through a series of switchbacks as it climbs the eastern side of the canyon. At 2.2 miles (3.5 km), the Wind Cave is first visible after turning right (in the uphill direction) on a switchback.

At 2.7 miles (4.3 km), the trail turns southwest and traverses across a wide, open area as it makes its way toward the west side of the canyon. At 3 miles (4.8 km), pass the unmarked junction to the Ice Cave and continue toward the Wind Cave. There is a plaque commemorating hikers killed at Darby Girls Camp at the base of the steep hike to the Wind Cave.

Hike the last 0.4 mile (0.6 km) up very steep switchbacks to reach the entrance of the Wind Cave. The first part of the cave before the first narrow passage is easy to explore. Return on the same trail.

Trail Notes

Entering caves can be dangerous. Wear a helmet. There are tight passages, blind drop-offs, and low ceilings in the Wind Cave. Bring a headlamp and spare lights. The first section of the Wind Cave is a rock scramble to a narrow tunnel that opens to a wider area and a drop-off. Turn around at this point unless you are experienced and properly equipped for cave travel in complete darkness.

In 2018, a couple got trapped at a cave waterfall and became dangerously hypothermic in the Ice Cave for two days before rescue crews saved them. They nearly lost their lives. Tell someone responsible where you are going and when to expect you back. Caves are dangerous. They require training and equipment.

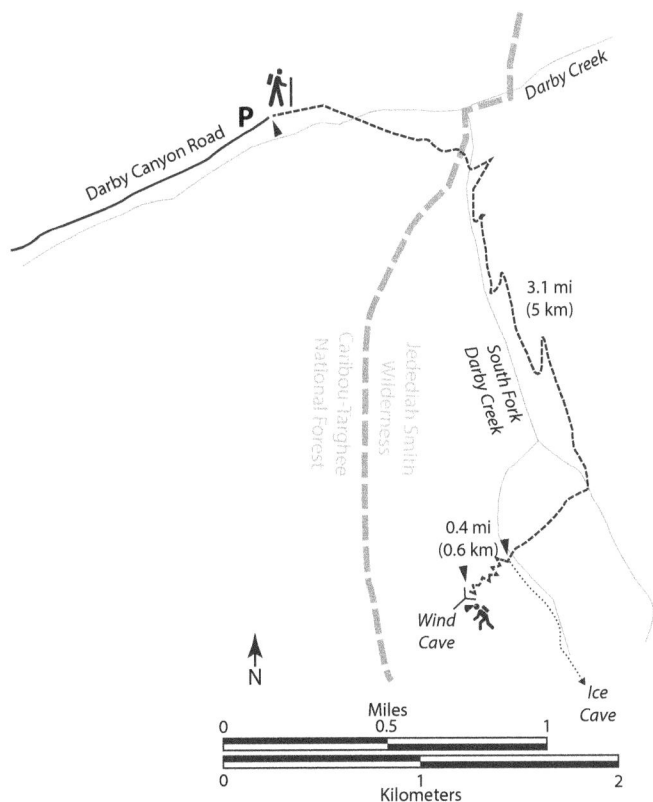

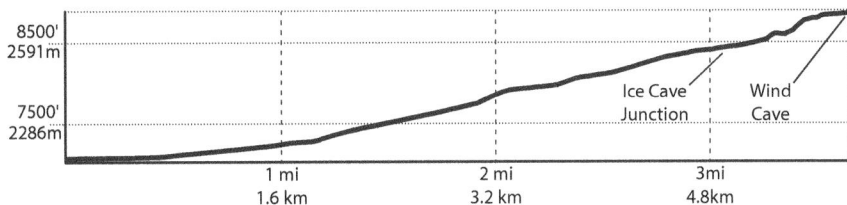

97 DEVILS STAIRS TO TETON SHELF
(9.2 mi / 14.4 km / Stren)

Overview: A continuous climb onto a shelf with stunning views.

Trip style: Out and back

Distance: 4.6 miles (7.4 km) one way, 9.2 miles (14.4 km) round trip

Elevation gain: 2,028 feet (618 m)

Max. Elevation: 8,987 feet (2,739 m)

Difficulty: Strenuous

Trailhead: Teton Canyon East Trailhead
43.7569°N, -110.9175°W / 43°45'25"N, -110°55'03"W
12T 0506644E 4844872N

Traffic: Heavy to the Devils Stairs junction, light on the shelf

Maps: Granite Basin, Mount Bannon 7.5' USGS Topos

Trailhead Directions

Drive 1.5 miles (2.4 km) west from the Town Square on Broadway to Highway 22 and turn right (N). Continue 24.4 miles (39.3 km) to Victor, Idaho. Continue north on ID-33 for 8.3 miles (13.4 km) and turn right on Ski Hill Road. Drive 6.6 miles (10.6 km) and turn on Teton Canyon Road. Continue 4.4 miles (7.1 km) on the dirt road to the east parking lot.

Trailhead Facilities

Restrooms, information kiosk.

Hike Description

Start from the parking lot on South Teton Trail 027. The start of the trail is broad and easy to follow as it immediately enters the Jedediah Smith Wilderness at the wooden sign. It meanders the open forest until it crosses the South Fork of Teton Creek on a wooden bridge at 0.8 mile (1.3 km).

The trail continues deeper south into Teton Canyon, staying on the west side of the South Fork of Teton Creek. It cuts through small patches of trees but is mostly exposed to the sun.

At 2.8 miles (4.5 km), turn right (SW) on trail 028 toward the Devils Stairs. The trail gains elevation before it encounters a series of steep switchbacks that makes its way up the cliff face.

Near the top, the path follows an exposed cliff with steep drop-offs. Be mindful of the trail surface, as it is slippery. At the crest of the trail, there is a short 0.2 mile (0.3 km) stub trail to a pond.

Continue for another 0.8 mile (1.2 km) to the first Teton Shelf overlook into Teton Canyon. From here, explore the Teton Shelf. It gently gains elevation for the next 2.4 miles (3.8 km) to the Teton Crest Trail. Return on the same path.

DEVILS STAIRS TO TETON SHELF

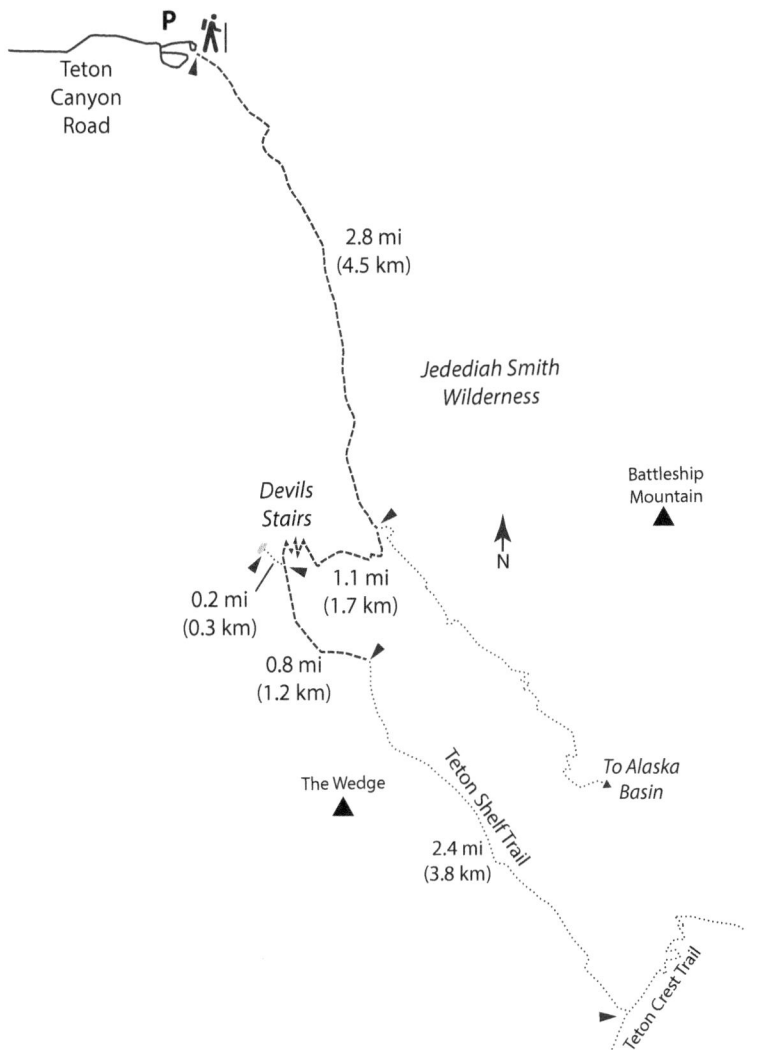

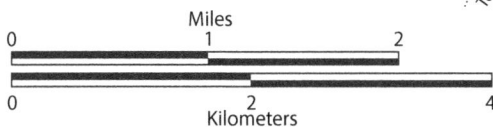

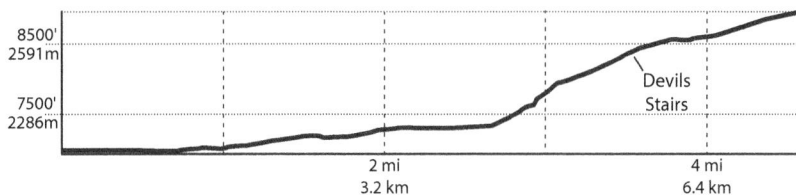

P

Teton
Canyon
Road

2.8 mi
(4.5 km)

Jedediah Smith
Wilderness

Battleship
Mountain
▲

Devils
Stairs

N

1.1 mi
(1.7 km)

0.2 mi
(0.3 km)

0.8 mi
(1.2 km)

Teton Shelf Trail

To Alaska
Basin

The Wedge
▲

2.4 mi
(3.8 km)

Teton Crest Trail

Miles
0   1   2

0   2   4
Kilometers

8500'
2591m

7500'
2286m

Devils
Stairs

2 mi
3.2 km

4 mi
6.4 km

DRIGGS

TETON VALLEY

98 FRED'S MOUNTAIN (6 mi / 9.6 km / Stren)

Overview: A ski hill climb to a northern valley summit.

Trip style: Out and back

Distance: 3 miles (4.8 km) one way, 6 miles (9.6 km) round trip

Elevation gain: 1,903 feet (580 m)

Max. Elevation: 9,862 feet (3,006 m)

Difficulty: Strenuous

Trailhead: Grand Targhee Ski area
43.7889°N, -110.9572°W / 43°47'20"N, -110°57'26"W
12T 0503446E 4848433N

Traffic: Moderate to heavy with mountain bike traffic

Maps: Granite Basin 7.5' USGS Topo

Trailhead Directions

Drive 1.5 miles (2.4 km) west from the Town Square on Broadway to Highway 22 and turn right (N). Continue 24.4 miles (39.3 km) to Victor, Idaho. Continue north on ID-33 for 8.3 miles (13.4 km) and turn right on Ski Hill Road. Follow the signs to the ski resort for 12 miles (19.3 km).

Trailhead Facilities

Restrooms, restaurants, information kiosk, and resort amenities.

Hike Description

Start from the parking lot and walk past the ski lift ticket booth to the Dreamcatcher chair lift. The sign for the Bannock Trail is the start of the path to the summit of Fred's Mountain. This path is also called the Summit Hiking Trail on some maps.

The trail initially zig-zags up the open ski slope toward the first patch of trees on the left (N) side of the slope. It continues under tree cover for 0.4 mile (0.6 km) where it crosses the ski slope to another patch of trees, exits, and works its way north for 0.8 mile (1.3 km).

At 1.4 miles (2.3 km), the trail reaches the ridge. It turns abruptly right (SE) and begins ascending a series of switchbacks and straight sections as it climbs toward the two summits of Fred's Mountain.

Near the first summit at 2.6 miles (4.2 km), the trail curves slightly to the right, works its way around the summit, then shifts back toward the ridge. It then passes the Dreamcatcher lift at 2.8 miles (4.5 km).

From here, continue 0.1 mile (0.2 km) to reach the summit of Fred's Mountain. The view from the ridge northeast toward the Cathedral Group is well worth the hike.

Return along the same trail to reach the trailhead.

FRED'S MOUNTAIN

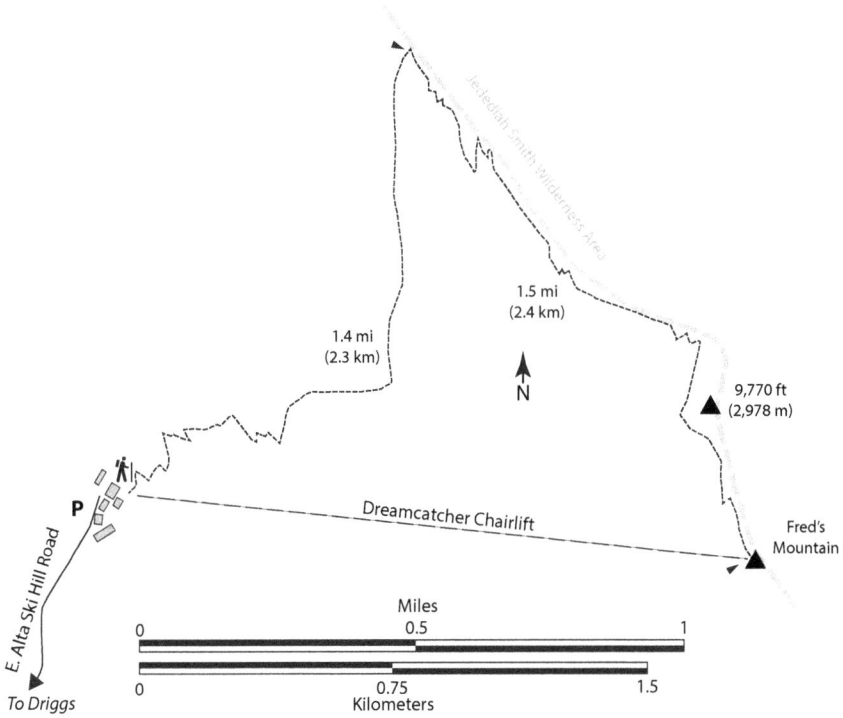

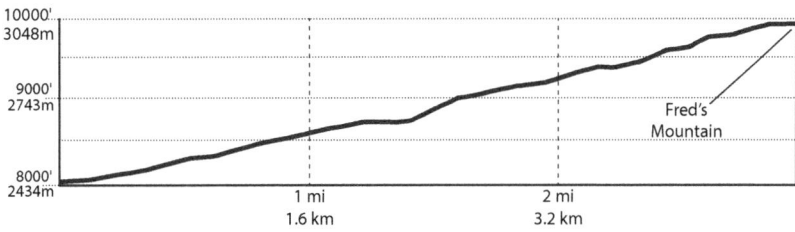

99 GRAND TARGHEE TRAIL NETWORK
(Varies / Mod to Stren)

Overview: A west-facing ski slope with a variety of trail options.

Trip style: Out and back or loop options

Distance: Varies

Elevation gain: Varies

Max. Elevation: 9,862 feet (3,006 m)

Difficulty: Moderate to strenuous

Trailhead: Grand Targhee Ski area
43.7889°N, -110.9572°W / 43°47'20"N, -110°57'26"W
12T 0503446E 4848433N

Traffic: Heavy with mountain bike traffic

Maps: Granite Basin 7.5' USGS Topo

Trailhead Directions

Drive 1.5 miles (2.4 km) west from the Town Square on Broadway to Highway 22 and turn right (N). Continue 24.4 miles (39.3 km) to Victor, Idaho. Continue north on ID-33 for 8.3 miles (13.4 km) and turn right on Ski Hill Road. Follow the signs to the ski resort for 12 miles (19.3 km).

Trailhead Facilities

Restrooms, restaurants, information kiosk, and resort amenities.

Hike Description

The Grand Targhee ski area has miles (kilometers) of hiking and adventure trails for you to explore. The highest elevation that can be attained on the main ski slope is at the top of Fred's Mountain at 9,862 feet (3,006 m).

Mary's Nipple offers hikers a farther afield option to hike to 9,920 feet (3,023 m), just shy of the 10,000-foot (3,048 m) mark. The trail to the top of this summit is more off-piste, requiring a bit of exploration and willingness to experience a minor amount of exposure. The view at the top is well worth the effort.

One of the big advantages of the Grand Targhee trail network is the freedom from large crowds. While Grand Teton will be crawling with people in the middle of July, you'll find that Grand Targhee offers plenty of views and adventure without the people.

If you are a mountain biker, driving to Grand Targhee is well worth the effort. It's possible to ride up the mountain or use one of the bike-equipped chairlifts to start at the top of the mountain and ride down.

The ski resort has all of the expected amenities with restaurants, snack bars, and restrooms.

100 TABLE MOUNTAIN (11.2 mi / 18 km / Ex Stren)

Overview: A hike to a summit with views of the Cathedral Group.
Trip style: Out and back
Distance: 4.2 miles (6.8 km) one way, 11.2 miles (18 km) round trip
Elevation gain: 4,134 feet (1,260 m)
Max. Elevation: 11,106 feet (3,385 m)
Difficulty: Extremely strenuous
Trailhead: Teton Canyon East Trailhead
43.7569°N, -110.9175°W / 43°45'25"N, -110°55'03"W
12T 0506644E 4844872N
Traffic: Heavy
Maps: Granite Basin, Mount Bannon, Mt. Moran, Grand Teton
7.5' USGS Topos

Trailhead Directions

Drive 1.5 miles (2.4 km) west from the Town Square on Broadway to Highway 22 and turn right (N). Continue 24.4 miles (39.3 km) to Victor, Idaho. Continue north on ID-33 for 8.3 miles (13.4 km) and turn right on Ski Hill Road. Drive 6.6 miles (10.6 km) and turn on Teton Canyon Road. Continue 4.4 miles (7.1 km) on the dirt road to the east parking lot.

Trailhead Facilities

Restrooms, information kiosk.

Hike Description

Start from the parking lot to the left (N) of the restroom on the signed trail, Face Trail 029. The trail immediately drops into heavy tree cover for the first 0.2 mile (0.3 km) before breaking out into a mostly exposed face. This trail is incredibly steep for the first 1.5 miles (2.4 km) before moderating somewhat as it moves in and out of tree cover. Past this point, the trail is often damaged by avalanches and may be difficult to follow. It is not well maintained and there is no water on the way up.

There is a sign that says "TRAIL NOT MAINTAINED. NOT RECOMMENDED." The trail is tough, technical, and rugged. It is a classic hardcore Rocky Mountains hike. There is often loose rubble obscuring the trail from rockfall and winter avalanches that tear up the trail.

At 2.7 miles (4.3 km), the Face Trail intersects the North Teton Trail (Huckleberry Trail, Trail 024). From here at 9,900 feet (3,018 m), the trail continues east toward the visible Table Mountain. There is no protection from weather or lightning above this point. Continue the 1.5 miles (2.4

km) to the summit. Often, hikers will turn around 0.7 mile (1.1 km) before the summit, underestimating the time, energy, and effort required to complete this hike.

The last 330 feet (100 m) may require scrambling and using your hands, depending on your skill and experience. At the summit, stunning views of the Teton Cathedral Group can be enjoyed. The summit is often windy and cold. Be prepared.

Turn around and follow the trail back to the intersection of the North Teton Trail and turn right (N). The trail rapidly drops into a heavily forested area. There are two creek crossings and often snow, challenging hikers until mid-summer when the snowmelt subsides. Some of this trail is often overgrown, making it difficult to follow. Leg protection is recommended.

The trail turns northwest and continues losing elevation, crossing the Teton Creek North Fork. The trail works its way around counterclockwise, continuously losing elevation. Bypass the intersection of Trail 023. Continue for another 1.4 miles (2.3 km) to the Teton Canyon parking lot.

Trail Notes

Many inexperienced hikers underestimate the difficulty of this trail. It is often covered in avalanche debris. Please pack out your doggie poo bags, as the level of trash has increased in recent years with the increased popularity of the trail.

Bring more water than you think you need and extra snacks. Some hikers report drinking 5 liters of water in the heat of summer. Also bring sunscreen, eye protection, extra clothing, blister first aid, and a hat. This one is a tough hike. The elevation gain makes the distance seem much farther than it is. Trekking poles are highly recommended. Hikers sometimes experience altitude sickness due to the incredible elevation gain.

In the morning, the Cathedral Group (Tetons) are backlit, so the views won't be as good. If you are fit, plan to summit mid-afternoon. Be mindful of afternoon thundershowers and lightning. There is no shelter above 9,900 feet (3,018 m).

Plan for minor scrambling to reach the summit. Expect to encounter snow in late June or early July. Frequent sunscreen application is highly recommended to prevent serious sunburn from high-altitude UV (ultraviolet) and also UV reflecting off the snow.

Expect moose and bear encounters on the North Teton Canyon Trail. Be prepared to walk through heavy brush, in creeks, and over unstable rocks.

The summit is often windy and cold. Many turn around before reaching the summit due to the altitude and overexerting themselves lower on the trail. The air is thin and you will feel it. Give yourself plenty of time and be prepared to turn back early.

TABLE MOUNTAIN

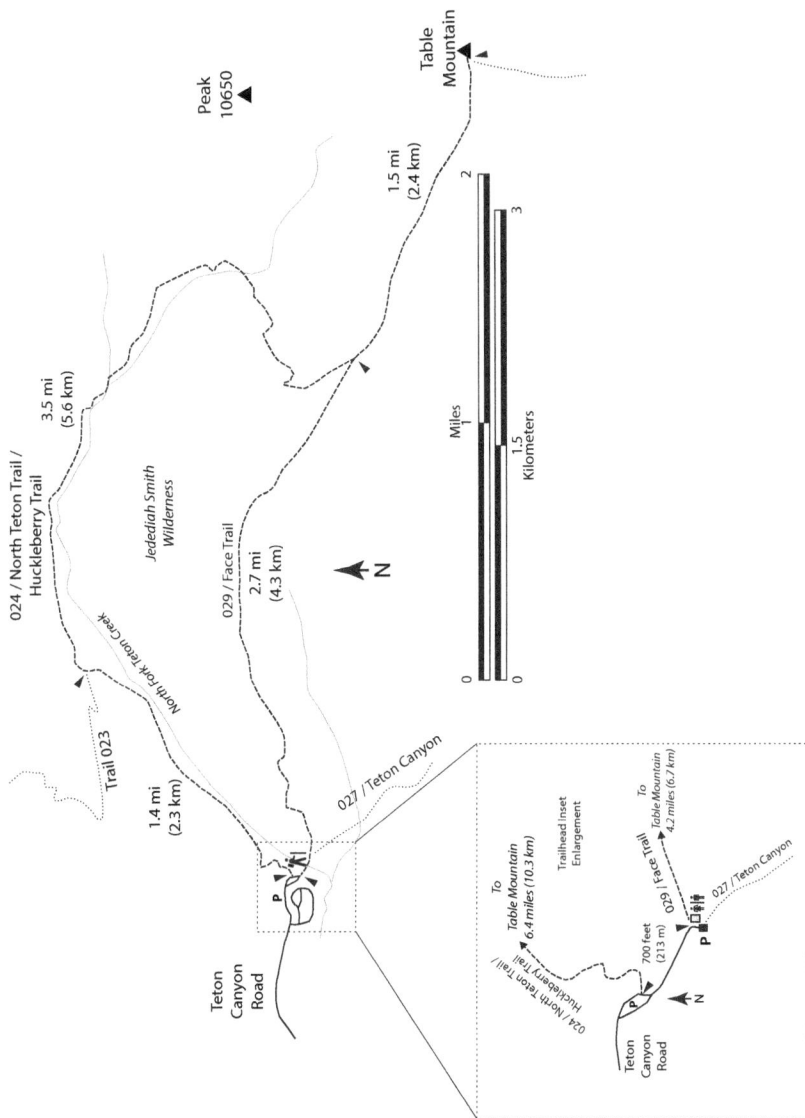

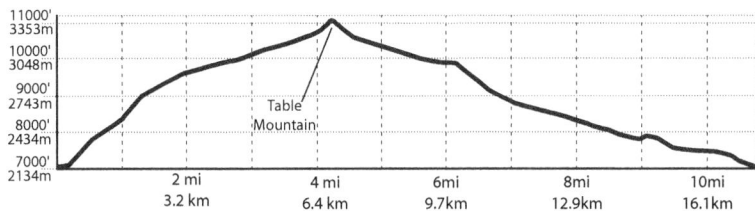

Table Mountain

Peak 10650

1.5 mi (2.4 km)

3.5 mi (5.6 km)

024 / North Teton Trail / Huckleberry Trail

Jedediah Smith Wilderness

029 / Face Trail

2.7 mi (4.3 km)

North Fork Teton Creek

Trail 023

1.4 mi (2.3 km)

027 / Teton Canyon

Teton Canyon Road

Miles

Kilometers

N

Trailhead Inset Enlargement

To Table Mountain 6.4 miles (10.3 km)

024 / North Teton Trail / Huckleberry Trail

To Table Mountain 4.2 miles (6.7 km)

029 / Face Trail

027 / Teton Canyon

700 feet (213 m)

Teton Canyon Road

N

11000' 3353m
10000' 3048m
9000' 2743m
8000' 2434m
7000' 2134m

Table Mountain

2 mi / 3.2 km
4 mi / 6.4 km
6mi / 9.7km
8mi / 12.9km
10mi / 16.1km

DRIGGS

101 TETON RANGE TRAVERSE
(20 mi / 32.2 km / Stren)

Overview: An epic, scenic traverse across the Teton Range.
Trip style: Shuttle
Distance: 20 miles (32.2 km)
Elevation gain: 3,541 feet (1,079 m) gain, 3,722 feet (1,134 m) loss
Max. Elevation: 10,532 feet (3,210 m)
Difficulty: Strenuous
Trailhead: Teton Canyon East Trailhead
43.7569°N, -110.9175°W / 43°45'25"N, -110°55'03"W
12T 0506644E 4844872N
Traffic: Moderate to heavy
Maps: Granite Basin, Mount Bannon, Grand Teton, Mount Moran 7.5' USGS Topos
Notes: Permits required to camp inside Grand Teton National Park.

Trailhead Directions
Drive 1.5 miles (2.4 km) west from the Town Square on Broadway to Highway 22 and turn right (N). Continue 24.4 miles (39.3 km) to Victor, Idaho. Continue north on ID-33 for 8.3 miles (13.4 km) and turn right on Ski Hill Road. Drive 6.6 miles (10.6 km) and turn on Teton Canyon Road. Continue 4.4 miles (7.1 km) on the dirt road to the east parking lot.

Trailhead Facilities
Restrooms, information kiosk.

Hike Description
Start from the parking lot on South Teton Trail 027. The start of the trail is broad and easy to follow as it immediately enters the Jedediah Smith Wilderness. It meanders the open forest until it crosses the South Fork of Teton Creek on a wooden bridge at 0.8 mile (1.3 km).

The trail continues deeper south into Teton Canyon, staying on the west side of the South Fork of Teton Creek. It cuts through small patches of trees but is mostly exposed to the sun.

At 2.8 miles (4.5 km), bypass the Teton Shelf via Devils Stairs Trail 028. The trail continues for another 1.1 miles (1.8 km) along a couple short switchbacks before encountering the end of the canyon.

From here, continue up a series of switchbacks as the trail gains elevation for 1 mile (1.6 km). The trail then continues east before encountering another series of switchbacks at 5.6 miles (9 km). It then turns south and climbs a gentle grade to 6.5 miles (10.5 km).

The trail then abruptly turns

northwest and follows another set of switchbacks as it intersects the Teton Crest Trail at 7 miles (11.3 km). Continue the last 0.2 mile (0.3 km) into Alaska Basin to explore the Basin Lakes and small creeks.

A short distance west of the Teton Crest Trail is the Jedediah Smith Wilderness area outside of the Grand Teton boundary where dispersed camping is allowed. Follow the signs to ensure the proper campsite placement.

Follow the trail signs for Hurricane Pass from Alaska Basin. Begin the climb toward Sunset Lake, 1.3 miles (2 km) north of Alaska Basin. Note that camping is not allowed near the shoreline. The climb from Sunset Lake to Hurricane Pass gains 880 feet (268 m) over this 1.5-mile (2.4 km) section. The southern view of the Cathedral Group is visible in its full glory at this stunning viewpoint.

Follow the exposed, steep switchback trail for 0.7 mile (1.1 km) into the South Fork of Cascade Canyon, dropping down to the jade-green pond at the bottom of Schoolroom Glacier. From here, the trail continues north, losing 2,190 feet (668 m) over the 4.2-mile (6.8 km) hike through this busy camping zone.

At the Cascade Canyon junction, take the right (E) fork toward Jenny Lake. The 3.3-mile (5.3 km) hike toward Jenny Lake from the fork is pleasant with a gentle downhill grade. Enjoy the views of the Grand Teton and Teewinot as they tower above the trail.

Take the left trail at the first junction that leads away from the boat dock for 0.7 mile (1.1 km). This section of trail follows a few switchbacks as it loses elevation. If the trail signs are not clear, simply continue to take the left fork as you continue in this section.

At the next junction, take the left trail fork to walk along Jenny Lake for 1.2 miles (1.9 km). This section of trail gains only a small amount of elevation and then loses it at the creek between String Lake and Jenny Lake.

Continue straight toward the String Lake parking lot and finish the hike with a 0.4 mile (0.6 km) nearly flat walk. You will cross a large wooden bridge over the outlet of String Lake to reach the parking lot.

Alternate Trail Ending

From the trail leading to the boat dock, take the right fork toward the south Jenny Lake parking lot. Follow the trail for 1.1 miles (1.8 km) to the upper and lower Jenny Lake Trail junction. Continue for 1.1 miles (1.7 km) following the lakeshore, past the boat dock, and to the South Jenny Lake parking lot.

Optionally, from the trail junction to Jenny Lake, follow the trail signs to the boat dock. If you arrive during operating hours, you can take the shuttle boat back. Be prepared to pay a fee on arrival at the Jenny Lake boat launch. From there, walk on a short paved trail to the parking lot.

TETON RANGE TRAVERSE

mi	km	Waypoints
0.0	0.0	Teton Canyon Trailhead
2.9	4.7	Devils Stairs junction
7.0	11.3	Teton Crest Trail
8.1	13.0	Sunset Lake
9.5	15.3	Hurricane Pass
10.3	16.6	Schoolroom Glacier
14.4	23.3	Cascade Canyon Fork
17.8	28.6	Inspiration Point cutoff
18.4	29.6	Jenny Lake Loop Trail
19.5	31.4	String Lake Loop Trail
20.0	32.2	String Lake parking lot

Falls in spring in South Teton Canyon.

Courtesy of Randy Isaacson

DRIGGS

TETON RANGE TRAVERSE

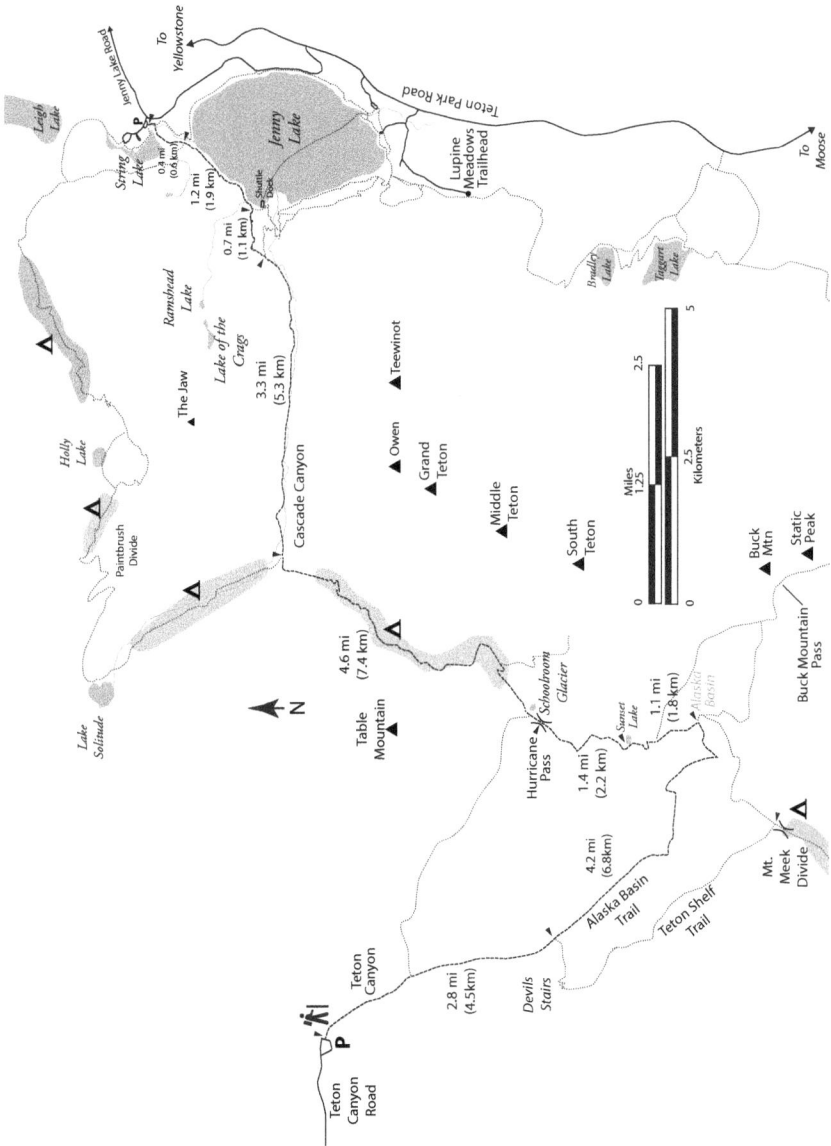

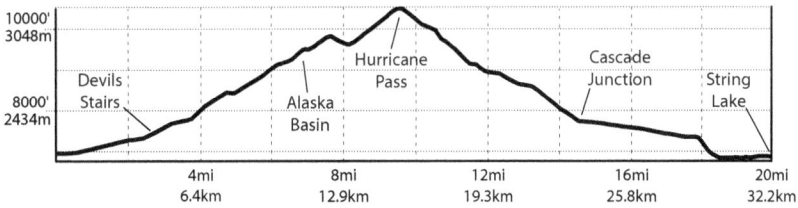

To Yellowstone

Jenny Lake Road

Teton Park Road

Leigh Lake

Jenny Lake

Lupine Meadows Trailhead

To Moose

Spring Lake

String Lake

0.4 mi (0.6 km)

1.2 mi (1.9 km)

Shadow Peak

0.7 mi (1.1 km)

Bradley Lake

Taggart Lake

Ramshead Lake

Lake of the Crags

3.3 mi (5.3 km)

The Jaw

Teewinot

Owen

Grand Teton

Middle Teton

Cascade Canyon

Holly Lake

Paintbrush Divide

South Teton

Buck Mtn

Static Peak

4.6 mi (7.4 km)

Lake Solitude

N

Table Mountain

Hurricane Pass

Schoolroom Glacier

Sunset Lake

1.1 mi (1.8 km)

Alaska Basin

Buck Mountain Pass

1.4 mi (2.2 km)

4.2 mi (6.8 km)

Alaska Basin Trail

Teton Shelf Trail

Mt. Meek Divide

2.8 mi (4.5 km)

Devils Stairs

Teton Canyon

P

Teton Canyon Road

Miles
1.25
2.5
0
Kilometers
2.5
0
5

10000'
3048m

8000'
2434m

Devils Stairs

Alaska Basin

Hurricane Pass

Cascade Junction

String Lake

4mi
6.4km

8mi
12.9km

12mi
19.3km

16mi
25.8km

20mi
32.2km

DRIGGS

Victor

Victor appears to be physically smaller than its sister town, Driggs, to the north. However, Victor has a larger population. The downtown of Victor is smaller but the population is slightly larger. Much of this large population is owed to the cheaper cost of living compared to Jackson and Wilson. Many Victor residents commute over the pass for work.

This is the first town travelers encounter when driving over Teton Pass from Jackson and Wilson. There is a general store, gas station, and several restaurant options in this Idaho community.

Only a few trails are located in the Victor vicinity due to the geography and access. There are many trails to the east of Victor near Pine Creek Pass.

The town also has a playhouse and a popular library available to residents and visitors alike. The Victor Valley Market (known locally as the VVM), a small store on the corner of ID-33 and ID-31, has groceries and supplies should you need them.

Darby Wind Cave seen from the eastern side of Darby Canyon, north of Victor, Idaho.

102 RUSH HOUR (4.2 mi / 6.8 km / Easy)

Overview: A short out and back easy roadside trail.

Trip style: Out and back

Distance: 2.1 miles (3.4 km) one way, 4.2 miles (6.8 km) round trip

Elevation gain: 191 feet (58 m)

Max. Elevation: 6,722 feet (2,049 m)

Difficulty: Easy

Trailhead: Old Jackson Highway
43.5611°N, -111.0672°W / 43°33'40"N, -111°04'02"W
12T 0494572E 4823131N

Traffic: Moderate to heavy

Maps: Victor 7.5' USGS Topo

Trailhead Directions

Drive 1.5 miles (2.4 km) west from the Town Square on Broadway to Highway 22 and turn right (N). Continue 19.1 miles (30.7 km) through Wilson and over Teton Pass. Turn right (N) on the Old Jackson Highway and drive 0.1 mile (0.2 km) to the trailhead. If you see the gated forest service road on the right, you have gone too far.

Trailhead Facilities

None.

Hike Description

Start north from the trailhead. In a short distance, the trail switchbacks and turns south, nearly folding on itself. It then begins following a curving path along ID 33 (WY 22).

There are several reversing switchbacks as the trail makes its way along the gentle grade. It travels up the hill toward the large turnout on the highway at the Idaho/Wyoming border where the welcome signs are. Return along the same trail.

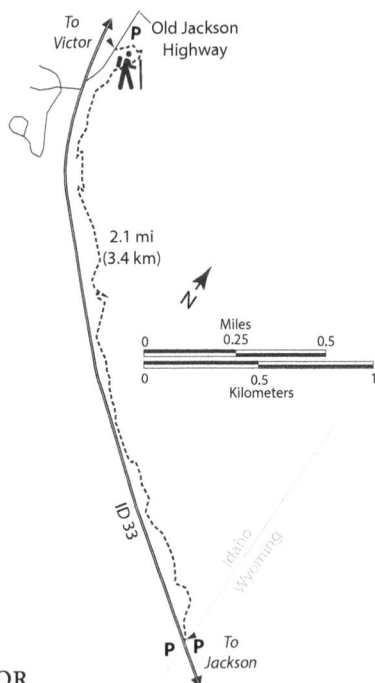

VICTOR

TETON VALLEY

GROS VENTRE

The Wyoming Gros Ventre range encompasses a large tract of land. For the hikes described in this book, this hiking area extends out of the Gros Ventre range for reader convenience. Some of the most spectacular landscapes and views in this book are outside of Grand Teton. Many of the best views of the Tetons are found in the Gros Ventre section of this book.

One of the most recognizable mountains in all of Jackson Hole, aside from the Grand Teton, is Sheep Mountain. Better known as the Sleeping Indian, it is the iconic 11,000 plus foot (3,353 m) summit on the eastern side of the valley.

This hike to this summit requires no technical skill or equipment. Hiking it simply requires stamina and strong lungs.

Much of the Gros Ventre area is laced with a network of trails that ventures deep into the range. Some of it even stretches out of Teton County and into Sublette County. Although some areas of the Gros Ventre range are technically outside of Jackson Hole proper, they are included in this book to offer readers and hikers an expanded view of what the region has to offer. As many of the hikes aren't too far of a drive from Jackson, they are well worthwhile.

The Gros Ventre Slide as seen from the Gros Ventre Slide Overlook Trail.

GROS VENTRE AREA HIKES

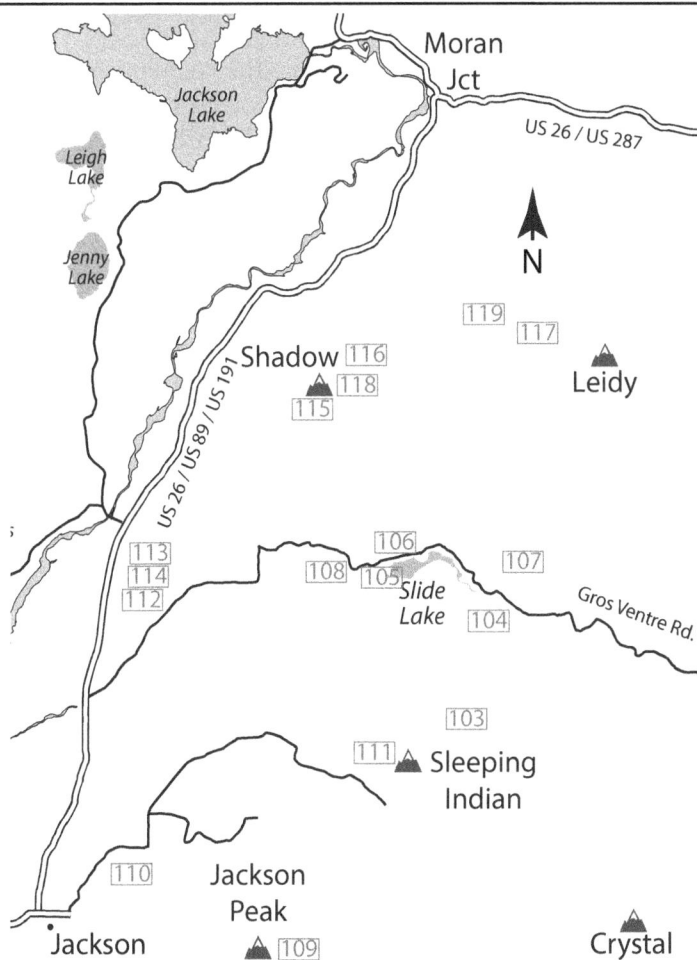

Gros Ventre Road

103. Blue Miner Lake
104. Grizzly Lake
105. Gros Ventre Slide Geology Walk
106. Gros Ventre Slide Overlook
107. Red and Lavender Hills Overlook
108. Wedding Tree

Curtis Canyon

109. Goodwin Lake and Jackson Peak
110. Miller Butte Trail
111. Sleeping Indian via Flat Creek

Blacktail Butte

112. Blacktail Butte Loop
113. Blacktail Butte Summit
114. Blacktail Butte Traverse

Shadow Mountain

115. 30340B Trail Picnic Hideaway
116. Grand View Overlook
117. Mount Leidy Lookout
118. Shadow Mountain Summit
119. Toppings Lake and Ridge

Gros Ventre Road

The Gros Ventre Road penetrates deep into the Gros Ventre range along a dirt track. It stretches nearly 25 miles (40 km) past Slide Lake. This unique geologic area is still active. The most noticeable activity can be seen at "The Slide," a massive landslide that occurred in 1925 that dammed the Gros Ventre River and created Slide Lake. Nearly two years later, the earthen dam failed, sending a torrent of water that altered the landscape. The flood destroyed the town of Kelly and killed several people.

Due to the nature of the geography of Jackson Hole and the Teton Range, the Gros Ventre Road area is much drier than its counterparts to the west. As a consequence, the unique soil strata can be observed.

One of the most picturesque spots in all of Jackson Hole can be found in the Gros Ventre Road area. The Wedding Tree is a unique and protected site. The hike is short but well worth the trip.

One of the enjoyable parts of the Gros Ventre Road area is the lack of crowds compared to Grand Teton. Most trails have easy and open parking at all times of the year that the road is accessible. After winter sets in, the gate at Slide Lake is closed. It only becomes accessible to snow travel, whether it be snowmobile, skis, or snowshoes. Slide Lake is often breezy in the afternoon.

There are ranger stations deep inside of the Gros Ventre Road area as well in case you require assistance in this stretch. As there is little to no cell phone service in the area, make sure to be prepared for that situation. This is especially important if you are relying on your device for maps that require cellular connectivity.

The Wedding Tree is one of the most famous Cathedral Group overlooks in Jackson Hole.

Gros Ventre Road

103 BLUE MINER LAKE (13.6 mi / 22 km / Mod)

Overview: A low-traffic hike to a hidden valley lake.

Trip style: Out and back

Distance: 6.8 miles (11 km) one way, 13.6 miles (22 km) round trip

Elevation gain: 2,752 feet (839 m)

Max. Elevation: 9,773 feet (2,979 m)

Difficulty: Light to moderate

Trailhead: Gros Ventre Wilderness Grizzly Lake
43.6113°N, -110.4387°W / 43°36'41"N, -110°26'19"W
12T 0545291E 4828860N

Traffic: Light

Maps: Grizzly Lake, Blue Miner Lake 7.5' USGS Topos

Trailhead Directions

Drive north from the square on North Cache Street which turns into US 191 for 6.9 miles (11.1 km) to an intersection. Turn right on Gros Ventre Road and continue 7 miles (11.2 km) to the town of Kelly. Continue on the road as it turns left (N) at Kelly and drive 1.1 miles (1.8 km). Turn right on the Gros Ventre Road and continue 11.5 miles (18.5 km) on Gros Ventre Road (FS 30400) to the large turnout on the right side (S) of the dirt road where the wilderness sign is visible.

Trailhead Facilities

Information kiosk.

Hike Description

Start at the trailhead on the south side of the road next to the wilderness information sign. Walk past the sign and continue southeast on the trail. At 0.4 mile (0.6 km), by-pass the unmarked trail that heads east. Continue southwest along the trail that partly travels along a buck rail fence.

At 1.1 miles (1.8 km), pass over East Miner Creek. The crossing may be dry, muddy, or have flowing water in early summer. The trail abruptly turns left (S) and gains elevation toward a ridge. It then switchbacks to the north and continues along the ridgeline, then drops down and crosses West Miner Creek at 1.6 miles (2.6 km).

Pass by an old dirt road along a fence and continue east. At 2.2 miles (3.5 km), take the left trail at the junction marked "BLUE MINER LAKE" on the wooden trail sign. There is also a sign in a tree just past the trail sign indicating the route.

At 2.9 miles (4.7 km), the trail enters the Gros Ventre Wilderness area. The trail then begins working its way along the top of a steep ridge for 1.5 miles (2.4 km). The landscape then widens out and the trail enters an open broad area south of the tree line.

From here, the trail works its way toward a seasonal creek bed for 1.1 miles (1.8 km) before momentarily entering a patch of trees. At 5.8 miles (9.3 km), the trail works its way up to a ridge where Blue Miner Lake becomes visible. At one switchback, an unmarked trail leads off to Sheep Mountain (Sleeping Indian). The trail drops 280 feet (85 m) to the lake on a moderately rocky trail.

Alternate route

Complete the hike as a shuttle trip. Continue from Blue Miner Lake to Sleeping Indian (Sheep Mountain), then drop down the western side of the mountain toward the Elk Refuge. Connect with a vehicle or bike left at the western Sleeping Indian parking area.

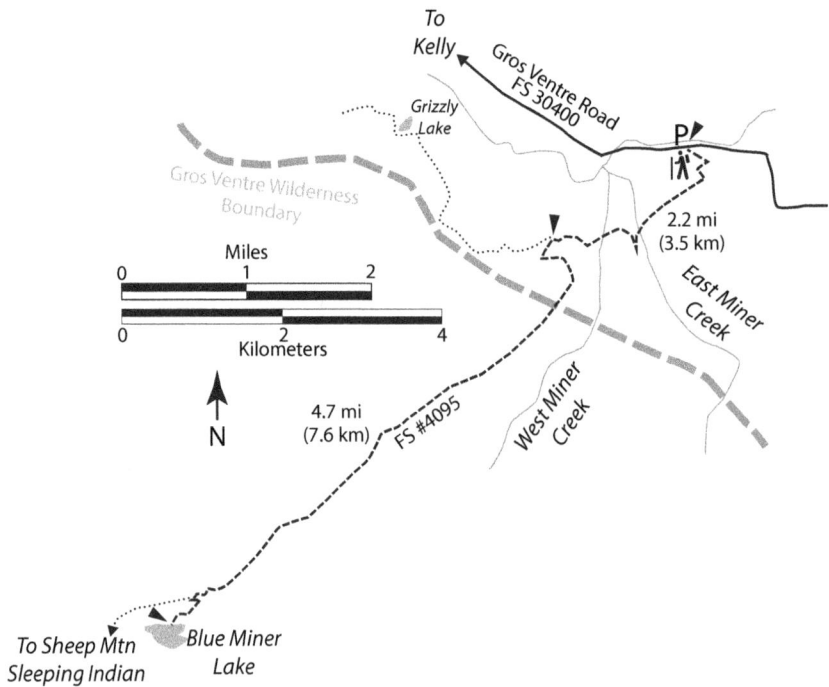

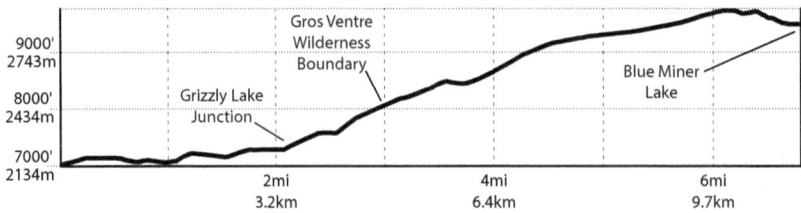

GROS VENTRE

GROS VENTRE ROAD

104 GRIZZLY LAKE (9.6 mi / 15.4 km / Easy)

Overview: A low-traffic hike to a turquoise-colored lake.

Trip style: Out and back

Distance: 4.8 miles (7.7 km) one way, 9.6 miles (15.4 km) round trip

Elevation gain: 613 feet (187 m)

Max. Elevation: 7,621 feet (2,323 feet)

Difficulty: Easy

Trailhead: Gros Ventre Wilderness Grizzly Lake
43.6113°N, -110.4387°W / 43°36'41"N, -110°26'19"W
12T 0545291E 4828860N

Traffic: Light to moderate

Maps: Grizzly Lake, Blue Miner Lake 7.5' USGS Topos

Trailhead Directions

Drive north from the square on North Cache Street which turns into US 191 for 6.9 miles (11.1 km) to an intersection. Turn right on Gros Ventre Road and continue 7 miles (11.2 km) to the town of Kelly. Continue on the road as it turns left (N) at Kelly and drive 1.1 miles (1.8 km). Turn right on the Gros Ventre Road and continue 11.5 miles (18.5 km) on Gros Ventre Road (FS 30400) to the large turnout on the right side (S) of the dirt road where the wilderness sign is visible.

Trailhead Facilities

Information kiosk.

Hike Description

Start at the trailhead on the south side of the road next to the wilderness information sign. Walk past the sign and continue southeast on the trail. At 0.4 mile (0.6 km), by-pass the unmarked trail that heads east. Continue southwest along the trail that partly travels along a buck rail fence.

At 1.1 miles (1.8 km), pass over East Miner Creek. The crossing may be dry, muddy, or have flowing water in early summer. The trail abruptly turns left (S) and gains elevation toward a ridge. It then switchbacks to the north and continues along the ridgeline, then drops down and crosses West Miner Creek at 1.6 miles (2.6 km).

Pass by an old dirt road along a fence and continue east. At 2.2 miles (3.5 km), pass the Blue Miner Lake junction and continue toward the Grizzly Lake Trail. To the right (N) of the trail is a large swan pond at this point. You have to look over your shoulder to see it.

At 2.8 miles (4.5 km), the trail crosses a muddy creek on a wooden bridge. Shortly past this point

GROS VENTRE

in 330 feet (101 m) is an unmarked junction. There may be debris on the northwest trail to discourage hikers from taking the wrong trail. There also may be a wooden arrow indicating the correct direction for travel. Take the left (SW) fork toward the trees where the trail climbs 215 feet (66 m) on broad switchbacks to the trail's high point.

The trail curves northwest. At 4.4 miles (7.1 km) there is an unmarked fork in the trail. These two routes reconnect together in a short distance. Continue for another 0.4 mile (0.6 km) to reach Grizzly Lake.

You may notice a wooden sign in the trees as you near the lake. The trail becomes fragmented for the last 325 feet (100 m) to the lake, making finding the return trail a slight challenge. Look over your shoulder to remember where to reconnect with the trail. There is an active spring at the northeast corner that feeds the lake. The trail continues past the lake for 0.6 mile (1 km) to an overlook hill.

Return along this route to reach the trailhead.

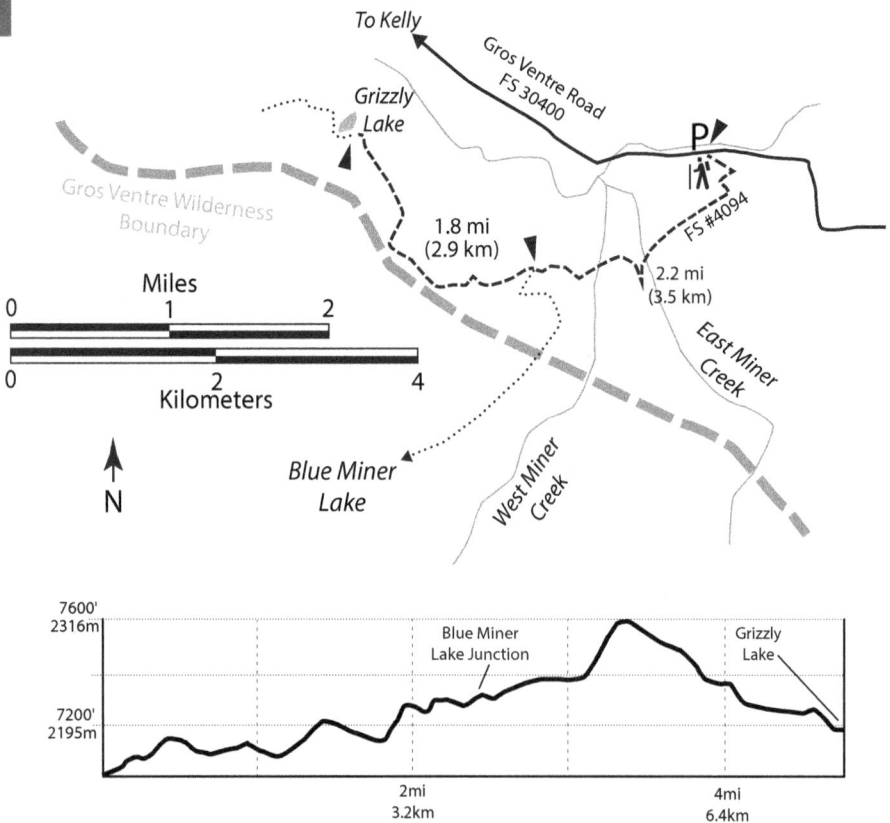

105 GROS VENTRE SLIDE GEOLOGY WALK (0.8 mi / 1.3 km / Easy)

Overview: A tour of the damage from the Gros Ventre slide.

Trip style: Loop

Distance: 0.8 mile (1.3 km)

Elevation gain: 195 feet (59 m)

Max. Elevation: 7,025 feet (2,141 m)

Difficulty: Easy

Trailhead: Gros Ventre Slide Sign
43.6339°N, -110.5473°W / 43°38'02"N, -110°32'50"W
12T 0536515E 4831315N

Traffic: Light

Maps: Shadow Mountain 7.5' USGS Topo

Trailhead Directions

Drive north from the square on North Cache Street which turns into US 191 for 6.9 miles (11.1 km) to an intersection. Turn right on Gros Ventre Road and continue 7 miles (11.2 km) to the town of Kelly. Continue on the road as it turns left (N) at Kelly and drive 1.1 miles (1.8 km). Turn right on the Gros Ventre Road and continue 4.6 miles (7.4 km) to the broad turnoff with the large wooden Gros Ventre Slide information sign.

Trailhead Facilities

Information signs.

Hike Description

Start at the east end of the parking lot at the trail sign. The trail immediately drops into a grove of trees as it wanders along a shaded pathway. There are benches for resting along the way as well as in-formational signs about the flora and fauna of the area.

Take the left trail fork if you wish to complete the entire loop. It passes by a sheltered view of Lower Slide Lake, then turns and enters the boulder field.

Take the right fork if you wish only to see the boulder field. There is no difference in difficulty with either route.

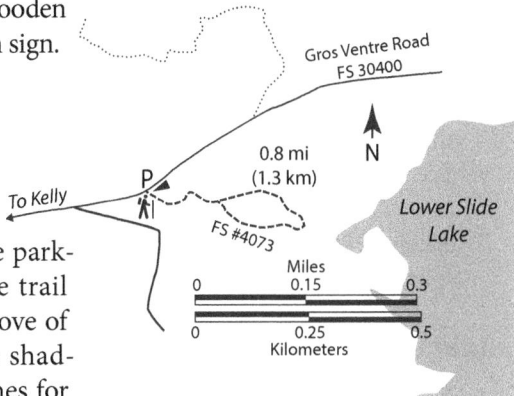

Gros Ventre Road
FS 30400

0.8 mi
(1.3 km)

To Kelly

P

FS #4073

Lower Slide Lake

N

Miles
0   0.15   0.3
0   0.25   0.5
Kilometers

106 GROS VENTRE SLIDE OVERLOOK
(0.8 mi / 1.2 km / Stren)

Overview: A hike to the best overlook of the Gros Ventre slide.

Trip style: Out and back

Distance: 0.4 mile (0.6 km) one way, 0.8 mile (1.2 km) round trip

Elevation gain: 489 feet (149 m)

Max. Elevation: 7,490 feet (2,283 m)

Difficulty: Strenuous

Trailhead: Gros Ventre Slide Sign
43.6339°N, -110.5473°W / 43°38'02"N, -110°32'50"W
12T 0536515E 4831315N

Traffic: None to light

Maps: Shadow Mountain 7.5' USGS Topo

Notes: High-clearance vehicle recommended.

Trailhead Directions

Drive north from the square on North Cache Street which turns into US 191 for 6.9 miles (11.1 km) to an intersection. Turn right on Gros Ventre Road and continue 7 miles (11.2 km) to the town of Kelly. Continue on the road as it turns left (N) at Kelly and drive 1.1 miles (1.8 km). Turn right on the Gros Ventre Road and continue 4.8 miles (7.7 km) and turn left on FS road 30361. Drive to the end of the narrow, rutted road and park. Do not block this dirt road if you are unable to negotiate your vehicle to the parking area.

Trailhead Facilities

None.

Hike Description

Start from the small parking and camping area and begin making your way up the rocky and steep jeep trail. IWW Creek may be flowing to the west of the parking area.

There are several fine viewing points for Lower Slide Lake along this route. At point 7490, the view opens up to a 270° panorama. The trail continues 0.1 mile (0.2 km) toward the cliffs and disappears.

The trail is incredibly steep and trekking poles are recommended for the descent.

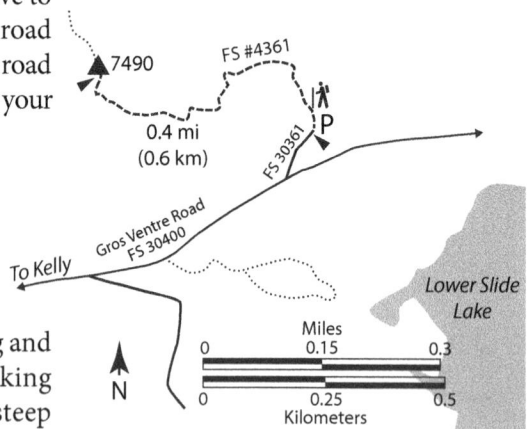

GROS VENTRE ROAD

107 RED AND LAVENDER HILLS
OVERLOOK (3.6 mi / 5.8 km / Stren)

Overview: Spectacular sunset viewpoint with broad vistas.

Trip style: Out and back

Distance: 1.8 miles (2.9 km) one way, 3.6 miles (5.8 km) round trip

Elevation gain: 1,570 feet (478 m)

Max. Elevation: 8,586 feet (2,616 m)

Difficulty: Strenuous, extremely steep for the last 0.3 mi (0.5 km)

Trailhead: Unmarked roadside grass and dirt pullout
43.6150°N, -110.4620°W / 43°36'54"N, -110°27'43"W
12T 0543414E 4829255N

Traffic: None to light

Maps: Grizzly Lake, Mount Leidy 7.5' USGS Topos

Notes: Bear scat is found on the trail. Unreliable water along the first section of trail. Steep and hot in midday. Gros Ventre Road turns to dirt east of Slide Lake.

Trailhead Directions

Drive north from the square on North Cache Street which turns into US 191 for 6.9 miles (11.1 km) to an intersection. Turn right on Gros Ventre Road and continue 7 miles (11.2 km) to the town of Kelly. At 1.1 miles (1.8 km) north of Kelly, turn right on Gros Ventre Road. Drive 10.2 miles (16.4 km) to a grass and dirt turnout on the south side of the road without blocking the steel gate.

Trailhead Facilities

No facilities available.

Hike Description

From the parking area, walk 60 feet (18 m) to an unsigned, well-worn dirt trail leading up the road berm toward the ravine.

The trail travels through an open sage field into the ravine, encountering a stand of aspen at 0.4 mile (0.6 km). Brush covers the trail in spots. Flowing water may be heard at 0.5 mile (0.8 km). The trail becomes steep from here.

At 0.9 mile (1.45 km), a trail splits and reconnects 150 feet (45 m) later. The left option is steep and open. The right option goes through deep brush and trees. At 1.1 miles (1.8 km), a trail leads to the left (west) toward the red rock cliff. Continue straight uphill toward the saddle.

The T-junction at 1.4 miles (2.3 km) lies at the top of the saddle. There are two options depending on your hiking ability.

To the right (southeast), an easy 0.1-mile (0.2 km) trail leads to an open overlook into the Gros Ventre Range.

The left trail leads to the top of the viewpoint. This trail is steep, gaining 432 feet (132 m) in 0.4 mile (0.6 km) in a series of rapid gains up 30° to 40° slopes. The crest of the trail offers several options.

Walk 160 feet (49 m) south to gain another vantage point. Continue north for 80 feet (24 m) to the apex of the ridge, though the western view is obscured by trees.

To reach the base of the climb to the high point of Lavender Hills, start at the Red Hills summit and hike north along the thin trail for 0.4 mile (0.6 km). Continue straight up or follow the contour around to the farther ridge for your ascent. Be aware either path is faint, crumbly, and potentially dangerous. Reverse the route to return to the parking lot.

Notes

The trail above the T-junction shown on the 1996-2017 USGS maps is either overgrown or the maps are incorrect. Follow the obvious trail to the northeast from the T-junction from the saddle at:
**43.6259°N, -110.4452°W
43°37'33"N, -110°26'43"W
12T 0544762E 4830477N**
to reach the viewpoint.

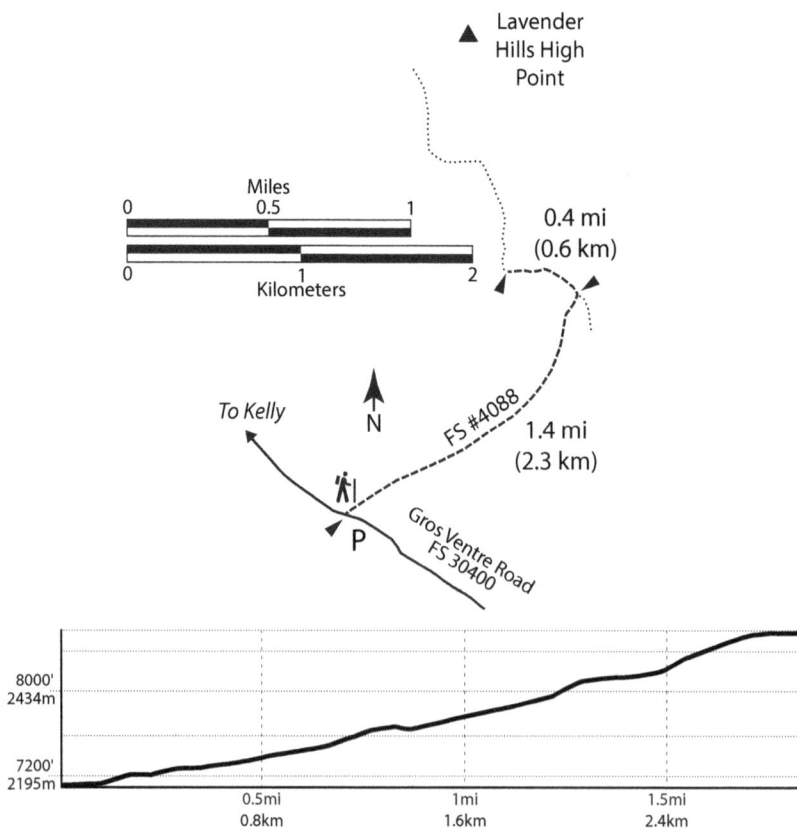

GROS VENTRE ROAD

108 WEDDING TREE (0.2 mi / 0.4 km / Easy)

Overview: A short hike to a picturesque overlook.

Trip style: Out and back

Distance: 0.1 mile (0.2 km) one way, 0.2 mile (0.4 km) round trip

Elevation gain: 13 feet (4 m)

Max. Elevation: 7,055 feet (2,150 m)

Difficulty: Easy

Trailhead: Gros Ventre Road Turnout
43.6312°N, -110.5648°W / 43°37'52"N, -110°33'53"W
12T 0535104E 4831000N

Traffic: Heavy

Maps: Shadow Mountain 7.5' USGS Topo

GROS VENTRE

Trailhead Directions

Drive north from the square on North Cache Street which turns into US 191 for 6.9 miles (11.1 km) to an intersection. Turn right on Gros Ventre Road and continue 7 miles (11.2 km) to the town of Kelly. Continue on the road as it turns left (N) at Kelly and drive 1.1 miles (1.8 km). Turn right on the Gros Ventre Road and continue 3.6 miles (5.8 km) to the small turnoff. If you see the large wooden Gros Ventre Slide sign, you have driven too far.

Trailhead Facilities

Information signs.

Hike Description

Start at the west end of the turnout where the trail starts. From here, the trail meanders over a few rocks before leveling out.

The trail then continues through sagebrush and conifers. If you are early in the season, there will be a cornucopia of flowers to make the hike more memorable. From the trailhead, the Wedding Tree will become visible in 250 feet (76 m).

Once you arrive at the end of the trail, the tree is unmistakable. Enjoy taking photographs and respect this irreplaceable landmark.

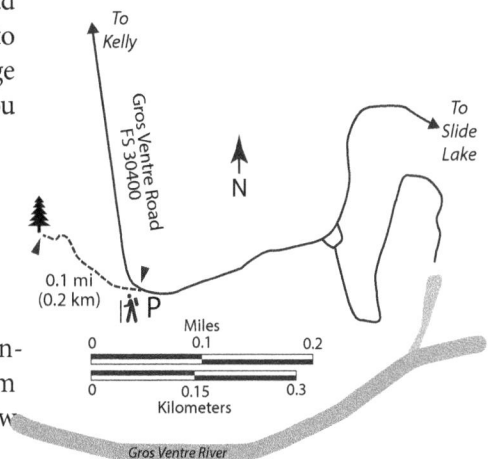

Curtis Canyon

Curtis Canyon has become a part-time home for transient travelers working in Jackson. Every morning and every evening, a steady stream of vehicles can be seen rolling along the dirt road to and from Curtis Canyon.

Accessed from the Refuge Road, Curtis Canyon is a rough road that is the primary access point for Jackson Peak, a popular summit for day hikers. One of the big advantages of this peak is the starting elevation. The trailhead is over 8,000 feet (2,438 m), meaning there is not as much climbing to achieve the unique summit. Once hikers reach Jackson Peak, they can see a broad swath of Jackson Hole. The hike to Godwin Lake is worth the effort, too.

Pronghorn, the fastest land animal in North America, roam the sagebrush fields of Jackson Hole.

Young bighorn sheep practice butting heads in the late winter along the Refuge Road.

109 GOODWIN LAKE AND JACKSON PEAK (10.3 mi / 16.6 km / Stren)

Overview: An accessible 10,000-foot (3,048 m) summit with views.

Trip style: Out and back

Distance: 5.2 miles (8.4 km) one way, 10.3 miles (16.6 km) round trip

Elevation gain: 2,628 feet (801 m)

Max. Elevation: 10,741 feet (3,274 m)

Difficulty: Strenuous

Trailhead: Goodwin Lake and Jackson Peak Trailhead
43.5026°N, -110.62811°W / 43°30'09"N, -110°37'41"W
12T 0530068E 4816699N

Traffic: Moderate to heavy

Maps: Gros Ventre Junction, Blue Miner Lake, Cache Cr., Turquoise Lake 7.5' USGS Topos

Notes: High clearance vehicle with 4WD recommended.

Trailhead Directions

Drive 1 mile (1.6 km) east from the Town Square to the end of the road. Turn left (N) onto the dirt refuge road. Continue 4.6 miles (7.4 km) past a hard left turn (N) at a ranch. Turn right at the Curtis Canyon Junction (marked as Sheep Creek on FS maps) that leads toward the mountains. Drive 4.8 miles (7.7 km) on the dirt road FS 30440 up an increasingly rutted and rough 4WD road. Bypass all spur roads.

If you do not have a 4-wheel drive vehicle, park completely off the road 1 mile (1.6 km) before the trailhead and walk. Driving the last mile (kilometer) has the potential for causing vehicle damage or becoming stuck with low-clearance vehicles (rental cars, sedans, minivans) and inexperienced drivers on the heavily rutted and washed-out road.

Trailhead Facilities

Information kiosk.

Hike Description

Start east from the parking lot on the trail that leads up into the tree cover, curving north. At 0.3 mile (0.5 km), the trail abruptly turns east and begins steadily gaining elevation. It switchbacks several times before reaching a ridge at 0.8 mile (1.3 km).

The trail continues along the ridge, mostly on the eastern slope, often with views of Sheep Creek peeking through the trees 450 feet (137 m) or more below the trail. Some parts of this section of trail feel slightly exposed, as it follows along the top of the steep ridge.

At 2.4 miles (3.9 km) the trail crosses into the Gros Ventre Wilderness Area. There is a sign indicating this boundary. Shortly past the edge of the wilderness area, the trail transitions off the ridge in heavy tree cover into a wider flat area while still gaining elevation.

The northern end of Lake Goodwin will come into view. The official trail travels on the eastern edge of the lake. Often, it is easy to end up on the western end of the lake with several fine lookout rocks above the lake's surface. This route is more interesting than the eastern side and is worth exploring.

Whichever route you choose, they both continue around the lake. The western branch may be slightly challenging to follow in a few spots but it's difficult to become lost. The trails merge up near the wide-open space above the lake. Above here, there is often snow well into mid-summer. Be prepared for wet and slippery travel.

The summit of Jackson Peak looms over to the trail to your right (W) as the trail continues gaining elevation. At 4.2 miles (6.8 km), the trail forks to the summit, breaking off from the trail that leads toward Cache Peak. Turn right (W) and begin working your way up toward the summit. This junction is at 10,000 feet (3,048 m) and hikers often feel the effects of the altitude from this point.

For the next 0.4 mile (0.6 km), the trail travels southwest away from the summit, working its way up toward the ridge. Though discouraging, this route is easier (and safer) to travel than scrambling directly up the loose boulders toward the summit ridge.

Once the trail reaches the ridge after a few short switchbacks, it turns sharply north. It works its way up along the top of the ridge. Often snow makes this portion of travel difficult. Hikers often find themselves on the east side of the ridge where a short climb up a patch of snow and ice is required to reach the ridge.

There is a short 0.1 mile (0.2 km) split in the trail near the summit. Take either route, as they reconnect 300 feet (91 m) before reaching the summit. This last section of hiking is mostly over scattered boulders and rocks with the sometimes vague trail. Continue gaining elevation until you reach the windswept summit. Return along the same path to the trailhead.

Nowlin Peak is 1 mile (1.6 km) west on a 261° true north bearing. The Grand Teton is 21.2 miles (34.1 km) northwest on a 335° true north bearing.

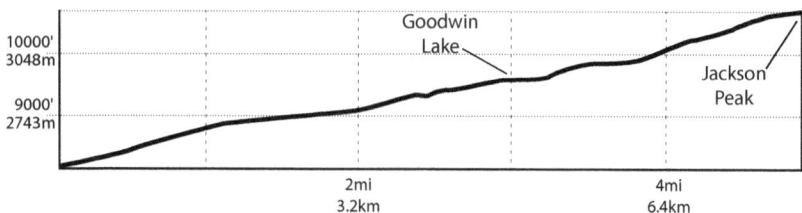

CURTIS CANYON

JACKSON PEAK AND GOODWIN LAKE

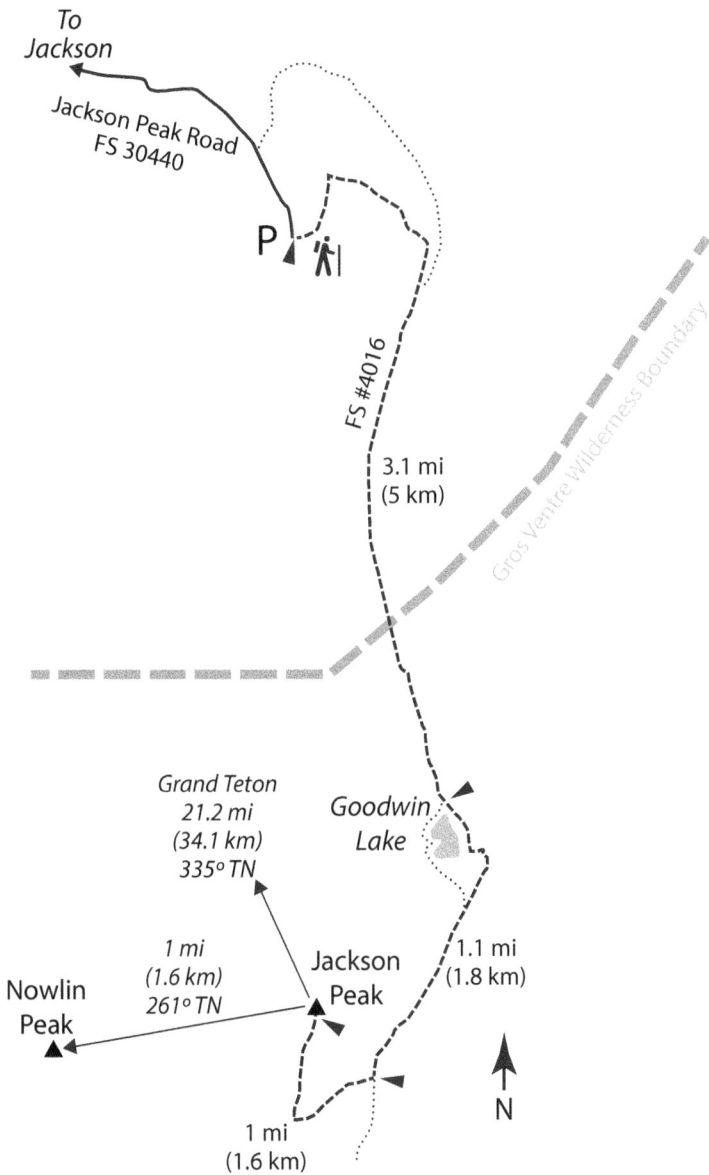

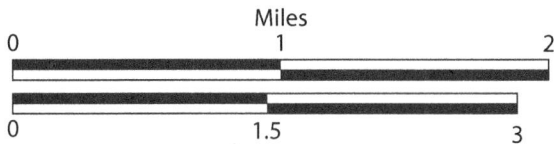

To
Jackson

Jackson Peak Road
FS 30440

P

FS #4016

3.1 mi
(5 km)

Gros Ventre Wilderness Boundary

GROS VENTRE

Grand Teton
21.2 mi
(34.1 km)
335° TN

Goodwin
Lake

1 mi
(1.6 km)
261° TN

Jackson
Peak

1.1 mi
(1.8 km)

Nowlin
Peak

N

1 mi
(1.6 km)

Miles
0   1   2

0   1.5   3

CURTIS CANYON

110 MILLER BUTTE TRAIL (4.8 mi / 7.8 km / Mod)

Overview: A short hike on a lightly traveled Elk Refuge trail.

Trip style: Out and back

Distance: 2.4 miles (3.9 km) one way, 4.8 mi (7.8 km) round trip (est.)

Elevation gain: 2,249 feet (685 m) estimated

Max. Elevation: 8,560 feet (2,609 feet)

Difficulty: Moderate with off-trail travel and navigation

Trailhead: Miller Butte Trailhead parking Area
43.5043°N, -110.7212°W / 43°30'15"N, -110°43'16"W
12T 0522536E 4816852N

Traffic: Light

Maps: Gros Ventre Junction, Cache Cr. 7.5' USGS Topo

Notes: Off-trail travel and route-finding required on the upper trail.

GROS VENTRE

Trailhead Directions

Drive 1 mile (1.6 km) east from the Town Square to the end of the road. Turn left (N) onto the dirt refuge road. Continue 2.1 miles (3.3 km) to the large parking area on the right (S) side of the refuge road. There are parking instructions and trail signs.

Off-trail travel is prohibited in the wildlife refuge.

Trailhead Facilities

None.

Hike Description

Start southeast from the trailhead, staying on the trail due to the refuge travel restrictions. Begin hiking toward the butte as the path works its way through the sagebrush. The trail exits the official National Elk Refuge boundary at 0.25 mile (0.4 km) which may be marked by signs (this has not been consistent over the years).

At 0.4 mile (0.6 km), the trail enters tree cover and then exits after a patch, beginning to work its way up a series of switchbacks that continue to gain elevation. The trail switches from traveling southeast to southwest for 0.5 mile (0.8 km), then curves back to the southeast. At this point, the trail becomes overgrown and is unmaintained.

At the invisible end of the trail, it's possible to cross-country travel to the summit of Peak 8776 in approximately 800 feet (244 m) or connect with the Crystal Butte Trail in the same distance. As the trail disappears before the unofficial ending, turn back or begin cross-country travel to the summit.

Though named, the trail does not climb Miller Butte.

MILLER BUTTE TRAIL

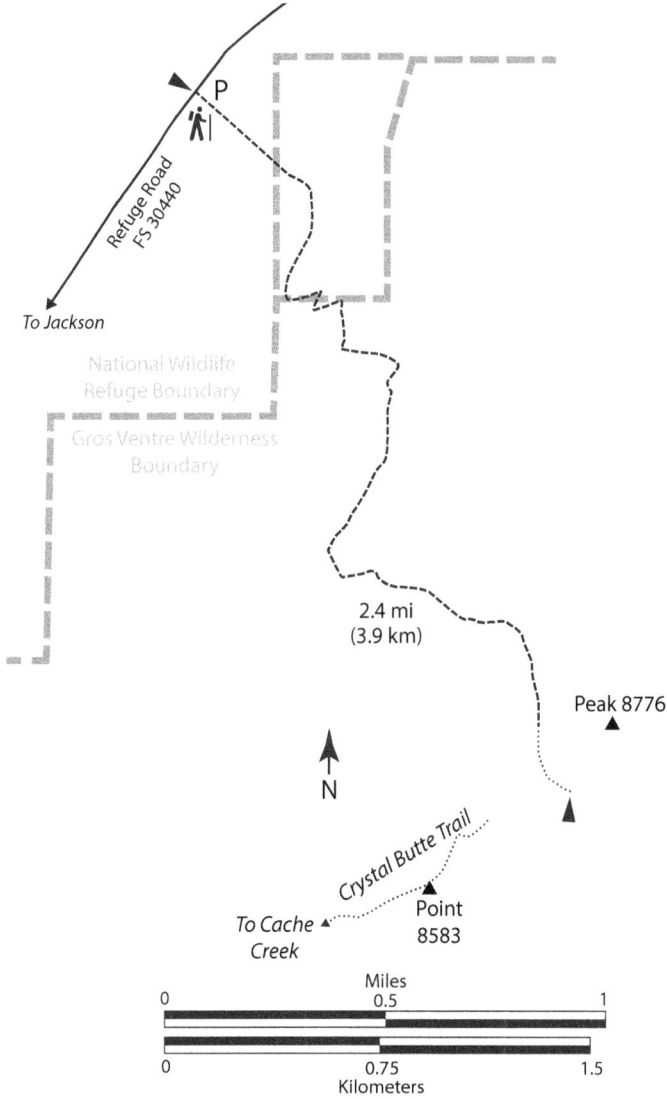

Refuge Road
FS 30440

To Jackson

National Wildlife
Refuge Boundary

Gros Ventre Wilderness
Boundary

2.4 mi
(3.9 km)

N

Peak 8776

Crystal Butte Trail

To Cache
Creek

Point
8583

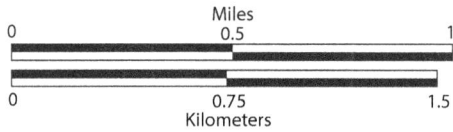

Miles
0   0.5   1

0   0.75   1.5
Kilometers

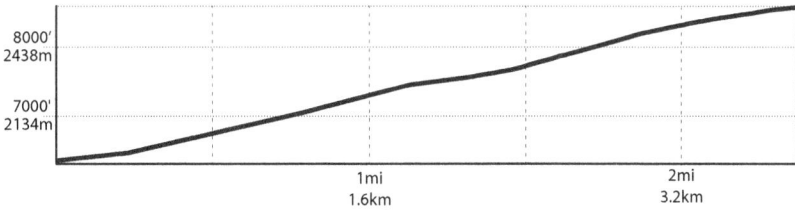

8000'
2438m

7000'
2134m

1mi
1.6km

2mi
3.2km

Curtis Canyon

111 SLEEPING INDIAN VIA FLAT CREEK
(10.6 mi / 17 km / Stren)

GROS VENTRE

Overview: A famous mountain summit with copious wildflowers.

Trip style: Out and back

Distance: 5.3 miles (8.5 km) one way, 10.6 miles (17 km) round trip

Elevation gain: 4,217 feet (1,285 m)

Max. Elevation: 11,239 feet (3,426 m)

Difficulty: Strenuous

Trailhead: Flat Creek, FS 30442 Sheep Mountain unofficial parking
43.5542°N, -110.6038°W / 43°33'15"N, -110°36'14"W
12T 0532005E 4822435N

Traffic: Light

Maps: Blue Miner Lake 7.5' USGS Topo

Notes: High-clearance vehicle recommended.

Trailhead Directions

Drive 1 mile (1.6 km) east from the Town Square to the end of the road. Turn left (N) onto the dirt refuge road. Continue 10.1 miles (16.3 km) along the dirt road (with a 90° left turn at Twin Creek Ranch). Continue past the Curtis Canyon/Sheep Creek turnoff where the road turns northwest and continues along an easily traveled dirt road toward a distant hill.

The road passes over Flat Creek and then makes its way around the southeast side of a hill. Slow down around the blind corner with steel speed bumps. Continue to the refuge boundary, driving past a large parking area.

From here the road is rough and a high-clearance vehicle is recommended. Continue one more mile (1.6 km) to the large pullout with logs and rocks marking the area. A two-track road leading toward the mountain is visible.

Off-trail travel is prohibited in the wildlife refuge. If you have a low-clearance vehicle (sedan, minivan, rental vehicle, etc.), park at the large parking area 980 feet (300 m) east of the refuge boundary marker. Continue 1 mile (1.6 km) on foot to the trailhead to avoid becoming stuck or inflicting vehicle damage.

Trailhead Facilities

None.

Hike Description

Start east from the trailhead. The trail initially follows a two-track old dirt road to the trees. It then enters a tree-covered area following a seasonal creek. The trail continues to wander on the northern edge of a stand of trees before it rises out of the small draw and into more open land where the trail enters the Gros Ventre Wilderness area.

At 1.2 miles (1.9 km), the trail passes through a stand of aspen trees before curving left (north) and entering a heavy stand of trees at 1.9 miles. There may be a significant number of fallen trees to negotiate, as heavy mountain storms have torn up this area before.

Around 3.4 miles (5.5 km) at 9,800 feet (2,987 m), the trees give way to a vast open area of short grasses and endless wildflowers. Although the summit appears close, most hikers feel the elevation from this point on and slow down.

It's often easy to lose the trail at this point, as the ground is rocky and there are multiple paths hikers have taken. When you are up higher, it's easier to follow the trail down than stay on it while climbing.

There are rock cairns all over the place from other hikers trying to be helpful. Be aware that these people who have come before you may not have known exactly where they were.

Should you lose the trail, proceed east across the open landscape toward the cliff. At roughly 4.5 miles (7.2 km), you will encounter the top of the ridge with a sheer drop-off to the east with Blue Miner Lake visible in the canyon.

Continue climbing toward the rocky summit from this point. Once you reach the broken rocks, there will be a climber's trail upward. It is relatively easy to follow.

It travels along a slight ridge as it makes its way toward the summit. Once you crest what seems to be the top of the summit, you need to continue for 0.1 mile (0.2 km) to reach the actual unmarked summit on the belly of the Sleeping Indian.

The nose of this formation is not accessible from this direction, as the rock is crumbly and dangerous. Return to the trailhead along this same path.

Trail Notes

The remains of a crashed aircraft may be seen along the trail. A C-130 cargo plane carrying nine people plus presidential support equipment slammed into the high mountain on August 17, 1996.

Though there was a cleanup in 2015, there may still be remnants of the crash. There is a marker nearby the trail where the aircraft crashed.

Please do not take souvenirs, as this is the site where many people lost their lives and should be treated as such.

The summit is windy and completely exposed. Bring layers. There is no reliable water on this trail past the seasonal creek at the beginning of the trail.

It is possible to make this hike into a traverse by using the hike to Blue Miner Lake. See Blue Miner Lake hike for more information on connecting these two trails into one grand adventure. It is usually done as an overnight backpack from the Gros Ventre Road side of this traverse.

GROS VENTRE

To Jackson

P

Flat Creek
FS 30442

P

Flat Creek

Flat Creek

0   0

N

Miles
Kilometers

1.5   1

5.3 mi
(8.5 km)

3   2

2.1 mi
(3.2 km)

To Flat Creek
Ranch

Gros Ventre Wilderness Boundary

11106

Sheep Mountain
(Sleeping Indian)

Blue Miner
Lake

Gros Ventre
Road

11000'
3353m

9000'
2743m

7000'
2134m

2mi
3.2km

4mi
6.4km

Sheep
Mountain

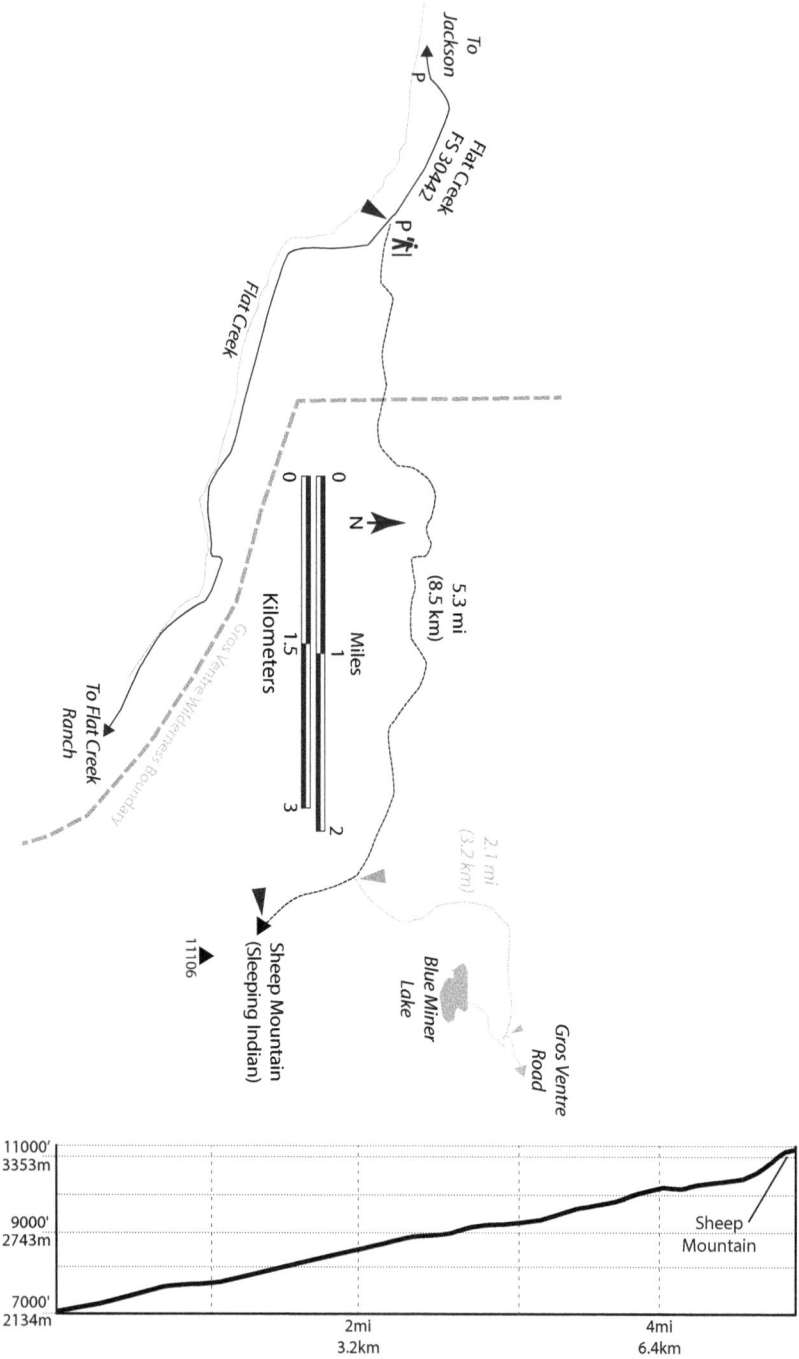

CURTIS CANYON

Blacktail Butte

Blacktail Butte is included in the Gros Ventre hiking area for mapping convenience. Geographically disconnected from the Teton Range, this unique butte defines the middle of Jackson Hole.

The broadleaf aspens that dot its flanks are the perfect backdrop for the picturesque Moulton Barn. It is one of the most photographed barns in the world and certainly the most photographed in Jackson Hole.

While being surrounded by millions of tourists every summer, Blacktail Butte sees surprisingly little traffic. Too often, hikers want to work their way into the Tetons. However, some of the best views of that majestic range are actually from Blacktail Butte.

As is often the case with many areas in Jackson Hole, visitors are not even aware that this location has hiking trails across it. The loop hike is fairly long but easy in terms of elevation gain. Once the steep approach is conquered, much of the travel across the butte is quite easy. For the stunning sunrise and sunset views afforded by this unique standalone feature, it's surprising it does not see more traffic than it receives.

GROS VENTRE

Climbing the eastern trail of Blacktail Butte with Sheep Mountain (Sleeping Indian) looming over the landscape in the upper right corner of the image.

112 BLACKTAIL BUTTE LOOP (9.9 mi / 15.9 km / Mod)

Overview: A tour of one of Jackson Hole's prominent features.

Trip style: Loop

Distance: 9.9 miles (15.9 km)

Elevation gain: 969 feet (295 m) gain/loss

Max. Elevation: 7,452 feet (2,271 m)

Difficulty: Moderate

Trailhead: Meadow Road
43.6249°N, -110.7199°W / 43°37'30"N, -110°43'12"W
12T 0522599E 4830248N

Traffic: Light

Maps: Gros Ventre Junction, Moose 7.5' USGS Topos

GROS VENTRE

Trailhead Directions

Drive north from the Town Square on Cache Street for 10.6 miles (17 km). Turn left (W) on Meadow Road and park to the side to avoid blocking the roadway.

Trailhead Facilities

None.

Hike Description

Start from the Meadow Road parking area, safely cross the highway, and hike east on the old overgrown two-track road. At 0.5 mile (0.8 km), the trail curves right (S) and works its way up an embankment onto the shelf for 0.3 mile (0.5 km) before curving left (E).

There is a marshy spring at 1 mile (1.6 km) to negotiate. The trail follows an old fence line for the next 2.3 miles (3.7 km) along the southern edge of Blacktail Butte. It travels to a stand of cottonwoods, past

old rusted pipes, and connects with Mormon Row.

Turn left (N) and walk on the dirt road for 0.4 mile (0.6 km), then turn left into the large parking area. From here, follow the two-track toward the first steep ridge where the trail begins ascending in earnest for 0.5 mile (0.8 km) before reaching a flat spot.

Continue for 0.4 mile (0.6 km) to a shady spot where the trail curves north, then travels another 0.3 mile (0.5 km) to the first junction. If you wish to reach the summit, turn left and continue for 1.2 miles (1.9 km). Otherwise, continue north past a second trail junction. Shortly after this point, the trail passes a notable sinkhole.

Hike an additional 0.3 mile (0.5 km) to the trail's high point. From here, the trail switchbacks into heavy forest cover. It then turns right (NW) where the trail begins rapidly losing elevation. At 5.7 miles (9.2 km), there is seasonal flowing water.

As you near the scree slope and large rock faces, mind your footing. The trail is narrow and crumbly, inviting twisted ankles and falls. Pass multiple rock faces and climbing areas until the trail exits the tree cover at 6.4 miles (10.3 km) and curves right (N). Hike an additional 0.5 mile (0.8 km) to reach the Blacktail Butte parking area and road.

From here, turn left (S) on the Jackson Hole pathway. Follow this paved path for 2.9 miles (4.7 km) to reach the Meadow Road parking area.

Faster return option

Before embarking on the hike, lock a bike at the Blacktail Butte parking area. Once you finish the descent off Blacktail Butte and return to the parking lot, retrieve your bike. Enjoy the quick ride back to Meadow Road along the protected pathway off the highway.

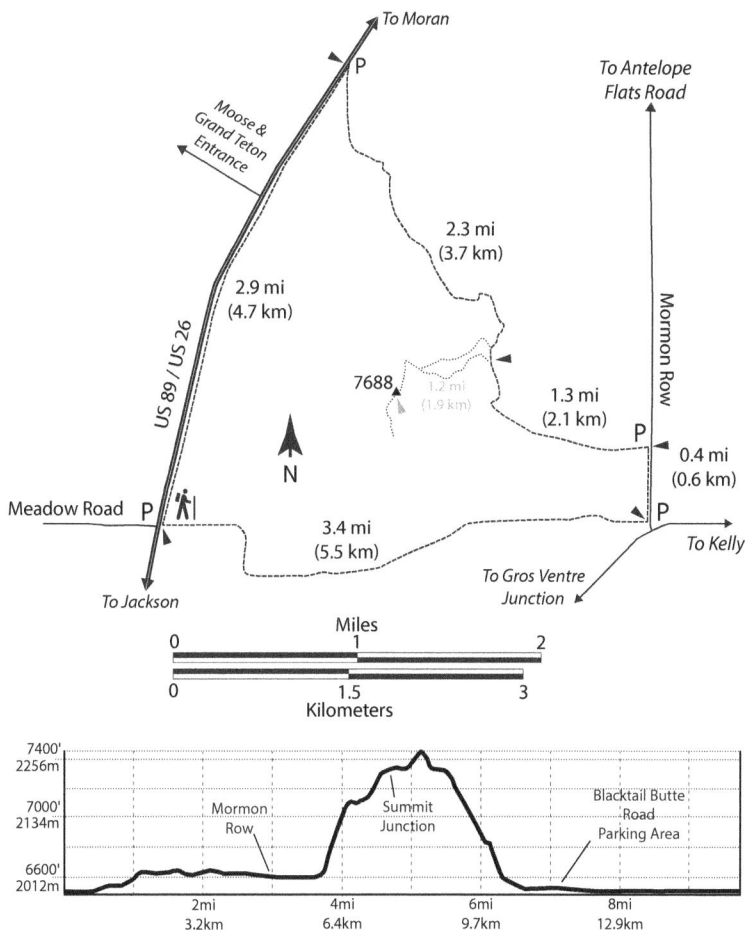

BLACKTAIL BUTTE

113 BLACKTAIL BUTTE SUMMIT
(4.8 mi / 7.7 km / Mod)

GROS VENTRE

Overview: A short hike to a unique Jackson Hole summit.

Trip style: Out and back

Distance: 2.4 miles (3.9 km) one way, 4.8 miles (7.7 km) round trip

Elevation gain: 1,090 feet (332 m)

Max. Elevation: 7,688 feet (2,343 m)

Difficulty: Moderate

Trailhead: Mormon Row Blacktail Butte Summit parking Area
43.6310°N, -110.6645°W / 43°37'52"N, -110°39'52"W
12T 0527064E 4830945N

Traffic: Light to moderate

Maps: Moose 7.5' USGS Topo

Trailhead Directions

Drive north from the square on North Cache Street which turns into US 191 for 6.9 miles (11.1 km) to the intersection. Turn right on Gros Ventre Road and continue 5 miles (8 km) to Mormon Row. Turn left (N) and continue for 0.4 mile (0.6 km) and turn left into the large parking area.

Trailhead Facilities

None.

Hike Description

From the parking lot, follow the two-track toward the first steep ridge where the trail begins ascending in earnest for 0.5 mile (0.8 km) before reaching a flat spot.

Continue for 0.4 mile (0.6 km) to a shady spot where the trail curves north, then travels another 0.3 mile (0.5 km) to the first junction. If you wish to reach the summit, turn left

and continue for 1.2 miles (1.9 km). Pass the stub trail to the false summit and continue into the trees, looking to your right (N) for the true summit in the trees. Hike up the rise and find the limestone rock with the bronze marker.

Continue past the summit for 0.35 mile (0.56 km) to a broad overlook on a ridge. Return on the same trail.

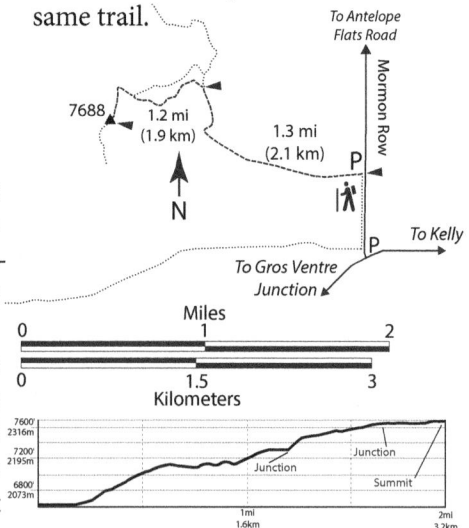

BLACKTAIL BUTTE

114 BLACKTAIL BUTTE TRAVERSE
(4.6 mi / 7.4 km / Mod)

Overview: A hike across a rarely-traversed yet famous Jackson Hole hill.

Trip style: Out and back with a loop option

Distance: 4.6 miles (7.4 km) one way traverse, multiple return options

Elevation gain: 861 feet (262 m)

Max. Elevation: 7,454 feet (2,272 m)

Difficulty: Moderate

Trailhead: Mormon Row Blacktail Butte Summit parking area
43.6310°N, -110.6645°W / 43°37'52"N, -110°39'52"W
12T 0527064E 4830945N

Traffic: Light to moderate

Maps: Moose 7.5' USGS Topo

Trailhead Directions

Drive north from the square on North Cache Street which turns into US 191 for 6.9 miles (11.1 km) to the intersection. Turn right on Gros Ventre Road and continue 5 miles (8 km) to Mormon Row. Turn left (N) and continue for 0.4 mile (0.6 km) and turn left into the large parking area.

Trailhead Facilities

None.

Hike Description

From the parking lot, follow the two-track toward the first steep ridge where the trail begins ascending in earnest for 0.5 mile (0.8 km) before reaching a flat spot.

Continue for 0.4 mile (0.6 km) to a shady spot where the trail curves north, then travels another 0.3 mile (0.5 km) to the first junction. If you wish to reach the summit, turn left

and continue for 1.2 miles (1.9 km). Otherwise, continue north past a second trail junction. Shortly after this point, the trail drops momentarily and passes a notable sinkhole. It then curves around to the northwest, gaining elevation.

Hike an additional 0.3 mile (0.5 km) to the traverse trail's high point. There is a short stub trail to the promontory to enjoy the view.

From here, the trail switchbacks into heavy forest cover, then turns right (NW) where the trail begins rapidly losing elevation. At 2.8 miles (4.5 km), there is seasonal flowing water.

As you near the scree slope and large rock faces, mind your footing. The trail is narrow and crumbly, inviting twisted ankles and falls. Pass multiple rock faces and climbing areas until the trail exits the tree cover at 3.9 miles (6.3 km) and curves right (N). Hike an additional 0.5

mile (0.8 km) to reach the Blacktail Butte parking area and road.

Return across the butte on the same trail.

Alternative Return Option

Before beginning your hike, drive to the Blacktail Butte parking lot and lock a bike. There are rocks with iron rings that you can lock your bike to. Return south along the highway, turn left at Gros Ventre Junction, and continue the driving directions.

Once you traverse Blacktail Butte, collect your bike. Follow the path north for 0.3 mile (0.5 km) to Antelope Flats Road and turn right (E). Ride 1.7 miles (2.7 km) to the Pink House intersection and turn right on Mormon Row. Ride for 2.4 miles (3.8 km) past the world-famous Moulton Barn and across the sage fields on the dirt road to the trailhead.

Be wary of bison, as they frequent this area. Keep an eye out for pronghorn, the fastest land animal in North America, as they lay in the sage during the heat of the day. Pronghorn have keen eyesight and will see you before you see them.

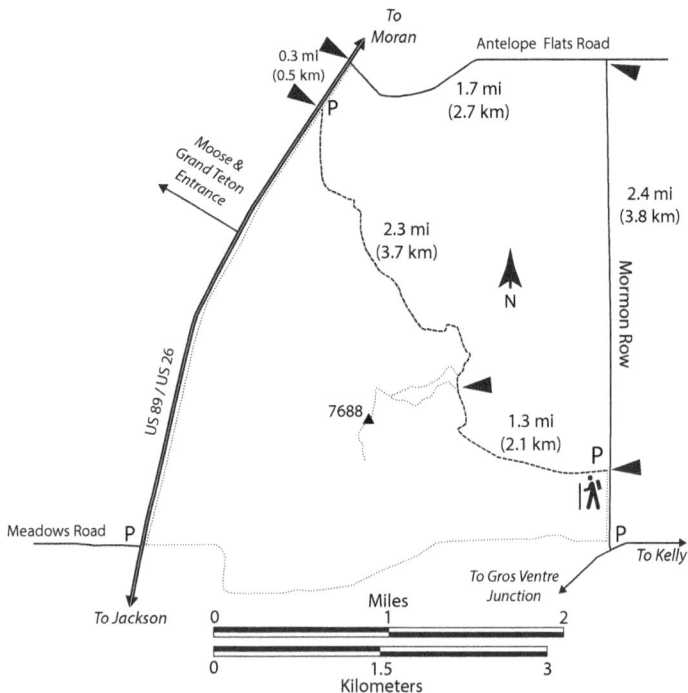

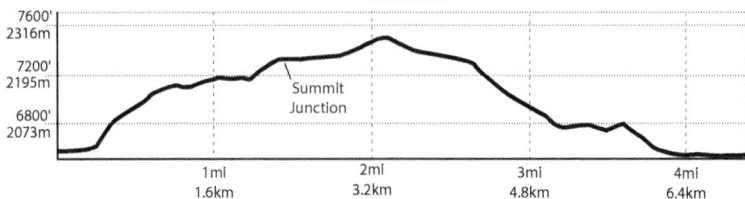

BLACKTAIL BUTTE

Shadow Mountain

Shadow Mountain has become a home away from home for many over the past few years. Once only known by locals, this mountain now shows up on many free camping device applications. As a consequence, the Forest Service has had to adjust its management of the area to reduce the impacts of increased overnight visitation.

If you know where you are going, a trip to Shadow Mountain is worth the diversion from other highlight locations. Just like with Blacktail Butte, some of the best views of the Tetons are enjoyed from the Shadow Mountain area. In fact, one of the author's favorite sunset spots can be found near Shadow Mountain.

As Shadow Mountain is outside of Grand Teton, mountain bikes and other conveyances are generally allowed. Check for updated regulations for any changes in the rules.

The road over Shadow Mountain can be impassible to vehicles without high clearance. Avoid taking an RV up this mountain, as becoming stuck is a major ordeal on the narrow Forest Service road. Scout out your path before committing to it.

Wildflowers along the old jeep track, not far from the 30340B Trail Picnic Hideaway Trailhead.

SHADOW MOUNTAIN

115 30340B TRAIL PICNIC HIDEAWAY
(0.8 mi / 1.2 km / Easy)

Overview: A short hike to a hidden picnic spot on Shadow Mountain.

Trip style: Out and back

Distance: 0.4 mile (0.6 km) one way, 0.8 mile (1.2 km) round trip

Elevation gain: 58 feet (18 m)

Max. Elevation: 7,236 feet (2,206 m)

Difficulty: Easy

Trailhead: Forest Service Road 30340B parking area
43.5611°N, -111.0672°W / 43°33'40"N, -111°04'02"W
12T 0494572E 4823131N

Traffic: None to light

Maps: Shadow Mountain 7.5' USGS Topo

Notes: High clearance or 4WD vehicle recommended. Minor route finding required on the lightly overgrown trail.

Trailhead Directions

Drive north from Jackson on Cache Street to US 191 for 13.6 miles (21.8 km) past Moose and turn right on Antelope Flats Road. Drive 3.3 miles (5.3 km), then turn left on Shadow Mountain Road and continue 1.6 miles (2.5 km) to the dirt road. Drive 0.8 mile (1.2 km) to the parking and camping area. Drive past the gate on the rough road for 1 mile (1.6 km) and turn right on FS 30340B and park.

Trailhead Facilities

None.

Hike Description

Two trails lead away from the parking lot. Follow the south trail into the stand of aspen and dead cottonwood trees. The trail travels south across an old jeep trail at 0.25 mile (0.4 km), then curves left (E) around a hill gaining elevation. It then drops into an aspen patch and then terminates at a flower-covered picnic spot.

The two-track trail leading southwest is an old jeep trail. At 0.3 mile (0.5 km), there is a fine flower-lined pathway leading directly to the Grand Teton. This is an excellent leading lines photography spot.

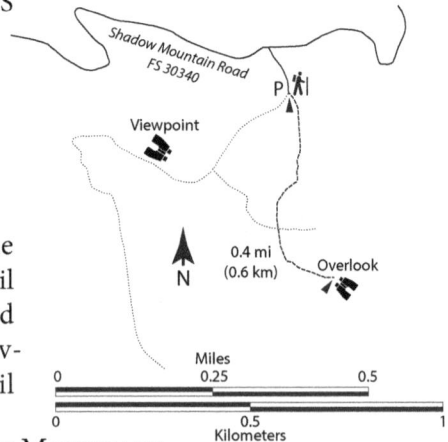

SHADOW MOUNTAIN

116 GRAND VIEW OVERLOOK (2 mi / 3.2 km / Easy)

Overview: A hike to a prime Gros Ventre sunrise viewpoint.

Trip style: Out and back

Distance: 1 mile (1.6 km) one way, 2 miles (3.2 km) round trip

Elevation gain: 149 feet (45 m) gain/loss

Max. Elevation: 8,129 feet (2,478 m)

Difficulty: Easy

Trailhead: Forest Service Road 30345 @ campsite 21/21A junction
43.7189°N, -110.5771°W / 43°43'08"N, -110°34'38"W
12T 0534062E 4840741N

Traffic: None to light

Maps: Shadow Mountain 7.5' USGS Topo

Notes: High clearance/4WD vehicle recommended. Narrow parking.

Trailhead Directions

Drive north from Jackson on Cache Street to US 191 for 13.6 miles (21.8 km) past Moose and turn right on Antelope Flats Road. Drive 3.3 miles (5.3 km), then turn left on Shadow Mountain Road and continue 1.6 miles (2.5 km) to the dirt road. Drive 0.8 mile (1.2 km) to the parking and camping area. Drive past the gate on the rough road for 4.3 miles (7 km), then turn right on FS 30345. Drive 0.3 mile (0.5 km) and park as far off the road as possible.

Trailhead Facilities

None.

Hike Description

Start hiking by walking through the wooden gate that blocks the old road to traffic. Pass the Trail 4211 sign and continue on the main path marked as Trail 4209 for 0.8 mile

(1.3 km). Turn right at the Grand View junction and hike up a slight rise for 0.2 mile (0.3 km) to Grand View Point. Return along the same path to the trailhead.

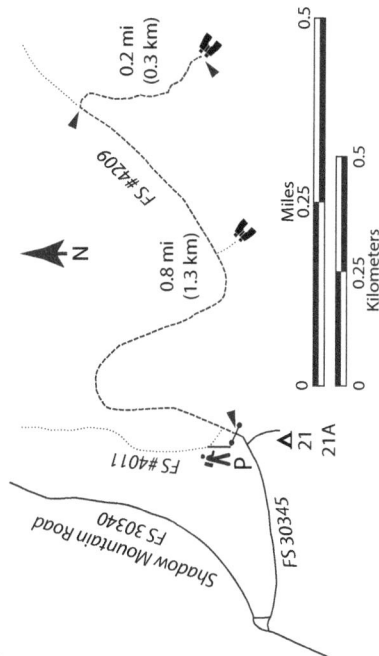

SHADOW MOUNTAIN

GROS VENTRE

117 MOUNT LEIDY LOOKOUT (5.6 mi / 9 km / Easy)

Overview: A rarely-hiked path to an overlook of a prominent summit.

Trip style: Out and back

Distance: 2.8 miles (4.5 km) one way, 5.6 miles (9 km) round trip

Elevation gain: 547 feet (167 m)

Max. Elevation: 8,493 feet (2,589 m)

Difficulty: Easy

Trailhead: End of Toppings Lake Road / FS 30310
43.7549°N, -110.49111°W / 43°45'17"N, -110°29'28"W
12T 0540971E 4844771N

Traffic: None

Maps: Mount Leidy 7.5' USGS Topo

Trailhead Directions

Drive north from Jackson on US 191 for 27.1 miles (43.6 km). Turn right on Toppings Lake Road / FS 30310 across the highway from the Cunningham Cabin. Stay on FS 30310 for 5 miles (8 km), bypassing the spur service roads. Park by the green steel gate. The road may require a high-clearance vehicle.

Trailhead Facilities

None.

Hike Description

Start by walking past the steel gate and continue on the old dirt road. The two-track trail passes by an old rusted forest service gate and continues on.

The trail passes by the outlet of Toppings Lake at 0.4 mile (0.6 km). The path begins curving right (S) and crosses over a large fallen tree (at the time of publication). At 1 mile (1.6 km), there is a faint road to the right that follows the extinct trail shown on the 2013 and 2016 forest service maps.

Continue on the main path as it turns east, winding back and forth along the contours of the mountain. Along this section, there is a large berm and drop-off on the road to prevent further vehicle travel. Continue beyond this short hill.

At 2.6 miles (4.2 km), the road terminates at a forested overlook into a wide downslope. Turn left (N) and continue along the faded path to the top of the ridge. From here, a fine view of Mt. Leidy can be enjoyed with Mt. Moran seen 180° opposite.

This last 0.1-mile (0.2 km) section of trail is not well defined, though it is relatively easy to follow. Stay along the ridge until you encounter a thick stand of timber just beyond the apex of the rise.

MOUNT LEIDY LOOKOUT

The summit of Mt. Leidy is 2.8 miles (4.6 km) from this viewpoint on a bearing of 118° true north. Return along the same path to reach the trailhead parking area. Toppings Lakes is a good side hike.

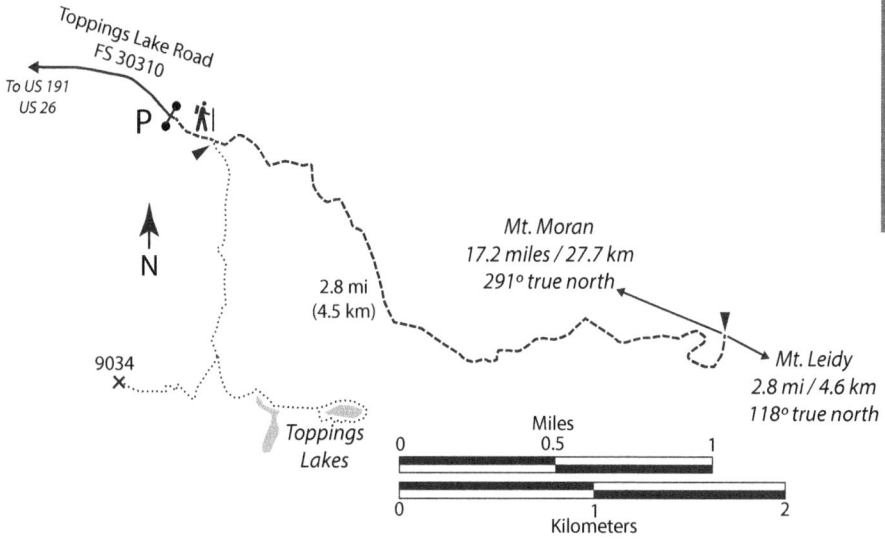

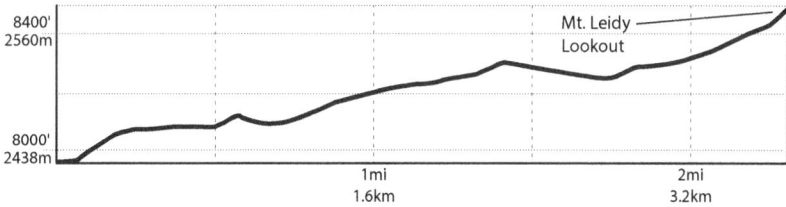

GROS VENTRE

118 SHADOW MOUNTAIN SUMMIT
(4.8 mi / 7.6 km / Mod)

Overview: A summit hike up a popular camping mountain.

Trip style: Out and back

Distance: 2.4 miles (3.8 km) one way, 4.8 miles (7.6 km) round trip

Elevation gain: 1,320 feet (402 m)

Max. Elevation: 8,252 feet (2,515 m)

Difficulty: Moderate

Trailhead: East Boundary Road from Lost Creek
43.7199°N, -110.6169°W / 43°43'12"N, -110°37'01"W
12T 0530862E 4840834N

Traffic: Moderate

Maps: Shadow Mountain 7.5' USGS Topo

Notes: High clearance vehicle recommended for the northern approach.

Trailhead Directions

Drive north from Jackson 21.6 miles (34.7 km) and turn right on Lost Creek Guest Ranch (FS 30340). (The turnoff is 0.17 mile (0.27 km) south of the Snake River Overlook turnoff.) Drive 1.5 miles (3.6 km) east, then turn right (S) at the metal sign that says "FOREST SERVICE ACCESS." Continue 2 miles (3.2 km) south along the base of Shadow Mountain to a broad unmarked turnout.

Trailhead Facilities

None.

Hike Description

Start hiking south along the flat trail toward the large aspen grove. The trail follows the edge of the grove to a junction at 0.3 mile (0.5 km) where the trail splits off from the old two-track road. Turn left (N) on the well-worn trail.

Continue hiking 2.1 miles (3.3 km) up the mostly forested trail to Shadow Mountain Road. Cross the road to reach the summit of Shadow Mountain. Return along the same path.

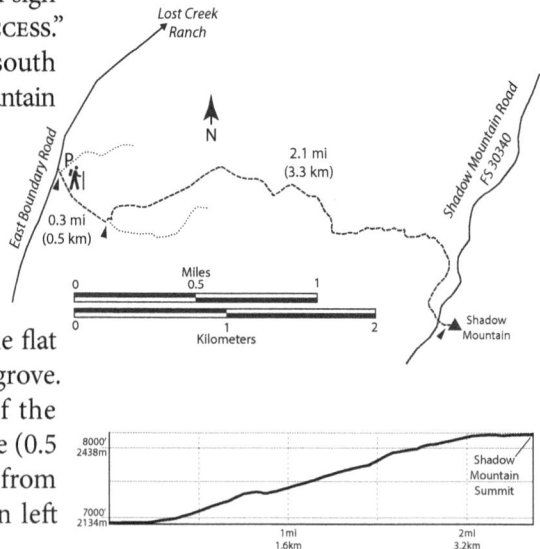

SHADOW MOUNTAIN

119 TOPPINGS LAKE AND RIDGE
(3 mi / 5 km / Mod)

Overview: A rarely visited pair of high mountain lakes and a ridge to watch sunsets from.

Trip style: Out and back

Distance: 1.5 miles (2.5 km) one way, 3 miles (5 km) round trip

Elevation gain: 664 feet (202 m) to Toppings Lake

Max. Elevation: 8,506 (2,593 m) Toppings Lake, 9,036 feet (2,754 m) Ridge

Difficulty: Moderate

Trailhead: End of Toppings Lake Road / FS 30310
43.7549°N, -110.4911°W / 43°45'17"N, -110°29'28"W
12T 0540971E 4844771N

Traffic: Light

Maps: Mount Leidy 7.5' USGS Topo

Trailhead Directions

Drive north from Jackson on US 191 for 27.1 miles (43.6 km). Turn right on Toppings Lake Road / FS 30310 across the highway from the Cunningham Cabin. Stay on FS 30310 for 5 miles (8 km), bypassing the spur service roads. Park by the green steel gate. The road may require a high-clearance vehicle.

Trailhead Facilities

None.

Hike Description

Start by walking past the steel gate and continuing on the old dirt road. Hike for 0.18 mile (0.29 km) to a trail junction on the right (S) side of the road. It may be marked with a rock cairn and orange poles. It is easy to miss the junction. Once you see it, the trail is well-traveled and apparent. The trail is easy to follow through the forest. Hike for 0.8 mile (1.3 km) along a heavily forested path to a junction. Take the left fork marked "TOPPINGS LAKE TRAIL" on a wooden sign. The right fork continues up to the ridgeline (a fine spot for watching a sunset).

Continue on the trail across the meadow for 0.2 mile (0.3 km) to the first Toppings Lake. The trail follows the north shore then enters heavy forest cover. In 0.2 mile (0.3 km) it passes by a marshy area and reaches the east Toppings Lake.

There is a loop around the eastern Toppings Lake. There may still be a swing on the north lakeshore of the east lake. Keep a sharp lookout for it.

Ridge Hike

Return to the single trail junction and turn left. The trail proceeds up a series of steep switchbacks to the ridge, gaining 570 feet (174 m). The trail disappears at the west end of the ridge which is a perfect sunset or picnic spot.

Return along the same trail to reach the parking area.

Hike Notes

The 2013 and 2016 forest service maps and the 1996 USGS 24k 7.5' map show a trail that does not exist anymore. The USGS Toppings 7.5' Topo maps (2012, 2015, 2017) show no trails to the lake.

Should you follow the faded road from the maps, you will encounter a ravine with a creek that drains Toppings Lake, then a cliff-like 50° slope. Avoid following this incorrectly mapped trail.

The climb is extremely steep, crumbly, and somewhat dangerous. There is a substantial quantity of fallen trees at the top of the ridge along the northern edge of the eastern Toppings Lake that makes for slow and difficult travel.

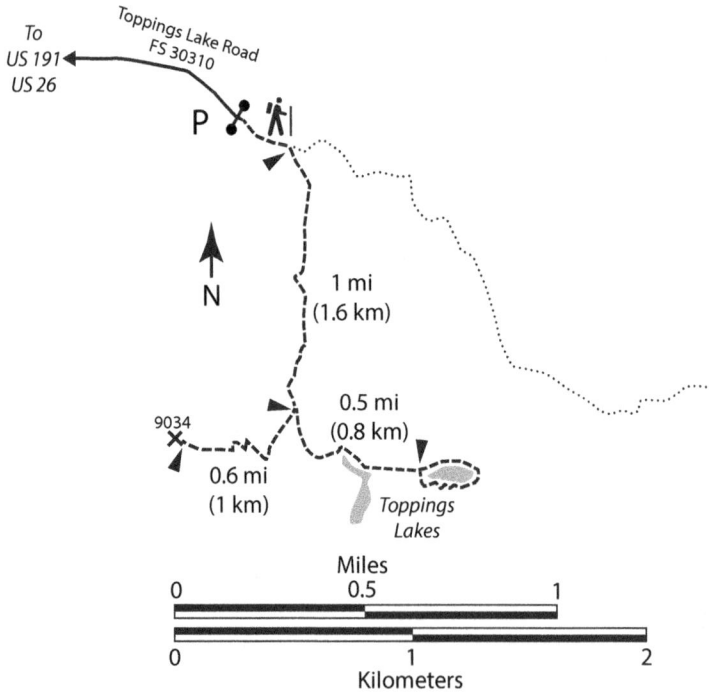

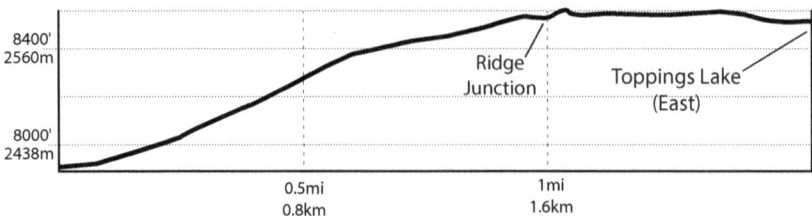

SHADOW MOUNTAIN

SOUTH JACKSON

The South Jackson hiking area is often overlooked by first-time visitors to Jackson Hole. Often, the focus is on visiting Yellowstone with a side trip to Grand Teton. Those areas certainly must be visited. However, with a little bit more time, some of the most enjoyable Jackson Hole hiking areas are in the opposite direction.

There are several highly popular trails with the locals for hiking, mountain biking, horseback riding, dirt biking, skiing, hunting, and general adventuring. Both the short and long trails of the South Jackson area have plenty to offer hikers. One of the biggest advantages is the lack of crowds. Most likely, you will only encounter locals in these areas.

Although the area often appears free of grizzly traffic, do not be lulled into a false sense of security. Grizzlies now roam throughout Jackson Hole. Be prepared with bear spray and make plenty of noise to prevent an unpleasant surprise encounter with a protective female bear and her cubs.

SOUTH JH

Panorama of the Big Munger Trail from the summit of Munger Mountain.

SOUTH JACKSON AREA HIKES

SOUTH JH

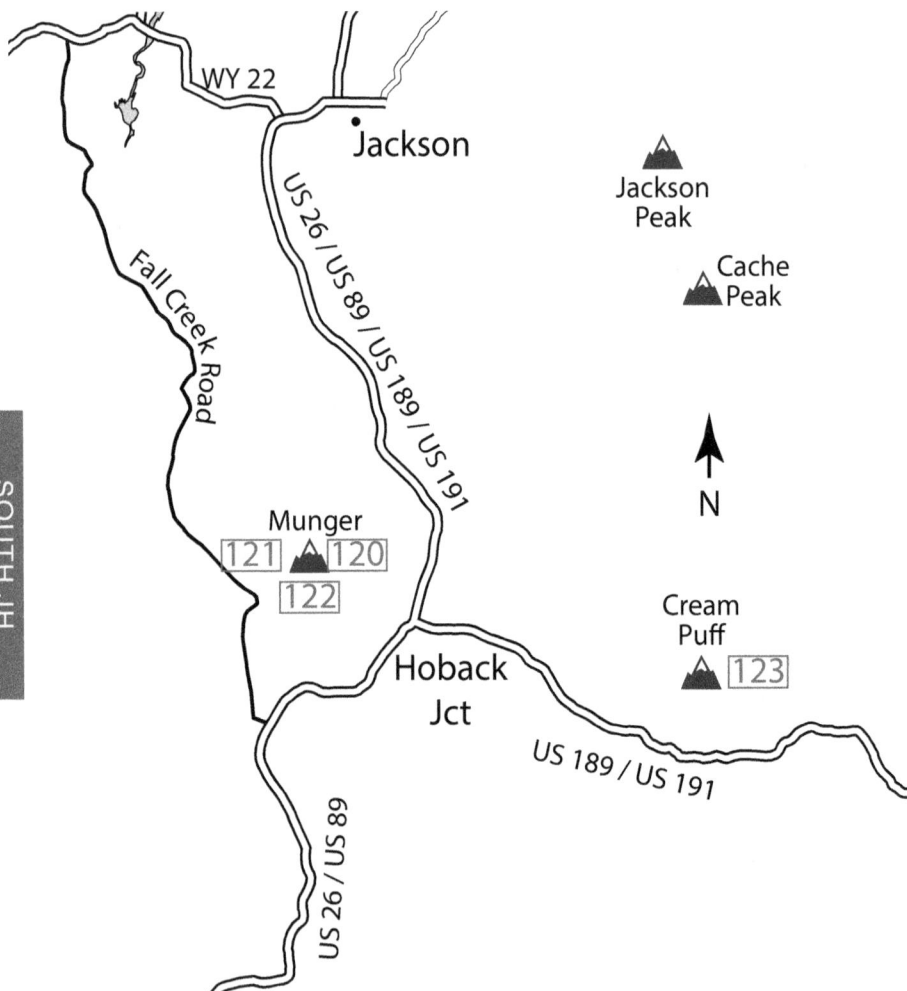

Munger Mountain

120. Big Munger Trail
121. Munger Trail Network
122. Munger Mountain Summit

South Gros Ventre

123. Cream Puff Peak

Munger Mountain

Munger Mountain is one of the best-kept secrets in all of Jackson Hole. Its broad vistas, enjoyable trails, and lack of big crowds make it highly popular with all types of visitors. One of the longest and most open stretches of trails in this entire guidebook can be found on Munger Mountain.

At over 6 miles (9.8 km) long from northwest to southeast, this large mountain dominates the southern end of Jackson Hole. Due to the nature of the area's geography, this mountain's mass isn't ap-parent until you are standing atop the summit. From here, you can see just how large the bulk of this mountain is.

One of the big advantages of hiking Munger Mountain is the Friends of Pathways signs at trail intersections. This organization has put substantial effort into mak-ing the complex network of trails more accessible to all users. Using the trail directions coupled with the trail signs, you can extend a short hike into an all-day affair and hardly backtrack on any trails.

Munger Mountain dominates the southern end of Jackson Hole.

120 BIG MUNGER TRAIL (11.7 mi / 18.8 km / Mod)

Overview: A big loop tour of a big mountain in south Jackson Hole.

Trip style: Loop with bike or vehicle shuttle

Distance: 9.3 miles (15 km) trail loop, 2.4 miles (3.9 km) road travel

Elevation gain: 2,960 feet (902 m) gain/loss

Max. Elevation: 8,383 feet (2,555 m)

Difficulty: Moderate

Trailhead: Munger Summit Trail
43.3438°N, -110.8195°W / 43°20'38"N, -110°49'10"W
12T 0514632E 4799008N

Traffic: Heavy

Maps: Munger Mountain, Jackson 7.5' USGS Topos

Notes: Watch for motor bike and mountain bike traffic.

Trailhead Directions

Drive west from Jackson on Broadway then turn northwest on Highway 22 toward Wilson for a total of 7.1 miles (11.4 km). Turn left (south) on North Fall Creek Road and drive for 12.9 miles (20.8 km) to the dirt lot on the left (east) side of the road to reach the Munger Mountain Trailhead.

Trailhead Facilities

None.

Hike Description

Be aware that motorcycles and e-bikes may be on the trail in specified seasons. Step off the trail.

Begin hiking east from the dirt lot up a small slope through open sagebrush toward a stand of trees on the south side of the trail. At 0.2 mile (0.3 km), the trail intersects the Rock Creek Connector that leads north to the Rock Creek Trail.

Continue another 0.4 mile (0.6 km) to a point where you may notice the original trail suffering from erosion leading straight up the slope in an open area. The dusty new trail section follows a series of switchbacks through a thinly treed area for 0.6 mile (1 km).

Once the new trail connects with the old, the path follows a vague ridge in partial tree cover for 0.6 mile (1 km) until the trail turns northwest. Forest service road 31015 and a parking area will be visible 0.7 mile (1.1 km) south and 1,000 ft (304 m) below your current position.

The ravine to your right (southeast) has an old overgrown trail that leads from the visible parking area toward the summit.

For the next 1.7 miles (2.7 km), the trail works its way toward the summit with little to no tree cover. If weather is threatening, do not continue on, as there are no hiding places past this point.

The new trail with easier switch-backs crisscrosses the old eroded more direct trail. There may be late-season snow patches on the north-facing slopes.

As you approach the summit, you may experience a large number of biting flies. Be prepared with insect repellent.

From the summit, you can see your next 4.5 miles (7.2 km) of travel leading off to the north along the wide ridge that the trail follows. This route, though initially a tough-er climb to the summit, allows hik-ers a continuous view of the Tetons. At the trail junction 0.3 mile (0.5 km) east of the summit, turn left (N). The right (SE) trail travels to the southeast sector of the moun-tain. This entire section is exposed, devoid of tree cover and there is no water. Be prepared for a long haul.

At 5.9 miles (9.5 km), the trail abruptly turns left (W) and initially parallels a heavily worn trail, then meanders away from it. The next 1.3 miles (2.1 km) is rough and may be in the process of rerouting due to the motorcycle and bicycle ruts.

The trail intersects the Squaw Creek Trail (4205B). Turn right and hike 1 mile (1.6 km) to the next junction with Tusky Ridge and Cosmic Carols. Turn right onto Cosmic Carols Connector and hike the short, exposed route for 0.2 mile (0.3 km) before turning right (N) on the Poison Creek Trail (4207) to continue descending.

Finish the trail hike with a 0.9-mile (1.4 km) walk along a section that gains and loses approximately 200 feet (61 m) over this section to end at the North Fall Creek Trail-head.

Return Plan

At the North Fall Creek Trailhead, you will need to walk 2.4 miles (3.9 km) south along Fall Creek Road to reach the Munger Moun-tain Trailhead. A more enjoyable option is to lock a bike to a tree out of view below the large parking area or leave a second vehicle.

Leaving transport at the north trailhead allows you to return to the starting trailhead in short order. This avoids an unexciting, dusty, and busy walk along the road.

Note the elevation profile does not include travel on Fall Creek Road, as there are multiple options.

SOUTH JH

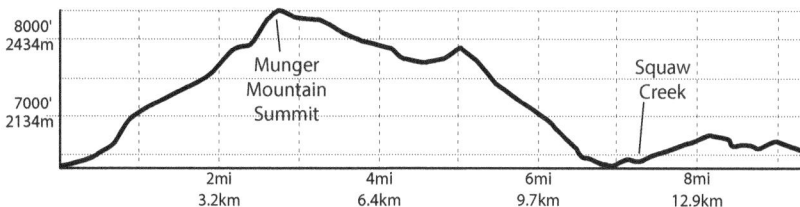

MUNGER MOUNTAIN

BIG MUNGER TRAIL

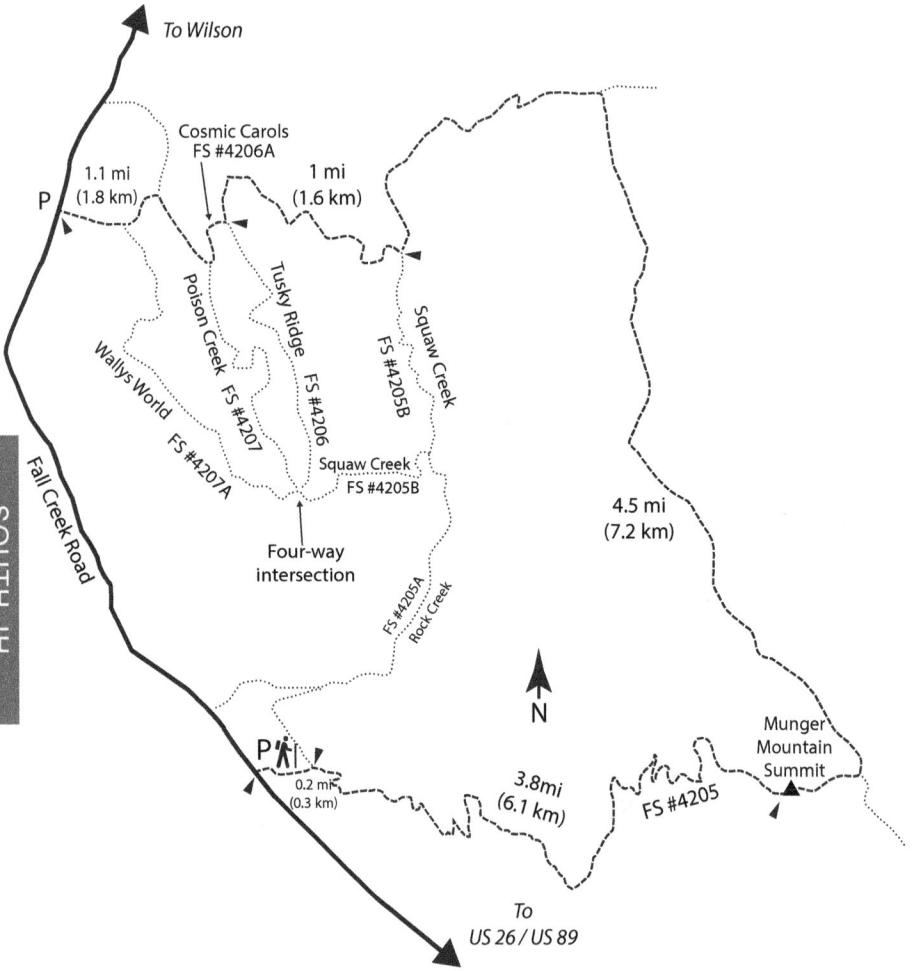

To Wilson

Cosmic Carols
FS #4206A

1.1 mi
(1.8 km)

P

1 mi
(1.6 km)

Poison Creek

Wallys World

FS #4207A

FS #4207

Tusky Ridge   FS #4206

Squaw Creek
FS #4205B

Fall Creek Road

SOUTH JH

Squaw Creek
FS #4205B

Four-way
intersection

FS #4205A
Rock Creek

4.5 mi
(7.2 km)

N

P

0.2 mi
(0.3 km)

3.8mi
(6.1 km)

FS #4205

Munger
Mountain
Summit

To
US 26 / US 89

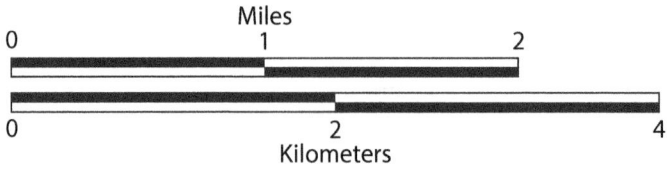

Miles

0   1   2

0   2   4
Kilometers

MUNGER MOUNTAIN

121 MUNGER TRAIL NETWORK (Varies / Mod)

Overview: A popular mesh of interconnected trails.

Trip style: Out and back or loop

Trailhead: North Fall Creek Trailhead
43.3438°N, -110.8195°W / 43°20'38"N, -110°49'10"W
12T 0514632E 4799008N
Rock Creek Trailhead
43.3470°N, -110.8229°W / 43°20'49"N, -110°49'22"W
12T 0514356E 4799363N

Traffic: Heavy

Maps: Munger Mountain, Jackson 7.5' USGS Topos

Notes: Watch for stock, motor bike, and mountain bike traffic.

Trailhead Directions

Drive west from Jackson on Broadway then turn northwest on Highway 22 toward Wilson for a total of 7.1 miles (11.4 km). Turn left (south) on North Fall Creek Road and drive for 10.7 miles (17.3 km) and park in the dirt lot on the right (W) side of the road.

To reach the Rock Creek Trailhead, continue another 2.1 miles (3.4 km) on a partial dirt road. Park on the left (E) side of the road.

Trailhead Facilities

None.

Hike Description

Be aware that motorcycles, mountain bikes, and e-bikes may be on the trail in specified seasons. There are two access points for the trail network. The first and most popular is the North Fall Creek Trailhead. This parking area is busy with hikers, motorbikes, mountain bikers, and horse riders.

The second access area is the Rock Creek Trailhead. The approach is far longer so this option tends to be far less busy. Plus, the parking is limited at this trailhead. The canyon that Rock Creek flows through is a more interesting and scenic approach to the Munger trail network.

Each of the trails described in this chapter have individual distances and elevations. Due to the relatively short distances these trails cover, they are separated for the reader's convenience.

Refer to the trail map to connect together an entire day's worth of hiking. If you want to hike the entire trail network with a minimum of hiking over the same trail twice, follow this suggested route. The total length is 7.7 miles (12.4 km) with only 0.5 mile (0.8 km) of total overlap over the whole route.

Hike from the North Fall Creek Trailhead, turn right (S) on Wallys World, turn left (N) on Poison Creek, turn right at Cosmic Carols, and connect to Tusky Ridge. Turn right (S) on Tusky Ridge, climb up the hill to the four-way intersection. Turn left on Squaw Creek, bypass the Rock Creek junction and continue on Squaw Creek to the Big Munger and Tusky Ridge junction.

Bypass the Big Munger Trail and continue on the Tusky Ridge Trail traveling west, turn right on Cosmic Carols, turn right on Poison Creek, pass the Wallys World junction, and return to the trailhead.

Poison Creek

Length: 2.03 miles (3.27 km)
Elevation gain: 505 feet (154 m)
Max. Elevation:
  7,034 feet (2,144 m)

Starting from the four-way intersection, the trail travels through a mixed aspen and conifer forest with low mixed plants and shrubs. At 0.4 mile (0.6 km), the trail passes by a log bench commemorating "MARK AMES." This is a fine viewpoint to stop and enjoy the open view before entering back into the forested area.

From the bench, the trail continues losing elevation, following a series of tight switchbacks as it works

its way along the creek. This steep trail quickly drops into the ravine and crosses the seasonal creek. In another 0.4 mile (0.6 km), the trail intersects the Cosmic Carols junction.

Rock Creek

Length: 1.83 miles (2.95 km)
Elevation gain: 510 feet (155 m)
Max. Elevation:
  6,829 feet (2,081 m)

Starting at the unmarked Rock Creek Trailhead on Fall Creek Road, hike past the no powered vehicle signs into the Rock Creek area. This wide canyon is quite open with little tree cover. At 0.5 mile (0.8 km), the trail passes through a wood post and wire fence. In a short distance, the trail crosses a seasonal creek over a wooden bridge.

From this point, the trail curves northward and continues on into a broad valley area with light tree cover. At 1.4 miles (2.3 km), the trail passes by a tall sign marked "TRAIL", then shortly crosses a seasonal creek over another wooden bridge.

The trail then enters a patchy mixed aspen and conifer area as it begins working its way up a hill. It gains some elevation in a thicker forest area. This area is still a patchy forest but is more dense with some shade. The trail switchbacks slightly a few times before finally reaching the Squaw Creek Trail junction.

![hiker icon]

Squaw Creek

Length: 1.58 miles (2.54 km)
Elevation gain: 638 feet (194 m)
Max. Elevation:
  7,037 feet (2,145 m)

From the four-way intersection, follow the Squaw Creek Trail for 0.7 mile (1.1 km) as it loses 200 feet (61 m) of elevation when it reaches the intersection with the Rock Creek Trail. This section is fairly open with plenty of sunlight penetrating the aspen and some mixed conifer forest. Bypass the Rock Creek Trail.

Continue on the Squaw Creek Trail as it turns north at the Rock Creek junction. The trail loses elevation along this section. It crosses over the seasonal Squaw Creek on a wooden bridge 0.3 mile (0.5 km) before the trail junction with the Big Munger and Tusky Ridge Trails.

![hiker icon]

Tusky Ridge

Length: 2.24 miles (3.61 km)
Elevation gain: 639 feet (195 m)
Max. Elevation:
  7,047 feet (2,148 m)

From the four-way intersection, the trail begins losing elevation in a mixed conifer and aspen forest area with low growing plants. This trail follows the path down a wide ridge as it loses elevation to Cosmic Carols junction at 1.21 miles (1.95 km).

From the Cosmic Carols junction, continue along the Tusky Ridge Trail as it begins making its way around a broad ridge for 1.03 miles (1.66 km) to the junction of Squaw Creek and Big Munger Trail.

Note that on some Forest Service maps, this trail is named the Tuscany Trail.

![hiker icon]

Wallys World

Length: 1.64 miles (2.63 km)
Elevation gain: 453 feet (138 m)
Max. Elevation:
  7,093 feet (2,162 m)

Starting at the northern end of the trail from the North Fall Creek Trailhead, begin working your way up the trail, slowly gaining elevation after the junction. The lower part of the trail is a fairly open conifer forest with many lodgepole pines and low plant growth. There are several sections of vibrant fireweed.

The trail is relatively smooth with sections of roots crisscrossing the path. There aren't too many rocks on the trail so it's quite easy to walk. Except for a few tight turns, it's fairly easy to see downhill mountain bikers.

SOUTH JH

On the upper part of the trail, the conifers give way to aspen trees with taller shrubs, shortening the view up the trail. Be mindful here and listen for bikes. This trail is highly popular with mountain bikers, as it's a great final downhill trip to the trailhead.

Once the trail breaks through the last aspen patch, it enters a sage and flower zone of no trees. This is where the views become enjoyable the rest of the way. The trail becomes more rocky here, making hiking a bit more challenging. Once the trail reaches the crest, it loses and then gains elevation to the last rise where a bench is. From here, travel downhill and back into the mixed aspen and conifer forest to the four-way intersection and the end of the Wallys World Trail.

Rock Creek Trail on Munger Mountain.

MUNGER MOUNTAIN

MUNGER MOUNTAIN TRAIL NETWORK

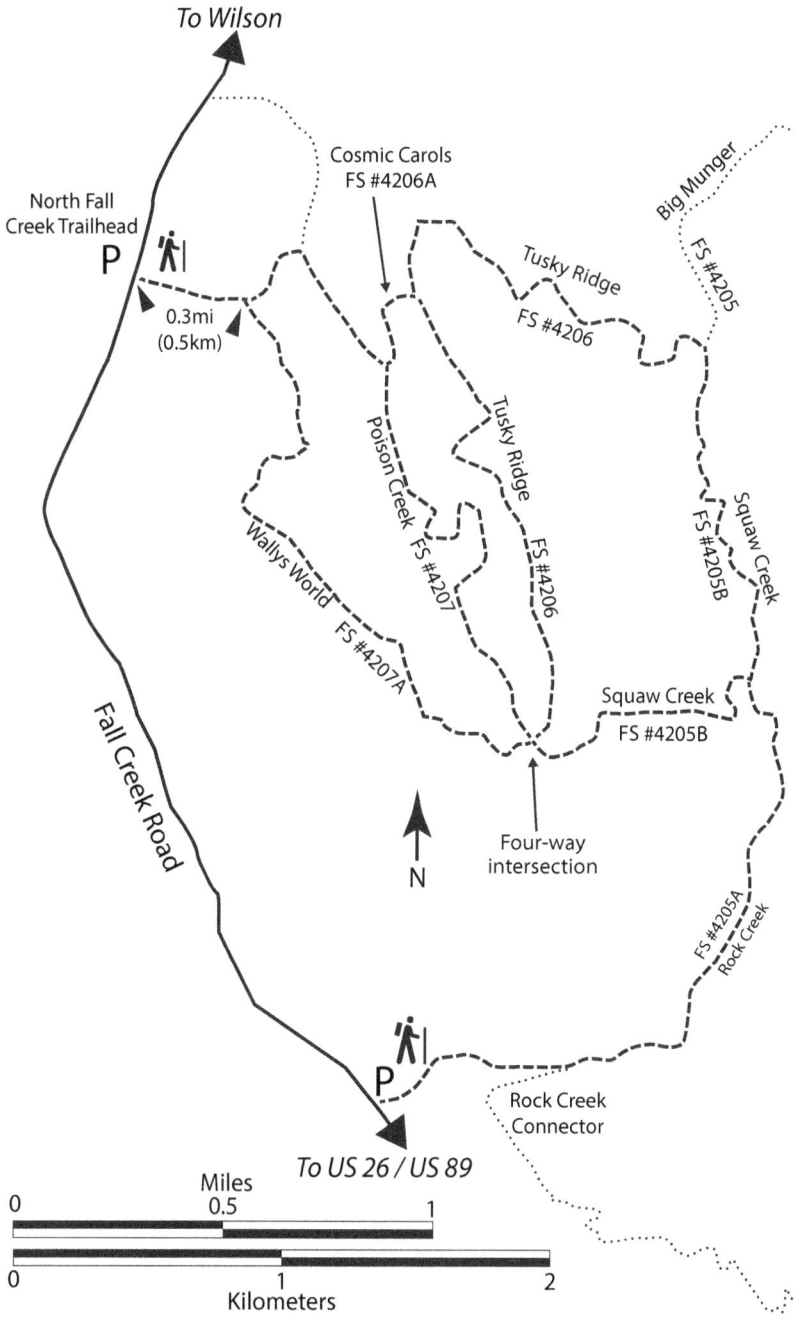

To Wilson

Cosmic Carols
FS #4206A

North Fall
Creek Trailhead

P

0.3mi
(0.5km)

Tusky Ridge

FS #4206

Big Munger

FS #4205

Poison Creek FS #4207

Tusky Ridge

FS #4206

Wallys World

FS #4207A

FS #4205B

Squaw Creek

Squaw Creek
FS #4205B

Fall Creek Road

N

Four-way
intersection

FS #4205A
Rock Creek

SOUTH JH

P

Rock Creek
Connector

To US 26 / US 89

Miles
0.5

0   1

0   1   2

Kilometers

MUNGER MOUNTAIN

122 MUNGER MOUNTAIN SUMMIT
(7.6 mi / 12 km / Mod)

Overview: A hike to one of the best sweeping views of the southern Jackson Hole area.

Trip style: Out and back

Distance: 3.8 mi (6 km) one way, 7.6 mi (12.0 km) round trip

Elev. gain/loss: 2,009 ft (612 m) / 95 ft (29 m)

Max. Elevation: 8,383 ft (2,555 m)

Difficulty: Moderate

Trailhead: Munger Summit Trail
43.3438°N, -110.8195°W / 43°20'38"N, -110°49'10"W
12T 0514632E 4799008N

Traffic: Heavy

Maps: Munger Mountain 7.5' USGS Topo

Notes: The trail was partially rerouted in 2019–2020 so it does not match the Munger Mountain, WY 2017 USGS Topo.

Trailhead Directions

Drive west from Jackson on Broadway then turn northwest on Highway 22 toward Wilson for a total of 7.1 miles (11.4 km). Turn left (south) on North Fall Creek Road and drive for 12.9 miles (20.8 km) to the dirt lot on the left (east) side of the road to reach the Munger Mountain Trailhead.

Trailhead Facilities

None.

Hike Description

Be aware that motorcycles and e-bikes may be on the trail in specified seasons. If you hear a bike approaching, step off the trail, as the rider may not see you early enough for a safe stop.

Begin hiking east from the dirt lot up a small slope through open sagebrush toward a stand of trees on the south side of the trail. At 0.2 mile (0.3 km), the trail intersects the Rock Creek Connector that leads north to the Rock Creek Trail.

Continue another 0.4 mile (0.6 km) to a point where you may notice the original trail suffering from erosion leading straight up the slope in an open area. The dusty new trail section follows a series of switchbacks through a thinly treed area for 0.6 mile (1 km).

Once the new trail connects with the old, the path follows a vague ridge in partial tree cover for 0.6 mile (1 km) until the trail turns northwest. Forest service road 31015 and a parking area will be visible 0.7 mile (1.1 km) south and 1,000 ft (304 m) below your current trail position.

The ravine to your right (southeast) has an old overgrown trail that leads from the visible parking area off toward the summit.

For the next 1.7 miles (2.7 km), the trail works its way toward the summit with little to no tree cover. If the weather is threatening, do not continue on, as there are no hiding places past this point.

The new trail with easier switchbacks crisscrosses the old eroded more direct trail. There may be late-season snow patches on the north-facing slopes.

As you approach the summit, you may experience a large number of biting flies. Be prepared with insect repellent.

The 8,383-foot (2,555 m) summit features a 1946 U.S. Coast and Geodetic Survey marker, the remnants of a fire tower, a pile of rocks, and rusty metal debris.

Trail Options

You can either return the way you came or continue north on the Big Munger Trail for 4.5 miles (7.2 km) to connect to the Squaw Creek and Tuscany Trails. See the Big Munger Trail loop description for more details.

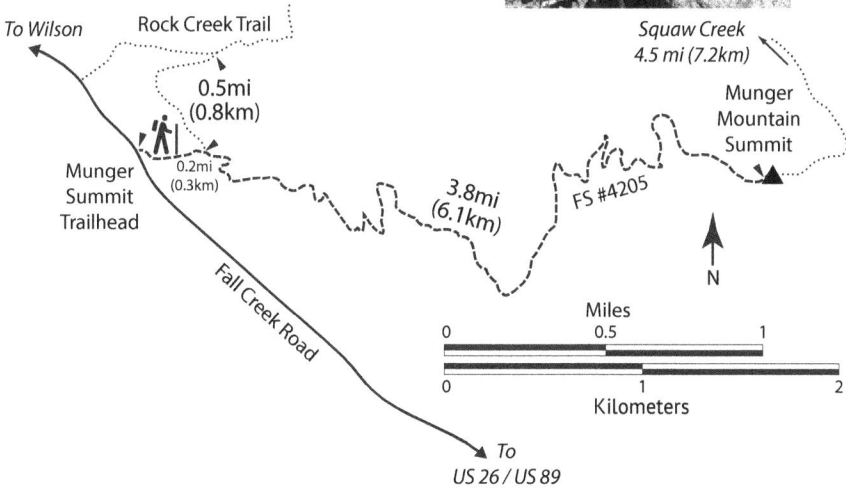

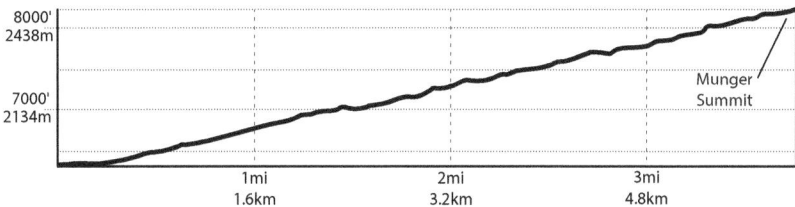

MUNGER MOUNTAIN

Hiking toward the Munger Mountain summit on a hot summer day.

A panoramic view from the summit of Munger Mountain looking north.
Previous page: The 1946 survey marker placed at the Munger Mountain summit.

MUNGER MOUNTAIN

South Gros Ventre

The South Gros Ventre hiking area is at the southern fringes of Jackson Hole. Although technically outside of the Jackson Hole area, the trails in this area are worthwhile and not too far of a drive from Jackson.

Just like the main part of the Gros Ventre range to the north, the southern part of the Gros Ventre range has a very different feel from the Tetons and Yellowstone area. The mountains are quite rugged and can be difficult to travel.

There are no roads inside of the South Gros Ventre range, meaning all access is by trails. As a consequence, this area sees far less traffic than the more popular destinations to the north. The big benefit is there is little vehicle or foot traffic. You can find yourself all alone for an entire day in the South Gros Ventre area.

Wildflowers with an insect along the trail to Cream Puff Peak.

SOUTH JH

123 CREAM PUFF PEAK (10.4 mi / 16.8 km / Stren)

Overview: A challenging hike to an isolated peak in south Jackson Hole.

Trip style: Out and back

Distance: 5.2 miles (8.4 km) one way, 10.4 miles (16.8 km) round trip

Elev. gain/loss: 3,229 feet (984 m) trailhead to summit

Max. Elevation: 9,665 feet (2,946 m)

Difficulty: Strenuous

Trailhead: Cow Creek Trailhead
43.2911°N, -110.5488°W / 43°17'28"N, -110°32'56"W
12T 0536603E 4793241N

Traffic: Light to none

Maps: Bull Creek 7.5' USGS Topo

Notes: The trail enters designated wilderness area.

Trailhead Directions

Drive south from Jackson on US 89 for 13.3 miles (21.5 km) to Hoback Junction. Continue east (marked south on the signs) on US 189/191 toward Pinedale for 10.5 miles (16.9 km). Turn left on FS 30497 (Bull Creek) and drive on the dirt road 900 feet (274 m). Park off the dirt road in the loop to access the Cow Creek Trail.

Trailhead Facilities

None.

Hike Description

Begin the hike from the western side of the dirt road 200 feet (61 m) north of the parking loop. The trail climbs up a small hill and passes through a small wall of trees. There is a wilderness sign at the edge of the stand of mixed trees.

The trail turns south then re-sumes traveling northwest for 0.5 mile (0.8 km) until it encounters the edge of the Gros Ventre Wilderness Area. An overgrown old two-track road intersects the trail at 0.1 mile (0.08 km).

The trail begins working its way up the south-facing slope of the hill to Cow Creek at 1.7 miles (2.7 km). This creek is a muddy crossing late in the season and has flowing water earlier in the summer.

For the next 1.7 miles (2.7 km), the trail continues gaining elevation through a series of flower fields and tree patches. An outfitter camp becomes visible before climbing a short hill. As the trail enters the trees, it forks left up the ridge. Finding the trail junction is difficult, as it is hidden in the shrubs and trees. Once you find it, the path is obvious as it begins making its way up the steep ridge.

Follow the trail up the summit of the ridge at 9,726 feet (2,964 m).

The trail marked on the 7.5' USGS topo does not match the current trail on the ground. If you follow this trail along the southeastern face of the ridge, you will reach a point where you have to climb directly up the loose face to reach the ridge. The climb is steep, loose, dusty, and unpleasant. Multiple trail websites and guidebooks show the trail as continuing below the ridgeline before climbing up to the saddle. If the trail is there, it's overgrown and difficult to follow.

The key to avoid missing this overgrown trail junction is to find it in the trees just above the outfitter camp. Take some time and effort to make sure you find the very clear trail up the ridge for far easier travel.

At the summit ridge, you will actually be at a higher elevation than Cream Puff Peak. Some hikers turn around at this point, as the trail to the outfitter camp is humid and quite buggy in the moist areas.

Should you continue on, you can see the trail from the top of the unnamed ridge as it works its way southwest toward Cream Puff Peak. This is a long and mostly easy-to-follow path to the summit. There are sections where the trail seems to disappear. Stay along the ridge the entire way on the eastern side of the tree line. This path is 1.8 miles (2.9 km) southwest along the ridge to Cream Puff Peak.

Note that the trail seems to terminate at a small false summit 900 feet (274 m) northeast of the official summit. Make sure to hike this short distance to the southwest to climb the extra 27 feet (8 m) to gain the actual summit after this tough hike. Walk along the same trail to return to the trailhead parking area.

SOUTH JH

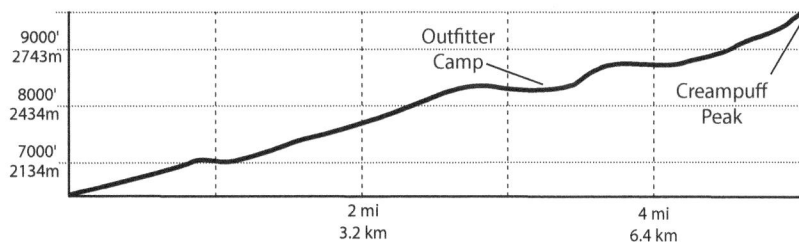

9000' 2743m
8000' 2434m
7000' 2134m

Outfitter Camp

Creampuff Peak

2 mi
3.2 km

4 mi
6.4 km

SOUTH GROS VENTRE

CREAM PUFF PEAK

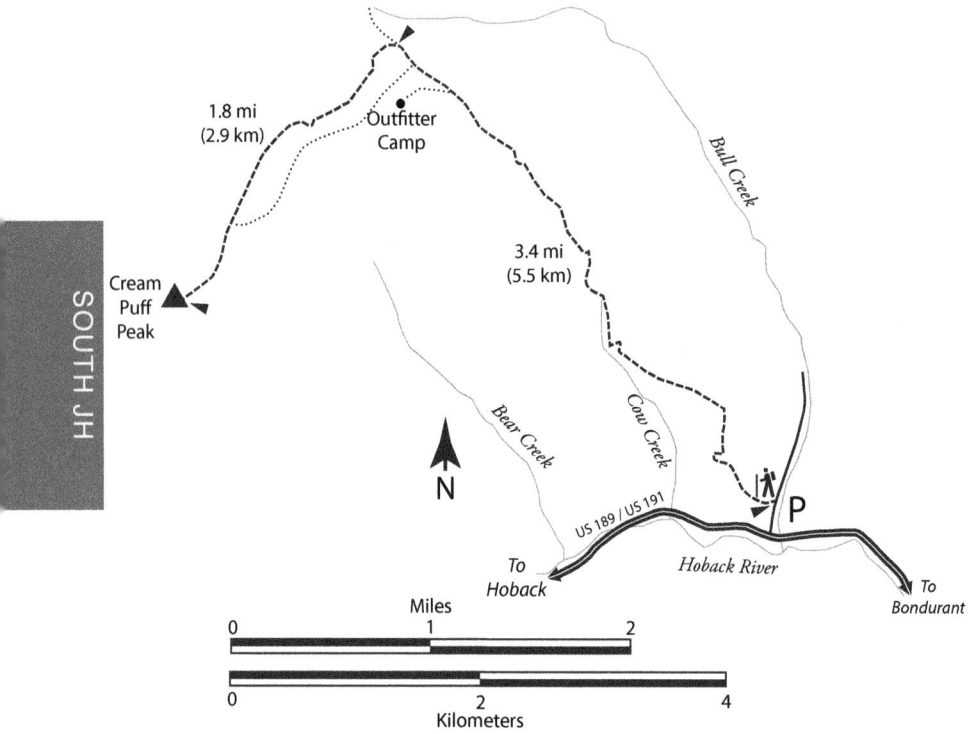

1.8 mi
(2.9 km)

Outfitter
Camp

Bull Creek

3.4 mi
(5.5 km)

Cream
Puff
Peak

SOUTH JH

Bear Creek

Cow Creek

N

US 189 / US 191

P

To
Hoback

Hoback River

To
Bondurant

Miles
0   1   2

0   2   4
Kilometers

SOUTH GROS VENTRE

TOGWOTEE PASS

Togwotee Pass is a high mountain pass at 9,655 feet (2,943 m) at its highest point. This pass is Jackson Hole's northeast access point to other locations in Wyoming, including the iconic Dubois and destinations farther east.

While the weather in Jackson Hole can be pleasant and clear, ice and snow will hang on Togwotee late into the summer season. Always be prepared with an extra jacket and overnight gear, as you never know what the weather may hold for you, even in the middle of summer.

There are many attractive areas to enjoy hiking on Togwotee Pass. There is a lodge on the western side of the pass that has a general store and supplies should you need them.

Note that the entire pass is prime grizzly habitat. The lighter amount of visitor traffic means that grizzlies are more likely to feel less pressure. They'll wander around at will and are often found by the roadside. Do not exit your car to photograph them.

These animals are powerful and unpredictable. Should they feel you are a threat, you will find yourself facing down an angry bear in short order. Always keep your bear spray at the ready. It is useless inside of your pack or awkwardly dangling from it. Be prepared to deploy the spray in two seconds.

SOUTH JH

Snowfall at Lost Lake on Togwotee Pass in late August.

TOGWOTEE PASS AREA HIKES

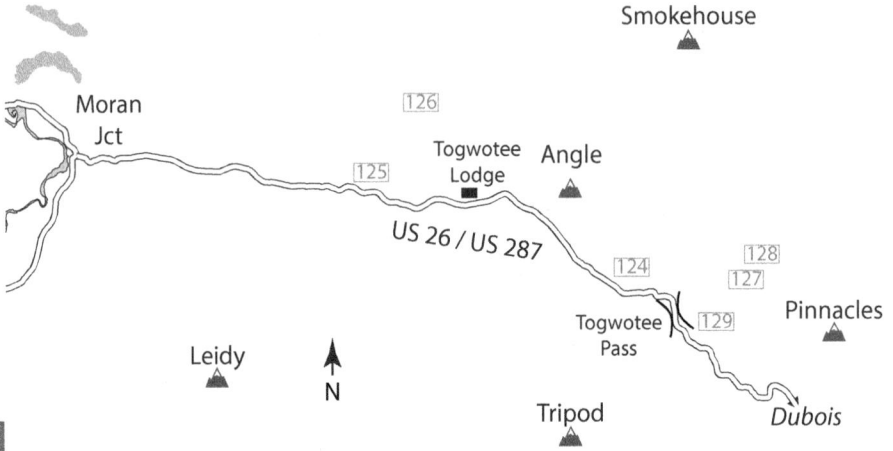

Smokehouse

Moran
Jct
126

Togwotee   Angle
Lodge
125

US 26 / US 287

124   128
127

Togwotee   129   Pinnacles
Pass

Leidy

N

Tripod   Dubois

SOUTH JH

Togwotee Pass West   **Togwotee Pass East**

124. Lost Lake   127. Jade Lakes

125. Rosies Ridge   128. Rainbow and Upper Brooks Lake

126. Turpin Meadows Ridge   129. Wind River Lake

Rosies Ridge Trail overlooking Blackrock Creek during light snowfall in August.

Togwotee Pass West

Hikes to the west of the Continental Divide are categorized into the Togwotee Pass West area. Several unique and little-known trails have interesting highlights found nowhere else in Jackson Hole.

One of the environmental features of the area is the relative dryness of the landscape. Although there are plenty of lakes, ponds, and creeks, the summer on Togwotee feels extra dry compared to the area around the Tetons.

The geography and geology of the Togwotee area is highly varied. There are meadows, high summits, and caves to be explored in the area. There are few roads off the highway, so much of the exploration in this area will be on foot.

Wherever you choose to go, make sure to be prepared for winter weather at any time. It has significantly snowed in July and August all along the pass. Cold weather catches many visitors unprepared.

Unmarked junction on the Turpin Meadows Ridge Trail.

TOGWOTEE

124 LOST LAKE (2.6 mi / 4.2 km / Easy)

Overview: An easy hike to a pretty, lightly visited high-altitude lake.
Trip style: Out and back
Distance: 1.3 miles (2.1 km) one way, 2.6 miles (4.2 km) round trip
Elev. gain/loss: 431 feet (131 m)
Max. Elevation: 9,551 feet (2,911 m)
Difficulty: Easy
Trailhead: Lost Lake Trailhead
43.7738°N, -110.1127°W / 43°46'26"N, -110°06'46"W
12T 0571411E 4847128N
Traffic: None
Maps: Togwotee Pass 7.5' USGS Topo

Trailhead Directions

Drive north from Jackson on US 191 for 30.3 miles (48.8 km) to Moran Junction. Continue past the junction, staying on US 26 / US 287, drive an additional 21.6 miles (34.9 km), past Togwotee Lodge, to the unmarked turnoff on FS 30200.

There have been signs for Lost Lake at this turnout in the past but at the time of this writing, there was no sign. Either park at the turnoff here or continue in your high-clearance vehicle on the forest service road for 0.4 mile (0.6 km) to the gated FS 30020. Falling trees have destroyed the old steel gate.

Trailhead Facilities

None.

Hike Description

Begin the hike at the old steel gate along the old forest service road. There may be a substantial number of fallen trees to discourage onward vehicle travel.

Hike along the obvious forest service road for 1.1 miles (1.8 km) to the high point of the dirt road. The road then drops steeply to the lakeshore. Slight steam and fog rise from this lake in cold and winter conditions.

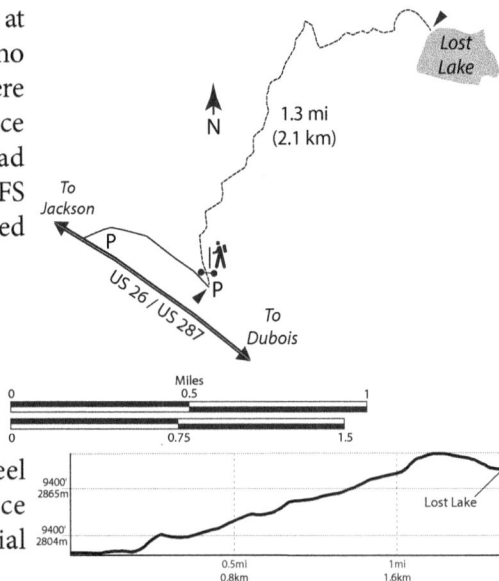

125 ROSIES RIDGE (8.8 mi / 14.2 km / Easy)

Overview: An easy longer hike with river views.
Trip style: Out and back
Distance: 4.4 miles (7.1 km) one way, 8.8 miles (14.2 km) round trip
Elev. gain/loss: 817 feet (249 m)
Max. Elevation: 7,939 feet (2,420 m)
Difficulty: Easy
Trailhead: Rosies Ridge parking area
43.8181°N, -110.2679°W / 43°49'05"N, -110°16'05"W
12T 0558873E 4851932N
Traffic: Light to none
Maps: Rosies Ridge 7.5' USGS Topo

Trailhead Directions

Drive north from Jackson on US 191 for 30.3 miles (48.8 km) to Moran Junction. Continue past the junction, staying on US 26 / US 287, drive an additional 13 miles (20.8 km) and turn left (N) on Turpin Meadow [Guest] Ranch Road (FS 30050). Continue 0.25 mile (0.4 km) and turn left on Rosies Ridge Road (FS 30060), then drive 0.2 mile (0.3 km) and park at the wide pullout area without blocking the gate.

Trailhead Facilities

None.

Hike Description

Begin the hike headed west on the well-traveled two-track road (FS 30060). In 0.2 mile (0.3 km), you will pass through a narrow brown steel forest service gate. It may be locked depending on the season.

From the gate, the trail travels 1.3 miles (2.1 km) northwest, then turns west. Along this section, there are several spur roads to campsites along the way.

The trail continues for 2.8 miles (4.5 km), passing additional spur roads that all terminate in areas useful for dispersed camping. Several are worth exploring. Many end in tranquil spots with excellent views of the valley to the south (highway side) of the ridge that Blackrock Creek meanders through.

To the north is a fine, broad view of the expansive Teton Wilderness area which is a prime grizzly habitat. The mountain summits appear to stretch to the horizon.

Once the two-track terminates at the end of the gate, enjoy the view from the rise. Note that the gate and fence protect an active facility. Do not pass the gate or go around the fencing.

ROSIES RIDGE

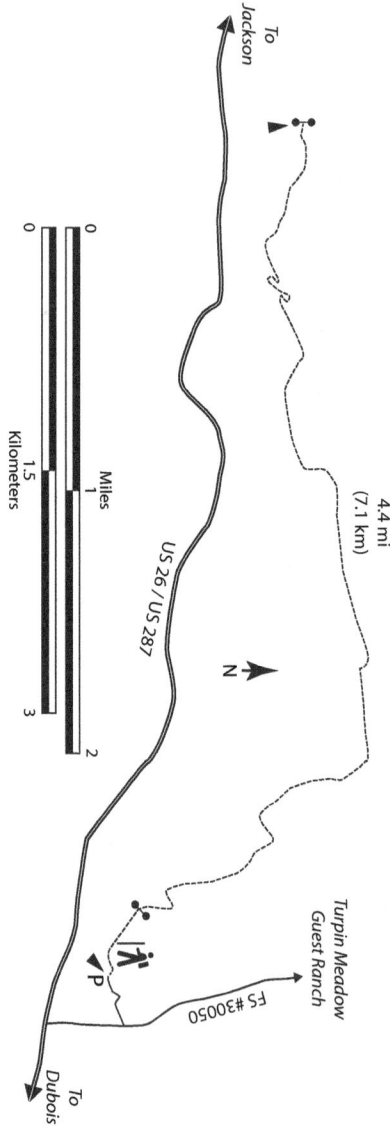

To Jackson

4.4 mi (7.1 km)

US 26 / US 287

N →

0
0

1.5
Kilometers

Miles
1

3
2

Turpin Meadow Guest Ranch

FS #30050

P

To Dubois

TOGWOTEE

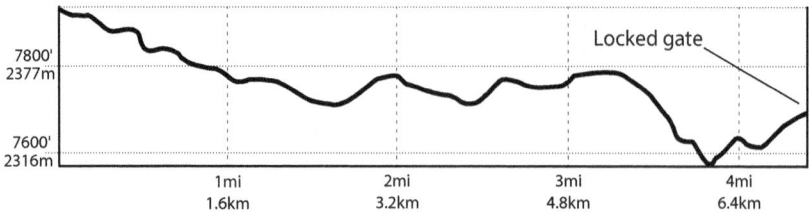

Locked gate

7800'
2377m

7600'
2316m

| 1mi | 2mi | 3mi | 4mi |
| 1.6km | 3.2km | 4.8km | 6.4km |

TOGWOTEE PASS WEST

126 TURPIN MEADOW RIDGE (5.2 mi / 8.4 km / Mod)

Overview: A loop circling a beautiful popular high-altitude meadow.
Trip style: Loop
Distance: 5.2 miles (8.4 km)
Elev. gain/loss: 817 feet (249 m)
Max. Elevation: 7,748 feet (2,362 m)
Difficulty: Moderate
Trailhead: Turpin Meadow Trailhead
43.8561°N, -110.2625°W / 43°51'22"N, -110°15'45"W
12T 0559271E 4856153N
Traffic: Light
Maps: Rosies Ridge 7.5' USGS Topo
Notes: Expect stock animals on the trail.

Trailhead Directions

Drive north from Jackson on US 191 for 30.3 miles (48.8 km) to Moran Junction. Continue past the junction, staying on US 26 / US 287, drive an additional 3.5 miles (5.6 km) and turn left (N) on Buffalo Valley Road (FS 30050). Continue 9.7 miles (16.6 km) past Tracey Lake to the Turpin Meadow Guest Ranch area.

Turn left (E) just before the bridge on FS 30065. The road transitions from pavement to dirt before the fork in the road. In 600 feet (183 m), turn right (FS 30066) at the fork marked "TURPIN MEADOW SUMMER HOME AREA." Continue 0.4 mile (0.6 km) to the Turpin Meadow Trailhead near the horse corrals.

Trailhead Facilities

Information kiosk, restrooms, camping areas.

Hike Description

Begin the hike past the kiosk on the trail marked North Fork Buffalo Trail (FS 6047). In 0.27 mile (0.43 km), take the unmarked left fork on the trail just before the main trail curves around a ridge. If you continue on the well-traveled horse trail, you will drop down to the river. The trail you want travels directly up the ridge.

In 0.5 mile (0.8 km), you will reach Point 7392 (on the 7.5' USGS Topo map). The view of Turpin Meadow at this point is sublime. The arcing curve of the Buffalo Fork cuts across the landscape. As the trail continues north, in another 0.3 mile (0.5 km), there is an unmarked junction. Take the left (W) fork that keeps you circling Turpin Meadow on a series of switchbacks.

At 1.8 miles (2.9 km), the path reaches the trail's high point. From here, the trail continues 0.6 mile (1 km) northeast, then curves around and heads west and southwest.

At 3.1 miles (5 km), the ridge trail intersects the Clear Creek Trail. Stay left, continuing to lose elevation into Turpin Meadow. At 4.1 miles (6.6 km), the trail intersects the Turpin Meadow Loop road. There is a sign for the Teton Wilderness and the trail is marked as the Clear Creek Trail.

Cross the road and continue following the trail south through the center of the meadow to the buck rail fence marked with a sign for the Clear Creek Trail. Reconnect with the dirt road and follow the loops around to the trailhead parking area.

Note that the grasses by the trailhead kiosk are full of small burrs that will stick to all clothing, even hardshell jackets. Avoid walking through the grasses here or placing any item on the ground. The burrs are small and difficult to remove from clothing, even from eVent and Goretex fabrics.

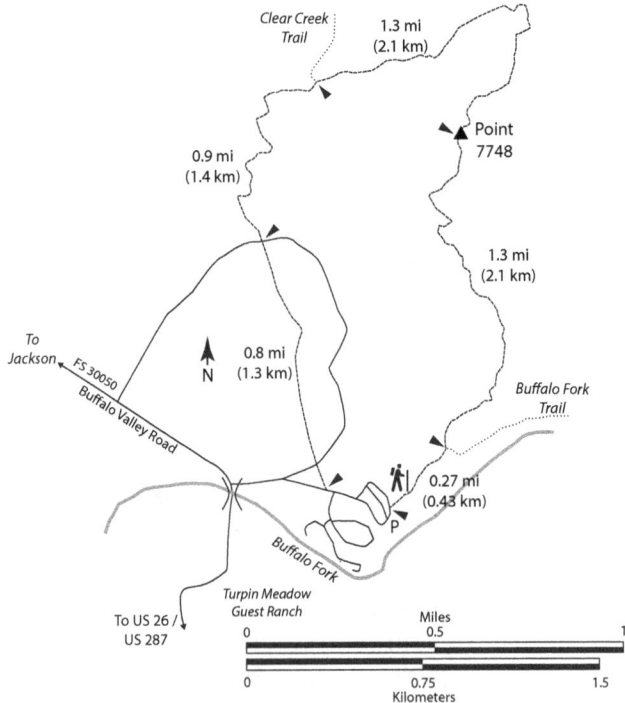

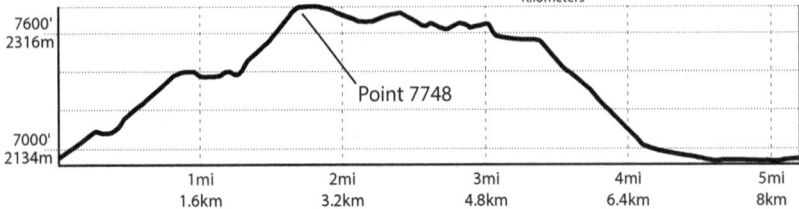

TOGWOTEE PASS WEST

Togwotee Pass East

Togwotee Pass East is one of the best and lightly-visited areas in this guidebook. Although technically outside of the Jackson Hole area, it is impossible to exclude some of the select hikes contained in this section.

One of the best fishing lakes in all of the region is located in the Togwotee Pass area. With your fishing license, a rod, and the appropriate lures or flies, you can find yourself enjoying an afternoon of angling like you never have anywhere else.

One of the easiest and shortest lake hikes is also contained in this portion of the book. The hike around Wind River Lake is pleasant and takes little time. Then, after the hike, enjoy the picnic grounds overlooking the lake. Should you be passing by, take the short walk. It is well worth your time.

The lakes in eastern Togwotee are beautiful and world-renowned. Anglers and backcountry enthusiasts often talk about Brooks Lake Lodge with reverent tones. Once you visit the area, you will better understand why others speak about this area with excitement and awe. It is worth the drive.

Snowfall on September 1 at Wind River Lake on Togwotee Pass.

TOGWOTEE

127 JADE LAKES (5.4 mi / 8.7 km / Mod)

Overview: Visit beautiful backcountry lakes with excellent fishing.

Trip style: Loop

Distance: 5.4 miles (8.7 km)

Elev. gain/loss: 589 feet (180 m)

Max. Elevation: 9,650 feet (2,941 m)

Difficulty: Moderate

Trailhead: Brooks Lake
43.75I3°N, -1I0.0059°W / 43°45'05"N, -1I0°00'2I"W
I2T 0580032E 4844736N

Traffic: Light to moderate

Maps: Togwotee Pass 7.5' USGS Topo

Trailhead Directions

Drive north from Jackson on US 191 for 30.3 miles (48.8 km) to Moran Junction. Continue past the junction, staying on US 26 / US 287, drive an additional 32.8 miles (52.8 km) and turn left (N) on Brooks Lake Recreation Area on FS 515. Drive 5.2 miles (8.4 km) to the western end of the dirt road at the boat ramp.

Avoid the western end of FS 151 unless you have a 4WD. This route is a narrow jeep trail suitable and may be impassable.

Trailhead Facilities

Information kiosk.

Hike Description

Begin the hike at the western end of the loop parking lot. The beginning section of the trail happens to follow the Continental Divide Trail, a trail that runs from Mexico to Canada along the Continental Divide. You may see signs marked "CDT" for this route.

The trail follows the western edge of Brooks Lake along a well-traveled pathway. At 0.5 mile (0.8 km), take the right fork and continue along the lakeshore for another 0.4 mile (0.6 km) where the trail departs the lake. This section of trail has many interconnects, splits, and junctions. Stay to the right and work your way along the broadest path heading north.

As the path departs Brooks Lake, it travels into a wide-open area. It stays to the west of Brooks Lake Creek. At 1.8 miles (2.9 km), you will reach the junction for Jade Lakes and Upper Brooks (and Rainbow) Lake. Take the left fork toward Jade Lakes.

Hike another 0.3 mile (0.5 km) to the next junction and take the left fork toward Lower Jade Lake. The trail climbs steeply and shortly

TOGWOTEE

encounters Lower Jade Lake.

The trail meanders along the west edge of the lake, then continues south to Upper Jade Lake. Following the eastern side of the lake, the trail leaves the lake and begins traveling southeast. It passes between two large hills, losing some elevation as it follows the creek. The trail then rapidly drops down the slope overlooking Brooks Lake.

The trail reconnects with the path that follows the western edge of Brooks Lake. Turn right and fol-low the last section of the trail to the trailhead.

There is great fishing potential at Lower Jade Lake, as trout tend to swim along the shoreline. A Wyoming fishing license is required.

Note that several popular trail map websites and applications have errors in their trails for this hike. Be prepared for some exploration and route finding.

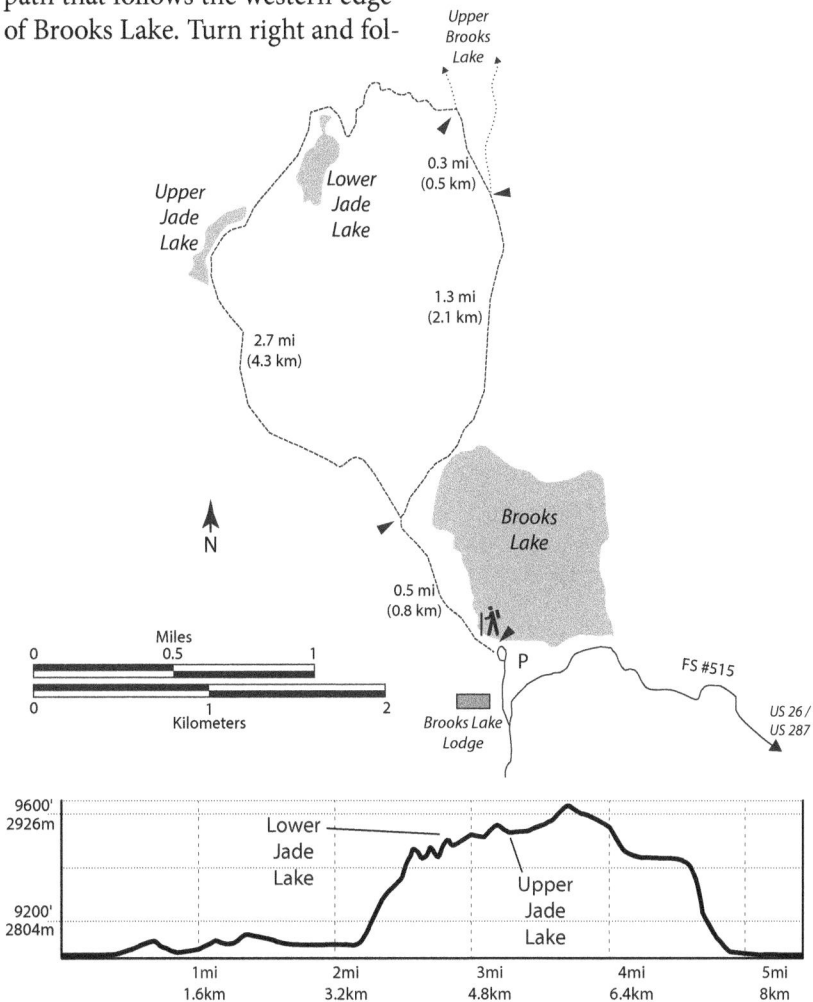

Upper Brooks Lake

0.3 mi (0.5 km)

Lower Jade Lake

Upper Jade Lake

1.3 mi (2.1 km)

2.7 mi (4.3 km)

N

Brooks Lake

0.5 mi (0.8 km)

Miles
0   0.5   1

0   1   2
        Kilometers

P

FS #515

US 26 / US 287

Brooks Lake Lodge

9600' 2926m

Lower Jade Lake

Upper Jade Lake

9200' 2804m

1mi   2mi   3mi   4mi   5mi
1.6km   3.2km   4.8km   6.4km   8km

TOGWOTEE

TOGWOTEE PASS EAST

128 RAINBOW AND UPPER
BROOKS LAKE (6.6 mi / 10.6 km / Mod)

Overview: A hike to secluded backcountry lakes with good fishing.

Trip style: Loop

Distance: 6.6 miles (10.6 km)

Elev. gain/loss: 172 feet (52 m)

Max. Elevation: 9,227 feet (2,812 m)

Difficulty: Easy to moderate

Trailhead: Brooks Lake
43.7513°N, -110.0059°W / 43°45'05"N, -110°00'21"W
12T 0580032E 4844736N

Traffic: Light to moderate

Maps: Togwotee Pass 7.5' USGS Topo

Trailhead Directions

Drive north from Jackson on US 191 for 30.3 miles (48.8 km) to Moran Junction. Continue past the junction, staying on US 26 / US 287, drive an additional 32.8 miles (52.8 km) and turn left (N) on Brooks Lake Recreation Area on FS 515. Drive 5.2 miles (8.4 km) to the western end of the dirt road at the boat ramp.

Avoid the western end of FS 151 unless you have a 4WD. This route is a narrow jeep trail suitable and may be impassable.

Trailhead Facilities

Information kiosk.

Hike Description

Begin the hike at the western end of the loop parking lot. The beginning section of the trail happens to follow the Continental Divide Trail, a trail that runs from Mexico to Canada along the Continental Divide. You may see signs marked "CDT" for this route.

The trail follows the western edge of Brooks Lake along a well-traveled pathway. At 0.5 mile (0.8 km), take the right fork. The trail continues through the broad area, gaining and losing some elevation for 1.5 miles (2.4 km). Take the left fork of the short split before the lake, staying along the western edge of the tree line. Be aware there are multiple paths along this trail that can make navigation difficult.

The trails merge before encountering the edge of Upper Brooks Lake. From this point, you can continue around Upper Brooks to reach Rainbow Lake or return directly along this path.

Note that the distances and elevation gains noted in the trail information are based on walking completely around Upper Brooks Lake.

RAINBOW AND UPPER BROOKS LAKE

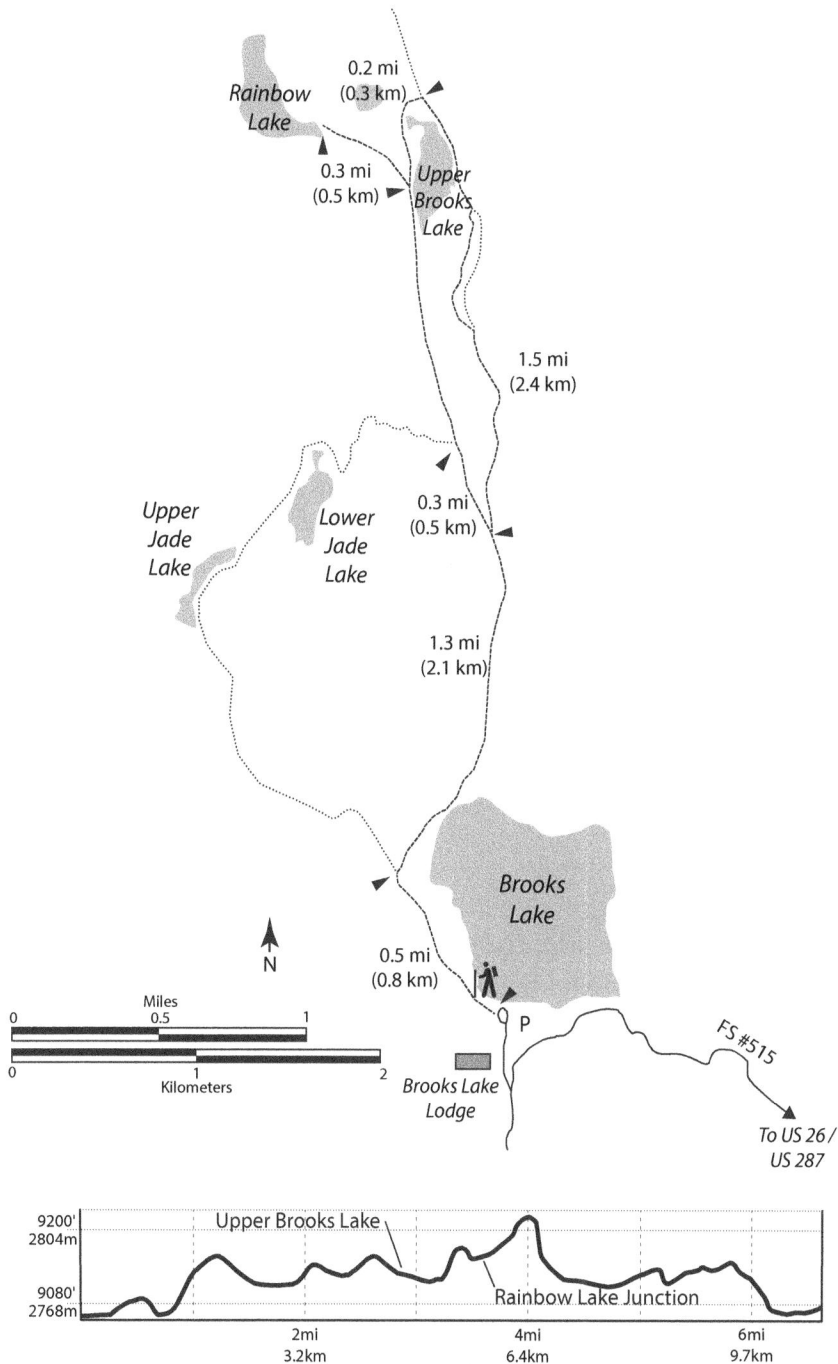

Rainbow Lake

0.2 mi (0.3 km)

Upper Brooks Lake

0.3 mi (0.5 km)

1.5 mi (2.4 km)

Upper Jade Lake

Lower Jade Lake

0.3 mi (0.5 km)

1.3 mi (2.1 km)

Brooks Lake

N

0.5 mi (0.8 km)

P

FS #515

Miles

Kilometers

Brooks Lake Lodge

To US 26 / US 287

TOGWOTEE

9200'
2804m

Upper Brooks Lake

9080'
2768m

Rainbow Lake Junction

2mi
3.2km

4mi
6.4km

6mi
9.7km

TOGWOTEE PASS EAST

129 WIND RIVER LAKE (0.7 mi / 1.1 km / Easy)

Overview: An easy hike around an accessible high mountain lake.
Trip style: Loop
Distance: 0.7 mile (1.1 km)
Elev. gain/loss: 31 feet (9 m)
Max. Elevation: 9,578 feet (2,919 m)
Difficulty: Easy
Trailhead: Wind River Lake parking area
43.7476°N, -110.0590°W / 43°44'51"N, -110°03'33"W
12T 0575761E 4844272N
Traffic: Moderate
Maps: Lava Mountain 7.5' USGS Topo

Trailhead Directions

Drive north from Jackson on US 191 for 30.3 miles (48.8 km) to Moran Junction. Continue past the junction, staying on US 26 / US 287, drive an additional 25.9 miles (41.7 km) to the Wind River Lake parking lot.

Trailhead Facilities

Restrooms, information kiosks.

Hike Description

Start to the left (NW) side of the lake and begin your hike. In 0.07 mile (0.11 km), the trail is somewhat overgrown by low shrubs. Avoid being guided to the lake's edge by the trail cut by other hikers. Instead, stay at the same elevation and work your way through the overgrowth. In 50 feet (16 m), you will exit the shrubs and find the trail again.

Follow the trail as it works its way east around the lake. At 0.3 mile (0.5 km), the trail requires a creek crossing on logs. Be careful, as the logs can be wet and slippery. It's easy to end up in the creek.

The trail curves southeast through a grassy marsh then works its way along the southern edge of the lake. This section is a bit steeper and is more dusty and slippery. Mind your footing as you make your way back to the trailhead at the parking lot.

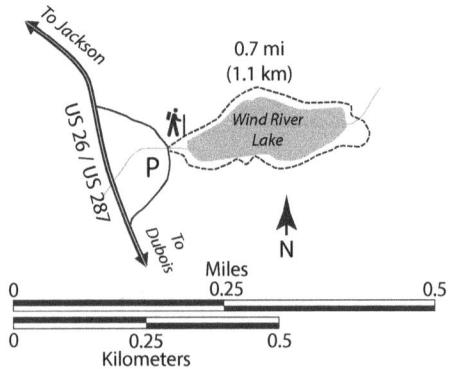

APPENDIX

Day Hiking Checklist

Bring these items with you on any hike you embark upon. When an unexpected event happens and you do need them, there is no substitute for these items in the wilderness.

☐ Map and compass ☐ Sunscreen
☐ Pocket knife ☐ Sunglasses
☐ Extra clothing ☐ Hat
☐ Rain gear ☐ Insect repellent
☐ Water bottle (with purification) ☐ Whistle/signal mirror
☐ Extra food ☐ Toilet paper
☐ Flashlight/headlamp ☐ Trekking poles
☐ First aid kit ☐ Bear spray
☐ Matches or fire starter ☐ Camera/phone

Let someone responsible know where you're going and when to expect your return. This small yet important detail has saved countless lives. If no one knows you're missing, they won't be looking for you when you're lost.

Overnight Hiking Checklist

Overnight trips equipment in addition to the above day hiking list.

☐ Tent or tarp shelter ☐ Ziplock bags
☐ Sleeping bag or quilt ☐ Toiletries
☐ Sleeping pad ☐ Stuff sacks
☐ Stove ☐ Small towel
☐ Cooking pot ☐ Pen/pencil and notebook
☐ Extra water bottles ☐ Warm night clothing
☐ Cup ☐ Spare socks
☐ Bowl ☐ Hiking boots
☐ Utensils ☐ Extra jacket
☐ Appropriate days of food ☐ Warm hat
☐ Bear-resistant food storage ☐ Gloves
☐ Trash bags ☐ Camping permit if required

Use synthetic, wool, or silk clothing. Avoid cotton. Cook 100 yards/meters away from your campsite. Store food the same distance away from your campsite at night. Pitch your tent in a safe location.

Enjoy the outdoor experience in Jackson Hole!

Hikes by Difficulty and Total Hiking Distance

Hikes are listed by difficulty and then the total hiking distance. The total hiking distance is from the trailhead to the objective and then back or the distance to complete the loop.

Difficulty	Total Hike Distance		Distance from Town Square		Trail #	Trail Name
	Mi	Km	Mi	Km		
Easy	0.2	0.4	18.6	29.9	108	Wedding Tree
Easy	0.3	0.4	6.6	10.6	94	Wilson Elementary
Easy	0.4	0.7	27	43.5	2	Cunningham Cabin
Easy	0.4	0.8	35.2	56.7	7	Lunch Tree Hill
Easy	0.4	0.6	13.9	22.4	43	Menors Ferry
Easy	0.4	0.6	7.3	11.8	92	Owen Bircher Wetland Trail
Easy	0.6	1	15.2	24.5	8	Potholes
Easy	0.6	1	17.6	28.3	34	Fabian Lucas Cabins
Easy	0.6	1	1.1	1.8	77	Nelson Knoll
Easy	0.7	1.1	56.2	90.5	129	Wind River Lake
Easy	0.8	1.3	19.6	31.6	105	Gros Ventre Slide Geology Walk
Easy	0.8	1.2	20.3	32.7	115	30340B Trail Picnic Hideaway
Easy	0.9	1.4	18	29.0	31	Bar BC
Easy	1	1.6	35	56.4	1	Christian Pond
Easy	1	1.6	5.8	9.3	93	Rendezvous Park
Easy	1.2	1.8	16.5	26.6	11	South Landing
Easy	1.4	2.2	2.3	3.7	72	River Trail
Easy	1.4	2.3	8.2	13.2	82	South Park Loop
Easy	1.8	2.9	35.4	57.0	5	Jackson Lake Dam Dike
Easy	2	3.2	23.9	38.5	116	Grand View Overlook
Easy	2.2	3.5	39.6	63.8	14	Lakeshore Loop
Easy	2.4	3.8	14.2	22.9	44	Sawmill Bench
Easy	2.6	4.2	52.3	84.2	124	Lost Lake
Easy	3	4.8	39.6	63.8	15	Swan Lake & Heron Pond
Easy	3	4.8	2.3	3.7	73	Sidewalk
Easy	3.2	5.2	17.4	28.0	45	Schwabacher Landing
Easy	3.6	5.8	20.2	32.5	22	Moose Ponds
Easy	3.6	5.8	15.9	25.6	36	Taggart Lake
Easy	3.8	6.1	24.5	39.4	30	String Lake Loop

HIKES BY DIFFICULTY AND TOTAL HIKING DISTANCE

Difficulty	Total Hike Distance		Distance from Town Square		Trail #	Trail Name
	Mi	Km	Mi	Km		
Easy	4	5.2	15.9	25.6	32	Bradley Lake
Easy	4.2	6.8	20.7	33.3	102	Rush Hour
Easy	4.4	7	5	8.1	91	Dike Trail
Easy	5.6	9	32.1	51.7	117	Mount Leidy Lookout
Easy	6.6	10.6	16.7	26.9	49	Phelps Lake and Jumping Rock
Easy	7.2	11.6	24.5	39.4	28	Leigh Lake
Easy	8.8	14.2	43.8	70.5	125	Rosies Ridge
Easy	9	4.5	24.5	39.4	24	Bearpaw and Trapper Lakes
Easy	9.6	15.4	26.5	42.7	104	Grizzly Lake
Easy	11.2	18	2.3	3.7	68	Cache Creek
Easy	13.9	22.3	18	29.0	35	River Road
Mod	1.4	2.2	0.4	0.6	63	Shade Monkey
Mod	2	3.2	17.7	28.5	52	Phelps Lake Overlook
Mod	2	3.6	1.1	1.8	67	Wildlife Drive Network
Mod	2.5	4	9	14.5	84	Big Rocks Loop
Mod	2.8	4.6	17.8	28.7	9	Signal Mountain Marina Cliff
Mod	2.8	4.6	24.5	39.4	27	Laurel Lake
Mod	3	4.8	16.7	26.9	48	Lake Creek and Woodlands Trail
Mod	3	4.8	2.3	3.7	70	Hagen Highway
Mod	3	4.8	9	14.5	86	Crater Trail to Old Pass Road
Mod	3	5	32.1	51.7	119	Toppings Lake and Ridge
Mod	3.2	5.2	35.2	56.7	6	Lookout Rock
Mod	3.4	5.5	16.7	26.9	47	Boulder Ridge Loop
Mod	3.6	5.8	36.1	58.1	4	Grandview Point
Mod	4	7.2	17.1	27.5	33	Burned Wagon Gulch
Mod	4	6.4	17.8	28.7	121	Munger Trail Network
Mod	4.2	6.6	11	17.7	89	Ski Lake
Mod	4.6	7.3	16.7	26.9	46	Aspen Ridge
Mod	4.6	7.7	12.3	19.8	114	Blacktail Butte Traverse
Mod	4.8	7.8	3.1	5.0	110	Miller Butte Trail
Mod	4.8	7.7	12.3	19.8	113	Blacktail Butte Summit
Mod	4.8	7.6	25.1	40.4	118	Shadow Mountain Summit
Mod	5.2	8.4	2.3	3.7	71	Hagen Trail
Mod	5.2	8.4	43.9	70.7	126	Turpin Meadows Ridge Loop

HIKES BY DIFFICULTY AND TOTAL HIKING DISTANCE

Difficulty	Total Hike Distance		Distance from Town Square		Trail #	Trail Name
	Mi	Km	Mi	Km		
Mod	5.4	8.7	68.3	110.0	127	Jade Lakes
Mod	5.6	9	20.2	32.5	19	Hidden Falls and Inspiration Point
Mod	5.6	9	1.8	2.9	64	Sink or Swim
Mod	6.2	10	36	58.0	12	Two Ocean Lake
Mod	6.6	10.6	68.3	110.0	128	Rainbow, Upper Brooks
Mod	7	11.2	12.2	19.6	85	Black Canyon
Mod	7.2	11.6	36.9	59.4	96	Darby Wind
Mod	7.5	12	24.5	39.4	20	Jenny Lake Loop
Mod	7.5	12.1	5.3	8.5	83	Wilson Canyon to Snow King
Mod	7.6	12	20	32.2	122	Munger Summit
Mod	8.8	14.2	1.1	1.8	78	Putt Putt and Town Overlook
Mod	9.4	15	17.8	28.7	10	Signal Mountain Summit
Mod	9.6	15.4	39.6	63.8	13	Hermitage Point
Mod	9.8	15.8	8.8	14.2	80	Game Creek to Snow King
Mod	9.9	15.9	10.6	17.1	112	Blacktail Butte Loop
Mod	11.4	18.3	33	53.1	3	Emma Matilda Lake
Mod	11.7	18.8	20	32.2	120	Big Munger Trail
Mod	13.6	22	26.5	42.7	103	Blue Miner Lake
Stren	0.8	1.2	2.7	4.3	61	High School Butte
Stren	0.8	1.2	19.8	31.9	106	Gros Ventre Slide Vista
Stren	1.2	2	1.1	1.8	76	Crystal Lite
Stren	2.2	3.4	1.8	2.9	62	Josie's Ridge
Stren	3.6	5.8	4.5	7.2	60	Adams Canyon
Stren	3.6	5.8	25.2	40.6	107	Red and Lavender Hills
Stren	3.6	5.8	0.4	0.6	66	Snow King Summit
Stren	4	6.4	9	14.5	87	History Trail
Stren	4	6.4	67.5	108.7	99	Grand Targhee Trail Network
Stren	6	9.6	67.5	108.7	98	Fred's Mountain
Stren	6.2	10	2.3	3.7	69	Ferrin's Trail
Stren	6.6	10.6	24.5	39.4	25	Hanging Canyon and The Jaw
Stren	8.6	13.8	21	33.8	37	Garnet Canyon Meadows and Spalding Falls
Stren	8.8	14.2	14.8	23.8	90	Taylor Mountain
Stren	9.2	14.4	45.2	72.8	97	Devils Stairs to Teton Shelf
Stren	9.6	15.4	21	33.8	40	Surprise, Amphitheater, Delta

HIKES BY DIFFICULTY AND TOTAL HIKING DISTANCE

Difficulty	Total Hike Distance		Distance from Town Square		Trail #	Trail Name
	Mi	Km	Mi	Km		
Stren	10.3	16.6	10.4	16.7	109	Goodwin Lake and Jackson Peak
Stren	10.4	16.8	23.8	38.3	123	Cream Puff Peak
Stren	10.6	17	11.1	17.9	111	Sleeping Indian via Flat Creek
Stren	11	17.7	24.5	39.4	17	Cascade Canyon Fork
Stren	12.6	20.2	55.2	88.9	16	Huckleberry Mountain
Stren	12.8	20.6	24.5	39.4	26	Holly Lake
Stren	13.3	21.4	2.3	3.7	74	Skyline Trail Loop
Stren	14.4	23.4	45.2	72.8	95	Alaska Basin via Teton Canyon
Stren	15.7	25.3	21	33.8	42	Valley Trail
Stren	16	25.8	24.5	39.4	21	Lake Solitude
Stren	17.2	27.6	17.7	28.5	51	Fox Creek Pass
Stren	18.2	29.2	14.3	23.0	56	Marion Lake
Stren	18.8	30.3	14.3	23.0	55	Granite Canyon to Open Canyon Loop
Stren	20	32.2	45.2	72.8	101	Teton Range Traverse
Stren	21.2	34	20.2	32.5	23	Schoolroom Glacier
Stren	23.4	37.7	14.3	23.0	54	Granite Canyon to Death Canyon Loop
Stren	23.6	38	17.7	28.5	50	Death Canyon Shelf to Alaska Basin Loop
Stren	32.7	52.6	20.2	32.5	18	Grand Teton Loop
Stren	37.5	60.4	14.3	23.0	57	Teton Crest Trail
Ex Stren	1.4	2.2	0.4	0.6	65	Snow King Bootpack
Ex Stren	1.6	2.8	12.2	19.6	88	Mount Glory
Ex Stren	2.4	3.9	5.3	8.5	81	Lower Valley Ridge
Ex Stren	5	8	21	33.8	41	Teewinot Apex and Glacier
Ex Stren	5	8	1.1	1.8	75	Crystal Butte
Ex Stren	5.6	9	1.1	1.8	79	Woods Canyon to Crystal Butte Loop
Ex Stren	11.2	18	45.2	72.8	100	Table Mountain
Ex Stren	12	19.4	21	33.8	38	Lower Saddle Grand Teton
Ex Stren	12.8	20.6	21	33.8	39	Middle and South Teton
Ex Stren	14	22.6	17.7	28.5	53	Static Peak & Divide
Ex Stren	14.2	23	12	19.3	58	Rendezvous Mountain
Ex Stren	18.1	29.1	12	19.3	59	Rendezvous Mountain to Granite Canyon Loop
Ex Stren	19.2	30.8	24.5	39.4	29	Paintbrush Divide to Cascade Canyon

HIKES BY DIFFICULTY AND TOTAL HIKING DISTANCE

Hikes by Distance from the Town Square

Hikes are listed by the distance from the Jackson Town Square. The total hiking distance is from the trailhead to the objective and then back or the distance to complete the loop.

Distance from Town Square		Total Hike Distance		Difficulty	Trail #	Trail Name
Mi	Km	Mi	Km			
0.4	0.6	1.4	2.2	Mod	63	Shade Monkey
0.4	0.6	1.4	2.2	Ex Stren	65	Snow King Bootpack
0.4	0.6	3.6	5.8	Stren	66	Snow King Summit
1.1	1.8	0.6	1	Easy	77	Nelson Knoll
1.1	1.8	1.2	2	Stren	76	Crystal Lite
1.1	1.8	2	3.6	Mod	67	Wildlife Drive Network
1.1	1.8	5	8	Ex Stren	75	Crystal Butte
1.1	1.8	5.6	9	Ex Stren	79	Woods Canyon to Crystal Butte Loop
1.1	1.8	8.8	14.2	Mod	78	Putt Putt and Town Overlook
1.8	2.9	2.2	3.4	Stren	62	Josie's Ridge
1.8	2.9	5.6	9	Mod	64	Sink or Swim
2.3	3.7	1.4	2.2	Easy	72	River Trail
2.3	3.7	3	4.8	Easy	73	Sidewalk
2.3	3.7	3	4.8	Mod	70	Hagen Highway
2.3	3.7	5.2	8.4	Mod	71	Hagen Trail
2.3	3.7	6.2	10	Stren	69	Ferrin's Trail
2.3	3.7	11.2	18	Easy	68	Cache Creek
2.3	3.7	13.3	21.4	Stren	74	Skyline Trail Loop
2.7	4.3	0.8	1.2	Stren	61	High School Butte
3.1	5.0	4.8	7.8	Mod	110	Miller Butte Trail
4.5	7.2	3.6	5.8	Stren	60	Adams Canyon
5	8.1	4.4	7	Easy	91	Dike Trail
5.3	8.5	2.4	3.9	Ex Stren	81	Lower Valley Ridge
5.3	8.5	7.5	12.1	Mod	83	Wilson Canyon to Snow King
5.8	9.3	1	1.6	Easy	93	Rendezvous Park
6.6	10.6	0.3	0.4	Easy	94	Wilson Elementary
7.3	11.8	0.4	0.6	Easy	92	Owen Bircher Wetland Trail
8.2	13.2	1.4	2.3	Easy	82	South Park Loop

APPENDIX

Distance from Town Square		Total Hike Distance		Difficulty	Trail #	Trail Name
Mi	Km	Mi	Km			
8.8	14.2	9.8	15.8	Mod	80	Game Creek to Snow King
9	14.5	2.5	4	Mod	84	Big Rocks Loop
9	14.5	3	4.8	Mod	86	Crater Trail to Old Pass Road
9	14.5	4	6.4	Stren	87	History Trail
10.4	16.7	10.3	16.6	Stren	109	Goodwin Lake and Jackson Peak
10.6	17.1	9.9	15.9	Mod	112	Blacktail Butte Loop
11	17.7	4.2	6.6	Mod	89	Ski Lake
11.1	17.9	10.6	17	Stren	111	Sleeping Indian via Flat Creek
12	19.3	14.2	23	Ex Stren	58	Rendezvous Mountain
12	19.3	18.1	29.1	Ex Stren	59	Rendezvous Mountain to Granite Canyon Loop
12.2	19.6	1.6	2.8	Ex Stren	88	Mount Glory
12.2	19.6	7	11.2	Mod	85	Black Canyon
12.3	19.8	4.6	7.7	Mod	114	Blacktail Butte Traverse
12.3	19.8	4.8	7.7	Mod	113	Blacktail Butte Summit
13.9	22.4	0.4	0.6	Easy	43	Menors Ferry
14.2	22.9	2.4	3.8	Easy	44	Sawmill Bench
14.3	23.0	18.2	29.2	Stren	56	Marion Lake
14.3	23.0	18.8	30.3	Stren	55	Granite Canyon to Open Canyon Loop
14.3	23.0	23.4	37.7	Stren	54	Granite Canyon to Death Canyon Loop
14.3	23.0	37.5	60.4	Stren	57	Teton Crest Trail
14.8	23.8	8.8	14.2	Stren	90	Taylor Mountain
15.2	24.5	0.6	1	Easy	8	Potholes
15.9	25.6	3.6	5.8	Easy	36	Taggart Lake
15.9	25.6	4	5.2	Easy	32	Bradley Lake
16.5	26.6	1.2	1.8	Easy	11	South Landing
16.7	26.9	3	4.8	Mod	48	Lake Creek and Woodlands Trail
16.7	26.9	3.4	5.5	Mod	47	Boulder Ridge Loop
16.7	26.9	4.6	7.3	Mod	46	Aspen Ridge
16.7	26.9	6.6	10.6	Easy	49	Phelps Lake and Jumping Rock
17.1	27.5	4	7.2	Mod	33	Burned Wagon Gulch
17.4	28.0	3.2	5.2	Easy	45	Schwabacher Landing
17.6	28.3	0.6	1	Easy	34	Fabian Lucas Cabins
17.7	28.5	2	3.2	Mod	52	Phelps Lake Overlook

HIKES BY DISTANCE FROM THE TOWN SQUARE

Distance from Town Square		Total Hike Distance		Difficulty	Trail #	Trail Name
Mi	Km	Mi	Km			
17.7	28.5	14	22.6	Ex Stren	53	Static Peak & Divide
17.7	28.5	17.2	27.6	Stren	51	Fox Creek Pass
17.7	28.5	23.6	38	Stren	50	Death Canyon Shelf to Alaska Basin Loop
17.8	28.7	2.8	4.6	Mod	9	Signal Mountain Marina Cliff
17.8	28.7	4	6.4	Mod	121	Munger Trail Network
17.8	28.7	9.4	15	Mod	10	Signal Mountain Summit
18	29.0	0.9	1.4	Easy	31	Bar BC
18	29.0	13.9	22.3	Easy	35	River Road
18.6	29.9	0.2	0.4	Easy	108	Wedding Tree
19.6	31.6	0.8	1.3	Easy	105	Gros Ventre Slide Geology Walk
19.8	31.9	0.8	1.2	Stren	106	Gros Ventre Slide Vista
20	32.2	7.6	12	Mod	122	Munger Summit
20	32.2	11.7	18.8	Mod	120	Big Munger Trail
20.2	32.5	3.6	5.8	Easy	22	Moose Ponds
20.2	32.5	5.6	9	Mod	19	Hidden Falls and Inspiration Point
20.2	32.5	21.2	34	Stren	23	Schoolroom Glacier
20.2	32.5	32.7	52.6	Stren	18	Grand Teton Loop
20.3	32.7	0.8	1.2	Easy	115	30340B Trail Picnic Hideaway
20.7	33.3	4.2	6.8	Easy	102	Rush Hour
21	33.8	5	8	Ex Stren	41	Teewinot Apex and Glacier
21	33.8	8.6	13.8	Stren	37	Garnet Canyon Meadows and Spalding Falls
21	33.8	9.6	15.4	Stren	40	Surprise, Amphitheater, Delta
21	33.8	12	19.4	Ex Stren	38	Lower Saddle Grand Teton
21	33.8	12.8	20.6	Ex Stren	39	Middle and South Teton
21	33.8	15.7	25.3	Stren	42	Valley Trail
23.8	38.3	10.4	16.8	Stren	123	Cream Puff Peak
23.9	38.5	2	3.2	Easy	116	Grand View Overlook
24.5	39.4	2.8	4.6	Mod	27	Laurel Lake
24.5	39.4	3.8	6.1	Easy	30	String Lake Loop
24.5	39.4	6.6	10.6	Stren	25	Hanging Canyon and The Jaw
24.5	39.4	7.2	11.6	Easy	28	Leigh Lake
24.5	39.4	7.5	12	Mod	20	Jenny Lake Loop
24.5	39.4	9	4.5	Easy	24	Bearpaw and Trapper Lakes
24.5	39.4	11	17.7	Stren	17	Cascade Canyon Fork

HIKES BY DISTANCE FROM THE TOWN SQUARE

Distance from Town Square		Total Hike Distance		Difficulty	Trail #	Trail Name
Mi	Km	Mi	Km			
24.5	39.4	12.8	20.6	Stren	26	Holly Lake
24.5	39.4	16	25.8	Stren	21	Lake Solitude
24.5	39.4	19.2	30.8	Ex Stren	29	Paintbrush Divide to Cascade Canyon
25.1	40.4	4.8	7.6	Mod	118	Shadow Mountain Summit
25.2	40.6	3.6	5.8	Stren	107	Red and Lavender Hills
26.5	42.7	9.6	15.4	Easy	104	Grizzly Lake
26.5	42.7	13.6	22	Mod	103	Blue Miner Lake
27	43.5	0.4	0.7	Easy	2	Cunningham Cabin
32.1	51.7	3	5	Mod	119	Toppings Lake and Ridge
32.1	51.7	5.6	9	Easy	117	Mount Leidy Lookout
33	53.1	11.4	18.3	Mod	3	Emma Matilda Lake
35	56.4	1	1.6	Easy	1	Christian Pond
35.2	56.7	0.4	0.8	Easy	7	Lunch Tree Hill
35.2	56.7	3.2	5.2	Mod	6	Lookout Rock
35.4	57.0	1.8	2.9	Easy	5	Jackson Lake Dam Dike
36	58.0	6.2	10	Mod	12	Two Ocean Lake
36.1	58.1	3.6	5.8	Mod	4	Grandview Point
36.9	59.4	7.2	11.6	Mod	96	Darby Wind
39.6	63.8	2.2	3.5	Easy	14	Lakeshore Loop
39.6	63.8	3	4.8	Easy	15	Swan Lake & Heron Pond
39.6	63.8	9.6	15.4	Mod	13	Hermitage Point
43.8	70.5	8.8	14.2	Easy	125	Rosies Ridge
43.9	70.7	5.2	8.4	Mod	126	Turpin Meadows Ridge Loop
45.2	72.8	9.2	14.4	Stren	97	Devils Stairs to Teton Shelf
45.2	72.8	11.2	18	Ex Stren	100	Table Mountain
45.2	72.8	14.4	23.4	Stren	95	Alaska Basin via Teton Canyon
45.2	72.8	20	32.2	Stren	101	Teton Range Traverse
52.3	84.2	2.6	4.2	Easy	124	Lost Lake
55.2	88.9	12.6	20.2	Stren	16	Huckleberry Mountain
56.2	90.5	0.7	1.1	Easy	129	Wind River Lake
67.5	108.7	4	6.4	Stren	99	Grand Targhee Trail Network
67.5	108.7	6	9.6	Stren	98	Fred's Mountain
68.3	110.0	5.4	8.7	Mod	127	Jade Lakes
68.3	110.0	6.6	10.6	Mod	128	Rainbow, Upper Brooks

APPENDIX

HIKES BY DISTANCE FROM THE TOWN SQUARE

Books by the author

Black Ice

Some missions don't have a way back. When a hypersonic drone crashes in northern Finland, Grant Colson races against the elements and unseen dangers before the mission—and his team—are erased by the Arctic. *Free download.*

www.aaronrlinsdau.com/sera/black-ice/

50 Jackson Hole Photography Hotspots

This guide reveals the best Jackson Hole photography spots. Learn what locals and insiders know to find the most impressive and iconic photography locations in the United States. This is an excellent companion guide to the *Jackson Hole Hiking Guide.*

www.sastrugipress.com/books/50-jackson-hole-photography-hotspots/

Adventure Expedition One
by Aaron Linsdau M.S. & Terry Williams, M.D.

Create, finance, enjoy, and return safely from your first expedition. Learn the techniques explorers use to achieve their goals and have a good time doing it. Acquire the skills, find the equipment, and learn the planning necessary to pull off an expedition.

www.sastrugipress.com/books/adventure-expedition-one/

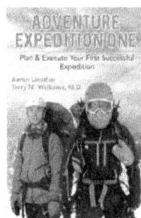

Antarctic Tears

Experience the honest story of solo polar exploration. This inspirational true book will make readers both cheer and cry. Coughing up blood and fighting skin-freezing temperatures were only a few of the perils Aaron Linsdau faced. Travel with him on a world-record expedition to the South Pole.

www.sastrugipress.com/books/antarctic-tears/

Lost at Windy Corner

Windy Corner on Denali has claimed fingers, toes, and even lives. What would make someone brave lethal weather, crevasses, and avalanches to attempt to summit North America's highest mountain? Aaron Linsdau shares the experience of climbing Denali alone and how you can apply the lessons to your life.

www.sastrugipress.com/books/lost-windy-corner/

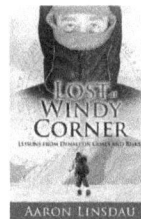

The Most Crucial Knots to Know

Knot tying is a skill everyone can use in daily life. This book shows how to tie over 40 of the most practical knots for virtually any situation. This guide will equip readers with skills that are useful, fun to learn, and will make you look like a confident pro.

www.sastrugipress.com/books/the-most-crucial-knots-to-know/

The Motivated Amateur's Guide to Winter Camping

Winter camping is one of the most satisfying ways to experience the wilderness. It is also the most challenging style of overnighting in the outdoors. Learn 100+ tips from a professional polar explorer on how to winter camp safely and be comfortable in the cold.

www.sastrugipress.com/books/the-motivated-amateurs-guide-to-winter-camping/

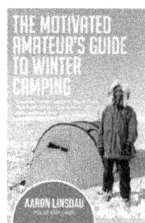

Two Friends and a Polar Bear
by Terry Williams, M.D. & Aaron Linsdau

Winter camping is one of the most satisfying ways to experience the wilderness. It is also the most challenging style of overnighting in the outdoors. Learn 100+ tips from a professional polar explorer on how to winter camp safely and be comfortable in the cold.

www.sastrugipress.com/books/two-friends-and-a-polar-bear/

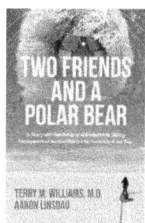

Use your smart device to scan the QR codes for website links.

Visit www.aaronrlinsdau.com/subscribe/ and join his email list. Receive updates when he releases new books and shows

Visit Sastrugi Press on the web at www.sastrugipress.com to purchase the above titles in print, e-book, or audiobook form.

About the Author

Aaron Linsdau is the second-only American to ski alone from the coast of Antarctica to the South Pole (730 miles / 1174 km). He set the world record for surviving the longest expedition ever for the Hercules Inlet to the South Pole route.

Aaron Linsdau at the South Pole.

Visit Aaron's YouTube channel: www.youtube.com/@alinsdau or scan the QR Code:

www.ingramcontent.com/pod-product-compliance
Lightning Source LLC
Chambersburg PA
CBHW060245100426
42742CB00011B/1645